KT-238-944

REHEARSAL FOR RECONSTRUCTION

The Port Royal Experiment

Winner of
The Allan Nevins History Prize, 1962
The Francis Parkman Prize, 1964
The Charles S. Sydnor Prize for Southern History, 1966

REHEARSAL FOR RECONSTRUCTION

The Port Royal Experiment

WILLIE LEE ROSE

With an Introduction by C. Vann Woodward

OXFORD UNIVERSITY PRESS
London · Oxford · New York

To My Mother
and
To the Memory of My Father

OXFORD UNIVERSITY PRESS

London   Oxford   New York
Glasgow   Toronto   Melbourne   Wellington
Cape Town   Ibadan   Nairobi   Dar es Salaam   Lusaka   Addis Ababa
Delhi   Bombay   Calcutta   Madras   Karachi   Lahore   Dacca
Kuala Lumpur   Singapore   Hong Kong   Tokyo

boilerplate>
COPYRIGHT © 1964 BY WILLIE LEE ROSE
LIBRARY OF CONGRESS CATALOG CARD NUMBER: 64-16720
FIRST PUBLISHED BY THE BOBBS-MERRILL COMPANY, INC., 1964
FIRST ISSUED IN A PAPERBACK EDITION BY VINTAGE BOOKS, 1967
THIS EDITION PUBLISHED BY OXFORD UNIVERSITY PRESS, NEW YORK,
1976, BY ARRANGEMENT WITH THE AUTHOR

PRINTED IN THE UNITED STATES OF AMERICA

ACKNOWLEDGMENTS

TO MY KIND FRIENDS AND ASSOCIATES IN THE JOHNS HOPKINS SEMINAR in American History, who for nearly four years bore in mind my special preoccupation with the Sea Island Negroes and their missionary tutors, and who have generously fed me clues and suggestions, I am most deeply grateful. Without in any way involving them with responsibility for my own mistakes of fact or judgment, I am in special debt to a number of people.

Professor C. Vann Woodward encouraged me to undertake the project, foreseeing, I believe, the exciting experience in scholarship that awaited me. He read the original manuscript, as well as my revision, and few pages are not the better for his interest, criticism, and careful attention. Professor Charles A. Barker also read the entire manuscript, much to its profit, offering numerous suggestions and criticisms.

I am in debt particularly to Mr. James McPherson and Mr. Tilden Edelstein, who read and criticized the entire manuscript, giving me the benefit of their special knowledge in the field. Mrs. Patricia Spain Ward has read nearly every chapter and has been an able consultant on questions of nineteenth-century medical practices. I am also obliged to Mr. Bertram Wyatt-Brown and Mrs. Perra S. Bell, who have read and commented upon the earlier chapters and offered helpful suggestions. Mrs. Bell brought important research materials to my notice, and Mr. Wyatt-Brown assisted me by microfilming relevant sections of the records of the American Missionary Association. My husband, William George Rose, has been at all times a willing listener, an honest critic, and an unfailing source of encouragement.

Generous grants from the American Association of University Women and the Social Science Research Council for the academic years 1958-59 and 1960-61, respectively, have provided the necessary free time for travel to libraries at a distance and for writing the dissertation. I also wish to thank the library staffs at The Johns Hopkins University, Harvard University, the Massachusetts Historical Society, the Boston Athenaeum, the University of North Carolina, the University of South Carolina, the South Carolina State Archives at Columbia, the South Carolina Historical Society, the Library of Congress, the United States Archives, the University of Wisconsin, and the Beaufort Township Library. Mr. and Mrs. Courtney Siceloff, of the Penn Community Center, made their collection of manuscripts and photographs available to me on the most convenient and friendly terms, and also gave me a guided tour of the Sea Island region that has occupied so much of my thought in the last few years.

The portrait of Mansfield French that appears following page 110 is reproduced here through the courtesy of The Dawes Memorial Library of Marietta College, from its copy of the original oil painting by Louise Coolidge Carpenter. The photograph of slave quarters on Edisto Island following page 334 and the two pictures on the following page are in the collections of the New-York Historical Society. All other illustrations came from the papers of Laura M. Towne and were made available to me through the courtesy of Mr. Courtney Siceloff, Director of the Penn Community Center on St. Helena Island. I am deeply grateful in each case for the kind permission to reproduce these pictures here.

                                                      W. L. R.

March 1964

CONTENTS

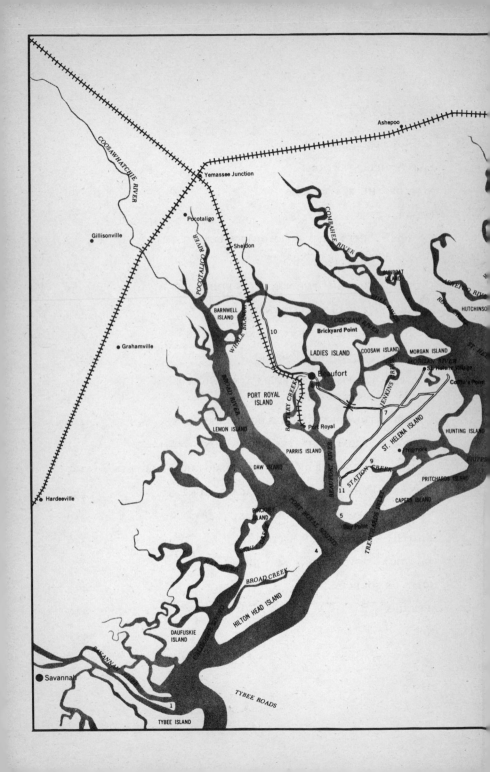

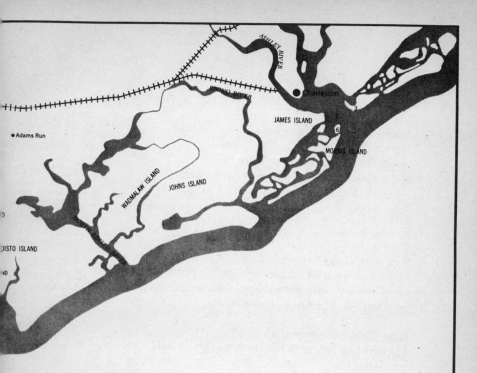

ATLANTIC OCEAN

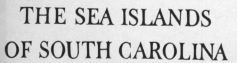

1   FORT PULASKI
2   FORT SUMTER
3   FORT MOULTRIE
4   FORT WALKER
5   FORT BEAUREGARD
6   FORT WAGNER
7   BRICK CHURCH
8   WHITEHALL FERRY
9   DR. JENKINS' PLANTATION
10 THE SHELL ROAD
11 LAND'S END

THE SEA ISLANDS
OF SOUTH CAROLINA
—during the Civil War and Reconstruction

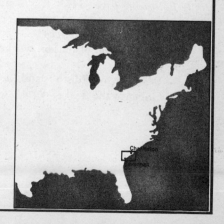

ILLUSTRATIONS

x

INTRODUCTION

THE HISTORY OF THE SOCIAL UPHEAVALS AND POLITICAL EXPERI-
ments called Reconstruction is ordinarily picked up by historians
at the end of the Civil War. It begins with the fall of the Confederacy and runs through the smoking ruins and social chaos left
by war, continues through a turbulent decade of revolution and
counterrevolution, and ends in frustration or stalemate. Abortive
as the revolution proved to be, it experimented with the most
drastic social changes ever attempted in American history. For
many reasons, its history is extremely hard to follow, interpret, and
understand. It involved millions of people and was complicated by
conflicts along racial, sectional, and partisan lines. The eleven
states of the defeated Confederacy provided the main theater for
Reconstruction, but the action shifted from coast to coast, and at
times the stage was nationwide.

The Port Royal Experiment, the subject of this book, was in
effect a dress rehearsal for Reconstruction acted out on the stage
neatly defined by the Sea Islands of South Carolina. It offers a rare
opportunity to review the vast spectacle in miniature and see it
in its germinal phase. It began not long after the war started, seven
months after the fall of Fort Sumter, and developed far behind
Confederate lines while the war thundered away on the mainland
in Virginia and along the Mississippi, hundreds of miles away. The
stage was cleared for the experiment by the United States Navy
on November 7, 1861, long remembered by the slaves as "the day
of the big gun-shoot." Under the command of Commodore S. F.

Du Pont, a fleet sailed into Port Royal Sound, opened a bombardment, quickly reduced the defending batteries, and on the following day landed troops to occupy the islands.

As soon as Commodore Du Pont's guns ceased fire, the slave-
owners and planters, as well as the entire white population, hur-
riedly loaded a few possessions and a few house servants on
flatboats, set fire to piles of cotton bales, and sailed away to the
mainland. Behind them they left their mansions, meals cooking
on stoves, along with their slaves and virtually all their possessions.
When the troops arrived in Beaufort, the only town of consequence, they discovered only one white man, and he was too
drunk to move. Some ten thousand slaves, more than eighty per
cent of the island population in 1860, remained behind, some to loot
the mansion houses and all to welcome the invaders and to determine—gradually and painfully—whether they came as liberators
or as a new set of masters. The troops and their commanders were
by no means clear on the point themselves. The old regime had
collapsed as suddenly as any in history, but the new regime was
not ready to take its place.

Into this island limbo between the old and the new sailed "Gideon's Band." The steamer *Atlantic* landed them at Beaufort in
March 1862. A band of fifty-three missionaries, the Gideonites
were mainly young antislavery people, about half of them from
Boston and its vicinity and half from New York. They were the
first of several hundred who came to the Sea Islands before the
end of the war. They were divided along sectarian lines, and time
was to prove them divided over the nature of their mission. But
they were united in their opposition to slavery and in their determination to give shape to liberation and guidance and help to the
liberated. At Beaufort, South Carolina, the abolitionists and the
slaves confronted each other on slave territory for the first time.
In store for both were some difficult and some painful adjustments.

It was a dramatic coincidence that abolition and reconstruction
should have struck first in the Sea Islands. The northern news-
paperman who called the islands "the exclusive home of the most

exclusive few of that most exclusive aristocracy" was guilty of some overstatement. But old Beaufort and its vicinity were the seedbed of South Carolina secessionism. Robert Barnwell Rhett, fire-eating secessionist, made his home there, and so did William J. Grayson, poet and champion of the slavery cause. James L. Petigru, another citizen, was tolerated as an eccentric unionist. The mansions of the Elliotts, the Heywards, the Coffins, the Fripps, the Barnwells, and the Seabrooks stood abandoned among their stately live oaks and festoons of Spanish moss. They were but a few of thousands of tangible reminders of the power and authority of the old order. The old masters had vanished quickly and completely, but they had left behind them a slave culture and social discipline that was the product of centuries and that would be slow to yield to the newly imported culture of freedom and free enterprise.

Mrs. Rose writes with rare perception, understanding, and detachment of both the old order and the revolutionary regime that took its place. Her main theme is the transition from the old to the new. Perhaps her clearest triumph is in her description of the nuances of change by which a slave became a free man, how a chattel became a person, and the changes in personality and identity that accompanied the transformation. She is successful also in portraying the philanthropists, the missionaries, the politicians, the military leaders, and the fortune seekers who crowded the Sea Islands to contest with each other over the destiny of the emancipated slaves.

Very little was settled about the slave's future when the experiment began: whether he was to be entirely free at all, and if free, whether he was to be a serf, a wage laborer, a landowner, a citizen, a soldier, a voter, an officeholder. What were his capacities? What were his rights? If slavery had indeed done the damage the abolitionists claimed, was the slave capable of the equality they promised? Nothing had been proved, and a hundred theorists came forward with plans, solutions, and panaceas to be tried out. Organized groups struggled against each other for the allegiance of the slaves, the support of the military, and the backing of Washington authorities.

In the midst of these rivalries on the Sea Islands, the rehearsal for Reconstruction went forward. Here the first troops were recruited among the late slaves and put to the test of battle; the first extensive schools for slaves got under way and the assault on illiteracy began; abandoned land was confiscated and freedmen took precarious title; the wage system received several trials and freedmen experimented with strikes and bargaining; political rallies and local politics first opened up an exciting range of experience.

The Port Royal Experiment became not only a proving ground for the freedmen, but also a training and recruiting ground for personnel of the postwar Reconstruction. Salmon P. Chase, Edwin M. Stanton, and Charles Sumner became champions of the experiment and were vitally concerned with its progress. In and out of the scene moved General O. O. Howard, future head of the Freedmen's Bureau; Harriet Tubman, the one-woman underground railroad; James Montgomery, ruthless lieutenant of old John Brown; Thomas Wentworth Higginson, colonel of a Negro regiment; Robert Gould Shaw, martyred leader of Negro troops; Robert Smalls, future Negro congressman and leader of his race. The schooling these and many others received on the Sea Islands was to bear fruit in the postwar years.

Mrs. Rose has made a rich contribution to the history of Reconstruction. Her study shows that the rehearsal on the Sea Islands not only played a part in shaping federal policy for Reconstruction, but that it also influenced the nation in adding to the initial war aim of Union, the eventual commitment to Freedom and, more hesitantly and halfheartedly, the still-unfulfilled commitment to Equality.

C. VANN WOODWARD

Rehearsal for Reconstruction

The Port Royal Experiment

one ❧ "INTO THE VORTEX OF REVOLUTION"

FALL CAME LATE TO SOUTH CAROLINA IN 1861. OCTOBER MADE WAY for November, and the gentility of Charleston began to drift away to their lowland plantations, but there had been as yet no killing frost, and all but the tenderest plants remained green in the oblique autumn sunshine. Away to the southwest, along the coastal estuaries and on the Sea Islands, Negro slaves were picking cotton, a crop that promised fair this year to be the largest most men could remember. Nature did not always consider the special needs of the fine long-staple cotton that grew in this unique climate, but in 1861 conditions had been perfect, and even the annual threat of fall hurricanes seemed by the end of October to be almost safely past.[1]

In ordinary times such a year was reason for deep thankfulness and enormous relief, for a great crop could move a planter out of the red and into the black with his cotton factor. But fall in 1861 was no ordinary time. Ardent patriots might read in the season's bounty a sign that King Cotton was going to win the war for the Southern Confederacy, as some had always said; but sober and practical men were undoubtedly wondering when, if ever, the cotton would reach its accustomed destination, the Liverpool market and the factories of England. In the seven months since the firing began in Charleston harbor, an ominous quiet had settled over the South Carolina low country. Local militia units drilled,

---

[1] Arney Robinson Childs (ed.), *The Private Journal of Henry William Ravenel, 1859–1867* (Columbia, South Carolina, 1947), p. 94; Elizabeth Ware Pearson (ed.), *Letters from Port Royal* (Boston, 1906), p. v.

and along the coast fortifications went up as speedily as possible. Offshore on any clear day the ships of the Federal blockading squadron were visible, but there were otherwise few overt signs of a state of war. While the blockade was not yet impenetrable, it was a humiliation. The ships were also an unsettling influence upon the slave population, just at the time when all hands were needed to pick the cotton. With a fine sense of history, the colored people seemed to know, despite Federal protests, that the Civil War was about slavery. Some of them deserted the fields and stole away to the blockade ships.[2]

There was an even graver matter for concern. For more than a month the newspapers had been carrying reports of a large fleet being prepared in New York Harbor for an assault on some undisclosed location on the Southern coast. With an uneasy awareness of having brought themselves most conspicuously to the notice of the Federal authorities, the inhabitants of Charleston were alarmed for the safety of their city. It remained to the most famous Unionist left among them to disparage these fears and to hold the cool opinion that the government at Washington could gain nothing at the moment by attacking Charleston. James L. Petigru, however, had lost his following. The witty old Whig lawyer, at seventy-two years of age, was just exactly as old as the United States Constitution, a document he had served loyally all his years, and he would have no part in a war against the Federal Union. There was now small demand for the opinion of Unionists, however, and the best they could expect from their neighbors was good-humored contempt.[3]

Away in the North Carolina upcountry, where he was vaca-

---

[2] Childs (ed.), *Ravenel Journal*, p. 93.

[3] *Ibid.*; James Petigru Carson, *Life, Letters and Speeches of James Louis Petigru* (Washington, 1920), p. 411; William Howard Russell, when he toured the South during the spring of the secession year, recorded the impression that Petigru, "a most lively, quaint, witty old lawyer," was regarded by his neighbors as "an amiable, harmless person. . . ." William Howard Russell, *My Diary North and South* (London, 1863), I, 170.

tioning, an old friend of Petigru was also pondering the possibilities of an attack on the Carolina coast. William Elliott reasoned well, and as early as September he sent warning to his sons concerning the safety of the numerous estates of the Elliotts in the island country southwest of Charleston. He advised the removal of slaves from the Hilton Head Island plantations, which were located near the mouth of Port Royal Sound. Elliott warned his sons not to overlook provisions, and to bring away "what cotton you can without exposing your hand." The Federal fleet would not attack the islands, he thought, just in order to occupy the little town of Beaufort, which was of little strategic importance, but rather, if they should do so, to strengthen the blockade by seizing command of the Port Royal Sound region *"for the war."* The national government could by that means "destroy the inland communications between Charleston and Savannah and blockade Savannah completely. . . ."[4]

Elliott had at least in part read the mind of the Cabinet. The urgent need for a coaling depot and a suitable anchorage for the South Atlantic blockading fleet had caused Secretary of the Navy Gideon Welles to run a speculative eye along the coast. As the largest deep water harbor between Cape Hatteras and Florida, Port Royal had indisputable attractions, and it would certainly be an easier mark than Charleston.[5] Port Royal had other advantages. A summer of military defeat and hesitation was reflected in the declining prestige of the Lincoln Administration. Even within the Cabinet there was chafing at the "do-nothing" policy. "We absolutely need some dashing expeditions," wrote Edward Bates, the Attorney General, "some victories—great or small, to stimulate the zeal of the Country." Bates had heard about the

[4] William Elliott to his son, William Elliott, September, 24, 1861, Elliott-Gonzales Manuscripts, Southern Historical Collection, Chapel Hill, North Carolina.

[5] Richard S. West, Jr., *Mr. Lincoln's Navy* (New York, 1957), p. 73; Bern Anderson, *By Sea and By River; The Naval History of the Civil War* (New York, 1962), pp. 38–40, 53–56.

great Sea-Island cotton crop and wanted to know why the government should not seize the islands and take the cotton, which would be "merchandise ready to our hand," and supply Northern factories. Ready cash, even a little, would be most welcome, for the Federal pocketbook was near the point of exhaustion. Salmon P. Chase, Secretary of the Treasury, complained that the daily drafts of his department were running during the month of October to "a million and three quarters at least," an amount "largely in excess of its means," he fretted.[6]

Port Royal's chances of receiving special attention from the United States Navy were therefore very good, as Elliott had supposed. In the actual event, the large fleet left New York with sealed instructions, which theoretically allowed Commodore Samuel F. Du Pont and General T. W. Sherman, in command of sea and land forces respectively, a choice of four possible points of attack. Both officers understood their destination, however, and knew that the choice was offered merely in an attempt to preserve secrecy—an attempt that was to prove notably unsuccessful. By November 1 the Confederate government had received reliable intelligence that Port Royal would indeed be the main focus of the attack, and the Secretary of War, Judah P. Benjamin, sent warning to the Governor of South Carolina.[7] There was now less than a week in which to make ready.

This region so well adapted to the culture of the highest quality cotton was level and sandy, cut into islands of greatly varying size by the extension of salt creeks and marshes, Port Royal Sound, and the Beaufort River. The unaccustomed New England eye sometimes missed the hills of home and saw the landscape at first

[6] Howard K. Beale (ed.), *The Diary of Edward Bates, 1859–1866,* in American Historical Association, Annual Report, IV (Washington, D.C., 1930), 194, 195; Bray Hammond, "The North's Empty Purse," *American Historical Review,* LXVII (October, 1961), 2.

[7] Daniel Ammen, *The Atlantic Coast* (New York, 1898), pp. 14, 16–17, and note p. 16. Ammen was a naval officer under Du Pont on the Port Royal expedition.

as "rather monotonous and uninteresting," but few lived long in the islands without responding to the somber spell of the great live oaks with their festoons of Spanish moss. In spring the islands became intoxicatingly beautiful, alive with lush greenery and the color and fragrance of yellow jasmine, roses, and acacia blossoms. In the fall the scarlet cassena berries gleamed along the roadside hedges with the white tufts of the mockingbird flower. The creeks abounded in fish, oysters, and crabs; on the outer islands wild deer and game birds grew fat and plentiful. One asset the visitor never failed to note was the remarkable song of the mockingbird.[8]

Beaufort, a pleasant little town on Port Royal Island, was the only community in the whole region above the size of a village. Located on the Beaufort River, where it reaches northward to the Coosaw River and St. Helena Sound, the place had no commercial importance. Beaufort's round-the-year inhabitants hardly numbered two thousand souls, but in summer, when the wealthy planters of the islands came to occupy their handsome houses, the population doubled. Flanked by magnolia and orange trees, furnished with mahogany and rosewood, these mansions attested to the prosperity of a class that had made the great staple crops of South Carolina pay well, if not at all times magnificently, over a number of generations. On any Sunday through the summer the casual visitor might have seen in the St. Helena Episcopal Church, built in 1724, as high a concentration of aristocracy per pew as gathered anywhere along the South Atlantic. In the galleries above the gentry were their counterparts in the black world, their house-servants, the Negro aristocracy. These were the "Swonga people," as the common field hands called them. In this sequestered region lived the Heywards, Barnwells, Elliotts, Coffins, and Fripps, along with the eleven thousand Negroes without surnames upon whose

---

[8] Edward L. Pierce, "The Freedmen at Port Royal," *Atlantic Monthly*, XII (September, 1863), 295; William F. Allen manuscript diary, University of Wisconsin, typescript copy, p. 8; Worthington C. Ford (ed.), *A Cycle of Adams Letters, 1861–65* (Boston, 1920), I, 126.

broad backs and nimble fingers rested the cotton culture and the well-ordered but static society of the islands.[9]

It is a remarkable fact that this quiet ocean-side backwater, whose place-names would soon become common newspaper property in the North, possessed a history as long and picturesque as that of any part of America. A hundred years before the pilgrims landed at Plymouth, Spanish explorers under the direction of Lucas Vásquez Ayllón found Port Royal Sound and called the country Santa Elena, a name that has survived in its Anglicized form as St. Helena Island. In 1562 the French briefly challenged the Spanish rule, when Admiral Coligny sent Jean Ribaut to the New World to prepare a refuge for persecuted Huguenots. Sailing onto the splendid sheet of water that bisects the island country, the delighted Ribaut named the place Port Royal. "We struck our sails and cast anchor at ten fathoms of water; for the depth is such, namely when the sea begins to flow, that the greatest ship of France, yea, the Arguzes [sic] of Venice may enter in there." After a friendly reception from the Indians, the Frenchmen built a fort, but its existence was precarious within lands claimed by the King of Spain. Four years later the first Protestant settlement in North America was destroyed.[10]

It was not until the English supplanted the Spanish late in the seventeenth century that the islands began to be settled by white men who came to build homes and carve out plantations. Many of the most prominent of the early settlers of Carolina came from the Barbados, and the attitudes and customs of the West Indies

[9] Thomas J. Woofter, Jr., *Black Yeomanry* (New York, 1930), p. 24; Guion Griffis Johnson, *A Social History of the Sea Islands* (Chapel Hill, 1930), pp. 112, 130.

[10] Paul Quattlebaum, *The Land Called Chicora* (Gainesville, Florida, 1956), is a good secondary account of the French and Spanish in the Carolinas. See page 46 for the quotation, which comes from the account of René Goulaine de Laudonnière, as included in Richard Hakluyt's *Collection of the Early Voyages, Travels, and Discoveries of the English Nation* (London, 1809–1812), III, 373.

toward slavery and plantations were in this way introduced. In time large holdings, staple crops, and Negro slavery became the characteristic economic features of the islands. By 1861 nearly 83 per cent of the total population comprised Negro slaves, who lived and worked under a harsh slave code that still bore the impress of its early origin in the West Indies.[11]

The special peculiarities of topography and climate had served over the years to isolate the island country from the mainland and to promote among the planters an inclination to identify their regional interests narrowly. The low country had produced more than its share of Revolutionary leaders in the war with England, and it had been the very seat of the most intense opposition to the tariff measures that rocked the Federal Union in the 1830's. William Elliott's constituents in St. Helena Parish had forced him, during that crisis, to resign as state senator, because he had stubbornly refused to join the stampede toward state nullification of the tariff. Elliott had warned the voters of his district, in a remarkably prophetic plea, against the pitfalls of over-hasty action. "When you have struck forward the ball of revolution, can you prescribe its path, and regulate its motion? . . . France! Poland! plead for me! Admonish them at least, to understand the true extent of their injuries before they fling themselves recklessly forward into the vortex of revolution."[12] At a time when humanitarian impulses stirred men everywhere, and at a time when Negro slavery was coming under particular attack, Elliott had reason to warn against starting brush fires. James L. Petigru expressed his

[11] Quattlebaum, *Chicora,* pp. 86–88. Edward Pierce wrote that only seven counties in the United States had a higher concentration of slaves than Beaufort, according to the Census of 1860, which gives the figure at 82.8 per cent of the total population. A. W. Stevens (ed.), *Enfranchisement and Citizenship; Addresses and Papers by Edward L. Pierce* (Boston, 1896), p. 69.

[12] Lewis Pinckney Jones, "Carolinians and Cubans: The Elliotts and Gonzales, Their Work and Their Writings" (unpublished doctoral dissertation, University of North Carolina, 1952), Part I, p. 9.

sympathy, writing Elliott that his course had been admired elsewhere in the state, and that he hardly knew what to think of
Beaufort. "For a quiet and rather dull place, it has become another
name for sedition."[13]

The tariff crisis was narrowly averted by President Andrew
Jackson's firm and tactful measures, but the southern tip of South
Carolina remained for the next thirty years a restless and grudging element in the Union. In fact, as the center of the influence of
the Robert Barnwell Rhett family, described by William Elliott,
who did not like them, as "unscrupulous, malignant, and influential," Beaufort became a very seedbed of the secession movement.[14]
As the islanders made ready for the invasion in the fall of 1861,
the younger William Elliott wrote his father, in some amusement,
that although most of the citizens of Beaufort were alarmed, such
was not the case with "old Mrs. Albergottie, who declared, when
she heard that Ed Rhett was at Bay Point, she felt no apprehension
whatever, for he, Mr. Rhett, would *prohibit* the fleet from coming
to Beaufort."[15] Secession leaders had long inflated the confidence
of the people by assuring them that cotton was an economic necessity throughout the world. On the fourth of March, 1858, in a
famous speech from the floor of the Senate, James Henry Hammond taunted his opponents: "Would any sane nation make war
on cotton? . . . England would topple headlong and carry the
whole civilized world with her to save the South. No, you dare
not make war on cotton. No power on earth dares make war upon
it. Cotton *is* King."[16]

[13] Carson, *Petigru*, pp. 98–99.

[14] Jones, "Carolinians and Cubans," Part I, p. 50. See also Laura A.
White, *Robert Barnwell Rhett: Father of Secession* (New York and London, 1931), pp. 109–110, 116.

[15] William Elliott to his father, William Elliott, October 7, 1861, Elliott-
Gonzales MSS.

[16] Elizabeth Merritt, *James Henry Hammond, 1807–1864* (Baltimore,
1923), p. 117. Despite the warmth of his statements, Hammond had become lukewarm about secession by the time the crisis came. See White,
Rhett, p. 170.

Such reckless arrogance reminded friend and foe alike, in early November, 1861, of what it is that pride goes before. On November 3 the ominous ships passed the outer bar at Charleston, and a few days later the fleet massed at Port Royal Sound. To Petigru it looked like a judgment: "On the islands a discovery is made which the inhabitants were slow in coming to, that in a war with an enemy that is master of the sea they are masters of nothing." A Northern newspaper reporter pondered the irony of proud South Carolina's being "attacked in the exclusive home of the most exclusive few of that most exclusive aristocracy . . . the concentrated essence of first-familyism."[17]

The morning sun of November 7 found the blue waters of the Sound as level as a mirror. Even Samuel Francis Du Pont, who was in command of the fleet, could have asked no more. In the Negro vernacular this cloudless day remained forever the "day of the gun-shoot at Bay Point." At 9:25 in the morning the war fleet approached the entrance to the Sound; it was fired upon; and the bombardment began. In a picture-book maneuver, the vessels sailed straight up the Sound, led by Commodore Du Pont's flagship, the *Wabash*. The vessels swept the eastern fort at Bay Point with fire, turned, and, still in perfect formation, moved deliberately against the western fortress on Hilton Head Island. The Union soldiers who watched the battle from the troop transports anchored just outside the bar had the best viewing. They covered the decks and clung to the masts and shrouds, eagerly following the action. The heavy guns rose to a steady and continuous roar as the vessels passed close to the works, pouring in their ammunition. Above the forts the shells burst into puffs of white smoke.[18] "I have seen a big battle," wrote Private E. O. Hill to his family, "but did not take any part in it." The big navy guns had done all

[17] Carson, *Petigru*, p. 413; New York *Daily Tribune*, November 15, 1861.

[18] *Official Records of the War of the Rebellion*, I, vi, 8, cited hereafter as *OR*; Hazard Stevens, *Life of Isaac Ingalls Stevens* (Boston, 1900), II, 347.

the work. "It looked kind of careless to see the old frigate Wabash pour in broad side after broad side into that little fort." Three such turns between the forts were sufficient. The Confederate flags came down, and evacuation began. The booming of the heavy gunfire rolling over the islands was the signal for flight and confusion. Negroes streamed in from the fields and found the white people hastily preparing for flight.[19]

The conflict of that day was recalled vividly after nearly three-quarters of a century by Sam Mitchell, who had then been a young slave of John Chaplin, living on Ladies Island. It was typical of scenes enacted on nearly every plantation. Sam's master, who had been in Beaufort, tore into the yard in his carriage and ordered out the flatboats that would carry his family to Charleston. The boat had eight oars, and the master wanted young Sam's father, the plantation carpenter, to man one of those oars. When Sam's mother heard of this, she shot out to her husband in the Gullah vernacular, as her son recalled, "You ain't gonna row no boat to Charleston, you go out dat back door and keep a-going." Master got the men for his boat, and the Chaplins went to Charleston, but one good slave carpenter and oarsman was not with them. Little Sam stood with his mother and listened to the big guns. The boy thought he heard thunder, but there was not a cloud in the sky. "Son," his mother explained crisply, "dat ain't no t'under, dat Yankee come to gib you Freedom."[20]

While posterity must applaud the accuracy of her instincts, from the point of view of purest fact Sam's mother was, as everybody knows, quite wrong. The problem of defining the status of

[19] E. O. Hill to "Brother Warren," November 12, 1861, Milton and Esther Hawks Manuscripts, Library of Congress; Johnson, *Social History,* pp. 54–55; Stevens (ed.), *Pierce,* p. 80.

[20] Account of Sam Mitchell, Slave Narrative Collection (WPA Federal Writers' Project), XIV, Part III, 202–203. Despite Mr. Mitchell's age, his memory seems to have been perfectly clear, for, except in one detail, the day of the week on which the battle of Port Royal took place, his story agrees with all the contemporary accounts.

refugee Negroes had vexed the government from the very onset of hostilities, but no firm policy had yet evolved. Anxious to hold the Border States from secession, President Lincoln had steadily maintained that the war was to preserve the Union, and only to preserve the Union. As late as the day following the First Battle of Bull Run, Congress had passed resolutions disclaiming any intention to interfere with "the rights or established institutions" of the states.[21]

On the other hand, the sequence of events was already in progress that would vindicate the confidence of Sam Mitchell's mother and the other Sea Island slaves who missed the boat to Charleston. It was much easier for the President and Congress to make policy statements and resolutions than it was for army officers in the field to carry them out. It was difficult to be blind to the fact that slaves were of great use to the states in rebellion, most especially when the convictions of the officer were all on the side of abolition, as was the case of General John C. Frémont. That radical officer had gone so far as to declare martial law throughout Missouri, and he proclaimed that the slaves of all those resisting Federal authority were thenceforth free men. Although Lincoln reprimanded him and forced the recall of the order, Frémont's bold action had fanned the hopes of abolitionists everywhere that the war would bring about emancipation.[22]

General Benjamin F. Butler had taken a more politic course in Virginia, at his command post at Fortress Monroe. Because it formed a direct precedent for the Federal formula as it actually emerged, the general's action is entitled to examination. Hardly a month after Sumter, three slaves who had been used to build a Confederate battery arrived within Butler's lines. Benjamin Butler had been a politician before he became a general, and he was quick to read the signs of the times. A few weeks earlier, his offer

[21] *Congressional Globe*, 37th Congress, 1st session (1861), XXXI, 222–223.
[22] Allan Nevins, *The Improvised War, 1861–1862*, Vol. I of *The War for the Union* (New York, 1959), pp. 331–336.

to use his troops to put down a possible slave uprising in Maryland had brought upon him the severest censure from the abolitionist wing of the Republican party in Massachusetts, Butler's home state. Therefore, when a Confederate officer arrived under a flag of truce to claim the runaway Negroes, the general was in a quandary. Having ascertained that the Negroes in question were about to be sent to South Carolina to help on the fortifications there, Butler borrowed a chapter from international law, declaring that the slaves were now "contraband of war," and refused to return them. In the subtle way of slave "intelligence" the news spread, and within three days Butler had $60,000 worth of human contraband on his hands.[23]

There was no denying the usefulness of the term, no matter what its legal shortcomings may have been. It had the distinct advantage of providing a rational ground for retaining Negro refugees without unduly irritating the political situation in the Border States, and it gave public opinion in the North time to take a positive direction. Official communications of the War Department immediately took up the convenient term.

Of even more importance was the reception of the "contraband idea" among Northern merchants and bankers. During the tense decade preceding the war, these men had often used their power and influence to reduce the impact of abolition agitation. Connected economically and politically, and often socially, with the Southern planting class, they thought they had much to lose by emancipation. In the months following Sumter, however, Northern merchants were forced to acknowledge that their efforts at compromise had failed; thereafter, the same economic considerations that had motivated them as compromisers impelled them to advocate a vigorous offensive. Awake to the fact that a serious

---

[23] Benjamin F. Butler, *Autobiography and Personal Reminiscences of Major-General Benj. F. Butler* (Boston, 1892), pp. 209, 211, 261–262; George R. Bentley, *A History of the Freedmen's Bureau* (Philadelphia, 1955), p. 2. For an able analysis of the legal aspects of the "contraband" definition, see Edward Pierce, "The Contrabands at Fortress Monroe," *Atlantic Monthly*, VIII (November, 1861), 627–630.

war was being waged against their financial interests, and stung by the Confederate embargo and nullification of debts owed in the North, merchants and trading men no longer felt their former solicitude for the slave property of their old allies. If confiscating slave property as "contraband" would help win the war quickly, leaders of trade would not object. One informed observer enlarged upon the value of "such technical terms in shaping public opinion." The implication of property rights and ownership in the word "contraband" was reassuring to "the venerable gentleman who wears gold spectacles and reads a conservative daily, [who] prefers confiscation to emancipation. He is reluctant to have slaves declared freemen, but has no objection to their being declared 'contrabands.' "[24] The Sea Island Negroes were, therefore, after November 7, in terms of current practice, neither slave nor free, but "contraband" property, subject to seizure by the Federal authorities.

Like many another middling position, this one was to prove exceptionally difficult to maintain; it would become increasingly so after the occupation of Port Royal, if for no other reason than the sheer numbers of Negroes involved. Although their masters had circulated a rumor that the Yankees would treat them as slaves and sell them to Cuba, few Negroes seem to have believed the story. Most of the field slaves left no stone unturned to remain on the islands. Whatever the intuitive source of Sam Mitchell's mother's information, thousands of Sea Island slaves shared in it. On the other hand, General T. W. Sherman did not take this advanced view of the matter; and on the day following the bombardment he made a public appeal to the white inhabitants to abandon their defiance, accept the protection of his forces, and rest assured that the Federal government had no intention to interfere with "social and local institutions." The Federal promise not

[24] *Ibid.*, p. 627; for business attitudes, see Philip S. Foner, *Business and Slavery* (Chapel Hill, 1941), pp. 217–223, 275–280, 318–320, 322, and Edith Ellen Ware, "Political Opinion in Massachusetts during the Civil War and Reconstruction," in Columbia University *Studies in History, Economics, and Public Law*, LXXIV, No. 2, whole number 175, p. 47.

to tamper with slavery was a familiar one, but this time nobody seems to have heard it. Certainly there was no response, and Sherman was obliged at last to report that "every white inhabitant has left the islands." He wrote that "St. Helena, Ladies and most of Port Royal [Islands] are abandoned by the whites, and the bountiful estates of the planters, with all their immense property, left to the pillage of hordes of apparently disaffected blacks. . . ."[25]

In the few days between the bombardment and the occupation of Beaufort, life took a turning on the islands that would never be retraced. Those who streamed off to the interior could not know that they would be away for four years, that some would never return. They could not know what changes would take place in their absence. They could not know that their particular part of South Carolina would undergo Reconstruction before the Civil War was over, or that their own social revolution would be accomplished before the process had fairly begun in other parts of the South.

The revolution began with considerable destruction of property. The Negroes on many plantations, thinking to release themselves from the next task in the cotton, broke the cotton gins. In other cases they began looting their masters' houses and furniture, an activity which the Federal soldiers took up enthusiastically until their officers restrained them. The inward significance of these destructive acts on the part of the colored people could scarcely be grasped aside from an understanding of their previous pattern of life, which only a few Northerners then on the islands had attained.[26]

The masters themselves were responsible for a large amount of destruction. Of the three sorts of property they were leaving be-

25 OR, I, vi, 4–6; Stevens (ed.), Pierce, p. 80.

26 See New York Times, February 24, 1862, and New York Tribune, November 20, 1861. There was much conflicting testimony concerning property destruction on the islands, but the most reliable sources concur in the opinion that there was a real Jacquerie following the flight of the masters. This will be dealt with more thoroughly in Chapter 4.

hind—land, slaves, and cotton—real estate seems to have given them least concern. Many came back under cover of darkness in the first few weeks of the Federal occupation in order to set fire to their cotton houses and to attempt, usually without success, to make their slaves come inland with them. Numbers of cotton barns were burned, but cotton in the field was difficult to destroy. One fugitive planter, an advocate of the scorched-earth policy who intended to "make hot work" of his own cotton, explained that the stakes were much higher than the crop itself. The Negroes could be put to work harvesting the crop for the Yankees if it were not burned. *With* the cotton the Negroes were an asset to the invaders; *without* it they were a liability. The slaves would, he thought, in the latter case go hungry, and return to their masters in preference to starvation.[27]

Despite the cluster of doubtful assumptions in the planter's reasoning, he had touched the salient point. For the first time in their long mutual history, the black man would find his relationship to King Cotton a fortunate thing. Although it would not immediately be apparent why this was true, in the long run the circumstance that the slaves and the cotton were taken together as "abandoned property" had more than a little to do with justifying the belief of many slaves that they could date their freedom from the day of the "gun-shoot at Bay Point." The collection of abandoned property was the responsibility of the Treasury Department, and Secretary Salmon P. Chase had emerged as "the mainspring of anti-slavery influence within the councils of the President." As a result of his official position, Chase had the opportunity to foster the first important experiment testing newly released slaves in the responsibilities of free laborers; because of his antislavery convictions, he seized it. At a time when "every member of the Cabinet and the President too looked coldly on," Chase

[27] Stephen Elliott to "My dear brother," November 26, 1861, and Thomas R. S. Elliott to his father, William Elliott, December 6, 1861, Elliott-Gonzales MSS; *Charleston Daily Courier*, November 11, 1861.

launched what came to be known as the Port Royal Experiment.[28]

The Secretary's correspondence during the months following the fall of Port Royal showed him that the government would gain the support of an ever-increasing segment of the public through sterner war measures: "Wagons, Cattle, Horses, Provisions, Negroes not excepted, in short everything useful to our army ought to be appropriated. . ." advised one correspondent, who sharply criticized the government for looking "more to a peace through compromise, than to a . . . victory of arms." He thought public opinion had outrun the Administration. Another correspondent criticized the government for taking pains "to show its loyalty to Slavery, the cause of all our evils, . . ." and for forbidding the army to free "a Rebel's slaves, while allowing [it] to take his life, and confiscate his property, as if a Rebel's right to Slavery was more sacred than his right to life or property." The capture of Port Royal was a "brilliant achievement," but one that would be to little purpose "unless the Government does aright with the institution of Slavery in the region thereabout." Another blunt informant briefed the Secretary on public opinion in northern Ohio, where, he wrote, "no one pretends to deny that Slavery is the cause of this Rebellion. And but very few hope to put down the rebellion and restore the Union without removing the cause of the war."[29]

No matter how clear-cut the issue appeared out in Ohio, from Chase's point of view in Washington it was not easy at first to see how the Port Royal situation could be used in the cause of emancipation. One close observer of the Washington scene thought President Lincoln was "frightened with the success in South Carolina, as in his opinion this success will complicate the question of

[28] Chase's antislavery influence in the Cabinet was unmatched before the appointment of Edwin Stanton to the War Department early in 1862. See Albert Bushnell Hart, *Salmon P. Chase* (Boston, 1899), p. 262; E. L. Pierce to James Miller McKim, McKim MSS, Cornell University.

[29] P. Lambrecht to Chase, November 15, 1861; Adam Jewett to Chase, November 16, 1861; and J. Cable to Chase, November 13, 1861, all in the Chase MSS, Vol. 52, Library of Congress.

slavery." Certainly the President's cautious treatment of the issue in his message to Congress offered little encouragement. He threw the problem of defining the new status of the Negroes at Port Royal and others in their situation into the lap of Congress, and then asked that provisions be made to colonize the liberated Negroes "in a climate congenial to them."[30] Small wonder it was that Chase turned his first attention to contraband cotton rather than to contraband Negroes.

In early December Lieutenant Colonel William H. Reynolds, an officer in the 1st Rhode Island Artillery, came to Secretary Chase with a letter from a family friend. William Sprague, the popular young governor of Rhode Island, thought Reynolds was the man Chase should send to South Carolina to collect the abandoned cotton. He wrote that Reynolds had "for many years occupied the most prominent position in the cotton trade" in his state and was an honest man, one admirably suited to serve the public interests, being, as Sprague had it, "religiously principled." The florid praise carried conviction because Sprague was himself a wealthy cotton manufacturer and because Chase counted the young governor among his personal friends. It was never one of the Secretary's strong points to ascertain integrity or the lack thereof upon short acquaintance, and he always had a kindly desire to please his friends. Time would prove that neither Governor Sprague nor Reynolds could withstand tempting opportunities to coin money from the war effort. But what the Secretary did not then know, he certainly would not suspect of the rich young governor who was soon to become his son-in-law. By the twentieth of December Colonel Reynolds was in Beaufort as the United States agent to collect contraband cotton.[31]

[30]Adam Gurowski, *Diary from March 4, 1861 to November 12, 1862* (Boston, 1862), p. 121; Lincoln's Message to Congress, dated December 3, 1861, in Roy P. Basler (ed.), *The Collected Works of Abraham Lincoln* (New Brunswick, N. J., 1953), V, 48.

[31] Sprague to Chase, December 1, 1861, item 10, Port Royal Correspondence, National Archives, hereafter cited as PRC; David Donald (ed.), *Inside Lincoln's Cabinet: The Civil War Diaries of Salmon P. Chase*

Once Reynolds was on his way, Chase applied himself to the humanitarian aspects of his problem, which were proliferating daily. The rapid change in their status was not working to the immediate advantage of many Sea Island Negroes, and their obvious hardship since the Federal invasion was embarrassing to the government. The army had made free use of plantation food stores, leaving many slave communities with little to eat. Commodore Du Pont ported that numbers of the nearly ten thousand Negroes on the islands were by late winter "almost starving and some naked or nearly so," because, he wrote indignantly, "the *one suit* allowed by the chivalry is made of such wretched quality that it does not hold out the year, and we came before the fall issue. . . ." Except for the plantations where the slave foremen, or "drivers" as they were called, had kept the keys to the storehouses and maintained their previous authority, there was little internal order on the plantations. There were no ordained ministers for the Negroes, and no doctors, at a time when sickness and death made heavy inroads upon them. Having no place to turn, they flocked to the neighborhood of the army camps. There they were as often treated badly as offered employment and help. The New York *Tribune's* correspondent reported that one enterprising and unscrupulous officer was caught in the act of assembling a cargo of Negroes for transportation and sale in Cuba, thus giving one example to bolster the late slave-masters' dire predictions. The situation had become so desperate that General Sherman and Commodore Du Pont were compelled to call upon Northern charity for food and clothing.[32]

(New York, 1954), p. 32; Hart, *Chase*, p. 421; Reynolds to Chase, December 23, 1861, item 24, PRC.

[32] Samuel F. Du Pont to Henry Winter Davis, February 25, 1862; Samuel Francis Du Pont MSS at the Eleutherian Mills Historical Library, Greenville, Wilmington, Delaware; New York *Tribune*, December 7, 1861; Mansfield French to Chase, February 16, 1862, item 65, PRC; *Annual Report of the New-York National Freedmen's Relief Association of New York, with a Sketch of its Early History* (New York, 1866), pp. 7, 8.

This desperate situation was watched with much anxiety by those who hoped to use the opportunities offered at Port Royal to advance the cause of freedom. Abolitionists in the North saw broad vistas opening quite as distinctly as did those who saw the victory in terms of cotton. George W. Smalley, a correspondent of the New York *Tribune* stationed at Beaufort, wrote Senator Charles Sumner describing the need of the Negroes and asking for help. Smalley wanted Sumner to see what could be done about getting public funds for the education of the Negroes "whom this war *must* lift into freedom." Smalley had not been a prewar convert to emancipation, but his abolitionist connections were excellent, for within five days Senator Sumner also heard from Wendell Phillips. The antislavery orator backed up Smalley's request and asked that an able supervisor be put in charge of the training of the liberated slaves.[33]

Something had to be done. If the land should lie fallow and the Negroes idle for long past the middle of February, there would be no cotton in 1862, and the Negroes would have to be supported by the government or charity, thus giving the opponents of emancipation a very good argument. Under the circumstances, it seemed fruitless and cruel to wait for Congress to act, and on the twentieth of December Secretary Chase wired a young Boston attorney named Edward L. Pierce, asking him to come to Washington "at once" if he wished to go to Port Royal to look into the contraband situation. The choice of Pierce was ordained by the coincidence of two facts: He was a close personal friend and political supporter of both Senator Sumner and Secretary Chase, as well as a man of strong antislavery conviction; and he had had more experience with "contrabands" than anyone else.[34] The

[33] Smalley to Charles Sumner, December 15, 1861, and Wendell Phillips to Sumner, December 20, 1861, in Charles Sumner MSS, Houghton Library, Harvard University.

[34] Chase to Pierce, telegram delivered December 20, 1861, Chase MSS; letter Chase to Pierce [n.d.] in Robert Bruce Warden, *An Account of the Private Life and Public Services of Salmon Portland Chase* (Cincinnati,

young lawyer had been among the earliest volunteers for military action and was stationed at Fortress Monroe when General Butler's first contrabands had come through the Union lines. Butler had assigned Pierce to the job of supervising the Negroes at their work, and on the strength of his experiences Pierce wrote an article that had appeared in the November 1861 issue of the *Atlantic Monthly*. In "The Contrabands at Fortress Monroe," Pierce had expressed the fullest confidence in the ability of the Negroes to aid in the war effort, and in their willingness to do so. He had also observed among them a widespread desire to learn to read, and he thought that the Negroes would certainly be no "less industrious, if free, than the whites, particularly as they would have the encouragement of wages." To Pierce it seemed that each Negro who served the cause of the Union "had vindicated beyond all future question, for himself, his wife, and their issue, a title to American citizenship, and become heir to all the immunities of Magna Charta, the Declaration of Independence, and the Constitution of the United States." Pierce saw no reason why Negroes would not make good and responsible soldiers.[35]

Chase wrote Pierce that he wanted him for the job at Port Royal not only because he knew him to be sympathetic to the welfare of the colored people, while he was not sure that Colonel Reynolds would have the inclination or patience to be so, but also because he knew Pierce to be a man of "cool and sound" judgment who would not be misled in his dealings with the Negroes by "mere sympathy" alone. He instructed Pierce that in his work he would prepare the Negroes "for self-support by their own industry hereafter," because, speaking only for himself, Chase could not see, he wrote, how the Negroes who had been "abandoned by their masters" and later "received into the service of the country" could

---

1874), pp. 395–396; for short biographies of Pierce, see Massachusetts Historical Society *Proceedings* [second series], XVIII, 363, and American Antiquarian Society *Proceedings* [new series], XII, 197–210.

[35] Pierce, "Contrabands at Fortress Monroe," pp. 639, 633.

be returned to slavery. They certainly could not be so dealt with, thought Chase, "without great inhumanity on the part of the government." After a conversation with Chase and a few days' reflection, the young lawyer wrote that he would leave for Port Royal immediately. Although he was free to work on the project for only a few months, he felt that this was an undertaking that he was not "at liberty to decline." He did not know Colonel Reynolds, Pierce wrote, but he hoped that there would be "no difference" between them as to "the system and principles of dealing with these people whom Providence has intrusted to our care."[36]

Pierce made the rough passage to Port Royal on the steamer *Baltic*, leaving New York on January 13. Although he remained on the islands more than two weeks, it took Pierce practically no time at all to see that he probably would not agree with Colonel Reynolds on all points. When Reynolds inquired carefully into his orders, he replied evasively that he did not yet know himself just what they were, but he intended "to look about for a week or so. . . ." Upon being pressed further, Pierce replied only that he had not come to interfere with what the Colonel was doing "efficiently and well." This shuffling resulted from Pierce's determination not to show Reynolds his own commission from Chase, which had ordered him to *report* to the Colonel. Pierce complained, perhaps on the basis of his experience as a private in the army, that this gave Reynolds the right, if he put a "military construction" on the word, to set him to work on "the most mechanical labor." He wrote hastily to Secretary Chase, asking him to forward new orders that would place him on an equal footing with Colonel Reynolds. He had misunderstood the purpose of his mission, Pierce wrote, if he was not to have a completely free hand in his investigations.[37]

[36] Chase to Pierce [n.d.] in Warden, *Chase*, pp. 395–396; Pierce to Chase, December 29, 1861, item 29, PRC.

[37] Pierce to Chase, January 19, 1862, item 36, PRC.

As the young lawyer visited the plantations, he had an opportunity to examine the arrangements that Reynolds had made for the collection of the cotton. The work had actually begun before the arrival of Reynolds, at the instigation of General Sherman, who had employed several cotton collectors, paying them a commission based upon the amount of property each secured. After some initial hesitation the Colonel decided to continue the system, merely reducing the percentage slightly. Offering the commission had the advantage, he wrote Chase, of providing the government with "the services of energetic men, who labor night and day. . . ." The Negroes were working at the cotton-picking for an allowance of one dollar for every four hundred pounds of unginned cotton delivered at the steamboat landing, being paid "partly in money and the bal[ance] in clothing and provisions." Some food supplies remained on the plantations, but Colonel Reynolds planned to provide the Negroes with such staples as "salt, molasses and other small stores in moderate quantities[,] deducting the cost of these articles from the am[oun]t due them for labor."[38]

Pierce was a shrewd observer, and he may have seen in these arrangements the outlines of a typical graft opportunity, to achieve its classic form in the "company store" of a later day. If he did, he did not yet think it wise to mention the fact to Chase. There was one open difficulty between the two Treasury agents, however, that was symptomatic of future trouble, and Chase soon heard of it. Reynolds wanted the cotton shipped to New York, to be ginned there rather than on the islands, and he had already approached manufacturers of cotton gins in the city concerning the work. Pierce objected promptly and strenuously, complaining that the advocates of sending the cotton to New York argued that this would help the unemployed classes of the North. He thought this unfair to the Negroes, for it was "of the utmost importance"

[38] Reynolds to Chase, January 1, 1862, item 30, PRC; see also Reynolds to Chase, December 23 and 28, items 24 and 28, in PRC.

that they should keep busy "at the work which they have been accustomed to do. . . ." Reynolds, argued Pierce, was looking to the rapid collection and shipment of the cotton as "the controlling consideration."[39] In any case Pierce avoided precipitating a showdown with Reynolds, allowing the matter to drop, saying that he was ready to defer judgment until he had a chance to study the problem further. The two Treasury agents were looking at the labor situation on the islands from widely differing points of view, and their respective areas of authority were not clearly differentiated. Only the most cooperative attitude could have overcome the problem, which was one that would plague all efforts on behalf of the freedmen throughout the war down to the establishment of the Freedmen's Bureau. Reynolds' orders to secure the cotton implied the use of contraband labor, but Pierce's instructions to observe how best to organize the Negroes for planting and how to address "their moral nature" and secure "their good will" certainly placed them primarily in his charge.[40]

Not only were the two Treasury agents at cross-purposes, but Reynolds had irritated the army officers, in ways not hard to imagine, through his broad construction of his orders to confiscate abandoned property to include household effects and furniture. A good example of this occurred when Reynolds frustrated General Isaac Ingalls Stevens' plan to open the Beaufort Library for the use of his troops. Reynolds' industrious agents confiscated it for shipment north.[41] The situation was not without amusing aspects for those who were not directly involved. It seemed to one sharp observer that the government had "sent out a cotton agent for every bale of cotton, with the rank of Captain." Com-

[39] Pierce to Chase, January 19, 1862, item 36, and Reynolds to Chase, December 28, 1862, item 28, both in PRC.

[40] Pierce stating his understanding of his commission, in letter to Chase, January 19, 1862, item 36, PRC.

[41] Chase to Hiram Barney, March 20, 1862, Restricted Commercial Intercourse, United States Archives; *New York Times*, February 24, 1862.

modore Du Pont wrote a Northern friend, "We have had all kinds of agents out here [,] cotton collectors, statistic collectors, humanitarians [,] philanthropists, etc., the best among them the people of God, starting schools. . . ." He wrote that they all came to visit him, that they differed with each other on nearly all points, "agreeing only on one, abuse of the *Generals*."[42]

In writing of humanitarians and philanthropists, Du Pont could not have been thinking of Colonel Reynolds, and it is unlikely that he referred to Pierce. Pierce would not have liked the label. There was, in all probability, only one visitor to the islands during February who would not have scowled at being called a "philanthropist," a word that carried, in the middle of the nineteenth century, unmistakable overtones of sentimentality and soft-headedness, at least wherever it was not preceded by such apologetic adjectives as "practical" and "common-sense." The Reverend Mr. Mansfield French, who arrived on the islands about a week behind Pierce, was no more ready than the next man to acknowledge a deficiency in common sense, but bad names bothered him little, especially when he was busy about the Lord's work.[43] This was a fortunate circumstance, for, if words could kill, the Methodist minister might not have survived his service in the Lord's army at Port Royal.

Mr. French had come south at the request of Lewis Tappan and George K. Whipple, prominent officers of the American Missionary Association, to discover what they could do in New York City for the Negroes at Port Royal. A commission to make an exploratory visit to the islands presented no difficulties, for French knew Secretary Chase personally, since he was a well-known itinerant evangelist in Ohio during the term of Chase's governor-

[42] Du Pont to Henry Winter Davis, February 25, 1862, Du Pont MSS; Stevens, *Stevens*, II, 368.

[43] For a short biographical treatment of Mansfield French, see Mansfield Joseph French, *Ancestors and Descendants of Samuel French the Joiner* (Ann Arbor, 1940).

ship and had shared with him the initial labors of raising funds for Wilberforce University. Born in 1810 in Manchester, Vermont, French had moved west in his youth and had come to maturity in Ohio during the years of the great religious revivals. Nourished on a yeasty mixture of evangelicalism and democracy, French had turned his hand to practically every good cause available. As preacher, teacher, and college president, he had long been especially interested in education and emancipation and had assumed an active part in establishing a number of colleges in Ohio, including an institution that later became Marietta College, Wilberforce for Negroes, and the Xenia Female Seminary, of which he was president. The outbreak of the Civil War found French in New York City, where he was editing, in cooperation with his wife Austa, a small religious monthly called *The Beauty of Holiness*. By virtue of his personal friendship with Secretary Chase and his important connections with the officers of the American Missionary Association and abolitionists of New York and the West, French had it in his power to be of great assistance to Edward Pierce, provided the two men should agree on the requirements of the situation at Port Royal.[44]

Although twenty years in age, and perhaps twenty leagues in temperament, lay between Pierce and French, they shared a hearty faith in the ability of the colored people to meet the demands of freedom. They also shared a mistrust of Reynolds' agents and were uneasy in mind about the local army officers, with the exception of Chief Quartermaster Rufus Saxton, the only officer much interested in the work for the contrabands. At the beginning of an unpopular undertaking, the two men were thankful for mutual support. Before leaving the islands, French and Pierce had come to an agreement that while Pierce was rallying the

[44] *Ibid.*, pp. 72–82; Beaufort (South Carolina) *Tribune*, March 22, 1876; *A History of the American Missionary Association: Its Churches and Educational Institutions among the Freedmen, Indians and Chinese* (New York, 1874), pp. 12–13.

support of Bostonians, French would marshal aid in New York City for the plan Pierce was proposing in his report to Secretary Chase.[45]

Because of its clarity, its searching survey of the morale of the lately-released slaves, and the obvious breadth of his investigation, Pierce's report of February 3 is a valuable document and a rare one.[46] The author's unmincing revelation of his own convictions on emancipation, combined with a temperate presentation of his conclusions and recommendations, gave it authority. While freely admitting that there were discouraging features in the social life of the erstwhile slaves, Pierce emphasized the positive aspects. Such defects as he had observed in the Negroes came from "their peculiar condition in the past or present, and not from constitutional proneness to evil beyond what may be attributed to human nature." The Negroes were easily influenced by such "higher considerations as duty and the love of offspring," religion, and love of their homes. A class of leaders already existed among them, men who could now exercise a "healthful influence" upon their fellows. Although many among the first Negroes Pierce met seemed anxious "to evade the inquiry whether or not they wished to be free" and seldom evinced the passionate affirmation that he had hoped to hear, Pierce soon found that there was a positive relationship between the amount of independence a slave had enjoyed in his work and his desire to become a free man. Earnest and intelligent Negroes impressed Pierce with their profound desire for freedom and told him how they had longed "to see this day." Negro river pilots had stood up well under fire when serving reconnaissance parties, and there were instances where slaves had armed themselves against Confederate cavalry units. Only those

[45] Report of Edward L. Pierce to Secretary Chase, February 3, 1862, Document 51, in Frank Moore (ed.), *The Rebellion Record*, Supplement, I, 314; Pierce to Chase, January 19, 1862, item 36, PRC; Saxton to French, February 10, 1862, published in the *New York Times*, March 2, 1862.

[46] Pierce's report to Chase, February 3, 1862, in Moore (ed.), *Rebellion Record*, Supplement, I, 302–314.

Negroes who had been most severely bound to the plantation routine seemed "but little awakened." Even those, wrote Pierce, were feeling the "quickening inspiration of present events." All the Negroes wished most earnestly to learn to read and write and to have schools for their children.[47]

Pierce reported that the Sea Island Negroes knew all the steps involved in the cotton culture and that the great majority of them were ready to work, "with proper inducements." They needed the help and protection of white men, however, in Pierce's opinion, and a good system of management. His proposal called for the appointment of a superintendent for each of the larger plantations, or groups of two or three smaller ones, a man who would be paid well and selected "as carefully as one would choose the guardian for his children." The superintendents would be granted authority "to enforce a paternal discipline," but only humane punishments should be administered. Whipping was to be prohibited under any and all circumstances. Control of the entire undertaking should rest with a Director-General or Governor, who should have ample authority to secure law and order on the plantations and to protect the colored people. He would be "a man of the best ability and character," and preferably one with an established public reputation.[48]

The Negroes were no longer slaves, either of their former owners or of the United States government. Although they were "as yet in large numbers unprepared for the full privileges of citizens," the islanders were to be managed "with sole reference" to preparing them for such privileges. If the experiment of a guided transition to freedom could work in the Sea Islands, where slaves had lived in such great isolation and ignorance, Pierce thought it could be "hopefully attempted" anywhere in the South.[49]

In his formal report Pierce omitted reference to an important unofficial part of his plan, that of sending ministers and teachers

[47] *Ibid.*, pp. 310, 308.
[48] *Ibid.*, pp. 310, 311.
[49] *Ibid.*, pp. 311, 310.

to the islands to preach and to open schools for the Negro children. These missionaries would not be "merely pietists or religious exhorters, but persons of good sense who could mingle with their religious exhortations advice and counsel as to how these people should act in their new condition, that is, be industrious, orderly, and sober." All Pierce asked of Chase for these teachers was authorization to go South, leaving their salary to private benevolence. His avowed reason for this was that government support too often detracted from a person's "efficiency and inspiration," but it is more likely that Pierce saw this as one means of maintaining direct abolitionist pressure at Port Royal, regardless of uncertain political influences that might affect the position of the superintendents.[50]

In any event, before leaving for the South Pierce had approached a few friends in Boston about his intention to ask for missionary teachers and had won the backing of the Reverend Mr. Jacob Manning, assistant pastor of the Old South Church. Manning was a radical spirit who, while pronouncing John Brown's raid on Harper's Ferry "an unlawful, a foolhardy, a suicidal act," nevertheless stood before it, as he said, "wondering and admiring." Manning entered into Pierce's project enthusiastically and promised to find both the missionaries and the means to support them. What Jacob Manning agreed to assist Pierce to do in Boston, the Reverend Mansfield French would accomplish in New York. In his report to Chase, French outlined his plan to organize an association in New York City to support the work at Port Royal "and all similar fields as they may be opened to our forces." He asked only for authorization and transportation for the missionaries selected by the association.[51]

[50] Pierce to Chase, January 19, 1862, item 36, PRC; Pierce to the Reverend Mr. Jacob Manning, January 19, 1862, Edward Atkinson MSS, Massachusetts Historical Society.

[51] C. Vann Woodward, "John Brown's Private War," in Daniel Aaron (ed.), *America in Crisis* (New York, 1952), p. 115; French to Chase, February 16, 1862, item 65, PRC.

Pierce returned North in mid-February and began a campaign to implement his proposals. His own report on the condition of the freedmen was his best advocate. It was published widely and read with interest by a public increasingly eager for authoritative information on that almost entirely unknown being who was slowly but surely being recognized as the key figure in the terrible civil conflict. Even those who derided Pierce's proposals as "a very mad scheme" admitted grudgingly that it had created "a stir and excitement in the North. . . ." An English publication carried the gist of the report under the title, "Mr. Pierce's Ten Thousand Clients."[52]

It seemed to one friend of emancipation, a close observer of the Washington scene, that "the active and acting abolitionists" could not do better than "concentrate all their efforts" on the Port Royal project, because "the success of a productive colony there would serve as a womb for the emancipation at large." Success there would certainly answer the first of two questions Pierce singled out as those that must be met before "the general sense of mankind" would confer upon the Negroes "permanent security in law or opinion." It was: "Will the people of African descent work for a living?"[53] The second question was a more direct product of that institutionalized form of human selfishness, the public interest, and it asked whether the Negro would fight for his freedom.

[52] *New York Times*, March 20, 1862; Stevens (ed.), *Pierce*, pp. 55–56.
[53] Gurowski, *Diary*, written sometime in January, 1862, p. 147; Stevens (ed.), *Pierce*, p. 57.

two GIDEON'S BAND

PIERCE REAPPEARED IN WASHINGTON PROPELLED BY THE KNOWL-
edge that he had no time to lose. Starting a free-labor experiment
with a full contingent of superintendents, agricultural supplies,
and tools for approximately two hundred cotton plantations would
be expensive, and getting the government to pay for it might not
be easy. Many persons would undoubtedly regard the Port Royal
venture as impractical and visionary, and Secretary Chase was
worried about money as never before. It was already well understood that unless the government bowed to the necessity of creating a paper currency and making it legal tender, an expedient
that was equated in some quarters with bankruptcy of the state
if not with downright immorality, it would be unable to meet its
debts.[1] Meanwhile, time was wasting, and every day's delay now
meant a day lost for the 1862 crop. The government would undoubtedly take steps to put the cotton lands under cultivation, but
Pierce was well aware that there was a plan alternative to his own
that had very serious backing. While he was asking the government to gamble on the success of a novel agricultural experiment,
Colonel Reynolds proposed leasing the plantations and the laborers
to a private organization. Reynolds' plan had the merit of simplicity and much better prospects of immediate revenue to the
government.[2]

[1] See Pierce's report of February 3, 1862, reproduced in Frank Moore
(ed.), *The Rebellion Record* (New York, 1866), Supplement, I, Document 51, 303, 312. Bray Hammond, "The North's Empty Purse, 1861–
1862," *American Historical Review*, LXVII (October, 1961), 2–4.

[2] Moore (ed.), *Rebellion Record*, Supplement, I, 310–311; William Reynolds to S. P. Chase, February 1, 1862, item 45, PRC.

The specific leasing proposal most seriously advanced, one that Governor Sprague of Rhode Island, always interested in everything pertaining to cotton, had recommended to Chase, and a plan that Colonel Reynolds had offered gratuitously to supervise, was not without certain trimmings that seemed to indicate a concern for the welfare of the Negroes. They were to have their housing, clothes, and food supplied without cost, and a chance to attend school during three months of the year. They were also to receive wages. These were to be at a low rate, however, and, as the plan was originally conceived, even these small wages were to be withheld until the expiration of the lease.[3]

Pierce recognized that these doubtful concessions did not add up to a free status, and in his widely-printed report he had attacked the leasing proposal briskly. Those anxious to obtain leases would have as their "leading object," he charged, the raising of "a large immediate revenue"; and those who succeeded in obtaining leases would be in a tortuous moral posture indeed. "No man, not even the best of men, charged with the duties which ought to belong to the guardians of these people, should be put in a position where there would be such a conflict between his humanity and his self-interest. . . ." While Pierce admitted that the leasing plan might in the short run be more profitable to the government, he insisted that this was of no moment compared with the possible loss of a great opportunity to inaugurate "a beneficent system which will settle a great social question, insure the sympathies of foreign nations, now wielded against us, and advance the civilization of the age."[4]

It was in later years a matter of personal pride to Pierce that he had blocked proposals which would have held the Negroes "*adscripti glebae*" and that he had set the initial work at Port Royal

---

[3] *Ibid.*; Ellis, Britton, & Eaton to Chase, February 3, 1862, item 46, PRC; Ellis, Britton, & Eaton, *Proposition to Employ Liberated Negroes*, a broadside (Springfield, Vermont, December 18, 1861).

[4] Moore (ed.), *Rebellion Record*, Supplement, I, 310–311.

"on a thorough anti-slavery basis."[5] Secretary Chase endorsed the general outlines of Pierce's plan and on February 15 sent Pierce to see President Lincoln. Harassed as he had been by those who wished to push him ahead of public opinion on the slavery question, and grieved personally by the critical illness of his young son, Lincoln's famous humor failed him entirely. He received Pierce with scant patience and, after listening a few moments, stated flatly that he did not think he ought to be bothered with such details. He asked irritably why there was such an "itching" to get the Negroes inside the Federal lines. When his young visitor explained that the Negroes at Port Royal had always lived where they now were and that it was their masters who had run away, not they, the President picked up a card and wrote Chase a crisp note authorizing him to give Pierce "in his discretion . . . such instructions in regard to Port Royal contrabands as may seem judicious."[6]

The young lawyer undoubtedly had hoped to hear some reassuring word from Lincoln about the future status of the Negroes at Port Royal. This was a point that had disturbed many prospective supporters of the educational work, for they feared that after being treated as freemen and trained to support themselves the Negroes might become the victims of "some unhappy compromise." Although Pierce could get no official commitment, some comfort was to be extracted from reports that Lincoln was saying privately that Negroes within the lines who had been engaged in the service of the United States should be defended in their freedom. There were no public statements, however, and the Port Royal plans drew from him at this time the exclamation, according to one account, that handling the slavery question was "a big job," one that he feared would "smother" the government. Congressmen whom Pierce buttonholed were more courteous listeners,

[5] Edward L. Pierce to James Miller McKim, December 13, 1866, McKim MSS, Cornell University.

[6] A. W. Stevens (ed.), *Addresses and Papers of Edward L. Pierce* (Boston, 1896), pp. 86–87.

perhaps, but no more encouraging than the President. They seemed, thought the young lawyer, either "to dread the magnitude of the social question" or to regard it as being, for the time at least, outside their area of responsibility.[7]

When Pierce returned to Boston, he found there all the enthusiasm he had missed at the national capital. But the enthusiasm proper to Boston was private and efficient, and it neatly avoided the unpredictable action of a public meeting. The Reverend Mr. Jacob Manning began by publishing the letter Pierce had written him from the islands, in which he called for teachers of "talent and enthusiasm . . . regulated by good understanding." The letter appeared in the January 27 Boston *Transcript*, and at the same time a handful of citizens who needed no introduction in Boston sent invitations to prospective supporters asking them to meet at Manning's house on February 4 to organize for the work at Port Royal. At this first meeting little was accomplished beyond the election of a chairman and secretary and the naming of essential committees. Three days later, a second meeting was held at the Young Men's Christian Association, with seventeen members present; and the group adopted a constitution, named themselves the Educational Commission, and declared their aim to be "the industrial, social, intellectual, moral and religious elevation of persons released from Slavery in the course of the War for the Union."[8] There seemed small danger that the Bostonians would cut the cloth too small or underestimate what the Negroes required of them. It was only at this juncture, after battle had been joined all along the line, that a public meeting was called for February 17

[7] *Ibid.*, pp. 86–88; Adam Gurowski, *Diary from March 4, 1861, to November 12, 1862* (Boston, 1862), p. 223.

[8] *First Annual Report of the Boston Educational Commission for Freedmen*, May, 1863 (Boston, 1863), pp. 4, 7; invitation, No. 2, in John Albion Andrew Manuscripts, Massachusetts Historical Society. The original of Pierce's letter to Jacob Manning, dated January 19, 1862, is in the Edward Atkinson Manuscripts, also in the Massachusetts Historical Society.

at Boston's Old South Church, where "leading clergymen" spoke and "warmly enlisted the people" behind the good work.[9]

Pierce wrote Chase that Boston was "profoundly moved" by affairs at Port Royal and that upon his return to the city he had "represented the facts quite fully to large numbers of persons specially invited to private houses where gentlemen of wealth and position have attended." He subsequently described these first backers of the educational work as persons of "much consideration" in their communities, "of unostentatious philanthropy" and "energetic and practical benevolence, hardly one of whom has ever filled or been a candidate for a political office." A more informative and less effusive analysis would have indicated that the professions most largely represented were the ministry and teaching, ably backed up by a contingent of public-spirited business leaders, among whom were some of the wealthiest men in Boston. In securing as president John Albion Andrew, the popular war governor of Massachusetts, the Educational Commission provided a distinguished exception to Pierce's generalization about political figures.[10]

Most of the members of the General Committee of the Educational Commission were recognized as being staunch opponents of slavery. Neither Wendell Phillips nor William Lloyd Garrison was included on this original committee, but several prominent citizens whose adherence to abolition went back as far as 1834 to the mobbing of Garrison were active leaders in the new work. Among these were Henry Ingersoll Bowditch and George B. Emerson. Most of the committeemen, however, were younger

[9] Papers of the Bureau of Refugees, Freedmen and Abandoned Lands (hereinafter cited BRFAL), Synopses of School Reports, I, 339, National Archives.

[10] Pierce to Chase, February 21, 1862, item 72, PRC; Stevens (ed.), *Addresses and Papers*, p. 89; John A. Andrew to Edward Atkinson, February 11, 1962, Atkinson MSS. A listing of the original officers of the Educational Commission is to be found in *Extracts from Letters Received by the Educational Commission of Boston from Teachers Employed at Port Royal and Its Vicinity* (Boston, 1862), p. 4.

and had come to the antislavery cause in the 1850's as a result of the intense opposition to the Fugitive Slave Act, the Free Soil movement, and the Kansas wars. Edward Everett Hale, the first chairman of the commission, had been a prominent officer in the Kansas Emigrant Aid Society, organized to arm and equip free settlers from New England to fight the proslavery influence in the new territories. Dr. Samuel Cabot had been one of the largest contributors to that movement, and young Edward Atkinson had been one of the most active solicitors. Most of the money that Atkinson had raised went to arm John Brown. Atkinson had also been a member of the Committee of Vigilants to help runaway slaves escape recapture, a cause with which several other members of the commission had been openly identified.[11]

Many of the leaders of the Port Royal Experiment had been too young at the beginning of the abolition movement to have any political views whatever. When their consciences were roused in the 1850's by the Kansas conflict, what they saw was a contest between two systems of labor, and in subsequent efforts to advance the cause of emancipation they frequently argued the practical economic advantages of freedom. Edward Atkinson, for instance, who was chosen secretary of the Education Commission, had recently attracted considerable attention by the publication of a pamphlet called "Cheap Cotton by Free Labor," a strong argument for emancipation as a war measure. The author was at this time treasurer and agent for six cotton-manufacturing firms in Boston, and he was rapidly becoming an authority on all phases

[11] Vincent Yardley Bowditch, *Life and Correspondence of Henry I. Bowditch* (Boston, 1902), I, 92–102, 272; John L. Thomas, *The Liberator: William Lloyd Garrison* (Boston, 1963), pp. 206–207; Jean Halloway, *Edward Everett Hale* (Austin: University of Texas Press, 1956), pp. 4–5, 196–213. For Cabot's part in the Kansas movement, see Oscar Sherwin, *Prophet of Liberty, The Life and Times of Wendell Phillips* (New York, 1958), p. 756. For Atkinson's part, see Harold F. Williamson, *Edward Atkinson, The Biography of an American Liberal, 1827–1905* (Boston, 1934), pp. 4, 7, 8. Garrison became active in the work of freedmen's education at a later date.

of the cotton business. Atkinson attempted to convince cotton manufacturers that emancipation would not *decrease* their cotton supply but *increase* it.[12]

To men like Atkinson, the opportunity offered at Port Royal was a godsend. The heaviest gun that conservatives, North or South, had ever had in their arsenal was the fearful question of what would happen if the Negroes were "turned loose" on society. What if they should prove unwilling to work? Atkinson and others of his persuasion among younger writers on economic subjects had been looking for just such an opportunity to demonstrate in a conclusive way the superior productivity of free labor. Far from the Border State area and safely insulated from interference from the old masters, the Sea Island conditions seemed ready and waiting for a real transplanting of Northern values.[13] The Port Royal Experiment would encompass political and social changes to equal the transition from slavery to freedom. The decadent South, with its antique civil arrangements, would be regenerated by the vigorous institutions of New England, the public-school system, "liberal Christianity," and even the town meeting, if possible. But most of all, its sponsors thought the Port Royal Experiment would prove that the fundamental precept of classical economics, progress through enlightened self-interest, was altogether color-blind. Much was expected of the Negroes at Port Royal.[14]

Veteran abolitionists of the 1830's had never been greatly absorbed in the question of slavery as one of two rival *labor* systems. For them it was primarily a moral question. Numbers of them joined in the Port Royal movement, however, and viewed the

---

[12] *Ibid.*

[13] *Ibid.*; Frederick Law Olmsted to Atkinson, October 31, 1861, Atkinson MSS.

[14] Edward S. Philbrick to [?], February 19, 1862, in Elizabeth Ware Pearson (ed.), *Letters from Port Royal* (Boston, 1906), p. 1; Pierce, "The Freedmen at Port Royal," *Atlantic Monthly*, XII (September, 1863), 291.

project as a culmination of their own mighty labors. Maria Weston Chapman, for instance, was ready to give credit where it was due. "Our lectures of 30 years' standing do not put the case so squarely and effectually as the rising generation," she generously acknowledged after hearing Pierce address a meeting. "We were trained to a preparatory work, and well we have performed it," she wrote, but now there was a new call, a summons "to the duty of expansion in freedom, as the flag goes forward delivering the blacks from slavery." Mrs. Chapman thought herself too old to be of much use at Port Royal but felt it her duty "to sustain that movement strongly." Lydia Maria Child sent a contribution and asked that she and her husband, David Lee Child, be enrolled as members of the Educational Commission. She suggested the names of others who might be interested and offered a little advice that was true to form: "Excuse me if I take the liberty to suggest," she wrote, "that no person even suspected of a pro-slavery bias ought to be employed." She was sure that "such habits of thought and feeling" would handicap a teacher greatly in dealing with the colored people.[15]

Quite aside from the exalted aims of remodeling Southern society and spreading New England civilization among the liberated slaves, there was also the simple but imperative call to provide for the physical needs of those who through no fault of their own were suffering as a result of the war. This offered a broader basis for popular support than all the branches of the anti-slavery movement combined. What reasonable citizen could shirk the responsibility pointed out so plainly by the Educational Commission: "The people of the North owe at least thus much to the subject-people of the South—that their condition shall not be the *worse* for our invasion." If the slaves did not gain something from their new liberty, then Northerners would stand convicted be-

[15] Mrs. M. W. Chapman to E. B. Chapman [February 16, 1862], Vol. 6, No. 92, Weston MSS, Boston Public Library. This letter has been dated from internal evidence; Lydia Maria Child to William Endicott, March 2, 1862, Atkinson MSS.

fore Southerners of "that spurious philanthropy" of which they had so often been accused. "We may hope . . . to do for these stepchildren of nature all their masters have failed to do, but we must certainly begin by doing what their masters did not and could not omit."[16]

So compelling were the obvious physical needs of the Negroes to the conscience of the general citizenry that the Reverend Mr. Mansfield French and his assistants in New York launched their main public drive on that basis. The original impetus for the organization in New York City came from Lewis Tappan, George Whipple, and other prominent officers of the American Missionary Association, men who had been following the contraband situation with interest and anxiety since the opening of hostilities. The AMA had actually launched the movement for aid to refugee Negroes in a small way in the preceding summer by sending to Edward Pierce the first missionary for the contrabands at Fortress Monroe. It had been at the suggestion of Lewis Tappan that Mansfield French made his exploratory visit to the Sea Islands.[17]

From its inception the American Missionary Association had been strongly antislavery, serving as an institutional channel for the energies of those evangelical abolitionists of New York City who had found it equally impossible to follow the Garrisonians up the high road to universal reform on the one hand, and on the other to work with the older church mission boards that were so often dominated by men they regarded as being too softhearted toward slaveholding. In the AMA they had their own organization, and because the antislavery conviction of the leading officers was never open to question, they were in an excellent position to

[16] *Address to the Public by the Committee of Correspondence of the Educational Commission* (Boston [c. late February, 1862]).

[17] *A History of the American Missionary Association; Its Churches and Educational Institutions among the Freedmen, Indians and Chinese* (New York, 1874), p. 13; Report of George Whipple, Synopses of School Reports, Educational Division, BRFAL, I, entry 158, 323–327; Beaufort *Tribune*, March 22, 1876.

launch the work for relief of the contrabands.[18] It seemed, however, to Tappan and George Whipple, when they discussed the problems of Port Royal with French upon his return from the islands, that this was a job too large for their organization to manage alone. Perhaps they grasped the idea that there was no better way to advance antislavery in the opinion of the public at large than to enlist public interest in preparing the slave to be a free man. In any event, the gentlemen decided that "the emergency required some further instrumentalities," which would be "likely to enlist a constituency that the Association could not reach." They therefore called a public meeting at Cooper Institute for the evening of February 20 and read a public appeal for contraband relief signed jointly by General Sherman and Commodore Du Pont. Largely attended by generous citizens who made financial contributions almost before being asked to do so, the meeting adopted resolutions to meet both the short-term physical needs and the longer-range educational requirements of the Negroes. A committee of organization was appointed, and two days later a constitution was drawn up and a program laid out aiming at the same broad goals that the Bostonians had espoused for "the relief and improvement" of the released slaves. The great objects would be to teach the Negroes "civilization and Christianity" as well as "order, industry, economy, and self-reliance; and to elevate them in the scale of humanity, by inspiring them with self-respect."[19]

Calling their organization the "New York National Freedmen's Relief Association" was undoubtedly a piece of presumption on

[18] For an able description of the origins of the AMA, see Richard Bryant Drake, "The American Missionary Association and the Southern Negro, 1861–1888" (unpublished doctoral dissertation, Emory University, 1957), p. 4. John L. Thomas, *The Liberator*, includes a good recent account of the split between the Garrisonians and the evangelicals. See pp. 291–293.

[19] *A History of the AMA*, p. 13; *National Freedmen's Relief Association Organized in the City of New York on 22nd of February 1862* (New York, 1862); William A. White to Edward Atkinson, February 21, 1862, Atkinson MSS.

the part of the New Yorkers, a species of municipal imperialism that was instinct in their hopeful resolution that "committees raised or about to be raised in other cities and towns throughout the free states, be invited to become auxiliaries to the committee organized in New York. . . ." There was small likelihood that the Bostonians would rush into the New York orbit on less than an equal axis; but shortly the two organizations began to act together in organizing the Port Royal mission, and within a few weeks a loose union had been effected.[20] There was good reason to hope that the organizations might cooperate more easily than the rival branches of the antislavery movement had been able to do, for the public interest encompassed a broader spectrum, and much of the fire had gone out of the burning issues of twenty years before. When it appeared that the course of the war might well bring an end to slavery, few would care to argue that good abolitionists should refrain on principle from participation in national politics. Another fruitful source of discord of other days had evaporated from the moment the slavery question eclipsed all others in immediacy. It was harder for abolitionists to be disagreeable now that they were no longer in a constant posture of hostility to the established social order. When so familiar an abolitionist as Maria Weston Chapman could go into Boston and hear numbers of people, "ex-pro-Slavery people," express "regret and repentance" for their former unenlightened views, assuring her that "you were right and we were wrong," there seemed to be only one threat to ultimate success, short of a possible military debacle, and that was overconfidence. Mrs. Chapman wrote Edward Atkinson to place her blessing on the Port Royal Experiment, and asked if, "from the high historic view, was ever progress so swift?—But thirty

[20] Articles of agreement signed on March 20, 1862, by Edward Atkinson and Jacob Manning for the Educational Commission and by Judge John W. Edmonds and William Cullen Bryant for New York. Philadelphia had also organized for the work by March 20, and Philip P. Randolph and Stephen Colwell signed for their organization, which was called the Port Royal Relief Committee. The document is in the Atkinson MSS.

years from the *start*, and you are organizing the leading slave state in Freedom!"[21]

Even Mrs. Chapman knew, however, that the antislavery crusade was not over, and that the organizers of the Port Royal work had never received the reassurances they had sought from the government as to the future status of the Negroes at Port Royal. "The flag," she wrote, "has to wait on the creation and consolidation of public sentiment for *permission* to go forward." But the committees in New York and Boston went to work, interviewed and selected their superintendents and teachers, and raised the funds to support them. They were "wisely determined to do what they could to prepare the freedmen to become self-supporting citizens," reported Edward Pierce, "in the belief that when they had become such, no government could ever be found base enough to turn its back upon them."[22] They worked with commendable speed and efficiency, for in two weeks following Pierce's return to Boston, on Sunday, March 2, fifty-three men and women were in New York preparing to leave for South Carolina on the following day. The thirty-five persons sent from Boston had been selected painstakingly from a total of one hundred fifty applicants. Pierce had from the beginning pointed out what a rare opportunity Port Royal provided a young clergyman who might wish to serve his country but who was "by his profession excluded from bearing arms." "From such labors," thought Pierce, "even genius and learning ought not to shrink."[23]

They did not. Pierce was more than satisfied, for he found among the young people heading for the islands "some of the choicest young men of New England, fresh from Harvard, Yale, and Brown, from the divinity-schools of Andover and Cambridge,

[21] Maria Weston Chapman to E. B. Chapman [February 16, 1862], Weston Family MSS, Vol. 6, No. 92; Maria Weston Chapman to Edward Atkinson [n.d., but probably late March, 1862], Atkinson MSS.

[22] *Ibid.*; Stevens (ed.), *Addresses and Papers*, pp. 88–89.

[23] *Ibid.*, p. 91; *Educational Commission*, a broadside (Boston, March 14, 1862); Pierce to Manning, January 19, 1862, Atkinson MSS.

—men of practical talent and experience. There were some," he wrote, "of whom the world was scarce worthy. . . ." The twelve women of the party had formed no part in Pierce's original plan for the Port Royal expedition, and he was not altogether easy in mind about their presence. Time would vindicate the ladies, but for the moment Pierce firmly and cheerfully assigned to the Reverend Mr. Mansfield French the full responsibility for all the women, "even those who go from Boston," remarking that since the "sending of ladies is as yet an experiment," its success should rest with Mr. French, who had proposed the idea. On the evening before their departure the missionaries assembled in the library of the home of Hiram Barney, the burly Collector of the Port of New York, where they placed their hands on the Bible, in groups of six, and took the wartime oath of allegiance. They received their passports to Port Royal.[24]

A cold northeast drizzle enshrouded New York City on the morning of March 3. On Canal Street, where the steamer *Atlantic* was loading for the Southern voyage, the customary confusion of embarkation was compounded by the nasty weather. Vanishing into the hold of the paddle-wheeled transport went large stores of clothing, medicines, supplies, farm equipment, and seeds, all destined for the cotton plantations. Collector Barney, who stood with his papers in the throng on the pier, ruffled through the red tape and administered the oath to those who had not been present the evening before. There was a bleak moment when Edward Pierce refused to allow aboard a lady teacher who had not obtained the proper clearance, and she became as damp and ungracious as the weather. At last the ship was loaded, however; the Collector bundled up his papers, the wharf emptied, and the *At-*

[24] Pierce, "The Freedmen at Port Royal," p. 299; Pierce to Chase, February 21, 1862, PRC; Henry Noble Sherwood (ed.), "The Journal of Miss Susan Walker," in *Quarterly Publication of the Historical and Philosophical Society of Ohio*, VII, No. 1, (January–March, 1912), 11; Pearson (ed.), *Letters*, pp. viii, 2.

lantic plowed away through a blanket of fog and freezing rain.[25]

Pierce's evangels of civilization, as they sometimes called themselves, were watched curiously by their fellow passengers and hardly less so by each other. "It is a queer farrago we are," wrote William Channing Gannett, a young teacher from Boston, "clerks, doctors, divinity-students; professors and teachers, underground railway agents and socialists," young and old, with "white hairs and black." There were "Unitarians, free-thinkers, Methodists, straitlaced, and the other Evangelical sects." The young diarist seemed relieved to add, however, that in spite of this denominational variety he had heard "no expressions of bigotry," and that everybody seemed "pretty earnest and quite fraternal." And so it was that if Miss Susan Walker, who had come as a friend and personal representative of Secretary Chase, heard an occasional "discordant strain" in the spirited hymns the evangels sang on the deck in the evenings, it was undoubtedly owing to a want of vocal rather than of spiritual harmony.[26]

Among the passengers outside Pierce's band was one prominent citizen who watched the "villiantropic society," as he denominated the missionaries in a conscious adaptation of Charles Dickens, with more than ordinary interest. John Murray Forbes of Boston was a man whose talent for business was written in his shrewd and sharp-featured yet genial face; he was the very quintessence of Yankee success. As an important mercantile and

[25] Descriptions of the embarkation for Port Royal are found in the following: Sarah Hughes Forbes (ed.), *Letters and Recollections of John Murray Forbes* (Boston and New York, 1899), I, 294–295; Edward S. Philbrick to Helen Philbrick, March 5, 1862, in Pearson (ed.), *Letters*, pp. 2–3; the manuscript diary of William Channing Gannett, entitled "Steamer Atlantic," entry for March 3, 1862, located at the University of Rochester. The supplies sent are mentioned in *Annual Report of the New York National Freedmen's Aid Society of New York with a Sketch of Its Early History* (New York, 1866).

[26] Gannett, "Steamer Atlantic" journal, entry March 7, 1862; Sherwood (ed.), "Walker Journal," p. 12.

railroad leader, he had thought long and hard about slavery but
had never been able to resolve his own personal dilemma regarding
abolition. Forbes hated the peculiar institution and feared its
extension into the territories, but he had never quite seen how
emancipation could be achieved without rending the fabric of
society beyond repair. Although he had contributed handsomely
to the Free Kansas cause and had used his Hannibal and St. Joseph
railroad line to transport men and Sharps rifles straight into the
troubled territories, Forbes had been unwilling to identify himself publicly with the antislavery movement. He had regarded
abolitionists as a class as "arbitrary and illiberal" and had once
equated emancipation with "murder, fire, and rape." As late as
August of 1861, he had feared that emancipation would cause a
slave insurrection, and he was not ready to accept that result.
Forbes was, in short, the sort of business leader who might have
sat for Pierce's verbal portrait of the man with the gold spectacles
and the conservative daily. He knew how to recognize necessities.
Although never a prewar abolitionist, he might well become a wartime emancipationist.[27]

There seemed small likelihood that John Murray Forbes's opinion of abolitionists would be revised upward en route to Port
Royal. His humor had not been improved by a long wait on the
dock in the raw weather, and his first impressions of the missionaries Collector Barney was swearing in were distinctly sour. He
described them as "bearded and mustached and odd-looking men,
with odder-looking women. . . . You would have doubted," he
wrote, "whether it was the adjournment of a John Brown meeting or the fag end of a broken-down phalanstery! . . ."[28]

Mr. Forbes may have been unaware that beards were returning
to fashion's favor, but it is probable, in any event, that his impressions were formed by subtler emanations of character. A brisk
young engineer from Boston named Edward Philbrick was also

[27] Hughes (ed.), *Forbes*, I, 239, 294–296, 317–318.
[28] *Ibid.*, pp. 294–295.

looking nervously about, and he perhaps came closer to the point than Forbes had when he wrote of his fellows that "a good many look like broken-down schoolmasters or ministers who have excellent dispositions but not much talent." He was afraid that they might not succeed at cotton-planting.[29] There must have been a certain seediness, a distillation of frayed cuffs and faraway expressions, which, taken together with their patent idealism, caused Forbes to set the missionaries down as the fag end of a reform. Through his characterization there flickered yet another image, however—a more significant one. As successors of old John Brown, a fanatic now reincarnate in the mold of the fighting prophets of the Old Testament, Pierce's little band could lay claim to a militant zeal to make war on evil. This was a conception of themselves that the missionaries were ready to honor. Like the "Puritans" of old, they would accept as an accolade a derisive nickname that the soldiers quickly fastened upon them.[30] As "Gideonites" they carried a pitcher of light and a trumpet apiece, and they were the more certain of victory because their numbers were few. They moved forward to another battle between freedom and slavery in the spirit of the free-soil settlers of Kansas, for whom John Greenleaf Whittier wrote a song in 1854:

> We go to rear a wall of men
> On Freedom's southern line,
> And plant beside the cotton tree
> The rugged Northern pine![31]

Edward Pierce would have been offended gravely to think that Mr. Forbes, a distinguished fellow-townsman from Milton, regarded his party even in the very beginning as a collection of

[29] Edward Philbrick to Mrs. Philbrick, March 2, 1862, in Pearson (ed.), *Letters*, p. 2.

[30] Hughes (ed.), *Forbes*, I, 300.

[31] *The Complete Poetical Works of John Greenleaf Whittier*, (Boston, 1894), p. 317.

fanatics. Pierce had himself taken pains to eliminate the lunatic fringe. Only two days before leaving New York he had rejected three applicants referred to him by no less a personage than Senator Charles Sumner, on the ground that they showed a reluctance to sign the oath of allegiance, claiming that they were "non-resistants." As members of Hopedale, a community of Christian perfectionists at Milford, Massachusetts, they were pledged to pacifism, and they feared that taking the oath might oblige them to break their rule. Pierce had not a doubt of his duty. He explained to the Senator that in an army post where soldiers were being trained to fight for their country "such views could be offensive." He also wanted people at Port Royal who would not take away from the Negroes the "little manhood left them by inculcating the doctrine of non-resistance."[32]

Pierce had been looking for the best, and eccentrics formed no part of his conception of what was best for Port Royal. The hand-picked young men Pierce brought from Boston were, in fact, so remarkable for their similarities to one another that one is forced to the conclusion that most of those who gave the anomalous complexion to Gideon's Band came from New York. The young men from Massachusetts were uniformly well educated; they were well grounded in the antislavery conviction, being in many cases sons and relatives of well-known abolitionists; and a large number of them were Unitarian. Of the thirteen described particularly by Pierce in a letter to Secretary Chase, only five were more than twenty-five years of age, and all but one of those over twenty had earned the college degree. In addition to the recent college graduates, there were two engineers and the two medical doctors. In view of the first assignment of the Gideonites, to plant cotton, the presence of only one young man bold enough to list himself as a *farmer* is noteworthy. T. Edwin Ruggles' farming experience must necessarily have been limited, however, for he was only

---

[32] E. L. Pierce to Charles Sumner, March 20, 1862, Charles Sumner Papers, Houghton Library, Cambridge, Massachusetts. The Hopedale community is described in Thomas' *The Liberator*, pp. 313–314.

twenty-four and had only recently received his degree from Yale. Four of the whole number of thirty from Boston went without salary, but the Educational Commission paid the others from $25 to $50 per month.[33]

Edward Philbrick wrote of his fellows, "Our Boston party improves upon acquaintance, and the longer I think of the matter the more wonderful does it seem that such a number of disinterested, earnest men should be got together at so short a notice to exile themselves from all social ties and devote themselves, as they certainly do, with a will, to this holy work. It must and with God's help it *shall* succeed!" Already thirty-four years old himself, married, and well-established in his career as an engineer and architect, young Philbrick was coming to Port Royal at considerable personal sacrifice. He not only volunteered his own services without charge but also contributed $1,000 outright to the initial funds of the Educational Commission. Philbrick was recognized promptly as "one of the most valuable men on the mission."[34]

As the son of a well-known abolitionist, Samuel Philbrick, who had been for many years treasurer of the Massachusetts Anti-Slavery Society and a friend of Garrison, young Philbrick had learned to hate slavery in his childhood. To one staunch woman abolitionist it seemed a wonderful blessing that Philbrick's dead father, who had "fought the thirty years' fight" for freedom, should have as his heavenly reward "a son like Edward to spring into the breach where he falls, and to enter the so-long-invested city."[35] Young Philbrick's youthful convictions had been

[33] Pierce to Salmon P. Chase, April 17, 1862, PRC; *First Annual Report of the Educational Commission, May, 1863* (Boston, 1863), p. 10.

[34] E. S. Philbrick to Mrs. Philbrick, March 6, 1862, in Pearson (ed.), *Letters*, p. 4. See also *ibid.*, p. viii; William H. Pease, "Three Years among the Freedmen; William Channing Gannett and the Port Royal Experiment," *Journal of Negro History*, XLII (April, 1957), 99; Henry Lee Swint, *The Northern Teacher in the South* (Nashville, 1941), p. 161.

[35] M. W. Chapman to Edward Atkinson, April 15, 1862, Atkinson MSS; Jacob Chapman, *A Genealogy of the Philbrick and Philbrook Families* (Exeter, N. H., 1886), pp. 58–59; Thomas, *The Liberator*, pp. 272, 282, 283.

reinforced by the economic arguments for freedom that were gaining ground in the years following his graduation in 1846 from Harvard College. Association with Edward Atkinson and other cotton manufacturers had kept him abreast of the body of opinion which held that more cotton could be produced at less cost by free labor than by slaves. It seemed to such men that the continued production of cotton was indispensable to national prosperity, and they therefore were most interested in proving for good and all that the abandonment of slavery did not imply the abandonment of cotton. This would be a most convincing argument for abolition. "You don't know what a satisfaction it is," wrote Philbrick, "to feel at last that there is a chance for me to *do something* in this great work which is going on."[36]

Although short in stature, Edward Philbrick was in every respect a man of impressive appearance. With a full growth of sandy beard, a broad forehead, and a level gaze, he had as well, according to one of his fellows, a stock of "ready information and practical good sense on all subjects." Philbrick characteristically spent the idleness of the sea voyage reading on cotton culture and enlarging his stock of "ready information." There was much about Edward Philbrick to commend itself to a man like John Murray Forbes.[37]

Among the Pierce group Forbes also recognized two of his own son's Harvard classmates, young men of distinguished Boston families. Samuel Phillips was a nephew of Wendell Phillips and was a medical student, while Edward Hooper, the son of Dr. Robert W. Hooper, had just taken his degree in law. A young person of great charm, Hooper rapidly gained friends among his fellows. He had volunteered to go to Port Royal without pay, and Pierce, who immediately recognized his qualities of judg-

[36] E. S. Philbrick to Mrs. Philbrick, March 6, 1862, in Pearson (ed.), *Letters*, p. 4.

[37] William F. Allen MS diary, November 8, 1862, University of Wisconsin Library, Madison, Wisconsin; Pearson (ed.), *Letters*, p. 6.

ment and tact, made him his personal aide and secretary.[38] Typical of this younger group of evangels was William Channing Gannett, twenty-two years old and a recent graduate of Harvard Divinity School. His father, Ezra Stiles Gannett, had succeeded the venerable William Ellery Channing to the highest post in Boston's Unitarianism when he became pastor of the Arlington Street Church. The elder Gannett had never been friendly to the abolitionists of the city, but the son had found their movement irresistible. With the outbreak of war the two men had come into serious conflict over whether William should enlist in the army. The arguments of the father took a pacifist line; the son was hard to convince. It was so difficult, he complained, for a young man "whose blood prompts him to action, while he has not yet solved the contradictions between right and apparent necessity . . . to sit still because he thinks he ought to while friends and companions are going to danger, to which they also think duty leads them." The Port Royal venture seemed ready-made to resolve such a conflict. Gannett, described by another passenger as quiet, energetic, and "very agreeable," had resolved to go to Port Royal, for the first month at least, without compensation from the Education Commission.[39]

Although the desire to strike a blow for freedom was the major force that had brought the Port Royal pioneers, there were other

[38] Hughes (ed.), *Forbes*, I, 296; for Phillips, see Ray Allen Billington (ed.), *The Journal of Charlotte Forten* (New York, 1953), entry for November 19, 1862, p. 135; for Hooper, see Rupert Sargent Holland (ed.), *The Letters and Diary of Laura M. Towne* (Cambridge, 1912), entry for August 24, 1862, p. 88, and Ward Thoron (ed.), *The Letters of Mrs. Henry Adams, 1865–1883* (Boston, 1936), p. 464; Harold Dean Cater (ed.), *Henry Adams and His Friends* (Boston, 1947), p. xl. Edward Hooper was the brother of Mrs. Henry Adams and was a close friend of the historian. He became a treasurer of Harvard College after the Civil War.

[39] William H. Pease, "William Channing Gannett" (unpublished doctoral dissertation, University of Rochester, 1955), pp. 35, 384–388; see also Pease, "Three Years among the Freedmen," *Journal of Negro History*, XLII (April, 1957), 98; Pierce to Chase, April 17, 1862, PRC.

inducements that made philanthropy attractive. A few had come largely from a sense of adventure, "to see a semi-tropical country," or hoping that "the climate would be good for their health."[40] Others undoubtedly were bothered by the matter of military service, as young Gannett had been. Although army service was not then compulsory, there was still a natural feeling that one should be doing something for his country. For the many who planned future careers in the ministry, going to Port Royal was preferable to enlisting in the army, especially if one had religious scruples about fighting. The salary of between $25 and $50 per month offered by societies, with subsistence provided by the government, was not token pay. The pay of a private soldier was $13 per month. One prospective missionary from the New York Association said that the whole proposition seemed to be "with many, a money-making or *business* operation—," and he concluded that although this was not the case with *him*, it was yet "imminently proper" that he too should "look out for No. 1."[41]

Bad weather continued to dog the passage of the *Atlantic*, and John Murray Forbes reported that as there was much seasickness among the passengers, the delicious food served aboard ship was "a terrible waste" for almost everybody. "We had an alarm of a countess," he wrote, "but neither captain nor purser knew of her, so it is doubtless a mistake, unless, like a wolf in sheep's clothing she has smuggled herself into Mr. Pierce's band of fifty!"[42] The twelve ladies Pierce had assigned with such patent relief to the mercies of Mr. French included a few possible suspects, but a close examination yielded no countesses. There were the wives of several congressmen, who had come merely to distribute the clothing and supplies that had been collected for the Negroes,

    40 J. Miller McKim, *An Address Delivered at Sansom Hall, July 9th, 1862* (Philadelphia, 1862), p. 17.
    41 Milton J. Hawks to Esther Hawks, April 11, 1862, Hawks MSS, Library of Congress; *First Annual Report of the Educational Commission, May, 1863* (Boston, 1863), p. 10.
    42 Hughes (ed.), *Forbes*, I, 297.

and there was Secretary Chase's friend Miss Walker. She possessed
the regal stature of a proper countess, being of a "somewhat mas-
culine appearance, with a large frame," and she was regarded as
being a very "strong-minded" woman for her time. On the other
hand, Susan Walker was much too well known for her association
with prominent American radicals and their movements to be
long mistaken for a foreigner. Among the younger volunteer
teachers, Miss Ellen Winsor was notable for her overriding determination to come to Port Royal. At the last moment Edward
Pierce had almost turned her away, when he saw how young she
was. Only the insistence of her sponsors from the Educational
Commission that she was "admirably fitted by character and experience" for the work and Miss Walker's willingness to look
out for her prevailed over Pierce's fears that Miss Nelly might
not be quite safe on the islands.[43]

To assist him in his missionary labors, Mansfield French brought
his wife, Austa, with him when he returned to Port Royal.
Although Mrs. French probably would not have been mistaken
for a countess, she was an exceptional person, and she came nearer
fulfilling the impression of fanatical zeal that had first struck
Forbes than anyone else aboard ship. The formidable mother
of seven had managed to rear her large family, teach school, and
edit a religious periodical without ever losing step with her husband in his itinerant evangelical labors. With the encouragement
of Mr. French she had attended Mary Lyons' first school for
women at Ipswich, Massachusetts, in the year before her marriage, and had returned to Ohio to share Mr. French's teaching
duties at the Xenia Female Seminary. It was at Miss Lyons' school,
presumably, that Austa French developed the ecstatic prose style
that conveyed her evangelicalism with such conspicuous effect.
She had co-edited *The Beauty of Holiness* with her husband after

[43] Sherwood (ed.), "Walker Journal," p. 4. Susan Walker included in
her journal a listing of all the members of Pierce's party; Gannett,
"Steamer Atlantic" journal, entry for March 2, 1862.

their move from Ohio to New York City but had left the little magazine behind her when the opportunity to come to Port Royal appeared. Mrs. French's special purpose was to report on the mission. She was determined to make an investigation of the condition of the slaves of South Carolina or, as she phrased it, to force open "the seals of the book of slavery."[44]

In the straight tradition of the sensational literature of abolitionism, Austa French's account exposed the worst horrors of bondage and related an incredible number of atrocities, a large proportion of them having to do in some way with sex. It was an unfortunate thing for Mrs. French's sincere humanitarianism that she had eccentric manners, for it was all too easy in consequence for more reserved individuals to dismiss her as "cracked."[45] She deserves the credit, nonetheless, for writing the first account of the Port Royal Experiment. Even a slight exposure to *Slavery in South Carolina and the Ex-Slaves; or The Port Royal Mission* makes clear the pervading influence that reminded John Murray Forbes of John Brown and communal phalanxes. In an outrageous metaphor Mrs. French wrote that the Port Royal Experiment had been started "as to earthly agency, in the brain of our own Moses, he having led this band of Ladies to this Red Sea," and that it was of the greatest urgency that they should get "the sacred ark" over without mishap. It seems certain that "the sacred ark" was the antislavery cause, but whether Moses was Edward Pierce, Mansfield French, or Secretary Chase is far from clear. Anyway, Mrs. French was shortly proclaiming a victory, with the expectation that the waters of the Red Sea were about to engulf "the proslavery host."[46]

There was no abatement of bad weather as the *Atlantic* con-

---

[44] Mrs. A[usta] M[ansfield] French, *Slavery in South Carolina and the Ex-Slaves; or The Port Royal Mission* (New York, 1862), p. 62; French, *Ancestors and Descendants of Samuel French*, pp. 72–77 *et passim.*

[45] Arthur Sumner to Nina Hartshorn, August 8, 1864, Arthur Sumner MSS, Penn Community Center, St. Helena Island, South Carolina.

[46] French, *Slavery in South Carolina*, p. 45.

tinued its way through the difficult waters of Cape Hatteras. Around noontime on Wednesday, after a slow passage, the ship passed Fort Sumter, and the passengers could see the church spires of Charleston in the distance. The vessel arrived at the entrance to Port Royal Sound on Thursday afternoon, and before her was Bay Point, which first appeared as "a seeming line of white sand, curving out into the sea and looking as if the next wave would erase it." Arriving too late for the high tide, the *Atlantic* was obliged to drift about at the entrance to the Sound all night, waiting for a pilot to come and bring her into Port Royal Harbor.[47]

In the evening a large meeting was held aboard ship, and Pierce issued some final advice to the Gideonites concerning their duties. He assured them that "not even the Mayflower" had borne a colony "on a nobler mission" than theirs, which was destined to be of such significance that its result might settle "one way or the other, the social question of the age." Pierce warned them that their work would be extremely hard and that they might be shocked by what they saw. The former slaves had no regular time for meals, for they were in the habit of receiving the weekly peck of corn, cooking it, and eating, each one, whenever he felt like doing so. Some of them would be found to be very dirty, "some even vermined," but they must be taught to assume responsibility for their own habits of cleanliness and health. Their new clothes should be paid for with their own labor, when possible, "to cherish in them feelings of independence." Whatever the offense, the Negroes should be punished by being locked up, never by whipping. They were being prepared "for all the duties of American citizens."[48]

Mr. French added to Pierce's remarks a few of his own, "in his vein of honest, earnest Methodism." "Only by divine grace," he

[47] *Ibid.*, p. 13; Hughes (ed.), *Forbes*, I, 298; Gannett, "Steamer Atlantic," March 6, 1862.

[48] Pierce, "The Freedmen at Port Royal," p. 298; French, *Slavery in South Carolina*, p. 26.

declared, could the evangels obtain "a true fitness" for their mission. He particularly cautioned the Gideonites that "any lack of appreciation, or especially any contempt manifested toward their religious opinions or feelings," would "wound [the Negroes] very deeply." After these words of advice and counsel there were Bible readings and prayer.[49]

Following this meeting, some of the Gideonites began to confide to their journals a certain concern over Mr. French's capabilities as a leader. The praise of his worthy Christian character was unanimous, but Philbrick set him down as being "not so practical as Mr. Pierce," a reasonably severe censure from a man of Philbrick's stamp; and William Gannett thought that Mr. French had "the spirit and theory of the work, without the hand that takes hold." Several of the Boston group began to think that French had not used much judgment in selecting the teachers and superintendents who came from New York, but Philbrick wisely concluded that it was too soon "to form any such opinions" and that, after all, the evangels were "yoked together and must pull together."[50]

At noon on Friday the tide reached flood and a pilot boat came to escort the *Atlantic* in to Hilton Head, where she came to anchor in the great harbor that was now the center of activities for the blockading forces. Philbrick estimated that there were some fifty transports at anchor there, and he also observed that the two forts reduced by Du Pont in the fall "are so inconspicuous as to be barely perceptible to a passerby. . . ."[51]

The nearer view of the Sea Island landscape produced upon the Northerners a general impression of flatness and a marked contrast to the New England coast. The line of sandy shore was backed by "long dark green masses of foliage" of the pine trees,

[49] Gannett, "Steamer Atlantic," March 6, 1862; French, *Slavery in South Carolina*, pp. 28–29.

[50] Pearson (ed.), *Letters*, p. 4; Gannett, "Steamer Atlantic," March 6 and 7, 1862; see also Sherwood (ed.), "Walker Journal," pp. 16, 18.

[51] Pearson (ed.), *Letters*, p. 5.

and the serenity of the landscape struck Mrs. French as being "oppressive" in its beauty. In her susceptible soul the sight of the islands produced "strange feelings" and the thought that even nature was implicated in the guilt of the "weird Spirit of Slavery" that pervaded the whole scene. "There steals over you the feeling that you are passing under a great cloud of accumulated wrongs, in which you seem mysteriously implicated, the vague feeling that you yourself have done something awful, somewhere in the dim past." Though *she* had fought slavery, her *country* had condoned it. "And is not my country myself?" "Slavery is written upon the shore, the trees, the sky, the air. . . . The enormous black hawks, with their screams, seem to be its very spirit. No wonder they caw, caw, over this land—mean vultures, waiting for blood."[52]

While Mrs. French thought grim thoughts about slavery, William Gannett was struck by the speed with which Hilton Head had sprung up following the Federal occupation. "Northern energy has changed the beach into a city. Fort Walker and a large low build[in]g,—the hospital—huts and barracks are in sight." But for Edward Philbrick, the engineer, these manifestations of Yankee enterprise were not so astonishing as to elicit comment; nor was he overwhelmed, as Mrs. French was, by the corrosive effects of slavery on the beauties of nature. The scenery reminded him of the Northern coast of Africa, but he commented that "even Egypt was sufficiently enterprising to line its coast with windmills, while this state has not yet arrived at a stage of civilization sufficiently advanced to provide them. So, there being no water power and no steam, every negro grinds his peck of corn in a handmill as in the year one."[53]

While waiting at Hilton Head for a permit to continue up the river to Beaufort, the missionaries saw their first "contrabands."

[52] *Ibid.*; French, *Slavery in South Carolina*, p. 14.
[53] Gannett, "Steamer Atlantic," March 4, 1862; Pearson (ed.), *Letters*, p. 5.

The black oarsmen who rowed the Provost Marshal out to meet the ship and put the Gideonites' papers in order were considered a "neat and smart looking set of fellows," but the crew of a plantation boat that came near produced a different impression.[54] Mrs. French saw on "those poor faces" the "distinct and iron impress of slavery," and she noted the slaves' self-consciousness of their own "deficiency in dress, manners, and respectability of appearance." She saw their "sly, keen observation of everything" and concluded that the slaves had been accustomed to "self-control and secrecy." To William Gannett they looked "wretched and stupid enough," but he added that "to those who are accustomed to many Irish faces, these except by their *uniformity* c[oul]d suggest few new ideas of low humanity. . . ." The Irish immigrant population of New England offered the only available comparison within the experience of most of the missionaries, and they used it often, nearly always to the disparagement of the Irish, possibly because so many Irish laborers had vigorously opposed the abolition movement.[55] As for the former slaves, it would take time for most missionaries to see beyond color and recognize individual personality.

Most of Saturday was spent in transferring freight and baggage to a small river steamer for the journey up the channel to Beaufort. Leaving Hilton Head in mid-afternoon, the *Cosmopolitan* had made about half the fifteen-mile trip when she ran aground on an oyster bed, causing a further delay and more impatience among the passengers. Philbrick thought the flat shores looked uninviting, so he continued his reading on cotton culture; but some of his companions went ashore in a small boat to explore the nearby plantations. They found "everything deserted, broken, and ruined; in the overseer's house we found a smashed piano,"

[54] Gannett, "Steamer Atlantic," March 7, 1862.

[55] French, *Slavery in South Carolina*, p. 17; Gannett, "Steamer Atlantic," March 7, 1862; Bernard Mandel, *Labor: Free and Slave* (New York, 1955), pp. 68, 69.

reported William Gannett. They returned with what Miss Walker called the "first offerings of Secessia," peach and orange blossoms, honeysuckle, and branches of palmetto. Edward Hooper mockingly mailed some of the "sacred soil" home in a letter. At about 9:30 the steamer freed herself and proceeded on her way toward Beaufort, "poking slowly along the crooked channel under the glorious moonlight." The missionaries sang hymns and "John Brown's Body," which caused the steamboat officials to cast baleful looks upon Gideon's Band.[56]

The party arrived at Beaufort at about midnight on what had turned quite suddenly into the coldest night of the winter. They chose to sleep aboard and wait until the next day for unloading. Philbrick, who was out early the next morning, noticed that the deck was covered with hoarfrost. But soon after sunrise the chill morning warmed into a "bright, beautiful, soft day," reminding Gannett of June in the North. Clinging to a bend and a point in the Beaufort River, the small town spread out to the early sun was on a slightly higher elevation than the surrounding landscape. On the eastern side, almost encircled by the channel, were many elegant houses, all facing due south, with no conformation to the curving line of Bay Street, which followed the river's edge. These spacious residences met on the west a grove of magnificent live oaks, which crowded upon a grassy bank close to the water.[57]

The first call of duty this particular Sunday morning was for the men to fall to and unload the steamer. This was accomplished with New England despatch, "much to the astonishment," wrote

[56] Edward Philbrick to Mrs. Philbrick, March 8, 1862, in Pearson (ed.), *Letters*, p. 6. In this important collection the recipients of the letters are seldom named, and the senders are identified by their initials only. In further references the writers will usually be identified in the narrative itself; Hughes (ed.), *Forbes*, I, 299; Gannett, "Steamer Atlantic," March 8, 1862; Sherwood (ed.), "Walker Journal," p. 12. French, *Slavery in South Carolina*, pp. 20–24.

[57] Pearson (ed.), *Letters*, pp. 6, 7; Gannett, "Steamer Atlantic," March 9, 1862; personal observation of writer.

Susan Walker, "of the idle onlookers, white and black." Pierce engaged an elderly Negro woman to prepare a simple breakfast for his party, which had to go across town to her cabin to eat. Beaufort was laid out in a rectangular pattern and, as Philbrick observed quickly, there were no sidewalks, but the streets were "ankle-deep" in a fine white sand that looked like ashes. "Dilapidated fences, tumble-down outbuildings, untrimmed trees with lots of dead branches, weedy walks and gardens" contributed to the look of "*un*thrift" characteristic "of the best of slaveholding towns." The deserted and neglected houses were "surrounded by heaps of broken furniture and broken wine and beer bottles. . . ." The great houses of the east end of town were described by Gannett as being built for the most part "on high open basements, or pillars . . . with large porticos. . . ." In the yards there were usually several cabins with "quantities of Negro children" out in the morning sunshine, "grinning at us as we passed," wrote Philbrick.[58]

Soon the men of Pierce's party were installed in the town house of Edgar Fripp, which young Gannett thought "a perfect palace!" Almost surrounded by water, the house had an excellent view of Ladies Island across the river. The interior reflected its former grandeur, with "Egyptian marble mantles, gilt cornice and counterpiece in [the] parlor, and bathroom. . . ." The evidences of plunder were all about, in the smashed furniture, driven-in door panels, and broken plumbing fixtures. It saddened the missionaries to see such waste. "We kindle our fires with chips of polished mahogany," wrote one evangel, "and I am writing on my knees with a piece of flower-stand across them for a table. . . ."[59]

Mr. French was not so prompt in securing a home for the women of the party, and they were housed temporarily for several days with a good-natured minister who had preceded the party to Beaufort. The murmurings regarding Mr. French's

[58] Sherwood (ed.), "Walker Journal," p. 13; Gannett, "Steamer Atlantic," March 9, 1862; Pearson (ed.), *Letters*, p. 7.

[59] Gannett, "Steamer Atlantic," March 9, 1862; Pearson (ed.), *Letters*, p. 8; Sherwood (ed.), "Walker Journal," p. 14.

competence increased in tempo, but the next week found the ladies ensconced in "Hamilton's superb mansion," next door to Pierce's party. It had first been necessary, growled Miss Walker, to have it "thoroughly cleaned," because "the 'chivalry' look not to corners and *cupboards*." The very idea of twelve women under one roof struck her as a "fearful" situation, and she complained that the " 'elegant' furniture promised us could not be found." With a straw mattress, a potato for a candlestick, and a small wooden bench for her only chair, Susan Walker attempted to make herself comfortable, and asked herself conscientiously if she really was too dependent on the physical comforts.[60]

There was no undamaged furniture, of course, not only because of the plunder but also because the cotton agents under Colonel Reynolds had expanded their activities to include all movables. Pierce had his problems. Although his plan had the nominal backing of the Army as well as the Treasury Departments, the on-the-spot story might well be quite different. All about them the missionaries saw the evidences of the military as first-comers to this "small Paradise." Guards were posted everywhere, and passes and countersigns were in constant demand; it was only natural that the missionaries should be regarded as interlopers.[61] Real abolitionism was almost as scarce in Lincoln's army as in Jefferson Davis' in the spring of 1862. Even an antislavery officer, however, was capable of writing scornfully of Pierce's band that they were "sentimentalists, who come out here to throw their arms around . . . [the Negroes] and call them brothers and sisters, and who are beginning to be astonished at finding so much gonorrhea in the family. . . ." He thought they were "making fools" of the contrabands.[62]

[60] Gannett, "Steamer Atlantic," March 12, 1862; Sherwood (ed.), "Walker Journal," pp. 12–16.

[61] Worthington C. Ford (ed.), *A Cycle of Adams Letters* (Boston, 1920), I, 124; Sherwood (ed.), "Walker Journal," p. 16; Gannett, "Steamer Atlantic," March 8, 1862; Hughes (ed.), *Forbes*, I, 300.

[62] H. B. Sargent to Governor John A. Andrew, April 13, 1862, Andrew MSS, Massachusetts Historical Society.

Another officer who thought the missionaries "had better have kept away," because they were trying "to force the course of nature," was at the same time conscious of the predicament of the government and admitted that he had no idea of a better way in which to approach the contraband problem. Remarking that the course of the war had now "left Port Royal in the shade," he was "much mistaken if at this minute Port Royal is not a point of greater interest than either Virginia or Kentucky," for here the "contraband question" had been encountered in such dimension that it could no longer be ignored.[63]

[63] Charles Francis Adams, Jr., to Charles Francis Adams, March 11, 1862, in Ford (ed.), *A Cycle of Adams Letters*, I, 117–118, 127.

three ❧ *TO PLANT*

THE NORTHERN PINE

THE COLORED PEOPLE ALWAYS REFERRED TO THE MONTHS FOL-
lowing the flight of their masters as the time of "confusion."
Accustomed to a clean-cut line of authority, they sought information. The Negroes of one plantation explained to Susan Walker
that they had "been so 'confuse'; they did not know what to do;
did not know where they belonged or 'anything about we.' " Miss
Walker told them that it was now the *government* they had to
obey, which was probably a good deal clearer to the lady than to
her inquisitors, for that abstraction had appeared at Port Royal
in three persons. Whether the military authorities, the cotton
agents, or Gideon's Band would grasp the responsibility for
managing "contraband" affairs was as yet an open question.
Edward Pierce fortunately was not the sort of man to admit defeat readily, and he entered the fray expecting to win. The
lateness of the season, the haphazard arrangements on the different
plantations, and the prior arrival of the army and the cotton collectors were admitted difficulties, but Pierce was soon congratulating himself upon having made a good start. Driving about the
islands in an army wagon, he delivered teachers and superintendents to their far-flung plantations, set up a headquarters for
himself, and established central supply depots. He even performed
weddings. In late April Pierce asked his brother Henry to send
him summer clothes and prepared himself for rather warm
work.[1]

[1] Sherwood (ed.), "Walker Journal," p. 35; E. L. Pierce to Henry L.
Pierce, April 20 and March 20, 1862, in E. L. Pierce MSS, Houghton

From the time of the occupation of the islands, the soldiers had been a demoralizing influence on the defenseless Negroes. The very presence of the blue-coated strangers who appropriated everything in sight was in a sense a violation of the manorial feelings of the erstwhile slaves, who regarded their plantations as their homes, if not as their property. One observant officer, who was "struck by the gloomy ebony scowl," thought it arose from "jealousy at the liberties, taken by us, with what they consider their own plantations and possessions," and added that "the unmedicined diseases from which they suffer, and which our army has not diminished," had created much dissatisfaction.[2] The Negroes naturally resented the army's appropriation of the corn stored for their own winter food supply. On plantations where the Negro foremen, or "drivers," as they were called, had attempted to maintain a vestige of order, the discipline was completely wrecked whenever troops were encamped in the vicinity. It must surely have been a demoralizing spectacle to the people of Coffin Point, where careful husbandry had always been the rule, to see the plantation house converted into an abattoir for all the livestock on the east side of St. Helena Island. Before the war any unauthorized slaughter of livestock had been a very serious offense, carried on exclusively by Negro "maroons" living in the swamps, outlaws who had nothing to lose. With the coming of the soldiers and sailors, sheep-stealing became common enough.[3]

The unveiled contempt of many soldiers must have been galling to the colored people. One young private, semi-literate himself,

---

Library, Cambridge, Massachusetts. The second letter is mistakenly filed as being written to Henry Wilson. See also *Bridport* [England] *News*, October 21, 1865, in Gannett MSS, Box XXVIII.

[2] H. B. Sargent to John A. Andrew, March 3, 1862, John Andrew MSS.

[3] E P[hilbrick] in *Second Series of Extracts from Letters Received by the Educational Commission of Boston* (Boston, 1862), p. 4. These pamphlets ran through five series, continuing down to October, 1864. For army requisitions, see William Reynolds to Chase, January 1, 1862, item 30, Port Royal Correspondence, National Archives; see also Milton Hawks to Mrs. Esther Hawks, June 15, 1862, Hawks MSS, Library of Congress.

referred to "the niggers," who "dont no as much as a dumb bruit." Scarcely less painful were the sententious views of men like Charles Francis Adams, Jr., who was convinced that the war would bring freedom to the Negroes, but that they would soon become extinct, "how no man can tell," when thrown into competition with the more vigorous Anglo-Saxons. It is safe to say that such implicit feelings of superiority found expression in ways familiar to the Negroes from association with their late masters.[4]

Strangely enough, from the standpoint of the "evangels of civilization," the most troublesome mistake the soldiers had made was that of spreading among the Negroes the idea that they were absolutely *free*—free to do just as they pleased.[5] With few exceptions, the missionaries were cautious in speaking to the Negroes about a point that the government had not made clear. Only the most doctrinaire abolitionist could regard a premature advertisement of their freedom as "a good thing." If the Negroes were to demonstrate that free labor was cheaper than slave labor, they would have to be organized and put to work on the old staple. Distrusting their powers of persuasion, the novice planters welcomed the assistance of a little authority at the start. In some cases the soldiers specifically set the Negroes against their new friends.[6]

At a lower level the abuse of the colored people took a more savage turn. On the very night the Gideonites came up the Beaufort River, a party of soldiers came ashore at the remote Gabriel Capers plantation and held a party that degenerated into an outrageous drunken brawl. When the superintendents came out to investigate the affair, "Cuffy," the Negro foreman, deposed that

[4] Warren Bulton to his parents, January 8, 1862, single letter in South Caroliniana Library, Columbia, South Carolina; Charles Francis Adams, Jr., to Charles Francis Adams, March 11, 1862, in Worthington C. Ford (ed.), *A Cycle of Adams Letters* (Boston, 1920), I, 117–118.

[5] *Second Series of Extracts from Letters* (Boston, 1862), p. 4.

[6] Laura Towne to "G's," [her sisters], May 13, 1862, Towne MSS at the Penn Community Center, St. Helena Island, South Carolina, but soon to form a part of the Southern Historical Collection at Chapel Hill, North Carolina. These letters and Laura Towne's diary are in typescript copy; T. Edwin Ruggles to E. L. Pierce, April 11, 1862, item 128, PRC.

two men named "Mike" and "Jim" were the chief culprits, and that they had killed a cow, beaten up several Negro men, and attempted to rape the women.[7] It was not an isolated incident.

Most army officers were resentful of the Port Royal mission, looking upon Pierce's band as interlopers who had come before the situation was ripe for them. Isaac Ingalls Stevens, General Sherman's subordinate commander at Beaufort, was scrupulously correct in his manner toward the new Treasury agents but entirely out of sympathy with their work. Later his son, Hazard Stevens, who had been an aide-de-camp to his father at the time, said that the Gideonites had descended "like the locusts on Egypt" upon the department, and he recorded that General Sherman had given the missionaries "a cold and ungracious reception," packing them off summarily to Beaufort, where General Stevens had had to deal with them. Officers and men who were impatient for military action blamed the failure to move against the Confederates across the marshes on the government's solicitude for civilian sentimentalists and Negroes. "Their time is not yet and they make us fight in fetters," complained Charles Francis Adams, Jr., in a letter to his father. Sheer boredom accounts in part for the prankish stories circulated by the young officers, stories designed to frighten the lady teachers into thinking that the post was in immediate danger of attack and that the Confederates were sure to abduct all the women.[8]

But in time Pierce felt that he had "got the right side" of Stevens, who cooperated with the missionaries even if he did have very little faith in a good outcome. Stevens even took to himself a little credit for "modifying" what he considered to be the "crude and extravagant notions" of Gideon's Band.[9]

[7] Account of William Park [n.d.], item 116, PRC.

[8] Hazard Stevens, *Life of Isaac Ingalls Stevens* (Boston, 1900), II, 369; Ford (ed.), *Cycle of Adams Letters*, I, 160–161; Towne MS diary, May 4, 1862.

[9] Pierce to Henry L. Pierce, March 20, 1862, Pierce MSS; Stevens, *Stevens*, II, 369–370.

The army gave at least grudging cooperation, which is more than can be said of the cotton agents under Colonel Reynolds. From the moment Pierce began locating the superintendents, the trouble started. Reynolds and his men were acting within their orders in expanding their confiscations to include furniture, livestock, and everything "movable," but their industrious prosecution of the matter created in Pierce's mind a positive conviction that Reynolds wanted to inconvenience him. When it was known that Pierce intended to make his headquarters at the strategically located Daniel Pope plantation, known as "The Oaks," and to bring there the ladies in charge of distributing the boxes of clothing they had brought South, one of Reynolds' agents rounded up the beds and chairs of the house and carried them away to Beaufort. Pierce objected bitterly to Reynolds, complaining that the agent had left only a handful of chairs in a house to be occupied by four women and two men. "One bedstead was taken, leaving only one for the entire party of ladies and gentlemen." It was embarrassing. Pierce added that, while the agents had been hauling away the furniture, they had said that they "had no sympathy with the movement of which I had charge."[10]

Within a few days the same assiduous collector appeared at another point, where Pierce wanted to place a physician, again confiscating the furniture. Pierce wrote another testy letter to Reynolds and reminded him haughtily that he was still "waiting an answer" to his last complaint. The whole problem boiled down to the fact that Pierce, to carry out his job, needed the furniture, livestock, and farm equipment, which Reynolds controlled. In his turn Reynolds needed the labor of the "contrabands," which Pierce controlled.[11]

In addition, some of the cotton agents were personally objectionable to the missionaries. Pierce complained especially of

[10] Reynolds to Chase, January 1, 1862, and Pierce to Reynolds, March 18, 1862, items 30 and 112, respectively, PRC.
[11] Pierce to Reynolds, March 21 and 23, items 112 and 113, PRC.

Colonel William H. Nobles, whose activities covered the northern end of St. Helena Island. Nobles had come into head-on conflict with Pierce and Edward Philbrick, who had been assigned to the large and troublesome district centered around the Coffin Point plantation, which also served as Colonel Nobles' headquarters. Nobles had done his best to prevent Philbrick's occupation of Coffin Point and had tried, asserted Pierce, to set the Negroes against the missionaries. Nearly all the cotton agents had been remiss in paying the Negroes who had helped them in collecting the cotton. Pierce informed Collector Barney that the Negroes had received nothing in cash for their labor until late April, and even then the payments were made "in part of orders on friends of the cotton agents for goods at exorbitant rates—as molasses for a dollar a gallon—lawn which is eight cents a yard at home for twenty-five—and shoes which are 87 cents a pair at home for three dollars and so on." These abuses occurred even at the plantation where Pierce had his headquarters, and he had entered no formal protest solely because he had already had so much trouble with the agents.[12]

By the end of March Pierce was pronouncing the Coffin Point situation "intolerable" and demanding the immediate removal of Nobles. He blamed Nobles with a determination "to thwart the entire movement" at Port Royal and told Reynolds he was sure that if Secretary Chase "could be here and witness his conduct, or even hear his talk in the presence of you and myself on Wednesday last, [he] would remove him at once from the territory."[13]

In the meantime, in response to inquiries from Chase, Reynolds had been presenting his side of the case, accusing Pierce of overstepping his authority and complaining of the high tone Pierce

[12] Pearson (ed.), *Letters*, p. 12; Pierce to Reynolds, March 23 and 29, 1862, items 113 and 114, PRC; Pierce to Hiram Barney, April 21, 1862, item 124, PRC. See also Holland (ed.), *Towne*, pp. 16–17.

[13] Pierce to Reynolds, March 29, 1862, item 114, PRC.

used with the agents and of his thinly-veiled presumption of superior influence with Chase. Attacking strategically, Reynolds said *he* was not responsible for the damaging comments on the missionaries that had already made their way into the Northern papers. "I am convinced that seven-eighths of these Gentlemen are *totally unfit* for the positions which they attempt to occupy." Everybody at Port Royal could see this, said Reynolds, and that was why, he supposed, "scribblers, or gossipers, have turned their attention to it."[14]

It was a sad truth that most of the army officers, and all the Treasury agents, *did* consider the missionaries "totally unfit" for cotton planting. The opinion of the Negroes, who might have been competent judges, is not on record. Nobles, in presenting his side of the argument, scolded those who spent so much time "writing long communications" trying to increase their authority, or those who went about "assuming the air of a Southern Planter, minus a solitary idea that could by any possibility be brought to bear on raising Sea-Island cotton in the aristocratic State of South Carolina." He denounced those of the missionaries who had saluted the Negroes with "Sisters and brothers you are free" and then used them "as they were wont to be used by their old masters, in the cotton fields, placing upon them the additional burden of having first to teach their new masters not only the science, but the most simple rudiments of plantation and labors." He drew a caricature of a missionary who carried an umbrella, rain or shine, because he had seen the old planters "thus represented in the picture books."[15]

There was enough truth in the lampoon to make it painful. Gideon's Band was meeting many problems arising from inexperience, and their solutions were not always perfect. Few blunders escaped the cotton agents. Richard Soule, superintendent at Frogmore, made the serious mistake of permitting the Negroes to use

[14] Reynolds to Chase, April 1, 1862, item 117, PRC.
[15] Nobles to Pierce, April 2, 1862, item 119, PRC.

the ginned cotton seed for manure and cattle feed, thus leaving too small an amount for planting. When Pierce ordered too large a shipment of seed from New York, Reynolds was on hand to inform him of his error, and Pierce had the embarrassment of returning most of it.[16] Whether Pierce or Reynolds knew best how much would be required was a small matter beside the obvious fact that both men knew Reynolds had superior experience in the cotton business.

Pierce had made a mistake of another kind that had piled fuel on the fire of military ridicule. His method of dispatching one teacher and one superintendent to each plantation only after he was free to take them there meant in practice that considerable time elapsed before he completed the work of assignment. Several judiciously selected subordinates could have gotten the superintendents to work much sooner and also effected the desirable end of removing the missionaries from Beaufort, where the bored reporters and young officers made great stories of their smallest eccentricities. Philbrick complained of "loafing about and waiting upon the movements of Government officials," which was the "hardest work" he had ever tried to do. But Pierce was impervious to suggestions, complaining to his brother that he was "troubled with men who proposed a grand system for me. I tell them I have none, that I don't look ahead the length of my nose—and am content with doing each day's work." Toward the end of March all the superintendents were at their posts, and Pierce's only problems were that there were not enough of them and that Chase still had done nothing about the cotton agents.[17]

It was high time some of the ladies were removed from the household the Frenches had set up in Beaufort, for Susan Walker had been quite correct in her premonition that friction would develop from such a close concentration of opinionated females

[16] Reynolds to Chase, April 1, 1862, item 117, PRC; Pierce to Barney, April 2, 1862, item 111, PRC.

[17] Pearson (ed.), *Letters*, p. 9; Pierce to Henry Pierce, March 20, 1862, Pierce MSS; Philbrick to Edward Atkinson, March 23, 1862, Atkinson MSS.

under one roof. French had employed a staff of seven servants, wrote young Gannett from his observation post next door, and he noted that two waiters "in white waistcoats attend at table. Everybody and nobody is head." He thought that the ladies had been "subjected to many annoyances" by the Frenches, who were inefficient and "arbitrary" and much given to the promulgation of rules and regulations. The evangelist was described as "driving around town, doing much, accomplishing little." A typical row ensued when Mrs. French gave Miss Walker a public call-down for not kneeling during the evening devotions and expressed her fervent hope that Miss Walker in the future "would *always* do it, and set such an example to the colored people."[18] Miss Walker huffily retreated to her room, and Gannett said "the two sisters . . . looked like two old pure angels"—angry ones. What the fellow-evangels noticed would not go unobserved by the young officers on Stevens' staff. One of them referred to the ladies from Boston as not wishing to associate with those from New York. "Indeed, some of the Boston ladies have been creditably informed that the New-York delegation is composed of nothing better than milliners." The New York ladies were in their turn impugning the motives of the Boston contingent, suggesting that in their case the monthly salary was more persuasive than sheer good will.[19]

The prolonged stay in Beaufort had served to emphasize these petty differences, create ridiculous situations, and expose them to the public view. In the high pitch of crusading fervor that the approach to such a vast field induced, under the impact of their first contacts with the colored people whose freedom they had earnestly sought for many years, the abolitionist missionaries were

[18] William Channing Gannett, "Steamer Atlantic" journal, March 20, 1862, William Channing Gannett MSS, University of Rochester; Sherwood (ed.), "Walker Journal," p. 17.

[19] Gannett, "Steamer Atlantic," March 20, 1862, Gannett MSS; William T. Lusk to his mother, March 10, 1862, William Thompson Lusk, *War Letters of William Thompson Lusk* (New York, privately printed, 1911), pp. 127–128.

in for trouble. It was a great pity that friction should have arisen so quickly over religious differences.

Gideon's Band had been, it would appear, somewhat premature in congratulating themselves on their freedom from sectarian prejudices. As soon as the good work began, thunderclouds appeared. Susan Walker's little tiff with Austa French may be taken as a straw in the wind, illustrative of the general attitude of slightly contemptuous suspicion felt by the Boston group toward the more evangelical New Yorkers. It may also be seen in the light of the old cultural antagonism between the two cities, for Susan Walker had promptly discovered that she had more in common with the young people from Boston than with the Frenches and their party.[20] New England antislavery thought, coached by Wendell Phillips and William Lloyd Garrison, had operated on a high plane of ethical principle, but it had developed outside the church organizations.[21] Evangelicalism had been, on the other hand, a primary force in the abolitionism of New York, and the church-connected Port Royalists from that city were markedly different in temperament and in the special sources of their inspiration from those of Boston.

In 1833, the wealthy and philanthropic Tappan brothers, Arthur and Lewis, had launched the New York wing of the antislavery movement, just at a time when revivalism and evangelicalism exerted a strong influence on the city. Abolitionism sprang out of this fund of benevolence, in partnership with such other causes as Sabbatarianism, Sunday schools, tract distributions, foreign and domestic missions, and temperance. The stormy and quarrelsome course of the antislavery crusade is in a considerable degree attributable to the fundamental difference between the outlook of the New York organization, which rapidly formed connections with

[20] Sherwood (ed.), "Walker Journal," pp. 3–4, 18.
[21] Two recent studies including analyses of the intellectual background of the New England abolition movement are Stanley M. Elkins, *Slavery, A Problem in American Institutional and Intellectual Life* (Chicago, 1959), pp. 147–193, and Irving H. Bartlett, *Wendell Phillips: Brahmin Radical* (Boston, 1961), pp. 54–58, 94–98.

the Western movement, and that of the Boston wing, which had grown up in intellectual partnership with transcendentalism and had its spiritual roots in "liberal" Christianity.[22] So it can be seen that the first signs of antagonism appearing among the Port Royalists were little more than a projection of cleavages that had developed in American abolitionism before the war.

In case it may be thought that these matters were too abstract to cause irritation on specific points, it should be stated at the outset that they would color the attitudes of the two groups on nearly every aspect of their work on the islands: the relative importance of the "free labor" experiment to the salvation of souls; the type of "education" to be provided; and the position the missionaries ought to take on the religious practices of the Negroes. The last of these matters came before Gideon's Band first, and the New Yorkers enjoyed a distinct advantage, promptly becoming the preferred preachers of the colored people. Moral discourses on duty, truth, cleanliness, and so on were apt to pale in interest beside the stirring message of the crucified Christ. Belonging almost exclusively to the Close-Communion Baptist denomination, the island Negroes regarded vigorous revivals and emotional conversions as necessary integers of faith.[23] These appeared to the evangelicals as the outward and visible sign of a deep spiritual life.

[22] The influence of evangelists upon the antislavery crusade is discussed in Charles C. Cole, *The Social Ideas of the Northern Evangelists* (New York, 1954), pp. 192–220.

[23] Of the Negroes French wrote, "The great majority are pious. Their hearts have an education in the knowledge of Christian experience that may well be coveted by many whose mental culture bears no comparison with the dark minds of most of them." He exhorted the people to speak of "the dealings of God with their souls" and, from what he heard, determined that he was listening to "some of the Johns and Marys, who are favored with the Master's special smiles." French to George Whipple and Simeon Jocelyn, March 18, 1862, uncatalogued package marked "1862–A–J," in American Missionary Association Manuscripts, Fisk University. Hereafter cited as AMA MSS. See also [William Channing Gannett and Edward Everett Hale], "The Freedmen at Port Royal," *North American Review,* CI (July, 1865), 10.

To the Bostonian Unitarians, and to their group in general, the emotional "excesses" seemed an easy way of paying lip service to a faith that did not require much in the way of behavior. Edward Pierce summed up a common attitude: "Those [Negroes] of most demonstrative piety are rarely better than the rest, not indeed, hypocritical, but satisfying their consciences by self-deprecation and indulgence in emotion,—psychological manifestations which one may find in more advanced communities."[24] For one thing, the Negroes' religion took too much of their time. Two Boston teachers found it hard to understand why their cook's "striving" after religion should have such a dreadful impact on the cooking. Another schoolmistress was at her "wit's end" over the effects of religious "seeking" on the youngsters who were up all hours of the night, wandering, as they said, "out in the wilderness."[25] A Port Royal Island superintendent complained that a religious revival could break up two weeks' work in the cotton field, and he did not approve.[26]

But the evangelical sermon was what inspired the Negroes, as Mansfield French informed Secretary Chase. He insisted that "the Unitarians don't get hold of things in the right way, for the people are mostly Baptist, and like emotional religion better than rational, so called." They could not understand a religion not based on the divinity of Jesus.[27] At least one young Unitarian minister acknowledged the strength of the opposition in the most

[24] Edward Pierce, "The Freedmen at Port Royal," Atlantic Monthly, XII (September, 1863), 312.

[25] Mary Ames, From a New England Woman's Diary in Dixie in 1865, (Springfield, Massachusetts, 1906), pp. 115–116; Elizabeth Hyde Botume's speech in First Mohonk Conference on the Negro Question, Held June 4, 5, 6 (Boston, 1890), p. 24.

[26] Reuben Tomlinson to James Miller McKim, October 5, 1862, in the James Miller McKim MSS, which form a part of the Antislavery Collection at Cornell University.

[27] David Donald (ed.), Inside Lincoln's Cabinet, The Civil War Diaries of Salmon P. Chase (New York, 1954), p. 71.

conclusive way, by imitation. Throwing off his intellectualism, young William Gannett "put in all of the Methodist" he could and "talked ahead without thought or fear," finding he rather enjoyed himself. Most of the liberal Christians could not compromise, and they criticized the fervent evangelicals instead. "Mr. French as is natural with him was too Methodistical in matter and manner, appealing too much to the Religious sentiment of the people and not aiming sufficiently to strengthen them in principle and purpose," was a typical comment.[28]

Fundamentally, it was a matter of temperament. The Boston contingent was too coldly intellectual in the good cause to suit the French party, and the enthusiasm of the New Yorkers sometimes embarrassed their fellows. Years later the story about Mrs. French's arrival at Hilton Head was still circulating. She had rushed upon an astonished Negro woman passing by, and throwing her arms about her, kissed her, sobbing "Oh my sister!" It was altogether as though Austa French had personally struck off the chains, and the missionaries who remembered the scene also recalled painfully that it had "excited the contempt and ridicule of the pro-slavery officers who saw it." Whether there was much or little truth in the tale, it remained alive to illustrate a host of more significant differences that made regular appearances.[29] Even though the two factions differed in their ideas of how best to promote the welfare of the colored people, they were still in the pre-dawn of emancipation, a fact that enforced a grudging cooperation even if it could not stop the quarreling.

In the meantime the Port Royal movement was about to receive new recruits, as a result of the organization in Philadelphia of the

[28] William H. Pease, "William Channing Gannett" (unpublished doctoral dissertation, University of Rochester, 1955), p. 53; Tomlinson to McKim, August 18, 1862, McKim MSS.

[29] Arthur Sumner to Nina Hartshorn, August 8, 1864, Arthur Sumner MSS at the Penn Community Center, St. Helena Island, S. C., typescript copy, but soon to form a part of the Southern Historical Collection, Chapel Hill, N. C.

Port Royal Relief Committee. Two days after the sailing of the *Atlantic* a public meeting was held in National Hall, and a committee was formed for receiving and forwarding contributions of food and clothing and for taking "such other measures for the benefit of the freed blacks in the Sea Islands, as they may deem expedient."[30] James Miller McKim organized the movement. An able, early, and prominent abolitionist, McKim had the assistance of several well-known ministers in Philadelphia and the financial support of a number of benevolent and wealthy manufacturers.[31] Stephen Colwell, an iron manufacturer, lawyer, and writer on political economy as well, long remained a faithful supporter of the work. Matthias W. Baldwin, a locomotive manufacturer, was famous in Philadelphia for his numerous benefactions.[32] McKim reported that the generosity of his city soon provided a fund of more than five thousand dollars and "a very considerable quantity" of new and used clothing. In April a ship carried southward a large store of provisions and, as special representative, Miss Laura Matilda Towne, whose duty it would be to oversee their distribution. In a short time the Committee had broadened its purposes to correspond with those of Boston and New York; the Philadelphians would also strive to teach the Negroes "the rudimentary arts of civilized life" and "to instruct them in the elements of an English education and the simple truths of the Bible divested as much as possible of all sectarian bias."[33]

With the three major Eastern cities engaged in the philan-

[30] "Synopses of School Reports," I, 327–329, in Records of the Bureau of Refugees, Freedmen, and Abandoned Lands in the National Archives, War Records Division. Hereafter cited as BRFAL MSS.

[31] William Still, *The Underground Rail Road* (Philadelphia, 1872), pp. 655–658.

[32] Philip S. Foner, *Business & Slavery* (Chapel Hill, 1941), p. 7; *Dictionary of American Biography*, III, 327, and I, 541–542. For a list of the original officers, see *Circular of the Port Royal Relief Committee, signed March 17, 1862* (Philadelphia, 1862), pp. 3–4.

[33] *Ibid.*; *An Address Delivered by James Miller McKim at Sansom Hall, July 9th, 1862* (Philadelphia, 1862), pp. 3–4.

thropic activity on the islands, teachers and superintendents began to arrive steadily in Beaufort. In April the steamer *Oriental* brought southward several important additions to the Boston contingent, including Edward Philbrick's wife, Helen, and her friend Harriet Ware. Harriet and her brother Charles, who shortly came to Port Royal as a superintendent, were the grandchildren of Henry Ware, the famous Unitarian clergyman whose accession to the Hollis professorship at Harvard had represented a landmark in the history of his faith. Arthur Sumner, of Cambridge, also came on the *Oriental*. Sumner was a teacher of elocution, extremely nearsighted and possessed of a crackling, somewhat cynical sense of humor that often amused and confused his fellow evangels.[34]

Laura Towne, representing the Philadelphia Port Royal Relief Committee, entered in her diary a word or two describing each of the voyagers bound for Port Royal. Beside her own name she wrote the simple word "abolitionist." For Laura Towne this was the controlling fact about herself; but nobody else would have been able to discern in the tidy, smartly dressed little woman a shred of the fanatical exterior comprising the public image of the antislavery crank. Although she was not a schoolteacher, her strong, quiet face and sympathetic eyes revealed her possibilities, and she had the additional advantage of some study of homeopathic medicine. The prankish soldiers handling the large amount of freight sent by the Philadelphia Committee and consigned to "Miss Laura Towne" could not have been further from the mark when they sketched the imaginary consignee on the numerous boxes, showing a large, rawboned female of frightful expression astride a keg of molasses.[35] Laura Towne could enjoy the humor of this, but

[34] Passenger list for "Steamer Oriental," in Towne MSS; Milton Hawks to Esther Hawks, April 13, 1862, Hawks MSS; Thomas Wentworth Higginson to his mother, January 2, 1863, in Higginson MSS, Houghton Library, Cambridge, Massachusetts.

[35] Passenger list of "Steamer Oriental," and photographs in Towne MSS; Holland (ed.), *Towne*, pp. 32, 104.

about her abolitionism she tolerated no levity. She constantly measured all her fellow workers by the purity of their convictions.[36] Having become a convert to the antislavery cause through hearing the sermons of Dr. William Henry Furness, a prominent Garrisonian abolitionist of Philadelphia, Laura Towne espoused the root-and-branch abolitionism of New England. Her sympathies quickly gravitated to the Boston teachers and missionaries. She moved to the Pierce headquarters on St. Helena Island soon after her arrival, little dreaming that she would call no other place home for the rest of her life.[37]

Other important arrivals from Philadelphia in early summer were James Thompson, with his pretty sister Matilda, and Reuben Tomlinson. Thompson and Tomlinson were introduced by McKim to Laura Towne as being "zealous" young men of "good anti-slavery" principles. Thompson formerly had been a newspaper reporter, and Tomlinson had been a bank clerk. They came as superintendents, and Miss Thompson planned to teach. Laura Towne's good friend Ellen Murray soon arrived, and a lifelong partnership began. Early in the summer McKim came to the islands himself and brought with him his daughter Lucy, to whose understanding of music posterity is indebted for much of its knowledge of Negro slave songs.[38] In the fall John Hunn, a Quaker from Delaware, arrived with his daughter Elizabeth. Hunn had earned his high standing in abolitionism the hard way. For his activities in assisting escaping slaves near Cantwell's Bridge he had been convicted in Roger Taney's District Court, in May of 1848, and left "utterly destitute" as a result of the heavy penalty. But Hunn had boldly assured the court, while awaiting his sentence, that he would never desist from aiding fugitive slaves. With the Hunns came Charlotte Forten, of a Philadelphia Negro

[36] Towne to McKim, August 2, 1862, McKim MSS.

[37] Holland (ed.), *Towne*, p. x; Towne to "R," April 21, 1862, Towne MSS.

[38] McKim to Towne, July 25, 1862, Towne MSS; Towne to McKim, October 13, 1862, McKim MSS; Holland (ed.), *Towne*, p. 66.

family well known for outstanding service to abolitionism.[39] Although not so numerous as the contingents from Boston and New York, the Philadelphia evangels were unsurpassed in dedication, talent, and tenacity.

The land held in relative security by the Federal forces in early summer of 1862 extended from Hilton Head Island on the south to Edisto on the north in a wide arc to the interior, following the rough line formed by the creeks that had carved the islands from the mainland so long ago. On these islands, within gunshot and shouting distance of the Confederate pickets, American anti-slavery men and women had met the American slave on his home ground and were asking him to work out his own salvation by working cotton—voluntarily.

The full impact of this load fell first and foremost on the plantation superintendents. It soon became clear that, in addition to the problems originating with the military officials and the cotton agents, the Negroes themselves had conceived a strong opposition to planting the old staple. On many plantations they had been willing enough to plant corn and potatoes, the food crops that had already served to keep the wolf from the door. But the advantages of the year-long tyranny of Sea-Island cotton had not been readily apparent to the simple people who had never received a cash reward for growing it.

In their efforts to restore King Cotton to its former place in the island economy, these abolitionist superintendents had a nearly impossible task. Throughout the islands the work went forward in the most improbable and various, often ludicrous, ways. The composite picture was of a young and inexperienced college graduate in charge of as many as four or five large plantations, in a treacherous climate. His only assistant would be an even younger companion teacher, male or female, whose primary contribution would be limited, perforce, to enthusiasm.

[39] Still, *Underground Rail Road*, p. 712; Ray Allen Billington (ed.), *The Journal of Charlotte Forten* (New York, 1953), pp. 121–123.

Edward Hooper wrote that when the superintendent and teachers arrived at The Oaks, all the Negroes gathered about the piazza, and there he explained what would be expected of them, "namely faithful work; and what they might expect from us—good care, justice, and to be taught to read." He promised them that accounts would be made of their work and "that upon their faithfulness their future good depended." The promise of pay was considerably weakened by the tardy record of the cotton agents, and so it came about that preaching to the Negroes and teaching them to read were the most persuasive guarantees the missionaries had to offer of their good intentions.[40]

The evangels hardly knew what to say to the Negroes about their status. Laura Towne thought that most of her fellows were too cautious in assuring the colored people that they were free; she favored proclaiming the antislavery intent loudly. But the government had not clarified the matter, and most evangels simply hinted at the "future good" in store. *Work* was the favorite subject for the sermons the Negroes heard on Sundays. Francis E. Barnard, on Edisto, wrote home that the text he had taken for his first sermon was "*Work* out your own salvation with fear and trembling; for it is God worketh in you both to will and to do of his good pleasure." Those who took a stronger line and told the Negroes that they must grow cotton or risk being re-enslaved were, Laura Towne thought, using an idle threat, and she may well have been correct in her guess that the colored people recognized it as such. One Sunday a Negro patriarch who had a well-defined notion of what a sermon ought to be broke into a hortatory discourse with the complaint that "The Yankees preach nothing but cotton, cotton!"[41] On many plantations, preaching was about all that could be done.

The most useful ally a raw superintendent could cultivate was

[40] EWH in *Extracts from Letters* [first series] (Boston, 1862); Richard Soule to Pierce, March 29, 1862, item 110, PRC.
[41] Holland (ed.), *Towne*, p. 20; FEB in *Extracts from Letters* [first series].

the Negro "driver." These colored foremen exerted varying degrees of control, but they knew more about the farm operations in every case than anybody else. On a small plantation such as the Thomas B. Chaplin place, the driver, named Robert, was extremely intelligent and was able to read. He had kept the quarters clean and in good repair and had already supervised the planting of a sufficient corn crop before James Thorpe, the new superintendent, arrived.[42] But on a sprawling plantation such as Coffin Point, the drivers had lost control and, as a consequence, the superintendent's job was difficult.

Edward Philbrick described eloquently some of the problems he met in the course of a day: "Sixty-eight hands in the potato field planting sweet potatoes, swing their hoes in unison, timed by a jolly song, words indistinguishable. They work with a good will, and plant about thirteen acres during the day." Walking to another plantation, he found the people there planting corn, and he gave them a reading lesson in the loft of the cotton house after their tasks were finished. With the assistance of a Negro carpenter he mended a broken-down sulky, took possession of it, and drove home in style, "with an old sore-backed horse and a harness consisting mostly of hemp." He settled an argument among the women of the plantation about why some had received clothing and others had not and engaged in a second bout among the people who resented working on Saturday. "I tell them they must work, or I shall report them to Massa Lincoln as too lazy to be free. The best part go into the field grumbling about 'no clothes, no tobacco, no molasses, no salt, no shoes, no medicine,' etc., which is all very true and unanswerable."

A bad day began deceptively:

April 11th—People all start for the cotton field in good humor. Driver is called off by Mr. S. [the cotton agent] to furnish him with a crew; while he is absent from the field, the people mostly women and children say among themselves, "Here are twenty-four of our

[42] JET in *ibid.*

husbands and brothers gone to work for their own selves, what's the use of our working for our driver or massa—let's go work for ourselves too," and away they scatter. The greater part go to work listing ground in detached patches, scattered all over 300 acres, in a most republican spirit, but not in a way to be encouraged at present. Some go catching crabs; some go planting corn on their own hook. All leave the field early.

Philbrick thought there would be nothing to object to in this situation if the islands "were in a more advanced state of civilization," but it had to be regarded "just now . . . as chaos and insubordination." His orderly bones aching, Philbrick showed no little impatience.[43]

By the end of the same week, Laura Towne heard of "a little rebellion" at Coffin Point. Two men had refused point-blank to work the four hours on cotton required of them daily and had insisted on working only on corn. "They threaten, if unprovided with food, to break into the corn-house. One man drew his knife upon his driver, but crouched as soon as Mr. Philbrick laid his hand upon his shoulder." Before long the people at Coffin Point had partially won their way, and in a subsequent description of how the first free-labor cotton crop was grown Philbrick ascribed what success he had achieved to having abandoned the "gang system" earlier than most of the neighboring superintendents. He had capitulated to the Negro resistance to working in squads for their driver and had decided "to throw each family on its own responsibility, assigning to each a definite portion of land, and allowing them to choose their own time and manner of working it."[44] This land the people were to look to for provisions; they were assigned in addition as much cotton land as they wanted to take and were paid for each unit of work performed upon it—so much for planting, so much for hoeing, and, later, so much per

---

[43] ESP in *Second Series of Extracts from Letters* (Boston, 1862).
[44] Holland (ed.), *Towne*, p. 9; ESP in *Third Series of Extracts from Letters* (Boston, 1863).

pound for picking. Since the Negroes were each familiar with all stages of the cotton culture, no problems were presented, with the exception of the increased difficulty of introducing "new and improved methods," a matter dear to Philbrick's heart. But he had come to see that the method had the advantage of "inspiring the laborers with a degree of self-reliance," even though it offended his sense of system and order.[45]

On other plantations other methods prevailed, and much labor was performed in the old gang system, with the driver supervising.[46] The fact that the superintendents were able, even in so loose a fashion, to organize the Negroes into a working force was a triumph of patience. Not a few of the marks of the old slave system were retained, much to the chagrin of certain missionaries. For instance, the free passage from plantation to plantation without permits was not usually allowed by the superintendents, and Mrs. French thought they were more strict on this point than the late masters had been. She also criticized some of the young men for not being "genuinely anti-slavery" and for bearing "a dislike to the Colored."[47]

This was hardly fair of Mrs. French, for it was far too early to judge, and no other job undertaken on the islands was quite so exasperating and exacting as that of plantation superintendent. This was just what Arthur Sumner discovered when he was shifted from his teaching duties to superintend the plantation during the illness of his partner. He had to distribute supplies to five hundred Negroes on the plantation, and he portrayed himself somewhat comically driving over an eight-mile district in a dilapidated mule-cart, delivering "five cases of clothing, one thousand pounds of bacon, and a half a barrel of salt." When he arrived at the quarters, the nearsighted young man found himself "sur-

[45] *Ibid.*
[46] *A Speech Delivered by James Miller McKim at Sansom Hall* (Philadelphia, 1862), p. 28.
[47] French, *Slavery in South Carolina*, pp. 223, 303.

rounded by an eager, ungrateful, and complaining crowd of darkies. I brandish my knife, to cut off the bacon. . . ." For lack of orthodox scales, Sumner had requisitioned some pre-weighed iron junks with which to "adjust the equal gravitation of the hostile pounds," using a fence rail for a balance. "Cuffee bows, scrapes his foot behind him. 'Tank yer, massa': and after I have given out that plantation's allowance, I drive off, hearing as I go, such talk as this: 'Hm! didn't give me half's much as Napoleon and I done plant lots of cotton for um. I got six chillun, and only three pounds o' bac'n fer de hull lot!' "[48]

Sumner complained that most of the time lost was "spent in removing impediments in the way of doing something useful." These included waiting for meals, for "the negroes are *so* slow"; superintending the horses, as "the boys are not to be trusted"; and patching up worn-out harnesses.[49]

Gradually, in spite of all the frustrations, the enterprise assumed the aspect of a going concern. Of vital assistance were the arrival of a large shipment of mules bought for Pierce by the Treasury Department and a strict order from the military commander forbidding depredations and requiring that permission be secured from Pierce for the removal of any livestock from the plantations.[50] By April 23 Pierce estimated that between two and three thousand acres of cotton had been planted, and five days later he received five thousand dollars with which to begin paying the Negroes. The effect was not all that could have been desired, for many Negroes thought the pay too small and did not understand Pierce's method of withholding part of the money earned, on account, to secure the future good care of the crop.[51]

[48] Arthur Sumner to Nina Hartshorn, May 18, 1862, Arthur Sumner MSS.

[49] Sumner to Nina Hartshorn, May 25, 1862, Arthur Sumner MSS.

[50] Pierce to Barney, April 21, 1862, item 124, PRC; H. W. Benham, General Order No. 3, April 17, 1862, item 125, PRC.

[51] Pierce to Barney, April 29, 1862, item 141, PRC; Holland (ed.), *Towne*, p. 21.

Pierce was probably surprised to discover how neatly the women he had so reluctantly accepted fell into the plantation routine. Besides distributing Northern bounty and teaching school, they also kept house for the superintendents. These Northern women who stepped into the plantation mistresses' shoes had no easy job. With no conveniences, little furniture or equipment, and army rations sparsely supplemented by plantation produce, the simple production of three meals a day was a large order. The women who undertook these duties were from the beginning appreciated in a way that spoke volumes for the role of the old mistress at the vortex of plantation life.[52]

The mere presence of "white ladies" brought reassurance to the Negroes. When there was complaint of the small payments Pierce had made to the workers, Laura Towne wrote that "we women have to be borrowed and driven around to . . . appease the eager anxiety. This is quite a triumph, after having been rejected as useless." When Helen Philbrick arrived at Pine Grove, the Negroes wanted to know the extent of her "learning" and meant by it her knowledge of medicine. Harriet Ware reported that the colored people were "uneasy till they discovered our first names, and were pleased that mine was that of the 'Old Missus.' " Whenever the Northern women visited the "nigger-house," as the slaves had invariably denominated their quarters, they returned with their pockets full of the conventional gift of friendship on the islands—fresh eggs. And then, when everyone felt more friendly, the little articles that the Negroes had appropriated one jump ahead of the soldiers and cotton agents would make their reappearance at the big house, a sure sign that the colored people were beginning to accept the Yankees.[53]

Where the superintendents met stubborn and passive resistance, the teachers were joyfully accepted everywhere. The Negroes

[52] *Ibid.*, pp. 12–13.

[53] *Ibid.*, p. 26; Pearson (ed.), *Letters,* p. 25; Sherwood (ed.), "Walker Journal," pp. 42, 45, 49.

evinced an eagerness to learn the alphabet that excited endless comment and was a strong guarantee to the Gideonites of ultimate acceptance and cooperation. Although most slaves knew nothing of reading and writing, they had a profound reverence for the written word. "They had seen the magic of a scrap of writing sent from a master to an overseer, and they were eager to share such power if there were any chance," observed young William Gannett. He felt the schoolbook would have justified itself if for no other reason than that it served as a "talisman" that secured the confidence of the Negroes in other matters.[54]

It is difficult to understand how a people systematically kept in densest ignorance for generations could have had such a keen and almost unanimous understanding of the power of the written language. The answer probably lies in the fact that, in spite of the South Carolina laws, it had been impossible to exclude the slaves completely from the world of letters.

By the fundamental Slave Code of 1740 the teaching of writing had been prohibited, leaving the teaching of slaves to read to the discretion of the individual master. Even reading, however, was proscribed in 1834, by terms of a law passed at a time of intense fear of servile insurrection and prompted specifically by a desire to put it out of the power of the slaves to read abolition literature. Many religious white people of South Carolina had protested the 1834 law on the ground that it was as necessary for a Negro Christian to read the Bible as for a white one, but they had never made their point with the legislature. Theoretically, by 1862 there should have been no former slaves in South Carolina able to write, and very few able to read.[55]

But despite the illiteracy of the vast majority, the teachers dis-

---

[54] [William Channing Gannett and Edward Everett Hale], "The Education of the Freedmen," *North American Review*, CI (October, 1865), 533.

[55] H. M. Henry, *The Police Control of the Slave in South Carolina* (Emory, Virginia, 1914), p. 166. See "Slavery Petitions and Correspondence," State Archives, Columbia, South Carolina, for white protests against the 1834 law against reading.

covered a number of plantation drivers who could read and write. That a few masters had seen fit to flout the law and teach their drivers to write in the period before 1834 is clear from the number of these foremen able to indite intelligent reports on the condition of crops.[56] It was a great deal more convenient to have a literate foreman than an illiterate one. Probably, most of the Negroes able to read and write in 1862 had acquired the skills before 1834, but this was not universally true. Some black children learned to read "a letter at a time" from their white playmates. Others had received secret instruction. Little Suzie King Taylor had attended a clandestine school kept in Savannah by a free colored woman. A slave girl from Wadmalaw Island reported that she had been taught to read by her master's daughter. The young mistress, had she been charged and convicted, would have been obliged to pay a $100 fine and to spend six months in jail.[57]

The untutored field hand ordinarily associated the knowledge of reading not only with the powerful and exclusive world of his master but also with the privileged upper class of slaves, the drivers and house servants. All were ready and willing to learn.

By the second week in May, William Gannett and Harriet Ware had enrolled 138 pupils at Coffin Point, and fifty-eight of them were adult field hands. Even though some of the children had to walk as far as four miles to the school, the attendance was regular and the interest was strong. The frustrated superintendents who occasionally resorted to coercion reported that the strongest threat they could use to oblige the Negroes to work their tasks was

[56] See Isaac Stephens to his master, William Elliott, October 22, 1849, and Jacob to "master," July 3, 1860, in Elliott-Gonzales MSS, Southern Historical Collection, Chapel Hill, North Carolina. See also JET writing April 1, 1862, in *Extracts from Letters* (Boston, 1862).

[57] William F. Allen manuscript diary, December 19, 1863, p. 62, typescript copy in University of Wisconsin library; Susie King Taylor, *Reminiscences of My Life in Camp* (Boston, 1902), pp. 5–6; Pierce, "The Freedmen at Port Royal," *Atlantic Monthly*, XII (September, 1863), 307; Henry, *Police Control*, p. 166.

to mention taking away their primers. "The Negroes . . . will do anything for us, if we will only teach them."[58] In Beaufort the school founded by the Reverend Mr. Solomon Peck had been in existence since January, and Peck reported excellent progress by early April. Of his original sixteen pupils, none had known the alphabet, but the best of them had progressed to "easy reading" within three months. His school had grown to more than one hundred scholars, and he had employed four Negro teachers to assist him and his daughter in the teaching.[59]

Most teachers decided very early that the colored children were fully as capable of learning the rudiments as "white children of equal age and circumstances." Of his 135 scholars, Gannett reported that ten "would anywhere be considered bright." At the same time he observed that "the lack of all mental discipline" was a great handicap. Certainly the lack of familiarity with the words used in the Northern primers was another disadvantage to children whose total means of expression was colloquial in the extreme.[60]

From the beginning the teachers had been instructed to interpret their duties broadly. Edward Everett Hale in his instructions to two Boston teachers had written, "You are to teach them everything which it is proper for free men to know," which included a great deal beyond the ABC's. Susan Walker had hardly arrived at The Oaks before taking occasion to visit the quarters, where she "preached industry and cleanliness." The use of the scrub brush and of whitewash was recommended, and the provision of good clothing soon effected a metamorphosis.[61]

One situation that agitated the consciences of the missionaries was the fact that under South Carolina law none of the "married"

---

[58] "School Report," May 10, 1862, in Gannett MSS, Box I; JET in *Extracts from Letters* [first series]; RS in *Second Series of Extracts from Letters.*

[59] SP in *Extracts from Letters* [first series].

[60] [Gannett and Hale], "The Freedmen," p. 3.

[61] Hale to "Mr. Boynton," February 10, 1862, Atkinson MSS; Sherwood (ed.), "Walker Journal," p. 20; Pearson (ed.), *Letters*, p. 24.

couples actually was married. Even those slave unions that were dignified by pious masters with a degree of solemnity had no legal standing, and during the period following the exodus of the planters even these dubious formalities had lapsed. Legalizing these numerous old and new arrangements seemed an almost hopeless task, but whenever the Negroes asked to be married the missionaries made much of the occasion and invested the ceremony with all possible significance. Pierce described performing the wedding of Archie Pope and Madeline, emphasizing smartly, "What God hath joined together, *let not man put asunder!*" He introduced some severe strictures against the loose practices prevailing, called "marrying in blankets" by the colored people, and gave out a certificate to the newlyweds. The sixty guests who attended the wedding enjoyed a repast after the ceremony that was impressive enough to cause Pierce to be "surprised at the resources of the people."[62]

Mr. French became the staunchest advocate of matrimony, not only from the standpoint of morality but also because he thought valid marriage would constitute a "barrier" against possible reenslavement should the islands be recaptured by the Confederates. French's energy sometimes outstripped the zeal of the harassed superintendents. Francis E. Barnard of Edisto Island made a pun when he said, "I think a fool must have in charge one branch of our mission. I hear of a lot of marriage certificates for all those who have heretofore been informally joined. If that is to be carried out I think we had better take *French leave* of these islands."[63]

For teachers, superintendents, and Negroes alike, the social high point of the week was the Sunday church service. Here the Negroes appeared in their most favorable aspect, and the teachers and superintendents gathered from their remote plantations to exchange letters, news, and gossip. On fine Sunday mornings throughout the spring, an astonishing array of dilapidated car-

[62] Pierce to Henry Pierce, April 20, 1862, E. L. Pierce MSS.

[63] French to George Whipple and Simeon Jocelyn, March 18, 1862, in uncatalogued package marked "1862—A–J," AMA MSS, Fisk University; F. E. Barnard to William Gannett, May 27, 1862, Gannett MSS.

riages could be seen winding over the dusty roads, converging on the "Brick Church," the Baptist fold on St. Helena Island. The unpretentious sanctuary was on these occasions filled to over-flowing with Negro worshipers who occupied every available space—windows, doors, and aisles.[64] Those who found no place inside sat under the oaks in the churchyard, leaning against the marble gravestones of masters truly departed forever. Susan Walker, given to romanticizing, saw such a tableau one Sunday and thought "the Great Master must have arranged them" to illustrate that they were "God's images cut in ebony."[65]

On a typical Sunday a superintendent would open the service with Scripture readings, and a Negro member would offer prayer. On St. Helena the sermons stressed the theme of faithful work, perhaps because most of the Unitarian superintendents were located there. When Edward Hooper told the Negroes the story of St. Christopher and the Christ Child, he sharply drew out the moral about faithful work in small things and was promptly followed by Edward Pierce, who "made some excellent remarks touching everyday duties." On another Sunday David Thorpe spoke, "told [the Negroes] . . . their duties, urged industry and patience, [and] pointed out the greater sufferings" of the Union soldiers. It undoubtedly became monotonous, and many an adult probably silently seconded Miss Walker's little scholar who protested, when pressed to learn the alphabet in Sunday school, "We study de Lord."[66]

But the most original and free expression of the spiritual life of the islanders was to be found not at the churches but on the plantations, where the colored people gathered at the "Praise House," a standard feature of each community. Sometimes this building was erected by the master for the specific purpose of

[64] Pearson (ed.), *Letters*, p. 49; Holland (ed.), *Towne*, p. 20; Sherwood (ed.), "Walker Journal," pp. 20, 44.
[65] *Ibid.*
[66] *Ibid.*, pp. 21, 28.

worship, and sometimes it was merely the home of the eldest Negro spiritual leader on the plantation. In all cases it was the meeting place for prayer, singing, and whatever version of the dance known as the "shout" was allowed by the village elders. A Praise House Harriet Ware saw on Port Royal Island was "a little chapel . . . made very roughly of boards whitewashed, inside an earth floor, covered with straw, rough wooden benches, the pulpit and altar made in the same way, but covered entirely with the grey moss. . . ."[67] No matter what the arrangements, it was here that the slave found in song and dance a unique aesthetic and spiritual release from his deadening toil, as well as his few slight opportunities for leadership and organization outside the realm of white domination.

From the first days in Beaufort the Gideonites began attending the religious exercises of the colored people, and after their arrival on the plantations the invitation would soon come "to jine praise" with the Negroes. At these meetings, after the praying, it was customary to sing the spirituals that embodied in their strong imagery the common yearnings of mankind. The leader would deacon out the lines, and other singers would respond in chorus. The singing would merge into a dance on the plantations where "the shout" was regarded as a part of the worship. Some of the elders who disapproved of dancing "out in de world" thought it suitable for those who had joined the church to "strive behind the Elders."[68] Sometimes a shout was a feature of a conversion.[69]

Whatever the occasion of its performance, the shout was to Northerners who witnessed it the most amazing and primitive manifestation of the Negro spirit. One chronicler enjoins us to

[67] Towne to "G's," April 25, 1862, Towne MSS; Pearson (ed.), *Letters,* pp. 17–18.

[68] *Ibid.,* pp. 26, 27–28.

[69] Gold Refined Wilson, "The Religion of the American Negro Slave; His Attitude Toward Life and Death," *Journal of Negro History,* VIII (January, 1923), 56.

picture the time as evening, when "a light-wood fire burns red before the door to the house and on the hearth," with the benches pushed against the wall. The constant and ever-repeated refrain of some familiar hymn would bring up the dancers, and to the accompaniment of "a regular drumming of the feet and clapping of the hands" they would circle about, "winding monotonously round someone in the centre" while the excitement and intensity of the dance spread. The basic step was a shuffling movement of the feet, described by Susan Walker as "very heavy." It was accompanied by a vigorous hitching motion that agitated the entire upper body, "bringing out streams of perspiration." One observer commented on the endless variations of this dancing: "Some 'heel and toe' tumultuously, others merely tremble and stagger on, others stoop and rise, others whirl, others caper sideways, all keep steadily circling like dervishes; spectators applaud special strokes of skill." Sometimes the dancing continued all night, and when the spell was at last broken it was "amid general sighing and laughter."[70]

Even the evangelical missionaries, to say nothing of the Unitarians, were troubled by the "shout." The Reverend Mr. Horton, the Baptist shepherd on St. Helena, confessed himself to be "very much puzzled what to do about the religious feeling of these people. . . ."[71] With a few romantic-minded exceptions, the missionaries disapproved of the shouting, regarding it as a survival of paganism, "the remains of some old idol worship," and were happy to state that the older and more pious Christians had nothing to do with it. Reuben Tomlinson said, "It was the most hideous

[70] New York *Nation*, May 30, 1867, quoted in Pearson (ed.), *Letters*, note and text, p. 27; Sherwood (ed.), "Walker Journal," p. 16; Thomas Wentworth Higginson, *Army Life in a Black Regiment* (Cambridge, 1900), pp. 23–24. There are numerous descriptions of the shout, and all correspond well on details. My quotations have come, in order, from the above sources.

[71] Pearson (ed.), *Letters*, p. 36.

and at the same time the most pitiful sight I ever witnessed." The Negroes disagreed among themselves as to its religious character, and the curious Northerners came up with varying responses to this question. Laura Towne said simply, "I never saw anything so savage"; and to such a sophisticated Northern Negro teacher as Charlotte Forten, the whole affair was "barbarous." She speculated that it was "handed down" by the Negroes' "African ancestors, and destined to pass away under the influence of Christian teachings." To another observer it was "one-sixth praying and five-sixths playing."[72]

Even while they pondered the "extravagant" practices in Negro worship, the Gideonites promptly understood that religion was the central fact in the lives of most of the colored people. "Not only their soul, but their mind finds here," wrote young Gannett, "its principal exercise, and in great measure it takes the place of social entertainment and amusements." He found that the minds of the Negroes "never appear to better advantage than in conversation on religious topics." When Gannett asked the Negroes for their scriptural authority for the "shout," they responded plausibly that " 'the angels shout in heaven'!"[73] There was nothing whimsical about such justification, for all the Sea Island slave songs reveal a conception of a heaven as tangible as the next plantation and as desirable as freedom. "Hurry on, my weary soul, and I yearde [heard] from heaven to-day," they sang. "I'll sing and pray my soul away, Heav'n shall-a be my home." "Dere's room enough, Room enough in de heaven, my Lord, I can't stay behind!" Composed in infinite variety and freely improvised upon, the religious songs of the slave were a fine creative expression, an

[72] Towne to "G's," April 25, 1862, Towne MSS; Boston *Advertiser*, June 3, 1872; Tomlinson to McKim, October 5, 1862, McKim MSS; WCG in *Extracts from Letters* [first series] (Boston, 1862); Charlotte Forten, "Life on the Sea-Islands," *Atlantic Monthly*, XIII (May, 1864), 593–594.

[73] [Gannett and Hale], "The Freedmen at Port Royal," *North American Review*, CI (July, 1865), 10.

art requiring no expenditure of two items the slave could not call his own, time and money. Songs were also infinitely portable.[74] Rowing, hoeing cotton, grinding corn, or at prayer, the Negroes sang of the heavenly home and of their Savior, who was as real as their master, and more kind.

> *Jesus make de blind to see,*
> *Jesus make de cripple walk,*
> *Jesus make de deaf to hear.*
> *Walk in, kind Jesus!*[75]

The tempo varied with the mood of the singers and the natural pace of the work at hand; the same song could carol happiness or sublimate misery. The young people sang a favorite song too fast for the taste of an older songstress whose life had been unhappy. "Dey just rattles it off—dey don't know how for sing it. I likes 'Poor Rosy' better dan all de songs, but it can't be sung widout *a full heart and a troubled sperrit.*"[76]

To understand the wisdom and fitness of the slave's spiritual life as expressed in song required an insight that some of Gideon's Band possessed and others did not. It was more than easy to be misled by the difficulties of a language they hardly understood

[74] William F. Allen, Charles P. Ware, and Lucy McKim Garrison, *Slave Songs of the United States* (New York, 1929). This collection was drawn primarily from songs the authors heard on the Sea Islands. The two men were superintendents, and Lucy McKim visited Port Royal with her father, James Miller McKim, in the summer of 1862. The first edition appeared in 1867, and both editions include an excellent Preface describing the manner of the singing. All the illustrations I cite come from this book, but other listings of songs frequently heard on the islands appear in Edward King, *The Southern States of North America* (Glasgow and Edinburgh, 1875), pp. 618–620; Higginson, *Army Life;* Forten, "Life on the Sea-Islands."

[75] Charlotte Forten first heard this song when the boatmen sang it rowing her to St. Helena Island for the first time. Forten, "Life on the Sea-Islands," p. 588.

[76] Allen, Ware, and Garrison, *Slave Songs*, p. xxiii.

and by the uninhibited rhythms of the ebony people who danced as they sang. Certain Northern visitors who witnessed these scenes for idle amusement could have taken a lesson from a former minister to the slaves of the islands. After the war, the Reverend Dr. Charles Hall spoke with undisguised irritation of the caricatures of Negro religious life that had appeared in Northern papers. He cited instances of the most sincere religious thought and action, and of the singing he recalled "a woman who knew nothing of the art of music go fluttering above the main current of the singing of a thousand voices with a soprano all her own. I do not know why the Holy Spirit may not touch their spirits then." He remembered especially an old deacon in one of his churches. One morning a slave woman had been overcome by tears during the sermon, and the deacon had seen it. "He would take his old horse and follow that case up. Before morning he would be on his knees beside her. I wish you Christians would do the same sort of work."[77]

Miss Ellen Murray observed in the simple faith of the islanders what she considered one significant result of "true religion. . . . The fear of death seems to be in a great measure obliterated by their own numerous songs of heaven. Those who sing joyfully,

> '*I want to die like Jesus died,*
> *To die and lie in the grave.*'

or '*Jordan's stream is a good old stream,*' are not likely to be afraid when the reality comes upon them. . . ." Miss Murray may also have understood that there was no more telling commentary upon the stringency of the life of the slave than this constant gazing upon heaven. Even the superstitions surrounding death were beautiful in her eyes. One day when a sudden gust of wind shook the window of her schoolroom, she heard one little girl say

[77] The Reverend Dr. Charles D. Hall, speaking at the *First Mohonk Conference on the Negro Question, June 4, 5, 6* (Boston, 1890), pp. 134–135.

to another, "Tha's Susie's soul going away. Susie was buried yesterday." A dying woman told Miss Murray that she felt happy and secure, for "Jesus would know that she was old and feeble and would come to meet her half way lest she should be frightened."[78]

William Gannett referred to the "fatalism" that characterized the Negroes' attitude toward death and said that "this tendency to abandon themselves to what seems the unavoidable explains much of the apathy with which they endured their lot."[79] The Christian religion, if it had not become precisely what Marx called the opiate of the masses, had at the least given the slave much needed solace for a troubled life, and he had taken it to his heart.

In no other social institution had the slaves been granted so nearly an equal participation with their former masters as in the Christian church, and it is in his religious life that the African had made his most striking accommodation to the white man's world. If the Negro continued to manifest in his worship certain distinctive echoes of his West African past, this fact was more a result of the tenacity of culture than a mark of his failure to assimilate the true spirit of the new faith. For he worshiped with the sense of the approaching heavenly kingdom possessed by the earliest Christians and by the downtrodden everywhere.

Outside the areas where the master class had taken such pains to interfere actively, however, there lay sufficient terrain for the survival of many customs, folkways, and superstitions that bear the distinct imprint of West Africa. The speech of the islanders long baffled the missionaries, who considered the almost incomprehensible Gullah dialect a simple corruption of English. A recent scholar of linguistics, however, has discovered a sounder basis for their confusion and, through a comparative study of the numerous languages used on the West Coast of Africa and the Gullah, maintains that thousands of African words were in

[78] *Pennsylvania Freedmen's Bulletin* (January, 1867), p. 12.
[79] [Gannett and Hale], "The Education of the Freedmen," CI (October, 1865), 8.

currency on the islands instead of the previous acknowledged handful.[80] When Miss Elizabeth Botume made up her pupil role-book, she was especially confused by the multiple names given her scholars by their parents and playfellows:

> In time I began to get acquainted with some of their faces. I could remember that "Cornhouse" yesterday was "Primus" today. That "Quash" was "Bryan." He was already denying the old sobriquet, and threatening to "mash you mouf in," to anyone who called him Quash. I reproved the boys for teasing him. "Oh, us jes' call him so," with a little chuckle, as if he ought to see the fun. The older people told me these were "basket names." "Nem'seys (namesakes) gives folks different names."[81]

These "basket names" were almost always of African origin. In naming children, Sea Islanders sought, as their ancestors had done, names which would describe the appearance, personality, or some special ability of the child. Sometimes circumstances surrounding the birth of the baby, such as the day of the week or month, the weather, or the place would influence the selection of a name. Harriet Ware in making up her class rolls was "often puzzled" about the children's names, and never knew why her scholar "Rode" was so named, until "old Maria . . . told me that one child was born in the *road* on the way from the field the day 'gun fire at Bay Point and I give him name o' Road'!"[82]

In time the evangels discovered beneath a surface of conformity a subterranean current in which swam a host of good and evil spirits. The lively intervention of the witch in the affairs of men gave the missionaries no end of trouble. The Sea Island "hag" had the agility to doff her skin and hie herself to any distance to "ride"

[80] Lorenzo Dow Turner, *Africanisms in the Gullah Dialect* (Chicago, 1949).

[81] Elizabeth Hyde Botume, *First Days Amongst the Contrabands* (Boston, 1893), p. 48; See also *First Mohonk Conference on the Negro Question* (Boston, 1890), pp. 22–23.

[82] Turner, *Africanisms*, pp. 40–41; Pearson (ed.), *Letters*, p. 209.

her victims, giving them nightmares. The conventional method of frustrating her was to scatter mustard seed, salt, or pepper about the room of the victim, or better yet, if it could be done, upon the vacated skin of the witch.[83] Sometimes the "hagged" took the more aggressive method of beating the "witch." Miss Towne reported that such was the case of "Mom Charlotte," who was so old and feeble that she "could not walk half the distance" her "victim" supposed her to have come on her wicked errand. Fortune tellers flourished and were freely consulted in matters ranging from ill health to the identity of a thief. Witches and conjurors are common enough, of course, in the folklore of Europe and America, but the direct correspondences between the "hags" of the Sea Islands and those of the West Indies and West Africa make it a practical certainty that they were near relations.[84]

The manifestations of superstition were sometimes disconcerting. Laura Towne, after curing a feeble old woman of an ailment that the patient had concluded from a vision would be fatal, came away with the distinct impression that her convalescent thought she had accomplished the miraculous result through witchcraft.[85] Whatever surprise the Gideonites may have felt at first vanished as they came to know more of the Negroes individually. They met numerous older people who had survived the terrible "middle passage" aboard a slave ship and could remember their youth in Africa. An old man whom Harriet Ware encountered on Morgan Island had been at least twenty years old at the time his brother

[83] Melville J. Herskovits, *The Myth of the Negro Past* (Boston, 1958), p. 259. For several "hag" stories, see Elsie Clews Parsons, *Folk-Lore of the Sea Islands, South Carolina* ("Memoirs of the American Folk-Lore Society," XVI; [Cambridge, 1923], 63–64, 213). Towne MS diary, December 31, 1862, states that the Negroes feared to sleep alone, "for fear 'the hag will ride we.'" Turner, *Africanisms*, pp. 275–279, gives a "hag" story told by Sanko Singleton, of John's Island. *American Freedman*, III (June, 1868), 431–432, includes a "hag" story.

[84] Holland (ed.), *Towne*, pp. 186, 232; Ames, *A New England Woman's Diary*, p. 44; Herskovits, *The Myth*, pp. 259–260.

[85] Towne MS diary, August 13, 1863.

had sold him to a trader to pay a debt. A man named "Monday" bore upon his forehead the markings of his African tribe and upon his back the marks of the whippings it had taken to reduce him to slavery. He remembered his trip to the New World and his arrival in Charleston. A woman named Daphne, whom Laura Towne estimated to be more than a hundred years old, remembered coming from Africa with her parents at the time of the revolution. "She had fifty grand-children, sixty-five great grandchildren and three great-great grandchildren." "Maum Katie" was also more than a century old, and she remembered "worshipping her own gods in Africa." Regarded as a "spiritual mother; a fortune-teller, or rather a prophetess," she exercised an enormous influence over her "spiritual children."[86]

The influence of the Maum Katies may be assumed to have strengthened the elements of the African past that had been retained on the islands. Certainly there were more of these cultural survivals here than elsewhere in the slave states, but only a few are capable of isolation and specific identification. This is in part owing to the similarity of West African life in certain respects to that of the dominant culture the slave encountered in the New World. Agriculture had been to the West African the usual means of earning his living. He had lived under a definable political system and within an accepted framework of law. A surprisingly well-developed economic system, based on money, markets, middlemen, and a degree of specialization for the production of goods, surely made the transition to a European-dominated

[86] Pearson (ed.), *Letters*, p. 203; Holland (ed.), *Towne*, pp. 176–177, 145; Forten, "The Sea Islands," *Atlantic Monthly*, XIII (June, 1864), 670. Towne MS diary tells also of a woman whose face bore the tribal cicatrizations, April 28, 1862. A correspondent of the Beaufort *Republican*, an antebellum resident, wrote that "slaves were also brought directly to this Port, and sold on account of the master of the vessel." For an interesting account of cultural survivals and acculturation on the Sea Islands, see William R. Bascom, "Acculturation among the Gullah Negroes," *American Anthropologist*, XLIII (January–March, 1941), 43.

culture less shocking than it might have been to more primitive people. The existence of slavery itself as a part of the institutional past of the African may be considered in a sense preparatory for his traumatic change of fortune. By no means so easily pinpointed as multiple naming of children and unusual superstitions, these other institutional inheritances armed the African for the experience of slavery and European cultural domination.[87] It is a good question, in fact, whether without this background the African could have endured enslavement successfully. The American Indian, of a more primitive social and agricultural organization, had not possessed the cultural resilience to do so.

When the special circumstances of slavery on the Sea Islands are considered—the great isolation of the region, the limited contacts with white people, and the direct importation of West African Negroes to a relatively late date—it is amazing not that there was a goodly number of identifiable African "survivals" but that there were so *few*. Only the severities of plantation slavery as it was practiced on the Sea Islands can explain these cultural losses.

In most of their observations on the effects of slavery upon the Negro, the missionaries stated that the institution had "degraded" him, had reduced him from his original state of independence to a childish reliance upon others.[88] The squalor, laziness, tendency to lies, theft, and immorality that the missionary-abolitionists observed (but seldom stressed in their public accounts) seemed

[87] John Hope Franklin, *From Slavery to Freedom* (New York, 1947), p. 43; Herskovits, *The Myth*, pp. 58, 62; Stanley M. Elkins, *Slavery; A Problem in American Institutional and Intellectual Life* (Chicago, 1959), p. 96.

[88] "In fact it is the opinion of all who know the South, that the negroes of these Sea-islands are the most degraded slaves South of Dixie's line." Arthur Sumner to Joseph Clark, January 23, 1863, in Arthur Sumner MSS; see also the testimony of James P. Blake, who wrote that the Negroes were inclined to extenuate their masters' faults and to explain their own on the basis of being inferior: "nuffin but a nigger noways!" *Freedmen's Record*, I (February, 1865), 28; Pierce, "The Freedmen at Port Royal," *Atlantic Monthly*, XII (September, 1863), 300–301.

to surprise them not at all. These defects were readily attributable
to the evil inherent in slavery. Firsthand experience in the land of
bondage had stiffened their original convictions about the peculiar institution but at the same time introduced real conflicts into
the antislavery argument, questions that had been entirely
theoretical before. The destructive aspects of slavery had always
been emphasized by abolitionists. Now one had to ask: Could
slavery as an institution have been so degrading to its victims as
to make them *incapable* of the immediate assumption of the responsibilities of free men? Nobody said yes to this, at least on the
record, but at the same time there were many evidences of a system of repression and toil, of a past life barren of many essentials
of civilized society. The professed necessity for mission work with
the Negroes affirmed the damaging effects of the institution. Fortunately for the missionaries' logic, their economic and social ideas
had prepared them for much of what they saw, and their faith in
the therapeutic effects of liberty gave them leave to hope for an
immediate and bright future. Cultural factors would hardly need
to be considered. Edward Pierce voiced a minority opinion when
he made the dreary suggestion that since it took three generations
to reduce a free man to a state of complete servitude, it might take
more than a single generation to reverse the process.[89]

Most missionaries were more optimistic and emphasized the
auspicious signs, the common-sense approach of the late slaves to
planting their own provision crops, the fact that they rarely swore
or drank whiskey, and above all their eagerness to learn. Francis
Barnard was so pleased with "the true moral position" of his

[89] Pierce, "The Freedmen at Port Royal," p. 315. Frederick Law Olmsted's opinions were esteemed by the missionaries, especially by men
oriented toward economics. Olmsted wrote that "A man will as a general
rule, always work harder, more skillfully and with more exercise of discretion, for himself than for anyone else; especially so if his work is not
wholly voluntary. . . ." Thus he held that slavery was "a very great hin-
drance" to the acquirement of "moral, aesthetic, and mental as well as
material wealth." Olmsted, *Sea-Board Slave States*, pp. 490–491, 447.

charges on Edisto Island that he invited one and all to see. "In work, in behavior, in everything good, I have almost said, I will put my people against any [,] not because of my influence . . . but because of their good training before." Although few missionaries produced an orchid for the departed masters, they were inclined to explain the superiority of the Negroes on certain plantations as resulting from their having had a "better" master than their neighbors.[90]

The Negroes' seeming absence of vindictiveness toward their former owners was an indigestible fact for many Northerners. They clearly saw that the ebony hands had grasped freedom with equal determination, whether roughened by the cotton hoe or burnished by housework; and the Negroes, when questioned, usually said they never wanted to see their late masters again. On the other hand, they charitably wished the fugitives well and hoped that "the old people" would not come to want.[91]

There was even a lurking suspicion that the Negroes might be making unfavorable comparisons. An antislavery officer thought that some of them were "half-wearied of their liberty, or rather pined for the old allegiance with its careful providences." Gannett wrote that, when paying for their new clothing, the Negroes were "apt to contrast present high prices with the old time when their masters *gave* them 'a whole suit at Christmas.' "[92]

The curiosity the missionaries evinced about the character of the vanished masters may have sprung from a species of professional jealousy, but it may have been an instinctive search for a key to understanding the Negroes as well. There was much the evangels needed to know about the conditions of life that had preceded their advent. The riddle of that life, they sensed, lay

[90] F. E. Barnard to William Gannett, May 27, 1862, Gannett MSS; see Tomlinson to McKim, September 20, 1862, McKim MSS.

[91] Mrs. A. M. French, *Slavery in South Carolina* (New York, 1862), p. 34; Pearson (ed.), *Letters,* p. 206.

[92] H. B. Sargent to John A. Andrew, March 3, 1862, Andrew MSS; William Gannett to Edward Atkinson, January 16, 1863, Atkinson MSS.

somewhere in the ambivalent relations of these one-time slaves to those white men who had erected and controlled the collapsing peculiar institution. It did not embarrass the evangels to pry into these matters. They read old correspondence and records found in attics and queried the Negroes, who did not mind talking.[93] As often happens in conversation, abstractions gave way to specifics, and the specific matter the Negroes liked best to talk about was the most exciting day of their lives, that day back in the fall when the guns had boomed at Bay Point and their masters had fled the islands.

[93] Allen MS diary, January 11, 1864, pp. 90–91, typescript copy; Pearson (ed.), *Letters*, pp. 31, 79, 126–127, 165, 205–206.

four ❧ *"THE OLD ALLEGIANCE"*

LAURA TOWNE STOOD ON THE VERANDA OF DR. JENKINS' PLANTA-
tion house on Station Creek and gazed across the salt flats to the
distant point where the blue waters of Port Royal Sound narrow
and flow past the straits of Bay Point and Hilton Head Island. It
was here on this porch, the Negroes told her, that the St. Helena
planters had converged on that Thursday back in November to
watch the battle of Port Royal. They had hoped to see their sons
and relatives in the Beaufort Volunteer Artillery drive off the
invading fleet, but although they possibly had been too far away
to hear the victorious strains of "Yankee Doodle," they had
realized early in the afternoon that the forts were falling. Hastily
mounting their horses, the planters had ridden away to spread the
alarm.[1]

For the few confused hours that followed, the missionaries soon
learned that every plantation had its own special story. A few
planters had succeeded in quickly driving their slaves and livestock to the Beaufort ferry, but for every one who had succeeded
in this, there were a dozen who failed. The Negroes too had heard
the guns, and some had hidden in the swamps and in the fields,
crouched low between the corn rows. Others had sensed their
power for the first time and had stubbornly stood their ground
before their masters, impervious to cajolery and threats that the
Yankees would sell them to Cuba. Master Daniel Pope's seam-

[1] Towne MS diary, November 12, 1862; J A J[ohnson's] account in
Beaufort *Republican*, June 26, 1873. Johnson remembered hearing "Yankee Doodle" struck up as he and his fellow Confederate soldiers prepared
to retreat from Bay Point.

stress, Susannah, told Laura Towne that she had asked her master when he urged and threatened, "Why should they [the Yankees] kill poor black folks who did no harm and could only be guided by white folks?"[2] The majority of the Negroes showed the shrewdness of a certain Dr. Sams's man Cupid, who recalled that his master had told his slaves to collect at a certain point so that "dey could jus' sweep us up in a heap, an' put us in de boat." The Negroes had taken to the woods instead. "Jus as if I was gwine to be sich a goat!" commented Cupid. Pompey of Coffin's Point informed Harriet Ware that some Negroes in his plantation would have been duped by the Cuba story but for the fact that the "poor whites" of Beaufort had made the slaves "sensible" to the fact that their own freedom was at stake in the conflict.[3]

Not every planter had even tried to remove his slaves. There were perhaps a few others who followed the course of Captain John Fripp of St. Helena Island. This remarkable man, who was at once one of the richest landowners in the district and a Union sympathizer, called his slaves together and explained the situation. He warned that they would probably starve if they followed him to the interior and advised them to hide until the Confederate soldiers had passed through the island. They should then keep together, work their provision crops as usual, and forget about the cotton. It was late in the day when Henry, the cook at Coffin Point, sounded the alarm on the northern end of St. Helena. He excitedly informed the overseer that he had better be off, for "all the Yankee ships were 'going in procession up to Beaufort, solemn as a funeral.' " The overseer left, but Henry did not.[4]

Henry had been wrong in thinking the gunboats were occupy-

[2] Rupert Sargent Holland (ed.), *Letters and Diary of Laura M. Towne* (Cambridge, 1912), p. 27; Towne MS diary, November 17, 1862; Elizabeth Ware Pearson (ed.), *Letters from Port Royal* (Boston, 1906), pp. 78–79, 127.

[3] Charlotte Forten, "Life on the Sea-Islands," *Atlantic Monthly*, XIII (May, 1864), 593; Pearson (ed.), *Letters*, p. 207.

[4] EP in *Second Series of Extracts from Letters Received* (Boston, 1862); Pearson (ed.), *Letters*, p. 127.

ing Beaufort so promptly. After effecting a lodgment at Hilton Head and making a few tentative explorations, the Federal forces had waited patiently several days for some response to General T. W. Hunter's proclamation of assurance and protection to the citizens of the district. Had Du Pont's gunboats occupied Beaufort immediately, they would probably have intercepted almost the entire white population embarking for Charleston on a steamer that was docked conveniently at the town landing.[5] Such action would also have frustrated the enactment of a most instructive morality play on the true character of slavery. In the few days that elapsed before Federal authority was consolidated throughout the island region, the social and legal bindings of the peculiar institution unwound with the speed and ferocity of a coiled wire spring.

The sack of Beaufort was one event that the Negroes did not discuss with their new friends. The looting of the houses probably began with the motive of plunder, but in a short time crowds of field hands descended upon the town and took it apart, presumably for the satisfaction of doing it. Whatever manorial pride the field hands may have felt in the country estates of their late owners, it did not encompass the elegance of the family town houses. It is quite probable that most of these plantation Negroes had never been inside their masters' fine homes in Beaufort, but they were not intimidated. Over the protests of the house servants who had remained, they broke up furniture, loaded valuables onto boats to carry away, and helped themselves to the wine.[6] Thomas Elliott, who returned to his Beaufort house the day following the November 7 attack on the forts, reported that he discovered

[5] J A J[ohnson] in Beaufort *Republican*, June 23, 1873.

[6] Certain of the missionaries who arrived later than the first summer at Port Royal attributed the sack of the town to the soldiers, exculpating the Negroes. All the evidence of those on the spot at the time, including the whilom masters who were clandestinely roaming the region, said the field slaves did the damage. See the New York *Tribune*, November 20, 1861; Daniel Ammen, *The Atlantic Coast* (New York, 1898), pp. 33–34; Hazard Stevens, *Life of Isaac Ingalls Stevens*, II, 354–355.

"Chloe, Stephens' wife, seated at Phoebe's piano playing away like the very Devil and two damsels upstairs dancing away famously. . . ." They were all plantation Negroes who had come into town. The houses had little furniture left and had been "completely turned upside down and inside out. The organs in both churches were broken up," Elliott reported, "and the churches themselves robbed of many articles which were deposited there for safe keeping."[7]

The correspondent of the New York *Tribune* described the destruction that Du Pont and his landing party found when they went up to Beaufort on November 12. "We went through spacious houses where only a week ago families were living in luxury, and saw their costly furniture despoiled; books and papers smashed; pianos on the sidewalk, feather beds ripped open, and even the filth of the Negroes left lying in parlors and bedchambers." The destruction had been "wanton," and much of it could have served "no purposes of plunder" but only a "malicious love of mischief gratified."[8] Nothing that happened illustrated better the frustrated hostilities of generations than the desecration of the stylish houses in the east end of town.

Commodore Du Pont was saddened by what he saw but at the same time remembered with contempt how South Carolina fire-eaters had said their own slaves "would drive out the Yankees." They had known very little, reflected the Commodore, "of the relations existing between master and servant. Oh my! It was with difficulty they could get away [with] a household domestic—the field hands remained to a man . . . and immediately commenced plundering until we stopped them."[9]

Du Pont heard other, darker things as well. The planters and

[7] Thomas R. S. Elliott to his mother, Monday night [November 11, 1861], Elliott-Gonzales MSS.

[8] New York *Tribune*, November 20, 1861.

[9] Samuel Francis Du Pont to Henry Winter Davis, December 9, [18]61, Samuel Francis Du Pont MSS, Eleutherian Mills Historical Library, Greenville, Wilmington, Delaware.

overseers were in some cases shooting down rebellious slaves who would not leave the plantations with them.[10] In a panic to retrieve the most portable part of his evaporating fortunes, each planter had, in his own way, borne witness by action to his private conception of chattel slavery. For every man like Captain John Fripp, who thought first of his slaves as people, there was another who thought of them first as property. During the revolutionary days before the Federal pickets were posted over the islands, numerous planters concluded that there was yet time to evacuate Negroes and burn their cotton. When Thomas R. S. Elliott returned to his plantation and found the Negroes idle, he attempted to force them away with him. He was unsuccessful and commented grimly, "I think we will have to make a terrible example of many of them." Although Elliott's meaning is not precise, it is clear that many "terrible examples" were made.[11]

William Elliott had once written, in a candid defense of slavery, that masters were usually kind and that slavery served the interests of civilization. "Against *insubordination alone*, we are severe."[12] That was precisely what the masters had been obliged to deal with when the islands were invaded. The only eye-witnesses of these atrocities were the Negroes themselves, but their accounts were complete in many cases with names and places and were sufficient to convince the naval officers who questioned them. Commodore Du Pont was horrified to hear from an army officer, whose information had come "from reliable testimony," of recalcitrant slaves being burned to death in their cotton-houses. George W. Smalley, the correspondent of the New York *Tribune*, concluded that "the horrible fact stands out with appalling clearness and certainty that the murder of slaves who cannot be compelled to follow their masters is a deliberate and relentless

[10] *Ibid.*

[11] Thos. R. S. Elliott to his mother, Monday night [November 11, 1861], Elliott-Gonzales MSS.

[12] Lewis Pinckney Jones, "Carolinians and Cubans: The Elliotts and Gonzales, Their Work and Their Writings" (unpublished doctoral dissertation, University of North Carolina, 1952), Part I, p. 14.

purpose." His informants too gave names and places. A responsible Negro named Will Capers told Laura Towne that he had known of thirty Negroes who were shot for resistance.[13]

In the early days at Port Royal the missionaries heard many such stories. When all possible allowance is made for exaggeration, understandable mistakes, and even for the possibility that Negroes met death by accident while hiding in burning cotton-houses, the sheer weight of the evidence leads to the belief that many white men were willing to go to extreme lengths to retrieve their human property. James Petigru, following the Port Royal story from Charleston, heard of a planter who had burned all the buildings on his plantation, including all stores of corn and cotton, "and by so doing compelled his negroes to follow him, as they were on an island without food and shelter."[14]

The masters' problems were by no means over if they succeeded in recovering their slave property. Petigru wrote, "They have to find new homes, and provide for their people for a whole year, while the abandonment of their crops just harvested leaves them penniless." For men in the Confederate army, obliged to conduct these affairs through their wives and overseers, the problem was acute. Sometimes, when hiring out failed and there were no funds to meet financial pressures, the sale of slaves was the only answer.[15]

Masters who owned slaves on the periphery of the territory held by the Union forces were faced with the possible loss of all their slaves through running away. John Berkeley Grimball, who owned slaves and plantations in Beaufort and Colleton Districts, recorded in his diary for the early days of March in 1862 the gradual depopulation of his estates. The forty-eight slaves who stayed, including the old and sick, had their reward at the end of

[13] Du Pont to Henry Winter Davis, December 9, [18]61, Du Pont MSS; New York *Tribune*, December 7, 1861; Holland (ed.), *Towne*, p. 27.

[14] James Petigru Carson, *Life, Letters and Speeches of James Louis Petigru* (Washington, D. C., 1920), p. 414.

[15] *Ibid.*, p. 416; John Jenkins to his wife, Marcy, January 1, 1863, and April 10, 1863, John Jenkins MSS, South Caroliniana Library, Columbia, South Carolina.

the season in being sold for the round figure of $820 each.[16] Some masters relied upon severe punishment to discourage running away. When Ralph Elliott frustrated the escape of his father's slaves from Oak Lawn, he had two of the leaders sold in Charleston, and "the others were punished by whips and hand-cuffing." Every night they were chained and watched while Elliott waited for the danger to pass.[17]

But the danger did not pass. To William Elliott the Negroes seemed "utterly demoralized" by Yankee propaganda. The missionaries saw it differently. The streams of Negroes were coming out of the interior as a result of their total dissatisfaction with the "patriarchal institution." Generations of servitude had not stamped out of these people the desire to do as they pleased, although any real understanding of the responsibilities of freedom must have been, for most of them, very remote. E. L. Pierce wrote, in a moment of insight, that "the slave is unknown to all, even to himself, while the bondage lasts." Not even the keenest outside observer, "much less the master can measure the capacities and possibilities of the slave, until the slave himself is transmuted to a man."[18]

He might have added that the moment of freedom revealed the essence of ownership as well. The barbaric behavior of certain of the masters was probably no surprise to the Negroes who had been their slaves. A slave's life was one long lesson in accommodation to his master, and the slaves *did* recognize their own economic value. The missionaries, on the other hand, demonstrated occasionally a real sense of shock at the more severe aspects of the slave system as it was exercised in the old Sea Island region. There were plantations where nearly every Negro's back showed the marks of whipping, and the testimony of the Negroes against certain of the old owners was remarkably consistent. Occasionally, the dis-

[16] John Berkeley Grimball MS diary, March 3, 8, 14, 25, 1862; December 17, 1862, Grimball MSS, Southern Historical Collection, Chapel Hill.

[17] William Elliott to his son, William Elliott, August 25, 1862, Elliott-Gonzales MSS.

[18] Pierce, "The Freedmen at Port Royal," *Atlantic Monthly*, XII (September, 1863), 301.

A sandy St. Helena Island road, scored by carriage wheels. Half obscured on the left is Laura Towne's pride, "a picturesque gothic schoolhouse— a New England contrivance pitched in a grove of live oaks."

Above left: Major General David Hunter, among whose virtues patience was not. He filled the 1st South Carolina Volunteers by draft. Above right: Major General Rufus K. Saxton, Military Governor of the Sea Islands, who wanted the freedmen to inherit their native earth.

Mansfield French, army chaplain and friend of the freedmen, who influenced the Lincoln Administration in their behalf. To Secretary Salmon P. Chase he once wrote, "Pray excuse my enthusiasm, but *honor my faith.*"

covery of a revealing letter in the correspondence of the vanished white people bolstered the verdict of the Negroes. The missionaries heard again and again the same condemnation of certain cruel men and virtually unanimous praise of others.[19] While concluding that the majority of the slaves had been treated decently, Arthur Sumner reported that all the Negroes agreed that a number of the planters had been "devils in cruelty." The fact puzzled Sumner, for he had thought that "wherever the country belonged to old families whose plantations were hereditary property," masters had been generous and kind.[20]

That Sumner was ill-prepared for what he saw indicates that the young teacher's conception of slavery had been conditioned, perhaps subconsciously, by certain tenets of the proslavery argument. This is hardly surprising, for a number of the most vigorous champions of the South's peculiar institution had been identified with the Sea Islands. Perhaps Sumner had read *The Hireling and the Slave*, the poetic contribution of a bluff St. Helena planter-poet named William J. Grayson. In eight hundred heroic couplets, Grayson had presented an idyl of plantation slavery, where labor was "safe from harassing doubts and annual fears," and "unassailed by care." The happy slave was spared those conditions of unlucky Northern workers, where

> Labor with hunger wages ceaseless strife,
> And want and suffering only end with life.[21]

A native son of Beaufort also had contributed to the theological defense of slavery. The Reverend Dr. Richard Fuller had written

[19] Towne MS diary, May 23, June 13, 16, 1862; Pearson (ed.), *Letters*, pp. 31, 79, 206; William F. Allen MS diary, January 11, 1864, pp. 90–91, typescript copy.

[20] Arthur Sumner to Nina Hartshorn, May 18, 1862, Arthur Sumner MSS.

[21] See Vernon L. Parrington, *The Romantic Revolution in America 1800–1860* ("Main Currents in American Thought" [New York: Harcourt Brace Harvest Book, 1954], pp. 98–103), for an analysis of and excerpts from Grayson's popular poem.

in 1845 a series of letters to the Reverend Dr. Francis Wayland, in which he developed a battery of scriptural justifications for slavery. Sticking closely to his main point, one which was then rending his Baptist domination, Fuller maintained that holding slaves was not necessarily a sin. That some masters behaved sinfully toward their slaves the minister was not prepared to deny; but he emphasized the benevolent aspects of servitude in his part of the country, where "the slaves are not only watched over with guardian kindness and affection, but prefer to remain with their masters. . . ."[22] A Northern visitor had been so much impressed by the conditions of life on the William Joyner Smith plantation just south of Beaufort that he had written *A South-Side View of Slavery*; he had gained the never-ending contempt of all good abolitionists by the favorable impressions he conveyed.[23]

Other visitors had not seen the "south-side view" at all. Certainly the European visitor who had witnessed in Beaufort the sale of a handsome young slave woman and her sad separation from her young husband when she left Beaufort in the possession of a slave trader had not been favorably impressed. Fanny Kemble, the famous English actress who had married Pierce Butler and gone in 1838 to live at his plantation on St. Simon's Island, was made miserable by what she saw.[24] Her saga was told almost as well by a family slave as Miss Kemble told it in her book, and more simply. "She was a great lady—a *very* great lady . . . she tell Mr. Butler if he give up the slavery, she would likes to live there, but she couldn't stan' that; but he wouldn't 'grees to that, so she goes 'way and she get a dewoce."[25]

---

[22] Richard Fuller and Francis Wayland, *Domestic Slavery Considered as a Scriptural Institution* (New York, 1845), p. 158.

[23] Nehemiah Adams, *A South-Side View of Slavery: or Three Months at the South in 1854* (Boston, 1854).

[24] Boston *Commonwealth*, October 4, 1862; Frances Anne Kemble, *Journal of a Residence on a Georgia Plantation in 1838–1839* (London, 1863).

[25] Pearson (ed.), *Letters*, pp. 271–272.

That there should have been so many conflicting assessments of Sea Island slavery was troublesome to evangels attempting to reconstruct the typical past of the people they had come to the South to help—troublesome but not surprising. As Fanny Kemble perceived, there was "one most admirable circumstance in this slavery; you are absolute on your own plantation." Each plantation reflected the essential character of its owner, acting within the extremely liberal bounds allowed him by the slave law of South Carolina. Even Dr. Fuller had washed his hands of the attempt to vindicate certain of the "oppressive and wicked" slave statutes, but he had at the same time regarded the slave law as being unimportant in the real practice of slavery and a "great and fruitful source of misconception."[26] Far from being unimportant, the South Carolina statutes regarding slavery had offered the owners every facility for the exploitation of their human property and denied the slave any personal rights whatever. That numerous masters were unwilling to exercise their full liberty under the slave laws is a tribute to their own benevolence, not a sign that the law was insignificant.

The fundamental code, enacted in 1740, underwent no important changes between its enactment and the outbreak of the Civil War. In an important 1812 decision, the case of the *Executors of Walker vs. Bostick and Walker*, a South Carolina court said that the slaves of the southern United States were in their condition more analogous to the slaves of ancient Rome and Greece than to the villeins of medieval Europe, and that for precedent and authority the Roman Civil Law rather than the English Common Law must be consulted. Slaves were, "generally speaking, not considered as persons but as things. Almost all our statute regulations follow the principles of the civil law in relation to slaves. . . ." This position was stated even more strongly as late as 1847, when the Court placed the slave well outside the protection of Com-

---

[26] Kemble, *Journal*, p. 294; Fuller and Wayland, *Domestic Slavery*, pp. 158–159.

mon Law and Magna Carta. Of the slave it was said, "In the very nature of things he is subject to despotism. Law is to him only a compact between his rulers. . . ."[27]

That compact decreed that a slave was a slave for the rest of his natural life, that he could be hired out, sold, or disposed of by deed or gift. He could not bring action in his own name in court but was obliged to seek a white man friendly to his cause, even when his own freedom was the question. A slave's testimony was neither sought nor accepted. His marriage had no legal standing, and families could be separated by sale or bequest. In this last respect slavery was more severe in the United States than in Latin America, where the Roman Catholic Church was an established institution. The Church required masters to respect Christian marriage and the relations of mother and child, husband and wife. No such institution operated in any slave state except Louisiana to ameliorate the conditions of bondage or to stay the hand of individual owners in making use of chattel property.[28]

Whenever the evangels thought of the old masters, and it was often, they were obliged to see them through the eyes of the late slave population. Sometimes the old relationship between master and man was very hard to understand. Upon occasion Susannah, in charge of the kitchen at The Oaks, urged Laura Towne to accept gifts of fresh fish and other native delicacies for the table, explaining firmly that she did not want *pay*. Susannah said "she always gave such things to her old massas, and then they in return gave a little sweetning or something good from the table. It was give and take, good feeling all around." By this time Miss Towne was well aware that Master Dan was not the gentlest of men, and

[27] H. M. Henry, *The Police Control of the Slave in South Carolina* (Emory, Virginia, 1914), pp. 10–11.

[28] Stanley M. Elkins, *Slavery* (Chicago, 1959), pp. 54, 73. Elkins' study probes deeply into the psychological impact of American Negro slavery as a "closed system" offering no recourse to the slave beyond his own master. He explains the servility and childlike qualities of the slave as resulting from the effects of this system.

she sniffed to herself, "All giving on one side I should think, all taking, nearly, on the other, and good feeling according to the nature of the class, one only content in grasping, the other in giving." How was William Allen to understand old Captain John Fripp's charm? Praised for his kindness and generosity by all his slaves, and called by one "the best man on the island—from Coffin's Point to Land's End," the old patriarch in his daguerreotype looked forbidding to young Allen. He had "sharp and restless features" and looked as though "there might be vinegar in him." There was a whipping post within twenty feet of the big house. And he did whip his slaves, as one of them, "Dick," told Allen, but mildly, "jes like a young chile whippin'." Evidently, the aspect of personality could transcend even the worst aspects of the peculiar institution.[29]

In his defensive writings on slavery, Dr. Richard Fuller, who had also been a very popular man not only with his own slaves but with all those to whom he preached, liked to compare the master's role to that of a father to his children. He had enlarged upon the "painfully responsible situation" inherited by the Christian master, whose duty was the moral and spiritual elevation of his bondsmen.[30] How many men had taken their responsibility seriously? Even in his own day, the low-country planter enjoyed the benefits of an attractive stereotype, but the missionaries began to ask if the majority of them had been in actuality men of vast wealth, men of culture, and followers of the genteel tradition.

The State Census of South Carolina for 1860 shows that in the four parishes comprising Beaufort District there were 939 property owners of estates containing 883,048 acres of improved and

[29] Towne MS diary, April 28, 1862; William F. Allen MS diary, December 13, 1863, typescript copy, p. 57. See also Allen's entries in his manuscript diary for December 5, 6, 1863, p. 47, and January 19, 1864, p. 102.

[30] Fuller and Wayland, *Domestic Slavery*, p. 151. See Whitelaw Reid, *After the War: A Southern Tour, May 1, 1865 to May 1, 1866* (New York, 1866), p. 104, for an account of Dr. Fuller's reception by the Sea Island Negroes in 1865.

unimproved land. The Negro population for the same district, including a negligible sprinkling of free Negroes, numbered 33,339, according to the United States Census for the same year. An average based on these figures would therefore place every owner of land and slaves in the great planter category. A closer examination has shown, however, that three-fourths of the slaveholders owned fewer than twenty slaves each, and that only 19.9 per cent owned more than fifty. It is curious to note that even in the heart of the Carolina low country the typical planter was a small planter. This did not prevent the typical *slave* from being the field hand on a great plantation, for most of the slave population was concentrated in the hands of the larger owners.[31] There was clearly one stubborn fact damaging to Dr. Fuller's picture of slavery: Most patriarchs had too many "children." It is to the great planters and the near-great that we must look for the most potent factors in the past of the Negroes whom the North had "turned loose" on society in 1861.

Young James L. Petigru, who came to Beaufort District as a young man in the first quarter of the century to study law and teach school, had lamented the somnolent and easygoing ways of St. Luke's Parish; these ways nearly overcame his good resolutions to continue his studies. The man who would become the great Unionist of South Carolina found that he longed to move "fairly within the vulgar pale, lording it over a farm, talking of venison, drumfish, cotton-seed, and politics," as others did. William Grayson, who also knew the region thoroughly, described the post-revolutionary society of Beaufort in these terms: "They were a jovial and somewhat rough race, liberal, social, warm-hearted, hospitable, addicted to deep drinking, hard swearing, and practi-

---

[31] The territory occupied by Federal forces early in the war comprised only a part of Beaufort District. My totals are from the South Carolina MS Census Reports, State Archives, Columbia, South Carolina. See David Duncan Wallace, *South Carolina, A Short History 1520–1948* (Chapel Hill, 1951), Appendix IV, p. 710; Guion Griffis Johnson, *A Social History of the Sea Islands* (Chapel Hill, 1930), pp. 36–37.

cal joking, and not a little given to loose language and indelicate allusions. . . ."[32] Enough of this rustic flavor remained on the islands as late as the 1850's to make the reader of the records suspect that among the plantation owners the rough-and-tumble Squire Western type predominated over such polished specimens of nineteenth-century culture as Harriet Beecher Stowe had created in Augustine St. Clare.

The meeting of the Agricultural Society was the grand occasion of the month on St. Helena Island. The entertainment would consist of horse racing or trading, a dogfight, or the awarding of premiums for the best corn or potato production. The most serious pursuit seems to have been eating and drinking. The members rotated the responsibility of providing dinner, and the provisions were so lavish that at one point in its history the Society decided to impose a fifty-cent fine on members who sent more than six courses of meat to the Club House, a precaution taken to "prevent competition." Grayson said that, at these meetings of the country squires to hunt and dine, "no man was permitted to go home sober." Nobody should have known more about that than Grayson himself. Thomas B. Chaplin, a neighboring planter who entertained the poet at dinner, said of him that he was "a whole-souled fellow who got corned as a matter of courtesy," took a spill out of his sulky, and had to stay all night. Chaplin had himself to confess all too often to overindulgence. He reported that, at a celebration held in 1848 for the troops departing for the Mexican War, he had drunk too much champagne, "like a fool, and as usual got boisterous and perhaps insulting, while the toasts and speeches were being given. . . ."[33] A Coast Survey officer who had visited the island gentry before the war told the Northern

[32] William J. Grayson, *James Louis Petigru* (New York, 1866), p. 51; Grayson, quoted in Wallace, *South Carolina*, p. 490.

[33] Thomas B. Chaplin MS diary, December 1, 2, 1852; February 5, 1846; May 3, 1850; June 25, 1848; July 5 and December 25, 1845; and December 31, 1848. The Chaplin diary is located in the South Carolina Historical Society, Charleston; David Duncan Wallace, *South Carolina*, p. 490.

teachers that the St. Helena planters had been "generally a hard, uncultivated set." Other visitors had absorbed the same impression.[34] The island gentry appreciated unmasked power to the extent that its ugliest symbol, the cowhide plantation whip, could be casually presented and received by men wishing to mark important occasions. Even the severest critics, however, acknowledged that there were "some exceptions of taste and refinement among the planters."[35] Taking the islands as a whole, there were a great many of these favorable exceptions, and among them were those who owned the greater number of the Sea Island Negroes.

At the very summit of the social and economic life of the low country were such men as William Elliott, head of a large family whose widespread holdings throughout the entire rice and long-staple cotton region were only partly indicated by their acres in Beaufort District. Among the other great landowners of the area were William H. Trescot, paying taxes on an estate valued at $40,000, and Micah Jenkins, whose lands were valued at $34,600. Captain John Fripp and Mrs. Mary Coffin held more than two thousand acres each on St. Helena Island. The Reverend Dr. Fuller was himself a large owner of land and slaves.[36]

It would have been impossible for such men to come into direct contact of any depth with many of their slaves. Not only were the Negroes too numerous, but many of the great planters were away from home a great part of the year. Dr. Fuller had since

[34] Sherwood (ed.), "Walker Journal," p. 36; Holland (ed.), *Towne*, p. 34; Kemble, *Journal*, pp. 387–388; Adolph B. Benson (ed.), *America in the Fifties; Letters of Frederika Bremer* (New York, 1924), p. 110.

[35] Chaplin MS diary, March 1, 1845, January 2, 1856; Sherwood (ed.), "Walker Journal," p. 36; Kemble, *Journal*, pp. 387–388.

[36] Jones, "Carolinians and Cubans," Part I, p. 52; S. C. MS Census Reports, Beaufort District, State Archives, Columbia; Johnson, *Social History*, pp. 42–43. Fuller lost no time in inquiring of Secretary Chase about his rights in his slaves and lands at Port Royal. See Donald (ed.), *Inside Lincoln's Cabinet*, p. 283, text and note.

1847 been the minister to the Seventh Baptist Church in Baltimore, and only visited his plantations on vacations.[37] Because of the prevalence of fevers during the hot months, planters who could afford to do so left the islands completely or settled in some healthy locality nearer by, such as Beaufort, or in one of the small settlements on the ocean side of the islands. The villages of St. Helenaville and Eddingsville on Edisto Island were a special boon to planters who wished to keep an eye on their crops.[38]

When the William Elliott family issued an invitation, they found it necessary to say first where they would be. They called the Oak Lawn plantation on the Pon-Pon River their "winter quarters," but toward the end of February "the gayer portion of the family" visited Charleston, returning to Oak Lawn only a short time before leaving in May for Beaufort, "our residence during the summer months." Sometimes Elliott took his daughters to the North, where at Newport, Boston, and Saratoga Springs, they met their New England counterparts in the social world. There was an occasional European tour.[39]

For these great planters much time was consumed in the pursuit of culture, politics, and the amusements of sport. The handsome collection of rare volumes in biography and history belonging to the Beaufort Library Society was ample testimony to the cultural interests of these gentlemen planters. These books, and the numerous private collections, had excited the admiration of the agents who busily packed them up for the long trip north atop bales of confiscated cotton. William Elliott had found time to write a widely-known book, *Carolina Sports by Land and Water* (New York, 1859); and his estate, Oak Lawn, became a mecca for prominent anglers who wished to experience the thrill

[37] *Ibid.*
[38] John Fripp MS diary, June 19 and July 6, 1857.
[39] William Elliott to Mrs. [?] Bayard, January 24, 1846; William Elliott to his wife, August 16 and September 11, 1844, and August 19, 1845, Elliott-Gonzales MSS; Jones, "Carolinians and Cubans," Part I, p. 32.

of fishing for the giant drum, or "devilfish." The English journalist William H. Russell described a fishing party organized for his benefit in the spring the war began. A swift boat approached his landing, "pulled by six powerful Negroes, attired in red flannel jackets and white straw hats with broad ribands. The craft itself . . . lay deep in the water, for there were extra Negroes for fishing, servants, baskets of provisions, water buckets, stone jars of less innocent drinking, and abaft there was a knot of great planters—Elliotts all—cousins, uncles, and brothers."[40] It is probable that for the great planters most of their personal contacts with slaves other than house servants occurred on such pleasant sporting occasions, almost as jolly for the Negroes as for their master. This may go far to account for a fact that the missionaries duly noted, that there was a tendency on the part of plantation Negroes to exculpate their masters from responsibility for the harsh policies enacted by the overseers.[41]

If the wealthier planters had fewer direct contacts with their slaves than did their poorer counterparts, they frequently provided superior physical accommodations. The housing of slaves could become a symbol of wealth and status for the master. Dr. Milton Hawks, an agent of Pierce stationed on Edisto Island and a man who would have preferred to see the worst in slavery, thought the cabins on the island were "as good" as the homes of poor white people in Georgia and South Carolina. Frederika Bremer, a fair-minded Scandinavian visitor to the region in the decade preceding the war, was pleased to see on some plantations "small, whitewashed wooden houses, for the most part built in rows, forming a street, each house standing detached in its little yard or garden," surrounded by flowering peach trees, and kept in neat and clean condition. The volume of the evidence, however,

---

[40] New York Times, February 24, 1862; William Howard Russell, My Diary North and South (New York, 1859), pp. 205–206.

[41] Pearson (ed.), Letters, pp. 165, 272.

evolves into a different picture, one of comfortless little two-room puncheon cabins about twenty-five feet square, with wooden chimneys, and without glass in the windows.[42] J. Miller McKim spoke in withering contempt of the homes of the "happiest of all peasantries," pronouncing them "indescribable and incredible." A great deal depended upon the eye of the beholder, but it is worth noting that Nehemiah Adams was himself put on the defensive about the slave cabins, admitting that they would "strike everyone disagreeably at first."[43]

Closely related to housing was the matter of slave health. We may assume that it was ever in the planter's best interest to see that his human property was kept in good condition, and the mention of the expense of having doctors in attendance upon slaves appears frequently in the records of the period. Planters also became adept at home remedies and quickly learned to perform routine vaccinations.[44] Despite the enlistment of the planters' interests on the side of good health, there was a depressing prevalence of disease and suffering. The symptoms are not always easy to identify, and specific diagnoses are seldom given. Thomas B. Chaplin, a St. Helena planter, lost seventy-four days of labor from his relatively small number of plantation hands in 1849 because of maladies ranging from stone bruises to a fatal illness that he could not identify. Fevers and pulmonary diseases were the most common afflictions, but there were certain ailments that seem to be directly related to hard labor, poor living conditions, and bad

[42] Hawks to Esther Hawks, April 30, 1862, Hawks MSS; Benson (ed.), *America in the Fifties*, p. 103; Towne MS diary, May 23, 1862; French, *Slavery in South Carolina*, p. 161; Forten, "The Sea Islands," *Atlantic Monthly*, XIII (May, 1864), 592; Allen MS diary, February 4, 1864, pp. 118–119, typescript; Kemble, *Journal*, p. 308.

[43] McKim to Charles Sumner, January 20, 1863, Charles Sumner MSS; Adams, *South-Side View*, p. 37.

[44] Fripp MS diary, July 7, 1857, April 2, 24, 25, 1858; Chaplin MS diary, January 28, 1845, February 11, 1854.

social attitudes. Among these were swollen and sore feet and joints, abdominal pains, syphilis, rupture, and prolapsed uterus.[45] The latter problem, wrote Fanny Kemble, affected nearly every other woman on her husband's plantation and was directly attributable to severe tasking and the return of female slaves to the field too soon after child-bearing. It frequently incapacitated the slave completely.[46]

Housing and health varied more from plantation to plantation than did the rations and clothing supplied to field Negroes. These issues were highly standardized; the Negroes stated them as clearly as did any planter's manual when they knew the Federal fleet was coming and they went singing down to Hilton Head to build the fortifications they hoped would be inadequate:

> No more peck o' corn for me, No more, no more; ...
> No more driver's lash for me ...
> No more pint o' salt for me ...
> No more hundred lash for me ...
> No more mistress' call for me, No more, no more ...
> Many thousands go.[47]

The weekly peck of Indian corn, with occasional allotments of approximately three pounds of salt pork, supplemented from time to time by fresh beef and vegetables in season, made up the bulk of the diet. There was a regular issue of salt and molasses. The

[45] "List of Sick Negroes for 1849," at end of Chaplin MS diary; *ibid.*, January 10, 1856, April 25, 1857; David Gavin MS diary, October 18, 1855, in Southern Historical Collection, Chapel Hill; Fripp MS diary, March 27, 1857, June 10, 1857, April 2, 1858. Kemble pronounced pleurisy and pneumonia "terribly prevalent" and rheumatism "almost universal." Kemble, *Journal*, pp. 44–45, 137–138; exposure and improper housing were probably responsible.

[46] *Ibid.*, pp. 45, 232, 241–243, 272, 321; Chaplin MS diary, January 2, 1852; Hawks to Hawks, May 17, 1862, Hawks MSS.

[47] Allen, Ware, Garrison, *Slave Songs*, p. 48.

Negroes ground their own meal with a stone hand mill and varied their diet with crabs and fish caught on their own time. Clothing was provided at the rate of one outfit twice yearly, at the change of the seasons, and was usually issued by the yard. Shoes were included in the fall distribution, and a new blanket might be expected once every three years.[48]

Whether the missionaries understood or not, the real significance of the song "Many Thousands Go!" lay in its simple unaccented statement of the conditions of slavery. The slave did not understand that he received his peck of corn and the pint of salt in *return* for his labor; it was rather a condition of his life, a regular issue. It was by no means the reward of superior service, for all received the same allotment. The slave's inducement to work was the negative one of evading the "driver's lash," another condition of life. At bottom, the free-labor argument rested on the assumption that the liberated slave would automatically replace the negative impetus of the lash with the goal of making his own daily hominy, which would be unlikely to surpass in quality the master's old ration until the chaotic conditions attending the breakdown of the old system crystallized into a new way of life. Would the knowledge of freedom, or the mere hope of it, be sufficient to carry the ignorant Sea Island slave through the lean years to the point at which the material rewards of free labor would be greater than the ration of a slave? That was for the missionaries the main question.

In their humanitarian zeal, however, the evangels emphasized this point to the exclusion of others fully as important. To understand exactly how large an order they were asking the Negroes to fill, they ought to have questioned more seriously the viability

[48] James Hammond Plantation Manual, typescript copy of manuscript, seen at the South Carolina Historical Society in Charleston; Fripp MS diary, November 27, 1857, May 10, 1858; Chaplin MS diary, October 7, 9, 1845, December 25, 1845; Charles Nordhoff, *The Freedmen of South Carolina* (New York, 1863), pp. 5, 6; Stevens, *Stevens*, II, 354.

of the economic system they were breaking down, not with the consideration of possibly maintaining it, but for the discovery of clues as to the best direction for the Port Royal experiment to take.

The old planters of the islands had been able, with the advantages of their long experience, highly regimented slave labor, and large-scale production, to make Sea-Island cotton profitable. It had not been easy, however; the profits had not been, on a year-in, year-out basis, very great, and many men had failed. It is doubtful if many new fortunes were made in the old region in the forty years preceding the outbreak of the war. Even the evangels most oriented to economic problems seem to have been unaware of the agricultural difficulties ahead of them.

The opening of the rich cotton lands of the western South in the second decade of the century had made it harder for South Carolina to compete in the world cotton market. Because it cost the eastern planter more to produce cotton on his depleted lands, he had been obliged to manage his estates carefully, to see that the fertility of his soil was maintained through rest, fertilization, and rotation, and to cut his costs by raising much of his provision crop at home.[49] The long-staple cotton grower had the advantage of a product that always brought a higher price than other cotton, but he also faced a very great disadvantage. Because of the extremely long growing season, the planter was greatly subject to the chances of nature; too much or too little rain, too late a spring, blight, the worm, or a fall hurricane could spell disaster. The culture of long-staple cotton has been aptly called a "lottery" and would have been economically impossible but for the occasional golden years when weather and market cooperated to bring the fabulous returns that helped the planter through lean times. The merchants and factors with whom a planter dealt took great risks in financ-

---

[49] For an able analysis of the agricultural problems of South Carolina during this period and the adjustment of planters to them, see Alfred Glaze Smith, Jr., *Economic Readjustment of an Old Cotton State; South Carolina, 1820–1860* (Columbia: University of South Carolina Press, 1958).

ing such an enterprise and gained correspondingly high rewards.[50]

To offset his disadvantages, the long-staple grower paid serious attention to developing fine strains. Certain planters who became experts in the art of seed selection were disposed to guard their secrets well and enjoyed considerable fame for their product. Because the English buyers were familiar with the consistent quality of certain great producers, it became one of the special features of the trade that cotton sold in large quantities under a well-known name like Fripp or Coffin could bring a higher price in the market. It is probable that the sheer satisfaction of producing so fine a staple, and marking it with a symbol denoting the plantation of its origin, did much to retain the loyalty of Sea Island planters to their temperamental crop.[51] One planter who calculated his income over a forty-year period decided that he had received 4.37 per cent on his investment. The last decade before the war had been exceptionally prosperous, and it looked as though the eastern region was adapting to its economic difficulties. One writer thought that if a planter were content to grow "reasonably good, though not the finest" staple Sea-Island cotton, thereby producing more cotton per acre, and would use improved equipment for cleaning cotton and plows for cultivation, he might expect a profit of between 10 and 12 per cent.[52]

But most planters had never availed themselves of improved machinery, and very few had exchanged the long, heavy cotton hoe for the plow. The economic reason given for this backwardness was that the large number of slaves required in picking time

[50] Johnson, *Social History*, pp. 65, 71.

[51] *Ibid.*, pp. 51–52; Lewis Cecil Gray, *History of Agriculture in the Southern United States to 1860* (Washington, 1933), II, 731–739. Sometimes, smaller planters used the seed of more famous plantations and pooled their crops for higher prices. See Chaplin MS diary, December 16, 1855; see also Chalmers S. Murray, *This Our Land: The Story of the Agricultural Society of South Carolina* (Charleston, 1949), p. 190; Smith, *Economic Readjustment*, p. 61, note.

[52] Johnson, *Social History*, p. 102; Gray, *History of Agriculture*, II, 739.

could not be fully employed in the growing season, especially
when plows were introduced. A willingness to diversify the crops
to a greater extent would have overcome this problem. The mistaken notion that their labor and lands were suited only to the
growth of cotton had prevented the planters from securing a
greater margin of profit from their total farming operations.[53]

Another characteristic and legendary failure in management
was the gradual accumulation of an excess of house servants.
This became a problem at the Chaplin plantation. The master complained, not without an implied criticism of the mistress, that
there were thirteen servants about the house and yard and only
nine in the field. All told, he had "30 head to feed—only 9 to work
—and make feed for them," not to speak of shoes and clothing.[54]

For those in the field the hard work stretched around the year,
with the only slack season occurring in midsummer before the
picking began. Plantation activity was at its zenith in the fall when
the crop was brought in, and the tension mounted steadily.
Owners anxious to save their crops from possible hurricanes urged
their slaves to greater exertion than at any other time, and they
often resorted to the lash. John Fripp (not the benevolent Captain John) reported with impatience that he "gave nearly all of
them a poping [sic] . . . they should go over more ground or bring
in more cotton." Chaplin thought of his slaves who were picking
slowly that "a little cowhide will make them do better." Edgar
Fripp, a wealthy and arrogant man, sometimes made his slaves

[53] Smith, *Economic Readjustment*, p. 88; Johnson, *Social History*, p.
102. There was a difference of opinion as to the economic feasibility of
more mechanization even among more successful planters. A consultation
of the South Carolina MS Census for 1860 shows that successful planters
like Thomas Aston Coffin and Richard Fuller had more money invested in
equipment in proportion to their improved acreage than did Thomas
Chaplin, a consistently unlucky manager. On the other hand, the same
information seems to show that William Elliott, a highly successful manager, was not using plows on his Beaufort District cotton lands.

[54] Chaplin MS diary, February 18, 19, 1850.

work all night by the light of the full moon during the heaviest part of the season.[55]

Pickers were obliged to exercise the greatest care in freeing the cotton of dirt as they picked, as well as in the final operations of ginning and packing. These last tasks were not finished before the hardier hands reported to the fields again to prepare ground for the next crop. The fertility of the fields was maintained by transporting "salt marsh" grass or mud to the fields, a step that was absolutely necessary to the production of the fine staple. No job, however, was hated more by the slave than this cold, dirty, and wet midwinter duty.[56]

The most grotesque aspect of plantation paternalism lay in the fact that if a planter took *too* complaisant an attitude toward the performance of field work, he courted financial failure, and with failure would come the sale of his slaves to pay his indebtedness. If a planter managed badly or was the victim of extravagant tastes, he had to endure the bitter experience of Thomas Chaplin, forced in 1845 to sell ten prime field hands to clear his debts:

Nothing can be more mortifying and grieving to a man, than to select out some of his negroes to be sold—you know not to whom, or how they will be treated by their new owners, and negroes that you find no fault with—to separate families. Mothers and daughters—Brothers and sisters all to pay for your own extravagances—People will laugh at your distress—and say it serves you right—you lived beyond your means. . . .[57]

Chaplin blamed himself most justly for extravagance, but South Carolina agriculture was in a state of crisis in the middle 1840's, and many slaves went the way of Chaplin's. It is probable that

[55] Fripp MS diary, October 16, 1858, September 8, 1858; Chaplin MS diary, October 1, 1852, November 8, 1849, November 6, 1853; Allen MS diary, December 5, 6, 1863, p. 48, typescript.

[56] Gray, *History of Agriculture*, II, 735; Johnson, *Social History*, p. 64.

[57] Chaplin MS diary, May 3, 1845.

more than 170,000 Negroes were removed from South Carolina between 1820 and 1860. More than 5,000 went West out of the four lower districts between 1830 and 1840. Large numbers of white people also departed for the West, seeking there a solution to their economic distress.[58] But most men met the challenge on the old soil, concentrating their advantages of experience and business ability upon raising the fine cotton.

The evangels were for the most part unaware of the special economic problems they were confronting. Had they understood them better, they might well have asked if long-staple cotton, temperamental and financially hazardous, was a crop suitable to smaller-scale production, if it might not have been a better course to follow the urging of ante-bellum agricultural authorities and attempt a greater diversification. Some of Gideon's Band were already dreaming of the time when the islands would become small farms, worked by freed Negroes who would own their own land. Edward Philbrick, the one evangel who thought hard about economics, did not at this time contemplate such a future; he expected to retain the plantation system with the simple substitution of wages for slave labor. Oriented toward the New England textile interests and dedicated to proving his own favorite abolition argument, that free labor could raise cotton more cheaply than slave labor, Philbrick was unlikely to take alternate crops under serious consideration. For most evangels, the humanitarian and social considerations excluded the hard facts of Sea Island agriculture, and they continued to regard the Negro's response to freedom as comprising the whole foundation of their anticipated success.

The Negroes of the islands, wrote Edward Pierce, "had become an abject race, more docile and submissive than those of any

[58] Smith, *Economic Readjustment*, pp. 110, 25, 26, 28. For the economic significance of natural increase among slaves in the slave states of the East, consult Alfred H. Conrad and John R. Meyer, "The Economics of Slavery in the Ante Bellum South," *Journal of Political Economy*, LXVI (April, 1958).

other locality." Nowhere else had "the deterioration from their native manhood been carried so far. . . ." Pierce was by no means alone in this conclusion, for all the missionaries were struck with certain childish qualities manifested by many of the Negroes.[59] Elizabeth Botume described a class of young adults:

They rolled up their eyes and scratched their heads when puzzled, and every line in their faces was in motion. If any one missed a word, or gave a wrong answer, he looked very grave. But whenever a correct answer was given, especially if it seemed difficult, they laughed aloud, and reeled about, hitting each other with their elbows. Such "guffaws" could not be tolerated in regular school hours. They joked each other like children; but, unlike them, they took all good-naturedly.[60]

A superintendent concluded that the Negroes were entirely dependent, lacking in initiative, and that they needed "the positive ordering that a child of five or ten years of age requires." The sum of these observations added up to a picture of the personality known in American literature as "Sambo," the plantation slave, "docile but irresponsible, loyal but lazy, humble but chronically given to lying and stealing."[61]

But it is well to remember that although "Sambo" finds many illustrations in the observations of the teachers on the islands, he remains a *statistical* concept, and the record contains as many stories of protest, disloyalty to the late masters, and manly independence as of servile acquiescence. The extent to which the personality of the common field hand had been fundamentally altered by the experience of slavery finds a good test in his response to the opportunities offered by the new order inaugurated in the wake of the Northern occupation. The first reaction can be found

[59] Pierce, "The Freedmen at Port Royal," *Atlantic Monthly*, XII (September, 1863), 300; see above, Chapter 3, note 89.

[60] Elizabeth Hyde Botume, *First Days Among the Contrabands* (Boston, 1893), p. 96.

[61] Holland (ed.), *Towne*, p. 9; Elkins, *Slavery*, p. 82.

in the large numbers of slaves willing to risk severe punishment
and even death by running away from their masters. The wild
sacking of Beaufort and the plantation houses and the complete
destruction of the cotton gins show a bitter and long dammed-up
hostility that, if perhaps childish in its discharge, is yet remarkably similar to the venting of spleen demonstrable among more
"civilized" peoples. Other and more positive tests as to the fundamental damage to the slaves' personality would be provided as time
went on in the success, or lack thereof, of the missionaries' labors
to make the people self-reliant.

A more probable and immediate explanation of the obsequious
and infantile behavior of the majority of slaves who demonstrated
childish traits is that playing "Sambo" had its rewards and that
failing to play him incurred many risks. That the role could be
one of conscious hypocrisy is illustrated by the case of Elijah
Green. This ancient veteran of slavery remembered with rancor,
many long years after his freedom came, having been obliged to
give an affectionate endorsement of the new brides and grooms
who joined his master's family, whether he liked them or not.[62]

The main effect of slavery was a thick residue of accumulated
habits and responses that a slave child learned early in life. It was
a culture, in short, that invested its members with a number of
character traits useful in slavery but unbecoming in free men.
The extent to which these traits developed in an individual slave
depended in part upon the class to which he belonged. It has been
a general assumption that more enlightenment and self-respect
were to be found among house servants and the Negroes of the
towns than among field slaves. The common corollary, however,
that these "Swonga" people, as they were denominated by the
field hands, also possessed a greater spirit of *independence* is, at
the very least, a debatable point. They had merely absorbed more
of the white man's culture, and they paid for it in daily contacts

[62] Slave Narrative Collection, XIV, Part II, 198, in Rare Book Room,
Library of Congress.

with the "superior" beings whose very presence was a reminder of their own inferior status. Sometimes the loyalty of a well-treated house servant could make war on the very notion of independence. There is considerable evidence to support the idea that, while the Swonga people had perhaps more self-esteem and were better dressed, the field hands had more self-reliance. It would be hard to conceive of a more independent spirit than that shown by the six strapping sons of "Mom Peg." They had all been field slaves, and they defied an overseer to whip them. When one brother was threatened, all took to the woods in a body and had to be guaranteed immunity before returning. Described as "tall and handsome," the brothers held "high rank in church and council" and were to enjoy a bright future in freedom. On the other hand, Laura Towne met two women in Beaufort, formerly house servants, who assured her that they would not have run away from their masters except for their desire not to be separated from their kin. But they were already feeling nostalgic for the old ways, with the coming of April, for in the spring they had always come to Beaufort with their masters' families and had had "such gay times." They hoped the teachers would not go away, for it "seemed like they couldn't be happy widout white ladies 'roun."[63]

The story of Lydia Smalls is most instructive. When she was a girl, her mistress had taken her away from field work on the Ashdale plantation on Ladies Island and had brought her to Beaufort, where she became a trusted house servant. When Lydia's own son was growing up as a pampered pet in the Prince Street house of their master, Henry McKee, Lydia was afraid he did not realize the meaning of slavery or the full indignity of his position. Ever a rebel in her heart, Lydia forced her son to watch a slave being whipped in the yard of the Beaufort jail. Then young Robert went himself to stay for a time at the Ashdale plantation. He had seen the seemingly dull and cringing plantation people every week when he had come with his master to bring their

[63] Holland (ed.), *Towne*, p. 225; Towne MS diary, April 17, 1862.

rations. He never understood much about them, however, until the day he stayed and his master rode away. The apathetic people suddenly found the spirit to grumble and complain heartily about their diet. It was on the plantation that Robert Smalls first heard about Frederick Douglass and decided that he too would become a free man.[64]

For many a servant, a close personal tie with a good master or mistress could go a long way toward reconciliation to a dependent condition. "Henry," formerly cook for Mrs. Thomas Aston Coffin, spoke affectionately of his former mistress to Harriet Ware and readily seized upon Miss Ware's offer to write to Mrs. Coffin for him. He had hesitated to make the request himself for fear "they wouldn't think it right to have anything to do with the old people—'but she's a Nort' lady, you know, Ma'am,' " he said to Miss Ware, " 'a beautiful lady, I would serve her all my life.' " When Thomas Chaplin's slave "Anthony" died, Chaplin wrote, perhaps a little self-consciously, "he is regretted by many—white and black—I miss him more than I would any other negro that I own," and added, "Peace be to his *soul*."[65]

Anthony had belonged, as a "driver," to the uppermost rank of plantation life. These foremen and the skilled laborers enjoyed an even more exalted position than the house servants. The driver held the most responsible position a slave could occupy. His job included maintaining order in the quarters as well as calling the Negroes to work, assigning the daily tasks, and seeing that the work was well done. That the driver was sometimes a cruel despot, as he was frequently portrayed in abolition literature, is undeniable; but there is little evidence in the Sea Island story to indicate that he was commonly such. If the driver developed a fine

---

[64] Dorothy Sterling, *Captain of the Planter, The Story of Robert Smalls* (New York, 1958), pp. 16, 24, 29–31. Written in a style to appeal to youthful readers, this biography of a prominent Negro leader in South Carolina Reconstruction politics is based upon sound research and is factual in essential details.

[65] Pearson (ed.), *Letters*, pp. 206–207; Chaplin MS diary, May 5, 1850.

knowledge of farming and enjoyed his master's confidence over a period of years, their relationship could become one of mutual esteem and friendly respect, contrasting most favorably with the often unstable and transient connections between plantation owners and their overseers.

Isaac Stephens, "master servant" to William Elliott, was able to keep his master informed of the condition of the crops on Elliott's numerous estates while the latter was on extended trips from home. He had been certain enough of his own standing to pass judgment on the relative qualities of the white overseers at the several plantations and to exchange social information with his master about the family at home:

> Old Mistress and Miss Mary are quite well. I was quite sorry that some of my young mistress and masters wear [sic] not in Beaufort to enjoy some of the fine dinners and Tea partys [sic] old Mistress has been giving for her grandchildren. . . .
>
> Master will be so kind as to give my love to my wife—all her friends are well—and say howdey to her and myself just like an old Buck—hearty and prime. . . .[66]

There must have been few Negroes on the islands who had enjoyed so relaxed a relationship with their masters, or who had had such opportunities to develop judgment and leadership. The evangels could count on these few, however, to provide an example for the rest in making an adaptation to freedom.

[66] Isaac Stephens to William Elliott, October 22, 1849, Elliott-Gonzales MSS. Another revealing letter in the same collection is that of "Jacob" to Elliott, July 3, 1860, showing that Jacob was carrying on the farming operations, borrowing necessary supplies on his master's credit, asking Elliott's advice, and requesting the assistance of a carpenter. Of all the evangels, Philbrick alone gave the "drivers" a poor rating on intelligence and responsibility. See his letter to Atkinson, June 15, 1863, Atkinson MSS. On a number of Sea Island plantations the drivers served as de facto overseers, for the planters seem to have disregarded freely the statute stipulating the residence of a white person on plantations of more than ten working slaves. See Turner, *Africanisms,* p. 4; Slave Narrative Collection, XIV, Part II, 88.

There had even been a few opportunities for slaves to develop special talents outside the economic hierarchy of the plantation. Religious leaders enjoyed special standing with their fellows, and women sometimes achieved status as midwives. For all the slaves there was a small economic venture open in the raising of poultry and a little garden crop, or perhaps a pig. The surplus was sold to the master for cash; occasionally, it was sold outside the plantation by the slave himself. Although a statute against trading with slaves existed, it was usually ignored.[67] Outside these limited interests, there was nothing for most slaves but the dull routine of the cotton field. The real trouble with slavery as a "school" for anything was that the institution provided so few directions in which to grow and so much necessity to conform.

The Negro child on a large Sea Island plantation began learning how to be a slave almost from the moment of birth. In view of the generally acknowledged impact of early childhood experiences upon personality, the restrictions of a slave's childhood may go further than institutions or laws to explain certain of "Sambo's" failings. When the slave mother emerged from her confinement and returned to the field at the end of the third or fourth week, she saw her baby in the day only long enough for feeding and had very little time for the affectionate caressing so important for the development of the child's personality and security.[68] On the other hand, the mother herself could not experience the happiest aspects of motherhood when the child was merely an additional drain upon a tired body. The missionaries frequently observed that numbers of mothers on the great plantations appeared to demonstrate very little affection for their offspring. Arthur Sumner complained that the children "are invariably spoken to in harsh and peremptory tones" by adult Negroes and were

[67] Johnson, *Social History*, p. 86; Henry, *Police Control*, p. 80; Fuller and Wayland, *Domestic Slavery*, p. 151.

[68] Kemble, *Journal*, p. 220; "Pat has baby [and] will be out on Monday as it's a month old today." Fripp MS diary, June 13, 1857; Towne MS diary, August 25, 1863.

"whipped unmercifully for the least offence." A stern system called for stern discipline, and an old Negro woman asked Elizabeth Botume "What the Lord Almighty make trees for if they ain't fur lick boy chillen?" Toys were little known, and games usually took the form of fighting and wrestling in lieu of more constructive play. But the numbers of tender stories of maternal love show that, even among the victims of such a severe regimen, the human instincts served to soften the general harshness of the lives of children.[69]

When the mother returned to the field the child usually went, on the large Sea Island plantations, to a nursery, where he joined numbers of other children under the supervision of superannuated "Maumas" or grannies. Frederika Bremer pronounced this system "repulsive." She had seen "sometimes as many as sixty or seventy or even more [small children] together, and their guardians were a couple of old Negro witches who with a rod of reeds kept rule over these poor little black lambs, who with an unmistakable expression of fear and horror shrunk back whenever the threatening witches came forth, flourishing their rods." Aunt Jane Grant recalled in her old age some vivid details of her childhood in Beaufort. The little children of her establishment were cared for by an old mauma who fed them thus: "Dey'd clean off a place on de ground near de washpot where dey cooked de peas, clean it off real clean, den pile de peas out dere on de ground for us to eat."[70]

For fortunate slave children there came a time when they might, as the chosen playmates of the master's children, be able to take a part in the free country life about them. Sometimes the white parents objected that "the little negroes are ruining the children,"

---

[69] Arthur Sumner to Nina Hartshorn, July 9, 1863, Arthur Sumner MSS; Botume, *First Days,* pp. 257, 253; EHP in *Third Series of Extracts from Letters* (Boston, 1863); Towne MS diary, April 5, 1864. Despite commenting upon severe discipline, Miss Botume thought that with Negro mothers the "maternal feeling was intensified." See her *First Days,* p. 163.

[70] Frederika Bremer, *Homes of the New World; Impressions of America* (New York, 1854), II, 449; Slave Narrative Collection, XIV, Part II, 179.

but sooner or later the democracy of childhood broke down parental resolutions. Mrs. Thomas Chaplin might complain of the "badness" little Jack was teaching her son Ernest, but shortly she would see the two riding off on the same horse to gather wild plums or mulberries. The slave child's formal education would consist of learning the catechism, on plantations where that was deemed important, and he was instructed that his duty to his master was faithful work and that he was responsible to God for a good performance.[71] An important lesson most small slaves learned early was their relation to the white race in general and to the master in particular. Little Jane, of the Robert Oswald household, learned it the day she objected to calling her mistress's small son "Marse" and was sent around to Wilcox's store for a cowhide switch.[72]

The plantation child quickly grasped other things also. He learned how the slave enjoys life a little more at his master's expense. Thomas Chaplin wrote with some sense of resignation:

More robery [sic].—discovered that my little rascal William, who I had minding the crows off the watermellons [sic] had been the worst crow himself, and does the thing quite sistematically [sic]. He turns over a mellon, cuts a hole on the under side large enough to admit his hand, eats out the inside, when he finds a ripe one, then turns the mellon back again, not breaking it off the vine, there it lays, looking as sound as ever. No one would suppose it hollow. In picking some—we found no less than 23 or 4 in this fix. *Cunning*, very.[73]

It is not surprising that the missionaries should have found the former slaves irresponsible. At no point in his passage to adulthood

[71] Chaplin MS diary, May 10, 1854; Adams, *South-Side View*, p. 85; Fripp MS diary, March 3, 1857; Rebecca Grant recalled that the children were given Sabbath School lessons every Sunday morning on the porch of the master's house, where they were taught the catechism and "to be faithful to the missus and Marsa's work like you would to your heavenly Father's work." Slave Narrative Collection, XIV, Part II, 185.

[72] *Ibid.*, p. 179.

[73] Chaplin MS diary, July 10, 1854.

did the slave youth have the experience of learning to accept responsibility. The peculiar circumstances of his life became most apparent at the time of marriage. Nehemiah Adams was usually blind to the worst aspects of slave life, but even he saw clearly that slavery was inimical to the family as an institution, and he wrote particularly of "the annihilation . . . of the father in the domestic relations of the slaves. . . ." The master supplied the necessaries of life, and what else there was to receive was far more likely to be in the power of the wife to dispense than in that of her husband. The cabin was regarded as hers, and the small poultry and garden operations were usually her primary responsibility. She converted the yard goods into clothing for herself and her family and did the cooking. Even the children were acknowledged to be the mother's and were usually known by her name, as in the case of "Binah's Toby," or "Moll's Judy."[74] Unless he had a friendly alliance with some good-natured woman, the male slave did without many conveniences. Laura Towne commented drily that the liberated Negro men were better satisfied about being released from domestic tyranny than about any other aspect of their freedom. It is worth mentioning that the family picture under slavery was actually a reinforcement of the West African family pattern, arising, as it had there, from the polygynous household. The individual wives in the African community no doubt had to bow to the will of the husband; but within her own hut, and to her own children, the mother had been the omnipotent reality. Rivalry for preferences and honors to her children had provided the African woman with political outlets not unknown in the courts of Europe.[75]

Despite the legal and social obstacles, marriage had a reasonable chance of lasting if it was honored and respected by the owners of the principals. Thomas B. Chaplin complained of the "tomfoolery" of his wife, who took care to make a special occasion of

[74] Adams, *South-Side View*, p. 85; Elkins, *Slavery*, p. 130; Johnson, *Social History*, p. 137.
[75] Herskovits, *The Myth*, pp. 64–65.

the double wedding of her two maids, "Eliza" and "Nelly." The girls were married by "Robert," the spiritual leader of the plantation, and the party was provided with "a grand supper." "They had out," Chaplin complained, "my crockery—Tables, chairs, candle-sticks, and I suppose everything else they wanted." Then there was some of Chaplin's "good liquor made into a bowl of punch" for the guests. Twenty-seven years later, Chaplin penciled into the margin of his diary that the two girls were still alive, well, and still married to "the very same husbands." Many owners did not devote this interest to their slave marriages, but some element of formality was usually present.[76] Without legal protection, however, marriages suffered real stress under the conditions of slavery, which often promoted transient unions and easy partings. The religious leaders among the slaves complained often of unchastity and tried, sometimes without good effect, to bring moral suasion to the aid of family stability.[77] An understanding of this situation requires only the remembrance that the social and legal forces at work to bind together unhappy nineteenth-century white couples were largely inoperative with the slaves. One major problem for the evangels would clearly be to strengthen the Negro family, encouraging the fathers to assume hitherto unknown responsibilities.

So many of the faults of the slave had been perversions of laudable impulses, impulses of protest; those who learned them best frequently comprised the most spirited people on a plantation. Even Master Chaplin had a species of respect for his small slave who had thought of a smart way to steal watermelons. Grown slaves learned how to gain a little time for themselves by idling

[76] Chaplin MS diary, December 26, 1849. Chaplin's subsequent notation in pencil is dated "Christmas, 1876." This slave wedding no doubt formed a part of the holiday celebration on the Chaplin plantation; Olmsted, *Sea-Board Slave States*, p. 449.

[77] Adams, *South-Side View*, p. 88. See Kemble, *Journal*, p. 263, for indictment of complaisance of masters and overseers toward promiscuity among slaves.

or pretending illness, and as often as not the matter simply had to be faced with resignation. "Jim and Judge both lying up today," complained their master, "they will have their time out."[78]

When a man carried protest to the passionate length of running away, he had to be prepared for extreme punishment. Sweet must have been the knowledge to a "prime" runaway, even while reflecting on the bitter cost, that he was depriving his master of a week's hard work in the cotton field. Overt rebellion indeed existed, but it was for the few. Most slaves had learned to accept their condition, as one evangel said, just as "sand receives the cannon-ball, neither casting it off nor being shattered by it."[79] For the majority, the humdrum and safe satisfactions of a well-timed lie, petty theft, or feigned illness had seemed the appropriate defenses of reasonable beings. This mood permeates a folk story that was long told on St. Helena, of an old slave who had never worked in his life because his master was convinced he was a cripple. His master caught him one day, however, strumming his banjo to the words:

> *I was fooling my master seventy-two years,*
> *And I'm fooling him now.*

The enraged master prepared to whip the old man, but the timely magic of a "Negro doctor" intervened. "When his master started to whip him, none of the licks touch: And he had freedom."[80]

Frederika Bremer wrote after her visit to the Sea Islands just

[78] Chaplin MS diary, May 21, 1857; see also entries May 10 and July 9, 1850.

[79] [Gannett and Hale], "The Freedmen at Port Royal," *North American Review*, CI (July, 1865), 7. For runaways and their punishments, see Chaplin MS diary, November 27, 1853; David Gavin MS diary, July 4, 1857; Towne MS diary, June 13, 1845.

[80] Elsie Clews Parsons, *Folk-Lore of the Sea Islands, South Carolina* ("Memoirs of the American Folk-Lore Society," XVI [Cambridge, 1923], 62).

before the war that she had not found a single plantation where the master was able to advance the social well-being of the slaves. Even the efforts of progressive men who tried to institute some means of self-regulation among the slaves had merely achieved a superior form of discipline. She concluded somberly, "In the darkness of slavery I have sought for the moment of freedom with faith and hope in the genius of America. It is no fault of mine that I have found the darkness so great and the work of light as yet so feeble in the slave states."[81]

There was hardly a plantation that had not a harsh old tale of abuse, and on many the abject fear the slaves had of all white men said all that needed to be told. In the final analysis, however, it was the institution in all its aspects, knowing and foolish, kind and cruel, that had created the prevailing problems confronting Gideon's Band: an exaggerated attitude of dependency; a weak sense of family; an inevitable tendency toward the classic faults of the slave—lying, theft, and irresponsibility. As one Gideonite clearly saw, the barbarism of exceptional slave masters did not really signify much in the total picture. "The real wrong in slavery did not affect the body; but it was a curse to the soul and mind of the slave. The aim of the master was to keep down every principle of manhood and growth, and this held for good and bad planters alike, and was the natural growth of slavery itself."[82] And that was why, despite the moving and testimonial exceptions of strength and character found among the slaves, the larger number of the liberated Negroes of the islands constituted, according to Gannett, "a race of stunted, misshapen children, writhing from the grasp of that people, which, in so many respects, is foremost of the age."[83]

[81] Bremer, *Homes of the New World*, II, 492.

[82] Clipping from the Bristol [England] *Post*, October 23, 1865, in the Gannett MSS, Box XXVIII. The quotation is from a speech Gannett made in Bristol after the war.

[83] [Gannett and Hale], "The Freedmen at Port Royal," *North American Review*, CI (July, 1865), 1.

five ❧ *"A DEPARTMENT OF EXPERIMENTS"*

THE GIDEONITES WOULD BE A LONG TIME LEARNING ALL THEY HAD to know about slavery, and their progress in the first months at Port Royal was difficult to evaluate. The enterprise had, however, made one signal conversion. John Murray Forbes returned to Boston pronouncing the venture "a decided success." He had seen signs that were most hopeful to a liberal businessman: "All those engaged in the experiment will testify that the negro has the same selfish element in him which induces other men to labor, and that with a fair prospect of benefit . . . he will work like other human beings." That this discovery should have seemed marvelous will doubtless surprise the modern reader. Its emphasis must be regarded fully as much as a commentary upon contemporary Northern attitudes as upon Forbes's own racial notions. He cited the large amount of land the Negroes had planted privately for their own food supply and said he had heard of numerous cases in which especially industrious "contrabands" had asked to plant on their own, *"where their work would show."* Pierce had begun "one of the noblest experiments which modern civilization has undertaken, by inaugurating a system of free labor combined with instruction for the freed slaves upon *their native soil.*" Forbes's letter, designed to counter the slurs cast upon the enterprise by half-informed traducers, appeared in the Boston *Advertiser.*[1] Even Forbes knew, however, that enormous problems remained unsolved.

As the month of May brought the island spring to its most

[1] Forbes's letter was dated May 23, 1862. See the Boston *Advertiser,* June 10, 1862.

141

perfect beauty and the first "free labor" cotton pushed its way above ground, a number of developments in Washington and Hilton Head worked together in such a way as to rid the missionaries of the cotton agents, to place the experiment on a better official footing, and to deepen the impact of the Port Royal area on the vital question of the future of the Negro in the war effort.

The conflict between Gideon's Band and Reynolds' cotton agents grew worse before it was resolved. Secretary Chase, in response to the numerous complaints that had reached him through Pierce and others, ordered Colonel Reynolds to meet with Pierce and hear the charges made against his employees. "Should you find that, in any case, laborers have been paid in goods at extravagant prices, you will deduct any excess taken from them in that way by the Agents, from their compensation, and divide the excess among the laborers from whom it was taken, as nearly as practicable."[2] It was an infuriating rebuff. The particular complaints against Colonel William H. Nobles made that violent man so angry that he gave Pierce, in the words of Laura Towne, his "touch of martyrdom." On the seventh of May, as Pierce stepped off the dock at Hilton Head, Nobles assaulted him and beat him badly before the soldiers nearby could break up the fight. Nobles claimed that Pierce had wanted to "drive" him "like a dog from the islands."[3] Now the military authorities took charge of that themselves, by sending Nobles off "in disgrace" on the next northbound steamer. In an angry note of the following day, Pierce reproached Secretary Chase for not having removed Nobles much sooner. "Let me now say that had the Department sustained me in the appeal . . . which considering the circumstances of my coming here, I do not see how you could have denied, this assault could not have occurred."[4]

[2] Chase to Reynolds, April 30, 1862, item 21, Restricted Commercial Intercourse Records, Treasury Department Archives.

[3] Holland (ed.), *Towne*, p. 60; Nobles to Pierce, April 2, 1862, item 119, PRC.

[4] [?] Boynton to Edward Everett Hale, May 13, 1862, Atkinson MSS; Pierce to Chase, May 8, 1862, item 155, PRC.

Free schoolboys.

Laura Towne, with her students.

Ellen Murray, with her students.

Susannah, of The Oaks plantation.

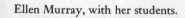

Hundreds of slave children, clad in rags and ignorance, were the human challenge of the Yankee schoolma'am.

Harriett Murray, with her students, Elsie on her left, and Puss on her right.

Chase had been waiting for an automatic clearing of conflicts that he thought would follow the completion of Reynolds' assignment. It was nearly finished. Bales and bales of rebel cotton, topped off by the elegant furniture of the fugitive owners, the books of the Beaufort Library, and all other "movables," had proceeded northward in overloaded steamers, gaining for the agents a fat 5 per cent commission on all property thus "saved" and at the same time opening a "cotton fund" that would provide a financial basis for carrying forward the plans of the supporters of the Port Royal experiment.[5] As their work was finished the agents departed, but Chase was to have no end of trouble with them. He ended by having to sanction payment of exorbitant and unreasonable fees to the agents, and there was more than a hint of outright fraud. Surprised by his sudden dismissal, Reynolds was caught short by 10 per cent in his accounts, and the circumstances were highly suspicious. The significant footnote to the affair was that Chase had gained no insight into the man who had so heartily recommended Reynolds for his job. For before many months were out, the Governor of Rhode Island—by now Chase's son-in-law—and Reynolds had joined several other disreputable partners and had used their connection with the naïve Secretary to promote an illegal private trade in guns and cotton with Confederate agents. It was treason, by almost any definition.[6]

[5] Hazard Stevens, *Life of Isaac Ingalls Stevens* (Boston, 1900), II, 367–369. A typical cargo was aboard the *Atlantic*, unloading at New York, March 16, 1862. "She brings as freight 95 bales ginned Sea-Island cotton, 28 bales Florida upland cotton, 1 mirror, 1 pianoforte, 21 hides, 30 cases of books, to Hiram Barney, Collector of the Port of New York." *New York Times*, March 20, 1862. See also Barney to Chase, August 22, 1862, item 85, and relevant items 76, 86, and 89, Letters from Collectors, H Series, Treasury Department Archives.

[6] Marva Robins Belden and Thomas Graham Belden, *So Fell the Angels* (Boston, 1956), p. 58 and note p. 362; see also Pierce to Chase, June 23, 1862, PRC. Chase did not grant the men permits to trade, but the well-known family connection between Chase and Sprague was of assistance to the plot, and Chase was slow to learn what was proceeding under his nose.

If Chase could have extracted a lesson about human nature from the cotton agents at Port Royal, and if the government could have thus early realized the problems inherent in placement of dual and conflicting authorities over the Negroes, much of the trouble that plagued all efforts in their behalf throughout the war and Reconstruction might have been averted. The government had set out upon a pragmatic course on these matters, a course that it would follow wherever it led, as long as the government felt obliged to have a course at all.

In the meantime, military affairs had assumed a new complexion. In mid-March of 1862 General T. W. Sherman was superseded in the command of the Department of the South by Major General David Hunter. Military gossip had it that this change resulted from abolitionist pressure on the War Department to bring to Port Royal a man whose views were more agreeable to their own.[7] Now that the change had been effected, the clear expectation of radicals was that Hunter would take some bold step in the direction in which John C. Frémont had abortively struck out, in Missouri, at the beginning of the war. In this Hunter's admirers got fully as much as they bargained for.

David Hunter was "very frank," Commodore Du Pont claimed, in his abolitionist convictions, "very independent in thought and action" and fearless in the face of responsibility. He was silent and rapid in effecting his plans.[8] On April 13, about two weeks after his arrival in the Department, Hunter clarified the standing of certain "contrabands" in the district he occupied by simply declaring them free men. This move drew little comment, for it was overshadowed by a more exciting development of the previous day—the successful assault on Fort Pulaski, the old Federal stronghold at the mouth of the Savannah River. Hunter's next

[7] Mrs. Samuel Francis Du Pont to Henry Winter Davis, May 16, 1862, Du Pont MSS.

[8] Same to same, May 21, 1862, quoting an earlier letter from Admiral Du Pont to Mrs. Du Pont, Du Pont MSS.

step was also relatively quiet. Interpreting his orders to organize Negroes within his command into "squads, companies, or otherwise," as actual authorization to raise Negro troops, he set about recruiting among the plantations. He inquired of the superintendents about the numbers of likely prospects and sent out James Cashman, probably the first Negro recruiter, to encourage enlistment.[9]

Lively rumors concerning Hunter's intention had been circulating for some time in the North. Edward Atkinson had heard of it from an officer of the Educational Commission who had just returned from Washington, and Charles Sumner wrote significantly to John Murray Forbes that 50,000 *"extra"* stands of arms were being sent to Port Royal, along with "50,000 red breeches." "This looks in the right direction," wrote Sumner. It is worth remembering that these steps could hardly have been taken without the knowledge and approval of Edwin Stanton, Secretary of War.[10] They were based, however, on ambitious expectations that little took into account the feelings of the late slave population of the islands. Susan Walker reported that she had "tried in vain to inspire a desire to fight but none [of the Negroes] wish to volunteer. This is a sad truth and full of deep meaning." Although the colored people had often demonstrated incredible feats of bravery in escaping their masters, they did not want to fight them. Miss Walker thought the Negroes might "be forced to fight, but none will volunteer to leave their homes." And there was another point. Laura Towne said the Negroes at her place would not volunteer to go to Hilton Head "as they think it is a

[9] *OR*, I, xiv, 333. This first order applied specifically to the Negroes within Fort Pulaski and on Cockspur Island; *OR*, III, ii, 29–30; Sherwood (ed.), "Walker Journal," pp. 36–37.

[10] Atkinson to Philbrick, April 23, 1862, Atkinson MSS; Charles Sumner to John Murray Forbes, April 28, 1862, Forbes MSS. The same news reached Admiral Du Pont. See Mrs. S. F. Du Pont to Henry Winter Davis, May 16, 1862, Du Pont MSS.

trap to get the able-bodied and send them to Cuba to sell."[11] Whatever the cause, the response was not heartening, and Hunter became impatient.

Abruptly, on May 9, he issued a short proclamation declaring *all* the slaves of South Carolina, Georgia, and Florida free men, on the grounds that these states were under martial law and that "slavery and martial law in a free country are altogether incompatible." The jubilation among the missionaries was boundless. It had not subsided before Hunter issued another short order. All able-bodied male Negroes between the ages of eighteen and forty-five who were capable of bearing arms were to be sent to Hilton Head at once.[12]

Hunter's orders left no room for discretion on the part of superintendents and no time for preparing the Negroes for the "draft." In fact, the general enjoined strictest secrecy until the morning of May 12, so that the Negroes could not take warning and run away. Early in the morning of that day several companies of soldiers moved rapidly over the islands, bringing consternation and fear to all plantations and outright panic to most. Harriet Ware reported that the soldiers at their plantation had "behaved admirably" and, "cheering the Negroes with tales of money and clothes, treated them most kindly."[13] There matters went off more smoothly than might have been expected. But on many plantations the Negroes became hysterical. Superintendent Samuel Phillips reported that the women broke "into the loudest lamentations" and clung to their departing husbands and sons "with the

---

[11] Sherwood (ed.), "Walker Journal," p. 37; Holland (ed.), *Towne*, p. 37. Despite the reluctance of the suspicious "contrabands," Hunter did obtain about 150 volunteers on Hilton Head Island through the cooperation of an influential colored minister, Abram Murchison. See Benjamin Quarles, *The Negro in the Civil War* (Boston, 1953), pp. 109–110.

[12] *OR*, I, xiv, 341, and III, ii, 52–53; French, *Slavery in South Carolina*, pp. 304–305.

[13] Pearson (ed.), *Letters*, p. 40.

agony of separation." They would hear no explanations but could only remember what their masters had told them about Cuba. At The Oaks, Laura Towne noticed that after the plantation people were brought together the soldiers "noisily" loaded their guns just at the point when the captain told them they must go to Hilton Head. It made her "blood boil" to witness "such arbitrary proceedings." She assured the people that Hunter was actually their friend, whether he appeared to be or not, and said she hoped that this meant they would soon return with their "free papers." If they were needed, however, she hoped they would "stay and help keep off the rebels." Each man's spirits were fortified with a half-dollar and a plug of tobacco, and the Negroes were hustled off to the new role designed for them by the white men whose ways were so incomprehensible.[14]

During the course of the day, five hundred men were taken to Hilton Head, where, according to Hunter's plan, they were to be held for a few weeks, instructed in army life and drill, and assured that they would afterward be free to go home if they still wished to do so.[15]

Pierce hotly protested the summary action, directly to Hunter and by letter to Chase. He pointed out what the reduction in manpower in the fields would do to the crops, described the misery that the action had caused, and voiced his fear that the damaged confidence of the Negroes in the good intentions of the Northerners might never be repaired. The only concession Hunter would make, however, was to return the plowmen and foremen; the government did not intervene to disband the unit. Neither did it acknowledge this first nucleus of a black regiment. In the government view, the organization simply did not exist.[16]

[14] Samuel Phillips' account is in *OR*, III, ii, 59–60; Holland (ed.), *Towne*, pp. 52–53; Sherwood (ed.), "Walker Journal," p. 39.
[15] *OR*, III, ii, 52–53.
[16] *Ibid.*; Holland (ed.), *Towne*, p. 83; Boston *Commonwealth*, October 4, 1862.

The missionaries resented Hunter's draft both because of the way it was managed and because they had planned other ways for the Negroes to demonstrate their capacity for freedom. But the obvious intention of the abolitionist general stilled the objections of many. Laura Towne, for one, angry as she was over Hunter's "headlong" order, refused to protest to Secretary Chase unless she was convinced Hunter was not "trying for freedom." John Murray Forbes, not directly involved, could see only the benefits. He wrote to Charles Sumner to induce the Senator to talk with Chase and modify the totally dark impression the latter was sure to receive from Pierce. He thought all would work out well. He had visited "the Black Cohort," had discovered that all the Negroes who "*were fit to serve*" had remained with the regiment and seemed happy in the military life. Their officers were optimistic, and Hunter was "hopeful" and "fully engaged" working for the success of the experiment.[17] For a man who regarded himself as a moderate conservative, Forbes was beginning to sound very like a radical abolitionist.

Abolitionists everywhere hailed Hunter's actions as of the greatest significance to the war effort. Edward Atkinson no doubt expressed the feeling of many New England supporters of the Port Royal movement when he comforted Philbrick for the loss of the field hands caught in Hunter's draft. "I hope you may get back enough to save your crop, but we feel here, that [that] is of little consequence now, as compared with the main question." Atkinson admitted that a "few remaining old hunkers" were displeased with Hunter's action, but he thought Philbrick would be surprised to see "the general approval" of the order.[18]

The larger issue was of course Hunter's emancipation proclama-

[17] Holland (ed.), *Towne*, p. 45; Towne MS diary, May 12, 1862; Forbes to Charles Sumner, May 16, 1862, Sumner MSS.

[18] Atkinson to Philbrick, May 19, 1862, Atkinson MSS. The word "hunker" was first applied to the members of the Democratic Party who fought the radical and reforming "Barnburner" faction. By the 1850's it was applied primarily to those who were soft on the slavery question.

tion. It was easy to ridicule the general's reasoning that martial law and slavery could not coexist. The *New York Times* pointed out that they were actually entirely compatible institutions, since both were based on force, and charged Hunter with having "largely transcended the sphere of his duty." An astonished Commodore Du Pont said that his first impulse had been to laugh, but that he could but wonder if Hunter would "take so much upon himself" if not authorized to do so.[19]

Governor Andrew of Massachusetts hoped that President Lincoln would sustain Hunter and "recognize *all* men, even black men, as legally capable of loyalty." People in the North would feel that the military draft was "heavy on their patriotism" as long as they saw Confederates using their slaves to advance the rebellion, while they could not themselves *"fire at the enemy's magazine...."*[20]

For men of Andrew's conviction, the time was not far distant when they would envision a vast throng of slaves passing through the lines to freedom to form a Negro army fighting for the Union. The South, largely depleted of its labor force, would then be torn also by the internal fear of servile insurrection.

Hunter's supporters on the islands could point to a dramatic illustration of what Andrew meant. The news of the military emancipation proclamation traveled swiftly through the Union lines and struck iron resolve into the soul of a young mulatto slave named Robert Smalls, a native of Beaufort and the islands, the pilot of a steamship called the *Planter*. Smalls quietly secreted his family and a few chosen associates aboard his master's vessel and in the faint dawn of Tuesday morning, the thirteenth of May, stole out of Charleston harbor, bound for Port Royal. Carefully giving the appropriate signal at Fort Sumter, two long whistles

[19] *New York Times*, May 16, 1862; Mrs. S. F. Du Pont to Henry Winter Davis, May 21, 1862, quoting an earlier letter from Commodore Du Pont, Du Pont MSS.

[20] Andrew to Stanton, May 19, 1862, in John Greenleaf Pearson, *The Life of John A. Andrew* (Boston, 1904), II, 11–12.

and a short, Smalls cut through the inland waterway until he encountered a blockade ship off Otter Island. The crew ran up a bedsheet and the Federal flag, and gave three cheers for the Union. In the evening of the same day Smalls reached Hilton Head, delivering his vessel and its expensive cargo of Confederate artillery to the authorities. He found himself a hero within the hour, and his story circulated widely through the newspapers.[21] This "slight and wide-awake" man with so much daring would surely be heard from again. John Murray Forbes wrote Charles Sumner, "I hope you legislators will see to it that he and his crew get full salvage irrespective of the Navys [sic] claim to prize money!" Such reactions to Hunter's proclamation should be encouraged, thought Forbes, for "the moral effect of such practical emancipation is worth much more than money!"[22] All would now depend upon executive support.

The Cabinet radicals, Chase and Stanton, also hoped that the President would support Hunter, but Lincoln was not ready. In a Cabinet meeting of May 17, they subordinated their judgment to that of the Chief Executive, and three days later Lincoln revoked Hunter's order. In an eloquent message, Lincoln made use of all the gentle arts of persuasion he knew so well. Showing no anger with Hunter but maintaining for himself the full authority to act in the sensitive matter of slavery, he also called upon the Border States, pleading that they take advantage of the joint Congressional resolution of March 6, which had proffered assistance to states undertaking voluntary emancipation. "I do not argue; I

21 There are numerous accounts of Robert Smalls's escape from Charleston. See excerpts from his log in the Boston *Advertiser*, June 18, 1862; Pearson, *Letters*, p. 47; [Justus Clement French], *The Trip of the Steamer Oceanus to Fort Sumter and Charleston, S. C., Comprising the Incidents of the Excursion, the Appearance, at That Time of the City, and the Entire Programme of the Exercises of Re-raising the Flag over the Ruins of Fort Sumter, April 14, 1865* (Brooklyn, 1865), pp. 85–87. A recent biography of Smalls written for young readers is Dorothy Sterling's *Captain of the Planter* (New York, 1958).

22 Forbes to Sumner, May 16, 1862, Sumner MSS.

beseech you to make the arguments yourselves. You cannot, if you would, be blind to the signs of the times. I beg of you to make a calm and enlarged consideration of them, ranging, if it may be, far above personal and partisan politics." Gradual emancipation in the Border States would "come gently as the dews of heaven, not rending or wrecking anything. Will you not embrace it?" But the appeal fell upon deaf ears, the sweetly disguised threat was ignored, and the "signs of the times" would have to work themselves out in their own way. The Borderland could not be persuaded to seize the "high privilege" to which the President beckoned it.[23]

The language of the revocation took much of the sting out of the message. Edward Atkinson was "sadly disappointed," even baffled, that the government had sent Hunter in the first place without the intention to support his "well-known views," but even he was confident that "the President's proclamation promises everything for the future." He believed that Lincoln meant "to make this a free country."[24]

The revocation of Hunter's order was the more surprising to the missionary-abolitionists because of the support and encouragement the philanthropic efforts at Port Royal were just then receiving from Secretaries Stanton and Chase. In order to close the

[23] *OR*, III, ii, 42–43. For opinions of Chase and Stanton, see Albert Bushnell Hart, *Salmon P. Chase* (Boston, 1899), pp. 262–263, and T. Harry Williams, *Lincoln and the Radicals* (Madison, Wisconsin, 1941), p. 137. Dr. LeBaron Russell, who was in Washington on the business of the Educational Commission at this time, returned to Boston with a story that may have been Capitol gossip but has an authentic ring. "Dr. Russell says," wrote Edward Atkinson, "that the President told Hunter to draw up his own instructions, [but] when he presented them, Abe struck out the proposed proclamation and told him it was not yet time for that. Stanton's comment on Hunter's proclamation was 'Damn him, why didn't he do it and say nothing about it!'" Atkinson to Philbrick, June 10, 1862, Atkinson MSS.

[24] Atkinson to Philbrick, a May 20 postscript to a letter dated May 19, 1862, Atkinson MSS.

breach between the Treasury agents and the military authorities, Chase delivered the control of Negro affairs to the War Department and cooperated closely with Secretary Stanton to effect a suitable arrangement. As early as April, a committee from the three freedmen's aid societies had come to Washington to get Chase to place Pierce in full charge of the Port Royal enterprise and give the missionary effort a better official footing. The committee had at the time received "assurances" that Pierce would be appointed military governor of the contrabands but had been told that the details had not been worked out.[25]

It became clearer later on, however, that the appointment should properly go to an army officer, who would have sufficient rank to protect him in his responsibilities. Pierce, Chase hoped, would take a position on the staff to assist the military governor. The Secretary assured C. C. Leigh, an officer of the New York freedmen's society, that "officers will be selected for the charge of the work . . . animated by the same spirit which had guided the action of Mr. Pierce." The man Chase recommended to Stanton was a career army officer who was elevated to the rank of brigadier general for the purpose of taking over the new command.[26]

On April 29, 1862, Rufus Saxton received instructions from Secretary Stanton to go to Port Royal and "take possession of all the plantations heretofore occupied by rebels, and take charge of the inhabitants remaining thereon within the department, or which the fortunes of war may hereafter bring into it," with full authority to make "such rules and regulations for the cultivation of the land, and for the protection, employment and government of the inhabitants as circumstances seem to require." Saxton was

[25] Atkinson to Philbrick, April 20, 1862, Atkinson MSS. See also Robert Bruce Warden, *An Account of the Private Life and Public Services of Salmon Portland Chase* (Cincinnati, 1874), pp. 424–425.

[26] Chase to Leigh, April 23, 1862, quoted in Warden, *Chase*, pp. 424–425; Chase to Pierce, April 23, 1862, item 2, p. 130, Restricted Commercial Intercourse, Treasury Department Archives. Hart, *Chase*, p. 260, gives Chase credit for recommending Saxton to Stanton.

responsible only to the War Department and to General Hunter himself, from whom he was to expect assistance and support. Saxton's appointment was a relief and a satisfaction to the missionaries, for he was known as a "thoroughgoing Abolitionist, of the radical sort," a rare military man who expressed, as Arthur Sumner put it, "a confidence in Absolute Truth, and let the consequences take care of themselves."[27]

Rufus Saxton was a native of Greenfield, Massachusetts, and had grown up in "the free air of the valley of the Connecticut." He was proud to have been a child of abolitionist parents, who had reared him in "an atmosphere of 'high thinking.' " Saxton had led an unusual career for a man of his antecedents.[28] He had been Chief Quartermaster for the Northern Pacific exploration, had served for a time as assistant instructor in military tactics at West Point, and had at the outbreak of the war volunteered for service in Missouri. The War Department had balked several opportunities for his advancement in rank through the volunteer service. Saxton first came to Port Royal in November of 1861, as Chief Quartermaster to General T. W. Sherman's forces. Small of stature, with luxuriant black hair and handsome side-whiskers, he was a man very accurately described as "narrow, but intense, not very profound in seeing the right, but energetic in doing it when seen. . . ."[29] His serious classical features and deep-set eyes were, to his generation, clear signs of straightforward character. Saxton was a man of few words; but kindliness and patience would be real assets in his new appointment, and of these he had a reasonable supply. Upon his slight shoulders would fall the total

[27] *OR*, III, ii, 27–28; Arthur Sumner to Joseph Clark, January 23, 1863, Arthur Sumner MSS.

[28] E. L. Pierce, "The Freedmen at Port Royal," *Atlantic Monthly*, XII (September, 1863), 300; Saxton to Thomas Wentworth Higginson, December 13, 1905, Higginson MSS, Houghton Library.

[29] Whitelaw Reid, *After the War: A Southern Tour, May 1, 1865 to May 1, 1866* (New York, 1866), p. 80; James L. Bowen, *Massachusetts in the War, 1861–1865* (Springfield, 1889), p. 978.

responsibility for the agglomeration of people, ideas, and conflicting interests at Port Royal.

The aid societies had further signs of government interest and support. There was a freer attitude toward supplying money for plantation equipment, clothing, and food, including salt, bacon, and other necessaries for the Negroes. The societies received reimbursements for their own previous expenditures of this kind, and future requisitions were now to be honored from the funds from sale of cotton. The cotton fund would also now provide money for salaries to the superintendents, releasing more of the private funds for the employment of teachers.[30] Under the new plan the plantations were grouped into districts, and over each island or group of islands comprising a district was placed a General Superintendent, whose job it was to report to Saxton and his staff. Edward Hooper, formerly Pierce's secretary, now became a captain on this staff and the officer most fully informed on the details of the Port Royal Experiment.[31] With only one serious modification, occasioned by the partial transfer of the lands to private ownership, this administrative system remained in effect until the end of the war and the establishment of the Freedmen's Bureau.

Despite the request of Saxton, the earnest persuasions of Secretary Chase, and the surprise of his friends, Pierce declined appointment on Saxton's staff. The Secretary had promised him every support and had said that, with Saxton at his side, Pierce could carry out his plans "with entire success, and great credit. It may be the germ," wrote Chase, "or at least the example of movements greater than we now dream of."[32] The Secretary was

[30] Pierce to Atkinson, May 10, 1862, Atkinson to Philbrick, April 24, 1862, Atkinson MSS; *Annual Report of the New York National Freedmen's Aid Society of New York, with a Sketch of Its Early History* (New York, 1866), p. 10.

[31] Holland (ed.), *Towne*, p. 76; Boston *Commonwealth*, January 22, 1864.

[32] Chase to Pierce, April 23, 1862, Restricted Commercial Intercourse Records, item 2, p. 130, National Archives.

hoping that Port Royal would become a proving ground for the reconstruction of the South.

But Pierce could not be moved. Laura Towne said she tried to persuade him that "his best interest consisted in identifying himself with this work, which he had begun so ably," and that Pierce had replied that he could not afford "to do work which did not and never could pay—that he was a poor man and needed money above all things." Pierce planned to return to his law practice in Boston, which had already been damaged by his long neglect.[33]

Miss Towne reported the scene at the Brick Church the Sunday in June when Pierce told the people of the new plan and of his own intention to leave. Nothing reveals more clearly the benevolent paternalism of the first phase of the Port Royal mission than his words. They also reveal how convenient it was for the missionaries, in simplifying explanations to the Negroes, to extol President Lincoln, whom they criticized among themselves as a foot-dragger on emancipation. The President's availability for the role of father and protector in this stage of semi-emancipation probably goes as far to explain his canonization after the war as the Emancipation Proclamation itself. The scene might have been a cherished page from the ante-bellum legend. Pierce explained kindly to the Negroes that President Lincoln was going "to send a much more powerful man than I am, a big general, to care for you—a man who has always been your friend. You must love him and obey him." When Pierce sat down the people began "to bless and pray for him aloud, to say they 'thanked massa for his goodness to we'"; and they pressed around to shake his hand. Pierce was moved to tears by the demonstration and may have, in that moment, regretted his decision.[34]

The initial phase of the social experiment was closing. A New England supporter who regretted Pierce's departure thought he was nevertheless deserving of the highest praise, for he had already

[33] Towne MS diary, July 2, 1862.
[34] Holland (ed.), *Towne*, pp. 61–62.

done "nearly the most important work of the war."[35] Unsettled and shapeless as the enterprise was in June of 1862, the worst conditions of poverty and neglect had been alleviated. Furthermore, the attention of the nation had been caught by what was going on. The third issue of the budding and ambitious Beaufort *Free South* praised the developments in the "Department of Experiments," boasting that the Department of the South was "second to none for the influence it has had upon the public mind and upon the general conduct of the war. Eminently, it has been the great experimental department of the country, and upon its stage have been advanced ideas which, more than any others have contributed to our national struggle." While no dramatic military developments had succeeded to the capture of the territory, Hunter's proclamation and the Negro recruitment had "done more (whether for good or evil) to set the mind of the country at work, considering the true issues of the war, than all the agencies of journalism, both houses of Congress, and all the executive branches of our country combined."[36]

On the national level, notice of the "experiment" was favorable or caustic depending upon the political complexion of the newspaper. The correspondent of the *New York Times* seriously questioned the advisability of granting Pierce and his missionaries so much authority when they knew so little of cotton planting. He poked fun at the missionaries who were naïve enough to arrive at a plantation, promptly ask the Negroes, "Do you want anything?" and make note of every request, great or small. The wagons would then roll in, said the reporter, loaded down with all sorts of provisions. "This is an expensive liberality and is no real kindness to the Negro." The New York *Herald* was heavier in its sarcasm, reporting on "The Abolitionists Among Their Colored Brethren," whose work was fraught with the "jealousies, reproaches and recriminations, which are the bane of all mis-

[35] Sarah Clarke to Laura Towne, June 19, 1862, Towne MSS.
[36] Beaufort *Free South*, August 23, 1862.

sionary societies, and which make the lives of Chadbands, Stigginses, Mrs. Jellybys and Mrs. Pardiggles a burthen to them." The *New York Times*, fairly enough, gave J. W. Edmonds, the President of the New York National Freedmen's Relief Association, an opportunity to refute some of the wildest charges made against the enterprise in the *Times*, the *Herald*, and the *Express*, but this did not stop the attempts of these papers to portray the missionaries as ridiculous visionaries who had come South with no more practical purpose than to brother and sister the former slaves.[37]

The criticism of much of the democratic press was bitter and contemptuous. William Channing Gannett's father wrote his son that the "representations" of hostile groups in the North were "atrocious. Some of the New York journals represent the whole work as a failure. . . ." The teachers had to stomach the fact that many Northerners would believe that they were selling goods to the Negroes for personal profit and that the Negroes were being cheated and abused. The very fury of the onslaught made Edward Atkinson take comfort in the notion that the "Satanic press" was doing "more good than harm."[38]

Harder by far to accept was criticism that came from a surprising source. Nothing reveals more clearly the continuation through the war of the old internal conflicts among abolitionists than their diverse attitudes toward the Port Royal work. One unnamed "tried and trusty" friend of the Negro cause wrote to the New York society that it was his "earnest conviction" that the missionaries' work would damage the cause of ultimate freedom. "I feel sure," he wrote, "that, while you will benefit individuals, you will, in the broad careless views which the world will take, exhibit a disastrous failure, and furnish a very strong argument

[37] *New York Times*, March 20 and 24, 1862; New York *Herald*, March 22, 1862.

[38] Ezra Stiles Gannett to William Channing Gannett, June 5, 1862, Gannett MSS; Holland (ed.), *Towne*, pp. 25–26; Towne to McKim, August 2, 1862, McKim MSS; Atkinson to Philbrick, April 30, 1862, Atkinson MSS.

against any method of emancipation."[39] The work of education and uplift stirred no enthusiasm in the bosom of Wendell Phillips, devoted as he was to the cause of freedom and despite the fact that he had been among the first to draw attention to the plight of the Port Royal Negroes. In May of 1862, at the annual meeting of the American Anti-Slavery Society, he declared the Port Royal work unimportant. "I ask nothing more for the negro than I ask for the Irishman or German who comes to our shores," he said. "I thank the benevolent men who are laboring at Port Royal—all right!—but the blacks of the South do not need them. They are not objects of charity. They only ask this nation—'Take your yoke off our necks;' . . . they ask their hands—nothing more; they will accomplish books, and education, and work. They have done so in the West Indies."[40]

Such men feared, of course, two things: the divisive effects on the antislavery movement of the work for the freedmen; and the repercussions that might arise from large-scale benevolence to the Negro. It was not the effect of charity upon the character of the newly released bondsmen that they dreaded, but its impact on the public opinion of the North. They could plainly see that the most characteristic feature of the initial phase of the Port Royal work was gift-giving. Charity was not a popular word with abolitionists, or with many other people for that matter, for the implications of paternalism and condescending benevolence it conveyed were antithetical to that equality of man upon which their ultimate arguments were laid. The abolitionists at Port Royal liked charity no better, for the most part, than did Wendell Phillips; but the practical aspects of their situation made a call upon the charitable instincts of the nation unavoidable. Those holding aloof from the enterprise could afford to claim that no help was necessary; those in the field could not, at least not at first. For the latter the claims

---

[39] An unidentified abolitionist quoted in the *Annual Report of the New York National Freedmen's Aid Society* (New York, 1866), p. 10.
[40] *The Liberator*, May 16, 1862.

of the newly released victims of slavery on the nation that had condoned their servitude for so long was clear. Later, as we shall see, the sterner evangels and those most dedicated to the principles of economic liberalism began to decry continued assistance except in the field of education. But for the time, the desperate immediate wants, the physical, emotional, and educational needs of the people, had to be met.

The implied criticisms that the work at Port Royal was heavily colored with benevolent condescension were well-founded but far easier to note than to correct. How easy it was, for instance, to slip into the habit of referring to the plantation people by the possessive pronoun.[41] The missionaries found themselves, almost in spite of themselves, in the same *social* relation to the Negroes that the late masters had occupied. While the missionaries perhaps did not protest this seductive arrangement as vigorously as modern democrats might have done, it is well, in all fairness, to examine

---

[41] "We have got to calling them *our* people and loving them really—not so much individually as the collective whole. . . ." Holland (ed.), *Towne*, p. 47. The occasional references to "niggers" strike the reader as an especially harsh manifestation of pride and superiority. The word was never used by the evangels in published accounts but makes an occasional appearance in private letters and diaries. A teacher sent to Beaufort by the AMA was subsequently fired on the ground that she frequently used this word, among other charges. [See a letter from Carrie A. Hamblin to Mrs. E. A. Lane, April 29, 1865, in the American Missionary Association MSS at Fisk University.] The letters of Arthur Sumner are marred by such references, frequently in an attempt at humor; but it is only fair to add that in his happy personal relations with Negroes, especially the school-children, there was no flinching whatever on grounds of skin color. His fondness and appreciation of his students is clearly genuine and apparently exceeds that of other teachers who were impeccable in their exterior forms. As is ever the case, the total attitude of an individual must be weighed, and individual slips must not be extracted and offered as *prima facie* evidence of bias. Nearly all the teachers referred to the cluster of cabins where the Negroes lived on the plantation as the "nigger-house," probably because the colored people themselves always used the phrase. See Pearson (ed.), *Letters*, pp. 18, 77.

some of the hurdles they encountered on the road toward the brotherhood of man. The Negroes had long dwelt in a strict hierarchy in which the ideal white man not only lived upon the labor of his slave but also accorded him a kindly protection and sometimes a vicarious experience in pride. The ingratiating dependence of "Sambo" had been a superb defense for the helpless slave, for it had both inculcated and rewarded a comfortable paternalism on the part of the master. As we have seen, there was an appreciable element of individualism on the plantation, and from the beginning many Negroes abjured this characteristic of dependence; but for large numbers of people the habit was strong and would not be cast away overnight. Failure of certain Gideonites to recognize this subservient role as being, in many cases, one of conscious play-acting accounts in part for their subsequent surprised resentment when the colored population began to show vigorous signs of independent thought.

For the time being, however, the introduction of democratic manners presented problems. There was the practical matter of stopping the Negroes from referring to the missionaries as "massas and missuses." What fortitude would have been required of Laura Towne to squelch a half-dozen delightful youngsters who clung to her skirts, quarreling amiably for the exclusive privilege of calling her "*my* missus?" Seemingly the possessive pronoun worked both ways. Or how withhold the titles of "Uncle" and "Aunt" from the venerable aged people who were universally so addressed? An incident serves to illustrate how difficult it was to inaugurate a widespread use of the proper form of English address among equals. "Joe doubled up and went off into convulsions when C[harles P. Ware] mentioned to me at table that he had been to call on Mrs. Jenkins (Wil'by) and did not find her at home." "Wil'by" Jenkins was Joe's wife.[42]

These battles were the harder to fight because of the Negroes' narrow exposure to the particular type of gentility they had

[42] Laura Towne to "T., R., and K.," August 26, 1862, Towne MSS; Pearson (ed.), *Letters*, pp. 122–123.

known in their masters. It was a formal and rigid pattern, and the Negroes understood its requirements very well. The way the white people lived reflected in a curious and inverted way upon the social standing of the whole plantation. "Rina," Laura Towne's cook, felt that "for the credit of the house" and "the honor of the establishment" gifts of food had to be dispatched occasionally to the neighbors, even when she was herself the unknown donor, and not Miss Towne. When Captain Hooper gave his comfortable seat in the carriage to old "Aunt Phyllis" for a Sunday trip to church and proposed to ride in the back, the dignity of "Harry," the coachman, was so confounded that he volubly protested what he supposed to be so inappropriate a seating arrangement.[43]

Harriet Ware wrote, "I daresay they think we are all 'poor white.' Mary . . . told Mr. G[annett] his clothes would be fifty cents per dozen for washing; that she used to have seventy-five in Charleston, 'for real gentle folks!' " Too rapid a rush toward democratic manners would obviously cost the missionaries a little in esteem.[44]

This snobbery of the plantation people was nowhere better demonstrated than at The Oaks when Charlotte Forten arrived to teach. Even Wendell Phillips could have been no more fiercely dedicated to the equality of man than was Laura Towne, who describes her difficulty in introducing the beautiful and delicate mulatto teacher into her household. "The people on our place are inclined to question a good deal about 'dat brown gal,' as they call Miss Forten. Aunt Becky required some coaxing to wait upon her and do her room. Aunt Phyllis is especially severe in the tone of her questions. I hope they will respect her. They put on this tone as a kind of reproach to us, I think."[45]

It is gratifying to note that the people at The Oaks promptly dropped their prejudice against Miss Forten's color when they discovered her talents. "When they heard her *play on the piano,*"

[43] Towne MS diary, February 10, 1864, and August 31, 1862.
[44] Pearson (ed.), *Letters*, p. 61.
[45] Towne MS diary, October 29, 1862.

reported Thomas Wentworth Higginson a year later, "it quite put them down, and soon all grew fond of her. Miss Towne says 'she is *the* pet and belle of the island.' "[46] A visiting Northern Negro who dined with the Wares at Coffin Point so threw off the calculations of an elderly colored woman named Grace that she almost addressed him as "Massa" but quickly retrieved the slip, substituting, "my dear." Another named Amaritta asked the visitor if he was a *free* man, saying, "I t'o't so, when I see you talk wi' buckra. . . ." The easy acceptance of this educated black man by the superintendent and his sister had given Amaritta something to think about.[47] It is only through the entry of such small vignettes in the diaries of the Northern teachers that we catch a glimpse of the severe reorganization of thought going on in the minds of these former slaves, who were at last seeing something new under the sun. Education was the answer, and not all of it would have to do with schoolbooks. Mary Ames writes tenderly of a sensitive little boy who slept, by conventional ante-bellum practice, at the foot of her bed. "One night, as he hung over my chair, he was uneasy, and I asked what troubled him. He whispered, 'Is the reason you don't kiss me 'cause I'm black?' I took him into my lap and held him till he slept."[48] Long would the hegemony of color warp the minds of black men and white alike, and only thousands of brotherly contacts would break its dominion. Slavery is indeed a matter of the mind as well as of the law.

For the time, however, it was naïve for theory-bound abolitionists like Wendell Phillips to claim that the Negroes needed no help, or "mercy," or even equal "justice." They needed, of course, all those things. Nonetheless, this question of the freedmen's aid societies showed a surprising indication of creating a division in the ranks of abolitionists. Whether the American Anti-

[46] Thomas Wentworth Higginson to Mrs. Higginson, October 25, 1863, Higginson MSS.

[47] Pearson (ed.), *Letters*, p. 225.

[48] Mary Ames, *A New England Woman's Diary in Dixie* (Springfield, 1906), p. 89.

Slavery Society should continue its frontal assault through the time-honored means of lectures and subscriptions or should shift to the newer work, on the assumption that the war itself was making an end of slavery, was serious indeed. J. Miller McKim, in stating his purpose to resign from the Pennsylvania Anti-Slavery Society, gave as his reason that "we have passed through the *pulling down* stage of our movement; the *building-up*—the constructive part remains to be accomplished."[49] McKim was no less an abolitionist for having taken the new direction. Before long, people who thought as he did began to show how the new social experiment could be put to service in the old cause. For one thing, publicity counted. At Port Royal the wicked dungeons of slavery on the remote plantations of cruel men were sprung to the stringent sunlight of abolitionist curiosity. Austa French saw all there was to see and set it forth in minute detail in her book *Slavery in South Carolina*, a volume in the straight tradition of the sensational literature of abolitionism.[50] J. Miller McKim also inquired

[49] McKim to Oliver Johnson, January 22, 1862, in *Anti-Slavery Standard*, May 3, 1862.

[50] Mrs. French's book presents problems. Her charges of barbarities perpetrated upon Sea Island slaves are so extravagant that only the most restrained style and irrefragable evidence would persuade belief. The preponderance of sexual atrocities and abuses of children, with the lurid and extravagant presentation, are both repelling and fascinating. But it by no means follows that Mrs. French should be given the lie direct. Sometimes the true circumstances were as lurid as a writer of cheap fiction could conceive. Thomas B. Chaplin, not squeamish himself about using the whip, records a case that made his heart grow cold. A "most *blood* thirsty tyrant," who had killed a slave for a trivial offense, was let off easily by the local jury of inquest. The reports of missionaries far more temperate than Mrs. French also corroborate much of her material. It would seem that the book is therefore more a product of the author's industry in ferreting out these stories than a triumph of pure invention. See also the Chaplin MS diary, February 19, 1849, and July 4, 1854. William F. Allen describes in his manuscript diary, January 11, 1864, the discovery of some correspondence of 1860 in one of the plantation houses, describing an atrocious slave murder and the deep shock felt by the author, an antebellum slaveowner.

into the treatment of slaves by their former masters when he visited the islands, inquiring particularly into the treatment of slaves by their whilom masters. "Such dreadful stories as they [the Negroes] told!" exclaimed Laura Towne, who accompanied him. McKim later expressed regret that he had not had the assistance of a photographer to record for the incredulous.[51]

Certainly, if the missionaries could demonstrate their thesis that free labor could grow more cotton more cheaply than slave labor, they would be giving the abolition cause a potent argument. But that would require time. Another economic argument was immediately available. Once the Negroes began to feel the comfortable clink of cash in their pockets, they began to want and to buy the things that make life more satisfying. McKim outlined this clearly in a public meeting in Philadelphia soon after his return from Port Royal. Citing Philbrick's sales at Coffin Point of $800 worth of goods, and the prompt disposal of $300 worth of clothing from Philadelphia, McKim asked his audience to reflect upon *"the enlarged market for Northern manufactures that will be created by an enlarged area of freedom."* Under the new order the Negroes did not live by bread alone, or by hominy and osnaberg clothes. "They begin to demand articles of household use also, such as pots, kettles, pans, brushes, brooms, knives, forks, spoons, soap, candles, combs, Yankee clocks, etc. etc." When the "ten thousand new customers" at Port Royal were multiplied by four hundred and the figure of the slave population of the South was considered, the future new market offered "an overwhelming economical argument" for pushing this Port Royal experiment to its logical conclusion.[52]

Austa French reminded her readers that in freedom the Negroes would not hoard money but spend it. "They will dress, and ride, in good style. The table and house, will be secondary, usually.

[51] Towne MS diary, June 16, 1862; McKim to Charles Sumner, January 20, 1863, Sumner MSS.
[52] *An Address Delivered by James Miller McKim at Sansom Hall, July 9th, 1862* (Philadelphia, 1862), pp. 21–22.

Imagine the trade set in motion the moment they get wages. What a brisk market for everything conceivable."[53] Mrs. French had made an inadvertent slip that neatly illustrates the pitfalls confronting the Port Royalists who were social reorganizers and abolitionists at the same time. It is doubtful that she intended to represent the released slaves as squanderers who cared more for clothes and carriages than for the more abiding comforts of home; she had simply permitted herself to be carried away by an economic argument for emancipation.

As long as abolitionists were not in direct contact with the victims of slavery, it had been easy to emphasize the destructive aspects of the institution. Now it was tempting to cite cases and offer proofs of their thesis. For every case of damaged character they offered, however, they gave aid and comfort to those who maintained that the slave was incapable of assuming immediately and successfully the responsibilities of freedom. Certain evangels introduced more formal logic into their arguments by conceding that slavery, on the islands at least, had not been so stringent in practice as they had formerly believed.[54] Others reacted conversely. Elizabeth Botume stated her credo flatly when she attempted to advise a harassed missionary woman whom she described as being "more enthusiastic than judicious." The lady was having trouble with a group of women who were clamoring over the distribution of clothing. Miss Botume expressed surprise at the missionary for allowing herself to be hoodwinked by one particularly aggressive claimant. To this the lady replied, " *'Do you think these poor colored people will lie? Do you think they would steal?'* (with a rising inflection to each sentence) 'Answer me that.' " Miss Botume replied, " 'My dear madam, they are human beings. If slavery produced only saints and no sinners, in Heaven's name let us leave them in their old estate! In all other conditions we find the good and the bad. I believe slavery engen-

[53] French, *Slavery in South Carolina*, p. 308.
[54] James Miller McKim represents Pierce as having formed this opinion. McKim to Towne, July 13, 1862, Towne MSS.

dered every vice under the sun. It is our mission to help these people to overcome evil, as well as to enlighten their ignorance.' "[55] Miss Botume cleared up her logic and let the political implications take care of themselves.

In the early days at Port Royal, none could be found to accuse the Negroes of making an unsatisfactory adjustment to their new condition, but for the most part, the assessments of Negro character had a certain hit-or-miss quality; the record is filled with contradictory generalizations, a tribute to the myriad forms of human personality and a witness to missionary confusion. The Negro could be a provident manager of his affairs or, as Mrs. French indicates, a lavish spender; he could be the lazy, slipshod workman slavery had made him or a docile and pliable laborer inured to toil and ready to make his way in the world. He could be a brutal parent roughened by a cruel life or an affectionate mother or father ready to care for his own. While numbers of missionaries did not at first believe that the Negro had enough valor to become a reliable soldier, this view would also undergo a striking change when the actions of the first Negro recruits and the alchemy of time made black regiments attractive to the North.[56] A full release from these perplexities could only come with what McKim referred to as the "logical conclusion" of the Port Royal experiment—emancipation.

In the meantime, the plantation people were themselves far less troubled by semantics. In their minds their freedom was most clearly related to the absence of their legal owners. Getting out of the master's power was the essence of freedom, and they reasonably concluded that his return was what they had to fear. In this

[55] Botume, *First Days*, p. 113. Since Miss Botume did not come to the islands until after the Emancipation Proclamation, her evaluation of the institution was not affected by the question of *nominal* freedom.

[56] The Philbrick group, including the Wares and William Gannett, were most vocal on this point, but they changed their opinion completely within a short time after Negro recruiting became public policy. See Pearson (ed.), *Letters*, pp. 42–43.

sense they had been free since the day of the "gun-shoot" at Bay Point. Except for times when the fear of Federal desertion swept over them, they were beginning to take their freedom for granted. Mrs. French tells us how Captain John Fripp's former coachman received the news of Hunter's emancipation proclamation. He was driving Mrs. French about Beaufort the day John Murray Forbes hailed her carriage to tell her the news. The pious lady was overjoyed, and she tells us that she clapped her hands and praised the Lord "over and over." Turning to her coachman, she asked him how he felt.

"Most beautiful, Missus; onspeakable."

"But why don't you say Hallelujah as I do?"

"I am burning inward, madam."

It would have been difficult for anyone to match Mrs. French's enthusiasm, and it may have been that the coachman meant a straightforward reply. It is probable, however, that he conveyed an attitude of ironic acceptance that the humorless lady could not comprehend.[57] Such a laconic response was amply vindicated by the subsequent revocation of the order, showing again how little words can do until time and politics are ripe for them. The status of the Negroes was as ambiguous as ever when General Saxton arrived in late June to assume charge at Port Royal.

Saxton arrived just in time to celebrate the first Fourth of July under military occupation. We may well believe that the national holiday was observed in this rebellious corner of South Carolina with more zeal than at any time since 1830. At The Oaks plantation the teachers were up at four o'clock in the morning to raise the flag, and after an early breakfast, at which they entertained the new general and his staff, they all went to the old Episcopal

---

[57] The coachman was probably amused. Laura Towne portrays him in her diary as "a shrewd man" with a tart but restrained sense of humor. He told her "with a very demure look" about Captain John's second wife, a very unpopular woman with the slaves. She was "a poor woman, who came home and was as much of a lady as anybody—couldn't get a glass of water for herself, nor nothing." Towne MS diary, April 28, 1862.

church on St. Helena. Miss Nelly Winsor obliged the little rebel organ to resound to "America" and the new "John Brown" song. Afterward, the teachers and superintendents took their places with Saxton and his staff on the platform in the churchyard under the moss-hung oaks. The Negroes, marshalled by two young superintendents, came down the roads leading to the church in great processions, bearing branches of greenery and singing one of their favorite songs, "Roll Jordan, Roll."[58] Arthur Sumner thought he had never heard such impressive music: "The singing was intrinsically good; the songs strange and beautiful; and their swaying to and fro had a sort of oceanic grandeur in it."[59]

Speeches were the ineluctable main course on such occasions. General Saxton greeted his new charges with a "manly" little talk, "straight-forward and encouraging," and then, as Miss Towne observed caustically, "Mr. Philbrick dilated upon work, work, and cotton, cotton." The lighter but more substantial part of the program followed, when the colored people were treated to crackers, dried herring, and molasses and water, which made them "happy as larks," while the white people, "we lords and ladies," as Arthur Sumner said, "rode off to Captain Hooper's headquarters where we had a fine lunch. . . ." As evening came on, the young Gideonites sang songs and were soon joined by the plantation people, who treated them to a "shout," thus ending the glorious celebration of the Fourth of July in South Carolina in 1862.[60]

[58] Holland (ed.), *Towne*, pp. 72–73.
[59] Arthur Sumner to Joseph Clark, July 7, 1862, Arthur Sumner MSS.
[60] *Ibid.*; Holland (ed.), *Towne*, pp. 72–73.

six ✤ IN JOHN BROWN'S ARMY

RUFUS SAXTON RODE BACK TO HIS HEADQUARTERS IN BEAUFORT after the Fourth of July celebration, having performed a fatherly part to a most obliging and happy group of people taking their pleasure in a typical Yankee holiday. It was a part that the general would play times without number in the next four years, and one that he always enjoyed. Perhaps Saxton had already arrived at his uncomplicated assessment of the islanders, that they were "intensely human."[1]

Saxton's assignment was unique. The war had convinced him that the abolitionist faith of his parents was grounded in the rock of truth, and he now had an opportunity to exert an influence, if he succeeded at his assignment, upon government policy in handling the thousands of slaves who would be released in the course of the war. There would come a time when resentful army officers would accuse Saxton of having taken up the "nigger business" as a safe berth toward official preferment by radicals.[2] A fear of such criticism could never have entered the general's head in 1863, for his sponsors were not omnipotent in national councils, and the army itself was as far out of sympathy with programs for

[1] Thomas Wentworth Higginson to Mrs. Higginson, in a postscript of May 10 to a letter of May 6, 1863, Higginson MSS.

[2] Henry Hitchcock, *Marching with Sherman; Passages from the Letters and Campaign Diaries of Henry Hitchcock* (New Haven, 1927), p. 226, quoted in George R. Bentley's *A History of the Freedmen's Bureau* (Philadelphia, 1955), p. 59.

Negro welfare as it well could be. Saxton was undoubtedly wise enough in the ways of military red tape to know that a letter from the Secretary of War was hardly enough to smooth his path at Hilton Head. As for the missionaries with whom he would now be expected to cooperate, Saxton had known such people in his youth in Greenfield but had never been obliged to work with them in the military harness. How would it all turn out?

In the last half of 1862, popular opinion in the North went through a rapid evolution on the question of the Negro's role in the war. Before the year had run its course the Port Royalists were not quite so far in advance of public policy as they had been in March. Radical ideas enjoyed a popular currency that offered Congress a sure footing for steps toward emancipation. The President himself, correctly charting the course of national thought, slowly and deliberately moved to meet the more radical spirit of the times. He moved too slowly and too deliberately to suit the Sea Island missionaries, but by the close of 1862 the war for the Union had indeed become a social revolution with the most far-reaching implications for the nation in general and Port Royal in particular.

And yet, to the first comers working in the island acres, all that was still to be achieved sometimes assumed an air of abstraction because the Sea Islanders were in their own minds free men. As E. S. Philbrick said, the "tad-poles" of the islands had "virtually shed their tails in the course of nature already." The initial problem of interesting the Negroes in working cotton was partially solved as faith in the government's intention to pay increased. Many of the physical hardships that the pioneers had suffered were also eased as they began to furnish the empty plantation houses with furniture left by the departing cotton agents. With the coming of summer the native produce provided a cheering improvement in the monotonous diet of army rations. "Yesterday I brought home two gentlemen from church," wrote Arthur Sumner, "and we sat down to chicken pie, . . . vegetables in abundance, chocolate and watermelons. This is now no uncommon style, for our table, at least." Turtle soup "and all such dainties" were to be had for "almost nothing."[3]

But the missionaries had no sooner begun to congratulate themselves upon their improved circumstances than a greater trouble than any they had known before descended upon them. On the twenty-fifth of July the thermometer on the porch at The Oaks stood at ninety-five degrees, and Laura Towne confided her sorrows to her diary. "Fleas and other vermin have been intolerable, but now the mosquitoes are almost unendurable. Night and day, sitting in the house or riding to the plantations, we have no rest. They bite in broad sunlight. . . ." Heedless of the repeated warnings of the Negroes that the islands were becoming unsafe for white people, the majority of the Gideonites had decided to stay through the summer.[4] Many suffered serious consequences. Laura Towne, who served as physician as well as teacher, reported that in the early fall many of the superintendents were ill of fever and that six or eight were going North to recover. Francis Barnard of Edisto was dying. He became the "first martyr" of Gideon's Band, and moving demonstrations of grief from the Negroes showed that he had won their affection and confidence. Three others lost their lives during the first season, including Samuel D. Phillips, the nephew of Wendell Phillips. The body of young Phillips was placed in a black coffin wreathed in camellias and evergreens and was laid to rest in the Fripp family tomb in the Episcopal churchyard on St. Helena. He was not the last missionary to await in the borrowed brownstone mausoleum his final voyage north.[5]

[3] Pearson (ed.), *Letters,* note on p. 69; Arthur Sumner to Joseph Clark, July 7, 1862, Arthur Sumner MSS; Laura Towne to [?], June 13, 1862, Towne MSS. Charles Ware wrote, "We live on the fat of the land. We are allowed $5.24 per month for rations, but I do not use even that." Pearson (ed.), *Letters,* p. 72.

[4] Towne MS diary, July 25, 1862.

[5] Towne MS diary, October 17 and 19, 1862, as well as July 23 and August 17, 1862; Jules de la Croix recalled that "The Negroes surrounded his house by the hundreds all night, praying for him." *Freedmen's Record,* I (February, 1865), 30.

The fevers lasted late into the fall, and when Arthur Sumner returned from the North in November he reported that the situation looked "a little dreary," for there was "a general feeling of insecurity" in the matter of health. "One of our company was dead, another has since died, and the gentleman whom we left in our house barely escaped with his life and is now at the North." He thought it "a little singular, that every white man who has lived in our house, (six, in all) has been ill of the local fevers. There is a cheerful swamp behind our house, within a stone's throw; and our windows are screened, by a grove of trees, from the full effects of the sun and wind."[6]

Some plantations were clearly more healthful than others, and although the lethal mosquito was never suspected, the missionaries quickly learned, as had generations of planters before them, that the places bordered by the ocean, with its stiff and continuous breezes, were relatively safe residences.[7] Illness and overwork took their toll of teachers and superintendents alike, and the constant attrition of these factors discouraged many well-meaning people who could not endure to wait for the alternate fates of martyrdom or better times. While many new workers were constantly arriving on the islands, there was also a quiet but steady procession of the departing.

Some among the earliest "evangels" did not remain to enjoy the auspicious changes that came with a degree of governmental recognition. In some lonely moment of decision for a Gideonite far from home and friends, perhaps isolated on a distant plantation, homesickness conquered zeal, and he was lost to the cause. Susan Walker's enthusiasm had dimmed early in June, when she concluded abruptly that she was "not prepared to accept this" as her "life-work." She doubted her suitability and did not "feel a

---

[6] Arthur Sumner to Nina Hartshorn, November 22, 1862, Arthur Sumner MSS.

[7] Philbrick wrote, "The health of every white man who has lived on the seaward side of St. Helena, from Coffin's Point to Land's End, has been perfectly good. . . ." Pearson (ed.), *Letters*, p. 135.

drawing toward it. . . ." William Park returned North for good after a session of fever and began to think of taking a commission in the army. "I think that it is more logical to thoroughly conquer the country before cultivating cotton and training the Negroes. . . ." J. Miller McKim spoke of "quite a number" of the approximately ninety who went to Port Royal in the spring and summer as having "proved incompetent." He mentioned that some had failed because they had come "in a spirit of sectarian religious zeal."[8] Some of the motives were less worthy. Reuben Tomlinson wrote McKim in the fall of a superintendent who claimed to have made a considerable amount of money "in a 'legitimate' way" by trading with the Negroes. Another man had been sent out of the Department for that reason. "Such things as these have of course a most disastrous effect upon the people. Then again some of the Superintendents, meaning very well, but hiring *very* young, and with little experience, their characters unformed, fall into the easy, shiftless sort of life so natural to the place, and allow things to take their course, trusting to luck and to the Negroes that all shall come out right." Edward Philbrick was also trenchant. "I don't believe in putting Reverends in places where prompt business men are required. Some of them don't get through morning prayers and get about their business till nearly noon, and then depend entirely upon their black drivers for their information in regard to plantation matters."[9]

The enterprise was not going to fail for lack of mutual watchfulness. At the time some of the superintendents were being accused of laxity, other critics found certain superintendents too whole-souled about growing cotton. It is certain that Laura

[8] Sherwood (ed.), "Walker Journal," entry for June 1, 1862, p. 45; William Park to William Gannett, August 13, 1862, Gannett MSS; McKim, *A Speech Delivered at Sansom Hall* (Philadelphia, 1862), p. 17; Luther P. Jackson, "The Educational Efforts of the Freedmen's Bureau and Freedmen's Aid Societies in South Carolina, 1862–1872," *Journal of Negro History*, VIII (January, 1923), 32.

[9] Tomlinson to McKim, September 20, 1862, McKim MSS; Pearson (ed.), *Letters*, p. 124.

Towne referred to Philbrick and his bustling New England colleagues so bent upon demonstrating the economy of free labor when she complained that "they have only changed the mode of compulsion. They *force* men to prove they are fit to be free by holding a tyrant's power over them." She agreed with Tomlinson that there was also "a little narrowness" among certain superintendents "on the subject of antislavery."[10] Surely the knowledge that their superintendents carried pistols and were known to use them in threatening recalcitrant Negroes must have reminded the black people strongly of the departed overseers. Whether he would or no, the superintendent found himself in a situation so analogous to that of the old planter that he not infrequently resembled him in outward behavior. As the only source of law, authority, and enforcement on the plantation, he sometimes resorted to strong measures—if not to achieve his own wishes, at least to prevent injustices and to secure order among the colored people. Unquestionably, he sometimes abused his power.[11]

The Negroes were not always easily managed. Scattered among missionary praise of their docility and of their eagerness to learn and to work were also complaints of lying, cheating, marital in-

[10] Towne MS diary, May 19, 1862; Tomlinson to McKim, September 20, 1862, McKim MSS.

[11] Anticipating a happier arrangement as a result of Saxton's arrival, Arthur Sumner wrote to Joseph Clark, July 7, 1862, Arthur Sumner MSS, "It will be perhaps no longer necessary to cow a turbulent black by drawing a pistol upon him, as we have been forced to do sometimes." See also Pearson (ed.), *Letters*, pp. 87, 95, 139; Towne MS diary, May 21, July 29, October 7, 1862; Tomlinson to McKim, September 20, 1862, McKim MSS. Arthur Sumner explained the predicament: "I think it most singular and unfortunate, that eight or ten thousand half-civilized people should be allowed to live without courts of law, either civil or military, without a police, and without sufficient means of enforcing order or punishing crime." Arthur Sumner to Nina Hartshorn, November 22, 1862, Arthur Sumner MSS.

fidelity, and laziness. We have seen that some of these conflicting assessments arose from the ambiguous ideological position in which the missionaries found themselves before emancipation became a reality. Another cause, of course, was the dominant tendency of mankind to simplify and to generalize from the particular. Some facts *did* stand behind the generalizations, however; and the only faulty logic was the inclination of each missionary to make his own observations cover too much ground. The Negroes were people, and including them in the human race meant that there had to be some troublemakers. William Gannett, who was removed from purely teaching duties and given charge of a group of plantations where the people were "acting badly," admitted he was having "a pretty hard time." He complained, "Now they work and then they stop—and some stop before they begin." For the first time in his life, he confessed, he had been obliged to knock a man down; "and I think I did right," he added defensively. On another plantation the people were taking the government corn without leave. A few days later Gannett wrote with relief in his diary, "A day without a row!"[12]

The situation varied from plantation to plantation. Reuben Tomlinson reported that the people on *one* of his Port Royal Island places were "very quiet, industrious and well-behaved" but that those on another were "sullen, indolent, unambitious and dirty." There was good reason to believe that the superintendents had more cooperation from the people on the plantations where they lived than from the Negroes on those at a distance.[13]

Sometimes the Negroes took advantage of the ignorance of the superintendents. Philbrick was chagrined to discover that the people on a certain Mr. Bryant's place had plumbed that gentleman's unawareness of the high standards customary in picking Sea-Island

[12] Pearson (ed.), *Letters*, p. 138; Gannett MS diary, November 14, 17, 1862, Gannett MSS.

[13] Tomlinson to McKim, September 20, 1862, McKim MSS; Pearson (ed.), *Letters*, p. 126.

cotton and had "taken the chance to shirk" by picking several bales of poorly moted, dirty cotton.[14]

Although the Northerners were winning a surface compliance with their plans, even the most successful superintendents knew that a real basis of confidence was not established. The Negroes still objected violently to the removal of corn from one plantation to another, and some of the people were saying that they yearned for the return of their old masters. Although winning their hearts was the easy result of "a cordial greeting, and patient friendliness," one superintendent said that the Negroes' gratitude "is that of smiles and promises, and votive offerings of eggs, and only lasts during fair weather. It is not their fault that suspicion of white men lies deeper than trust of this or that individual."[15] And indeed it was not.

The instincts of the newly-created black peasantry were not at fault, and the whole chain of suspicion and distrust at Port Royal did not begin or end with the Negroes. "Ignorance and want of confidence are the two evils from which we suffer," wrote Charles Ware, "want of confidence by the powers in us, by us in the negroes. It is painful to note how distrust must be the rule; how everyone must take it for granted that those under him are cheats and liars." He complained especially of the red tape involved in carrying on the plantations under the new regime.[16]

The high hopes of great improvement to result from the transfer of the "experiment" to military supervision had simply not materialized. All the sincere abolitionism of the "good little General," as Saxton soon came to be called, could not obscure the fact that he understood very little about cotton planting. One superintendent thought it "a great pity" that he did not "come onto the plantations himself and learn something, personally,"

[14] *Ibid.*, p. 116.

[15] [Gannett and Hale], "The Freedmen at Port Royal," *North American Review*, CI (July, 1865), 5; Gannett MS diary, November 11, 1862; Billington (ed.), *Forten*, p. 134.

[16] Pearson (ed.), *Letters*, p. 85.

about these matters. Another thought that Saxton and his staff knew "little or nothing of the real wants of the plantations. . . ."[17]

Although the superintendents had more official standing than before, most of the worst problems of Treasury Department control remained. Saxton promptly handed around small shoulder insignia to the superintendents, but the little cross surrounded by a band of gold did nothing to assure prompt payment to the laborers, who had to live by faith. The work done in May and June was not paid for until the second week in August, and in early October there was still "no prospect" of payment for July and August for six weeks to come. Philbrick preferred to advance pay to his workers from his own funds rather than wait longer than the end of October, but his solution was personal, and most superintendents surely were in no position to do this. The superintendents by this time were thoroughly aware of the practical limitations of their own power; when an order came to restrict the movements of the Negroes without passes, Charles Ware said, "I have no idea of making a rule I cannot enforce." He complained that there was no working system and that "general plans are usually determined just too late."[18]

Particularly irritating was the inability of Saxton to prevent the Union soldiers from stealing and killing the Negroes' livestock. The pickets on Ladies Island were such a menace to the poultry that the people took their chickens into their cabins at night, and it was reported that the pickets "shoot their pigs and in one case have shot two working mules! All these things are duly reported to General Saxton, but it does no good." The soldiers tore up fences by the mile to burn for firewood and even took the new rails freshly split for new fences. On Port Royal Island, "whole fields of corn, fifty acres in extent, have been stripped of every ear before hard enough to be stored." On the same island the General Superintendent, Mr. Judd, had also been asked to

[17] *Ibid.*, pp. 83-84; Towne to "T., R., and K.," August 26, 1862, Towne MSS.

[18] Pearson (ed.), *Letters*, pp. 83, 91; Towne MS diary, October 19, 1862.

supply ten thousand bushels of corn for the army. Small wonder that the superintendents feared such inroads would throw the people again upon government support.[19] One perceptive army officer explained the prejudice of the other officers and the white soldiers as being founded upon an "opinion that in some way the negroes have been more highly favored by the Government and [that] more privileges [have been] granted to them than to the volunteer soldier."[20] Behind the jealousy stood a host of frustrations accumulating as a result of relative inactivity and an ill-defined notion that the Negro was somehow, at bottom, the cause of the war. Whatever the source, the prejudices and abuses were real and were extremely difficult for Saxton to handle.

If Saxton did not understand the superintendents' problems, they only half understood his. Stranded amid unsympathetic or openly hostile fellow-officers whose duties could not always be clearly differentiated from his own, Saxton found his efforts on behalf of his small army of schoolteachers and civilian employees considered unimportant or openly ridiculed. Even among his own staff officers, only Captain Edward Hooper was in complete accord with the work of the missionaries. Although Hooper understood the problems from his former plantation experience with Pierce, he could not obviate all the snares and snags set by his opponents or handle every matter himself. When guns were ordered to the plantations for the Negroes to use in defense against threatening rebel raids, they were held up in delivery—intentionally, thought the missionaries—by a hostile officer.[21]

The most severe conflicts occurred between Saxton and Briga-

[19] Pearson (ed.), *Letters*, pp. 94, 118–119, note on p. 119; Towne MS diary, October 5, 1862.

[20] Ormsbie M. Mitchel to Edwin Stanton, September 20, 1862, *OR*, I, xiv, 384–385.

[21] Towne to "T., R., and K.," August 26, 1862, Towne MSS; Towne MS diary, July 14 and September 1, 1862; Arthur Sumner to Joseph Clark, October 4, 1863; John Chipman Gray and John Codman Ropes, *War Letters, 1862–1865* (Boston and New York, 1827), p. 230; Pearson (ed.), *Letters*, p. 93.

dier General John M. Brannan, who as Hunter's second-in-command was in full control whenever Hunter was out of the
Department. When he had the power, Brannan worked out re-
sentments he had accumulated when he and Saxton were fellow
subordinates. By closing access to equipment, housing, and supplies, he could frustrate the abolitionist general in a hundred petty
ways. Upon one occasion he had the General Superintendent of
Port Royal Island moved bag and baggage into the streets of
Beaufort and took over the house the superintendent had occupied. He was overtly, even "ostentatiously," as Governor Andrew complained to Charles Sumner, opposed to the policy Saxton
had been sent South to carry out. Eventually, the complaints
added up to a pressure Stanton could not ignore. He finally agreed
to the removal of Brannan from the Department, but not before
the confidence of the missionaries in Saxton's ability to withstand
the power of the regular military establishment had been seriously
weakened.[22] Hunter himself cooperated with Saxton, but he had
an undisguised distrust of the plantation superintendents, dating
from the time they had so vigorously criticized his summary
Negro draft. He obviously credited the superintendents with discouraging the Negroes from volunteering because of their own
selfish interests in the cotton crop.[23]

In desperation, the superintendents plagued the generals about
what appeared to be petty details. Once, when two of them went
to Hunter about Negro soldiers' being "quartered in their garden," Saxton was very angry at the "extreme disrespect" they had
shown in going over his head. The moody Hunter threatened

[22] Ormsbie Mitchel to Edwin Stanton, September 20, 1862, *OR*, I, xiv,
384–385; Pearson (ed.), *Letters*, pp. 108, 122; Tomlinson to McKim,
October 17, 1862, McKim MSS; John A. Andrew in a postscript addendum
to a letter from John Murray Forbes to Charles Sumner, urging Brannan's removal, November 29, 1862, Sumner MSS. See T. W. Higginson to
his mother, November 28, 1862, Higginson MSS; Donald (ed.), *Inside
Lincoln's Cabinet* (New York, 1954), pp. 137, 301.

[23] Holland (ed.), *Towne*, pp. 83–84.

grimly "to send them home in irons" if they continued their opposition to the Negro regiment.[24] There were too many chiefs
and too few Indians at Port Royal.

The missionaries were more than satisfied with Saxton as a
person, but he had a besetting character defect that from first to
last caused considerable trouble. Instead of maintaining a sympathetic but aloof position, he allowed himself to become attached
to factions developing within the missionary community. Even
his most devoted admirers could see that Saxton was prone to align
himself with people whom he regarded as having superior political
influence. The most serious implications of this involvement were
to materialize at a later date, but from the beginning Saxton's
naïve and sympathetic disposition encouraged individual missionaries to give him too much advice and to complain too freely. The
general became the first recourse in all disputes, great or small, and
his interest and willingness to intervene in matters of detail gained
him a popularity with the teachers that he did not always enjoy
with the superintendents.[25] A typical incident occurred when the
Negro Baptist congregation on St. Helena Island decided, under
some coaching from their Northern Baptist minister, to institute
"closed communion," thus excluding the preponderantly Unitarian teachers and superintendents on the island from the Lord's
Table. The teachers, who sagaciously foresaw that a failure to
take communion would lead to embarrassing questions from the
colored people, such as "Are none of the Northern gentlemen and
ladies Christians?" and reminders that their masters had drunk
out of the same cup with them, complained to Saxton. The general
suggested to the congregation that their minister might not be
just the right man for them and had his knuckles rapped politely
by an elder who reminded Saxton that their word was already
pledged to call the minister. The objectionable Mr. Horton was
eventually squeezed out of the Department, but not before the

24 *Ibid.*
25 Tomlinson to McKim, November 24, 1862, February 13, 1863,
McKim MSS.

Negroes, informed of Unitarian theology, had decided upon "closed communion" on their own.[26]

Saxton apparently enjoyed playing *pater familias* to his large and frequently troublesome tribe despite the many frustrations he endured on points of authority. He certainly cannot be held responsible for the most drastic impediments to the work, which were actually no more than hitches along the endless chain of cause and effect that bound Port Royal to the national war effort.

Frequent rumors of rebel attack and probable evacuation had an unsettling effect upon the Negroes, the missionaries, and the whole agricultural enterprise. These rumors often had no more basis in fact than brushes along the picket lines, where the meandering lines of river and marsh brought the blue and the gray within shouting and shooting distance of each other. In early June a typical little fray at Port Royal Ferry threw Beaufort into a panic. All women and other fearful civilians boarded a waiting steamer for a retreat to Hilton Head and the protection of Du Pont's gunboats. The authorities opened the old arsenal on Craven Street and told the remaining civilians to seize guns for the defense of the town. This skirmish came to nothing, and within a few days people were protesting that "*they* were not frightened at such an unlikelihood" as a rebel attack; those who had packed their trunks regretted their trouble. Although Laura Towne said the missionaries had behaved manfully and shouldered their guns to assist the scouting parties, she heard that the soldiers were "swearing at the 'nigger-lovers' " who had, they said, "run away at the first danger."[27] It was a slander, but the Gideonites were accustomed by now to ridicule. Small indeed was the danger of a full-scale Confederate assault, for just as the Federal army at Hilton Head was reduced to strengthen General George McClel-

[26] Towne MS diary, June 22, 29, 30, August 3, 1862; Towne to McKim, July 1, 1862, McKim MSS.

[27] Holland (ed.), *Towne*, p. 67; Tomlinson to McKim, August 18, 1862, McKim MSS; Sherwood (ed.), "Walker Journal," p. 47; Towne MS diary, June 7, 1862.

lan's peninsular campaign, so had many South Carolina Confederate units been ordered North to meet him before Richmond.[28]

A heavier blow to the Port Royal cotton-planting enterprise resulted from McClellan's failure. His procrastination and mismanagement of his large forces below Richmond had given Robert E. Lee his first opportunity to display the brilliant generalship that soon made him the most feared and respected of all Confederate opponents. Pressing hard on McClellan's retreating army, Lee drove him back to Harrison's Landing on the James River, and for several days sheer panic gripped Washington. In a series of frantic orders Secretary Stanton scoured all available commands for reinforcements to save McClellan's army; on July 3 he asked General Hunter to send ten thousand infantrymen to Virginia.[29] With his forces thus drastically reduced, Hunter immediately ordered a concentration of his forces on the most readily defensible of the islands, abandoning the extensive and rich lands of Edisto, where the superintendents had planted a very promising crop of seven hundred acres of cotton and even greater fields of corn and potatoes. The missionary-planters knew that this would cut their total achievement seriously and at the same time call for the evacuation of the Edisto Negroes, without a subsistence. Protests, under the circumstances, were vain.[30]

Sixteen hundred colored people of all ages, with their pigs, chickens, and personal effects, followed their superintendents to St. Helena Island aboard large flatboats camouflaged with branches of trees for protection against rebel sharpshooters. These

[28] *OR*, I, xiv, 480–482, 518; and I, xi, Part III, 511.

[29] *OR*, I, ii, Part III, 290–291.

[30] Saxton to Stanton, August 16, 1862, *OR*, I, xiv, 364–366; Mrs. S. F. Du Pont to Henry Winter Davis, August 2, 1862, reports her husband as regretting "extremely" the abandonment of such "valuable property to the *raids* of the secessionists"; Holland (ed.), *Towne*, pp. 73–74; Milton Hawks to Esther Hawks, July 16, 1862, Hawks MSS. A Confederate raider, native of Edisto, attested to the excellence of the crops thus abandoned. See John Jenkins to his wife, August 24, 1862, John Jenkins MSS, South Caroliniana Library, Columbia, South Carolina.

displaced people resettled at St. Helena Village, the summer watering place of the island, and remained there throughout the war. They readily agreed to take over the cotton fields that had been abandoned in May when Hunter drafted his black regiment. Remaining idle persons were seized by force, in the cruel and arbitrary manner that was fast becoming a pattern, and carried off as laborers to Fort Pulaski. Beautiful Edisto became from this time a no-man's-land that was raided sporadically by scouting parties from each army.[31]

Edward Pierce bitterly protested the abandonment of Edisto. He wrote Salmon P. Chase that there was small inducement to work for the social experiment at Port Royal so long as the government ignored its existence in the disposition of troops. Chase could only agree with Pierce but said that the action could be seen as the natural consequence of Lincoln's "revocation of Hunter's order and the McClellan infatuation" and, by clear implication, of the President's too-conservative opinions on the whole question of the Negro's role in the war. "The colonization delusion and the negrophobia dread are too potent yet. . . ." He referred to the President's idea that the Negroes might be carried abroad, and to the fear of servile insurrection. Chase was deeply discouraged about the war. "The darkness is dense enough," he moaned, "to herald the brightest of dawns. But while the dawn delays, my heart aches sadly."[32]

What the North needed most was a military victory, and Chase wanted it soon; his hopes for Negro emancipation rested upon such a victory. On July 22, shortly before Chase wrote his letter to Pierce, President Lincoln convened his Cabinet and, in a truly historic session, read a draft of his Preliminary Emancipation Proc-

[31] Holland (ed.), *Towne*, pp. 75–76, 92; Maria Middleton, an aged survivor of the journey, recalled the use of tree branches and the flats. See Elsie Clews Parsons, *Folk-Lore of the Sea Islands, South Carolina* (Cambridge, 1923), p. xxii.

[32] Chase to Pierce, August 2, 1862, James Freeman Clarke MSS, Houghton Library. The letter is clearly in response to complaints from Pierce.

lamation. The President's decision had been reached weeks before, in the growing certitude that the Border States would not avail themselves of his plan for compensated emancipation and with the knowledge that the outcome of McClellan's thrust had expunged all hopes for an early end to the fighting.[33]

Most of the Cabinet had been surprised at what appeared on the surface to be a sudden move on the part of the President, but the members readily agreed to the step without important modifications except for William Seward's well-considered suggestion that the President wait for a military victory before making his public announcement. The Secretary of State believed that the Proclamation would assume the air of an act of desperation, "our last shriek on the retreat," if it were made when the war was going so much against the Union.[34]

The war had indeed approached a crisis in late July. There had been little encouraging news from the Western theater since April, when the victory at Shiloh had been followed by the occupation of New Orleans. These victories were disappointing in that they seemed to be leading nowhere. The high hopes accompanying McClellan's advance up the peninsula below Richmond had been cruelly dashed. Waiting for victories, the Cabinet received news in late August of the most humiliating defeat of the entire war. General John Pope allowed his army to be trapped at Manassas, Virginia, practically on the doorstep of the Capitol, between the armies of Longstreet and Jackson; it was hurled back toward Washington in a retreat that was actually a rout.[35]

When the full impact of this latest disaster was at last known in the North, a real desperation gripped the public. "That we are in

[33] Donald (ed.), *Insiae Lincoln's Cabinet*, pp. 99–100.

[34] Allan Nevins, *War Becomes Revolution, 1862–1863* (New York, 1960), p. 165, quoting Francis B. Carpenter, *Six Months at the White House with Abraham Lincoln* (Boston, 1866), p. 22. Nevins' book mistakenly dates the meeting as being on August 22 instead of July 22.

[35] The impact of these events upon public opinion and political developments is well described in Nevins, *War Becomes Revolution*, Chapters 6 through 10.

serious danger of being whipped cannot be denied," wrote Edward Atkinson, "and there is scarce a man now in Boston, who would not thank God to hear of a successful insurrection among the slaves, such a change has this disaster wrought." Dr. Milton Hawks, perhaps the most fanatical missionary at Port Royal, repeated his belief that, unless emancipation were the goal of the war, the South would establish her independence. "The greatest kindness that a man could do this government today," he wrote furiously, "would be to assassinate Pres. Lincoln—He stands directly in the way."[36]

Lincoln's course was mysterious to the general public in the days between July 22 and the official pronouncement of the Preliminary Proclamation on September 22—dark days that saw the rout of Pope's army and the invasion of Maryland by Robert E. Lee. When the tide was turned at Antietam in a dubious and militarily unexploited victory, the President seized the slim occasion for his Proclamation and on September 22, at one stroke, lifted the struggle to a new plane. The war for the Union had become a war for freedom.

The President's Proclamation was a modest document to be freighted with so much significance. Its terms and limitations are well known. It was in effect a promise, or more properly speaking a threat, that in such states as remained in rebellion after the first of January, 1863, all slaves would be regarded as free by the Federal government and that no steps would be taken to hinder them "in any efforts they may make for their actual freedom." The latter part of the document was a specific injunction to "all persons in the military and naval service of the United States" to observe and enforce two Acts of Congress of March 13 and July 17, 1862.[37] The first Act prohibited the return of fugitive slaves by military officers, and the second, in its tenth section, was a repeti-

[36] Edward Atkinson to E. S. Philbrick, September 13, 1862, Atkinson MSS; Milton Hawks to Esther Hawks, September 11, 1862, Hawks MSS.

[37] For the text, see Roy P. Basler (ed.), *The Collected Works of Abraham Lincoln* (New Brunswick, New Jersey: Rutgers University Press, 1953), V, 433–436.

tion of this injunction. The ninth section of the Act of July 17, known as the Second Confiscation Act, declared that all slaves of persons "hereafter engaged in rebellion against the government of the United States" or giving aid and comfort to the rebellion, who should make their escape from their masters, be captured during the course of the war, or be found within areas occupied by the Federal forces, were "forever free of their servitude."[38] Radicals had been waiting for a sign that the President intended to enforce the Act, because the liberating clause embraced numbers of those who heretofore had been labeled "contraband." The President's original hesitation about signing the Act and his reference to the problem of determining in individual instances whether the terms of the ninth section applied, whether the master of a given fugitive was in fact engaged in rebellion, had created a doubt of his intention to execute its provisions. This was Horace Greeley's signal accusation in his famous open letter to the President entitled "The Prayer of Twenty Millions," in which he implored Lincoln to take action.[39] The President had acted.

For Negroes within the Federal lines, as were those at Port Royal, the Second Confiscation Act may be considered the initial step in liberation. It is doubtful, however, that the Act alone could have afforded actual freedom to a considerable portion of the people there, because of the difficulty of establishing by law whether the fugitive masters were actually engaged in rebellion or giving aid and comfort to it. Certainly the large numbers of slaves held by Dr. Richard Fuller, who was, as we have seen, a loyal resident of Baltimore, were not embraced in its liberating clause. The Preliminary Emancipation Proclamation of September, while in no way providing a means of determining the master's status, did, in its use of the war powers of the President, give

[38] *United States Statutes at Large*, 37th Congress, July 17, 1862, XII, 591.

[39] See Basler (ed.), *Lincoln*, V, 329–331, for the text of Lincoln's message to Congress, expressing his objections to the original bill. Greeley's letter appeared in the New York *Tribune* of August 20, 1862, and is summarized and presented with the text of Lincoln's reply of August 22, 1862, in Basler (ed.), *Lincoln*, V, 388–389.

additional force to the Act.[40] Congress had passed yet another measure on July 17, 1862, which had an emancipating clause with a bearing on the islanders. The thirteenth section of the Militia Act provided that Negroes who rendered military service were free and that the mothers, wives, and children of soldiers were also thereafter free. But this provision again had the disadvantage of depending upon whether the master was engaged in rebellion.[41]

The President and the Thirty-Seventh Congress had taken important steps that held promise for the future but had not struck at slavery in an unequivocal way, even in the Department of the South. So it was that by the end of the year, as the hundred days of waiting were running out, Port Royal Negroes were in very much the same ambiguous condition in which they had been when they had celebrated their first "free" Fourth of July.

The winds of revolutionary change were rising, however, and not long after the secret decision of the Cabinet, even before the public announcement of the Proclamation, the Department of the South felt at once the changing current of government policy. Because emancipation during wartime was inevitably connected with the use of the Negro to *win* the war, the most immediate result was a decision to raise Negro troops. But it came too late to preserve Hunter's plan.

Although the evangels had vigorously opposed General Hunter's high-handed impressment of the first Negro regiment, most of them had shortly become reconciled to the result if not the method, and they regarded the First Regiment of South Carolina

[40] I follow here the reasoning of James G. Randall, in his *Constitutional Problems Under Lincoln* (New York, 1926), pp. 358–364. "On close analysis, therefore, it is hard to see by what process any particular slaves could have legally established that freedom which the Second Confiscation Act 'declared.' " See page 363. Henry Winter Davis, an able constitutional lawyer, and later a foremost radical, considered the measure "a confession of intellectual bankruptcy" and feared that such extreme measures could well be "equally fatal to free institutions and a government of law" as to slavery. Davis to Samuel Francis Du Pont, [?] July, 1862, transcript, Du Pont MSS.

[41] Randall, *Constitutional Problems*, p. 363.

Volunteers as an auxiliary of their own efforts to prove what the Negro could do. Laura Towne, who visited the encampment, exclaimed that the men "looked splendidly," and she thought that "the great mass of blackness, animated with a soul and armed so keenly, was very impressive." They did Hunter credit. But not all in Gideon's Band were converted. Superintendent Charles Ware, unconvinced as yet that soldiers could be made of the late slaves and perhaps still harboring a grudge at the loss of the plantation laborers, commented that Hunter's methods were "such as to prejudice . . . [the Negroes] against military duty under any circumstances." He reported that one of the officers, "who is a terror to the whole black population," had abused the men, and that they had suffered greatly from the sudden change of diet "and quite as much from homesickness."[42]

A correspondent of the Boston *Advertiser* described the regiment as numbering about eight hundred men in the month of June. Each man wore a dark blue coat and trousers, a cone-shaped broad-brimmed hat, and "a stout unbleached cotton shirt." The general effect was "decidedly dark," but the men impressed the reporter as "clean and fresh in appearance." The Negro soldiers received the regular rations, and also, the reporter supposed, "the regular pay."[43]

He guessed wrong about that. Hunter kept his men at drill through June and July and strove mightily to obtain recognition and pay for them, but to no avail.[44] When an irate Congressman from Kentucky wanted to know if it was true that a regiment of black men, "fugitive or captured slaves," had been formed in

[42] Holland (ed.), *Towne*, pp. 69–70; Pearson (ed.), *Letters*, p. 96. Philbrick wrote, "Many of their officers abused them, and they were generally insulted by every white man they met." *Ibid.*, p. 100.

[43] Boston *Advertiser*, June 21, 1862. The men were subsequently uniformed in the famous red trousers that so offended Thomas Wentworth Higginson, as he records in his *Army Life*, p. 22.

[44] Holland (ed.), *Towne*, p. 83; George W. Williams, *A History of the Negro Troops in the War of the Rebellion 1861–1865* (New York, 1888), p. 95.

the Department of the South, Secretary Stanton denied having given any such authorization. But he cleverly permitted Hunter to reply directly to the challenge, and he sent the general's letter to Congress. By this inspired stroke Stanton was able, shrewd politician that he was, to maintain his standing with the radicals while at the same time appearing to comply with the demands of the conservatives.[45] In a communication considered saucy and irreverent by his opponents but brilliant by the friends of Negro enlistment, Hunter declared that his regiment was not composed of "fugitive slaves" but "of persons whose late masters are 'fugitive rebels.' " Far from running away from their masters, his men were "one and all, working with remarkable industry to place themselves in a position to go in pursuit of their fugacious and traitorous proprietors." Hunter claimed that his authorization to do as he had done had existed from an earlier order given by Simon Cameron, Stanton's predecessor in the War Department, "to employ all loyal persons offering their services in defense of the Union." He pointed out that there were no restrictions placed "on the character or color" of such persons or on "the nature of the employment, whether civil or military, in which their services should be used."[46]

But in the end Hunter had to surrender because he could obtain no pay for the men, and in early August he disbanded his entire regiment with the exception of one company, which he assigned to guard duty on St. Simon's Island. This company, made up of former slaves, was a part of the first Negro regiment, and it had the longest continuous existence of any colored unit in the Union army.[47]

Hunter had no sooner thrown up his hands and sent the other

[45] *Ibid.*, p. 92; James G. Sproat, "Blueprint for Radical Reconstruction," in *Journal of Southern History*, XXIII (February, 1957), 30.

[46] *House Executive Documents*, No. 143, 37th Congress, 2nd session, serial 1138.

[47] Williams, *Negro Troops*, note on p. 95, p. 181; Higginson, *Army Life*, pp. 1–2; Benjamin Quarles, *The Negro in the Civil War*, p. 119.

companies home to "gather crop" when the course of events shifted drastically and Port Royal immediately felt the new drift of policy.[48] Popular desperation over the defeats of the summer had prepared the ground for a new appeal. General Saxton was ambitious to try his hand where Hunter had failed, and in late August he sent Mr. French to Washington with "a very important plan to lay before the Secretary of War," a plan proposed by Saxton and sanctioned by Hunter and Admiral Du Pont. Saxton's plan was to raise Negro troops to increase the effective forces on the islands, offer greater security to the working Negroes on the plantations, act in their defense "in the event of any emergency," and encourage desertion of slaves of the rebels. He envisioned expeditions into the coastal districts to capture enemy salt works and to destroy property, and pointed to the offensive action taken by the Hunter troops on St. Simon's Island, driving rebels off and suffering casualties in action.[49] Small-scale guerrilla fighting of the kind familiar to the veterans of the Kansas struggles was perhaps the very best that could have been obtained for Negro soldiers at this time.

In his talks with Stanton and Chase, occurring within weeks after Lincoln's historic cabinet meeting of July 22, French made his points and "accomplished," he wrote, "*all* I came for." He had traveled to Washington with Robert Smalls, the hero of the *Planter* episode, who regaled Secretary Chase for "nearly an hour" with his "*thrilling story*."[50] French was inclined to dramatize, and it is altogether probable that bringing Smalls to Washington was his idea. It was probably an effective one. Smalls was an object

[48] Holland (ed.), *Towne*, p. 83.

[49] French to George Whipple, August 23, 1862, AMA MSS, in an uncatalogued box labeled "1862—A–J"; Saxton to Stanton, August 16, 1862, *OR*, I, xiv, 375–376.

[50] French to George Whipple, August 28, 1862, AMA MSS, in an uncatalogued box labeled "1862—A–J." See Dorothy Sterling, *Captain of the Planter, the Story of Robert Smalls* (New York, 1958) for an account of Smalls's talk with President Lincoln while in Washington (pp. 107–112).

lesson on what the incentive of emancipation would induce slaves to do, for his flight from Charleston had resulted from the news of Hunter's ill-fated Proclamation of May. French and Smalls returned triumphantly to Beaufort with full authorization from Stanton for Saxton "to arm, equip, and receive into the service of the United States such volunteers of African descent as you may deem expedient, not exceeding five thousand." Saxton was empowered to assign officers to drill and instruct the men and was promised the regular pay of volunteers for officers and men.[51]

Now the Port Royal Islands would indeed become a testing ground for the full panoply of an ever broadening radical program for the Negro. The black man would be given his chance as a free soldier of the Union as well as a free laborer upon the land where he had toiled as a bondsman. Relying upon patient persuasion rather than force, General Saxton went eagerly to the work of recruiting.

Throughout the fall, officers visited the plantations, talked with the people, and spoke in the little country churches. Saxton enlisted the influence and cooperation of the teachers and missionaries. Mrs. Francis D. Gage, abolitionist turned missionary, told the people how the slaves of Santa Cruz had risen and conquered their masters, proclaiming their own freedom. She urged

[51] Stanton to Saxton, August 25, 1862, *OR*, I, xiv, 377–378. Stanton implied in his letter that it was superfluous for Saxton to call for specific authorization to raise Negro troops, for "It is considered by the Department that the instructions given at the time of your appointment were sufficient to enable you to do what you have now requested authority for doing." In the light of Hunter's experience, Saxton seems to have been exercising no unnecessary caution in binding the wily Stanton firmly. There is a curious ambivalence in the instructions as to the pay for Negro volunteers. Those taken in as volunteer *laborers* were to receive $5.00 per month for common labor and $8.00 for skilled labor. But those who were to be drilled as soldiers were to "receive the same pay and rations as are allowed to [other] volunteers in the service." Classifying the Negro volunteers as laborers provided a very shabby foundation for consistently underpaying the Negro soldiers organized in the Department of the South.

the mothers to encourage their sons to enlist. Prince Rivers, the handsome and talented Negro sergeant from Hunter's original regiment, took an active and influential part, and General Saxton pointed to the example of Robert Smalls, who was giving up a good job storekeeping in order to join the regiment. "How can I expect to get my freedom if I'm not willing to fight for it?" he quoted Smalls as asking. The plantations took on a martial air as the teachers ran up their flags and drilled the field hands, giving them a foretaste of military life.[52]

In the beginning these concentrated efforts met with small success. Hunter's bungling and arbitrary methods in the original draft, and the summary conscription of the Edisto people to work at the forts, had embittered the gentle islanders against the prospect of military duty. They loved their homes and hated to leave their families and growing crops. The white soldiers discouraged recruiting by circulating "doleful tales" among the plantation women of plans for putting the Negroes in the front ranks of the fighting. On some plantations, the men would not listen to the recruiters and avoided church "at the sight of epaulets."[53] It was surely unrealistic to expect a people to emerge from a slave system of such isolation and repression as theirs had been, without a trace of the servility of their former condition. It is an everlasting tribute to the strength and resiliency of the Negro race in particular and of human nature in general that the colored people were able to encompass, in so short a time, so vast a social change.

Slowly, the first few companies were formed, and the worst suspicions were overcome. Laura Towne reported that the men from The Oaks were all going to volunteer, many willingly, but she added that "with some there is a dismal forlornness about their consent to go." Saxton had much greater success outside the area that had felt the direct effects of the Hunter draft. From St. Simon's Island large numbers of volunteers arrived, and the coastal

[52] Billington (ed.), *Forten*, p. 138; Pearson (ed.), *Letters*, pp. 89, 93, 104.
[53] *Ibid.*, pp. 96, 97, 100–103, 104; Billington (ed.), *Forten*, p. 138; Holland (ed.), *Towne*, pp. 93–94.

Negroes of Florida responded warmly to the challenge.[54] In early November the first full company was mustered in, and it was reported that the regiment numbered four hundred men and was "filling fast." By mid-January the strength of the regiment was nearly eight hundred men.[55]

Saxton, in looking about for the proper colonel to command his pet regiment, decided upon Thomas Wentworth Higginson, a well-known Massachusetts abolitionist who had been a prominent backer of John Brown during the Kansas struggle. On the fifth of November he wrote Higginson, then with the 51st Massachusetts in training at Worcester, and offered him the job.[56]

Higginson came within the month and immediately decided that this was a work tailored for him. He considered the arming of the Negroes "a vast experiment in indirect philanthropy," one upon which the destiny of the Negro race and the outcome of the war might well depend. Years later, Higginson wrote of his feelings at this time that he "had been an abolitionist too long, and had known John Brown too well, not to feel a thrill of joy" upon discovering himself at the head of a black regiment, where the martyred Brown had "merely wished to be." In reality, the men were too little alike to justify so close an identification as Higginson implied, and in 1862 the idea would not have occurred to the new colonel. Yet the same romantic streak that brought the parallel to mind in later years caused Higginson in 1862 to relish his position at the head of a unique regiment, to enjoy the exotic features of the climate, and to savor the irony of his new scene of activity in the homeland of the old slaveocracy. Although

[54] *Ibid.*; Higginson, *Army Life*, pp. 21–22; Suzie King Taylor, *Reminiscences of My Life in Camp* (Boston, 1902), p. 46. The 1st South Carolina Volunteers, then forming, was subsequently renamed the 33rd U. S. Colored Troops.

[55] Pearson (ed.), *Letters*, pp. 106–107. On November 12, 1862, Saxton reported to Stanton that he had enlisted 550 men. *OR*, I, xiv, 190; Arthur Sumner to Joseph Clark, January 23, 1863, Arthur Sumner MSS.

[56] Higginson, *Army Life*, p. 1.

there were a few critics of Higginson's appointment on the grounds of his lack of experience, in one respect no better man could have been found.[57] Higginson was a writer of no mean skill, and he did much to publicize the exploits of his black regiment.

Soon there were exciting things to report. Saxton himself had already written in glowing terms of the conduct of the Hunter regiment in a stand-up fight against rebel guerrillas on St. Simon's Island in midsummer. The men had suffered casualties and driven off the Confederates. In early November another excursion to the Georgia coast had yielded evidence of the fighting capabilities of the 1st South Carolina Volunteers. Enemy saltworks were demolished, slaves and property brought off, and prisoners taken. The general praised his Negro soldiers highly.[58]

The Gideonites well knew that they had much to gain from the presence of the black regiment. The islands would increase in national significance as the setting of a serious effort to raise a Negro army. Furthermore, the fear of immediate evacuation of the islands, a fear that had persisted throughout the summer, was now removed. Even the most skeptical missionaries were ready now to admit that the matter was "very important." Others could look with real pride on the promising regiment.[59] There was too great a kinship between the two projects for Negro advancement for either to ignore the other. Since the spelling book was as popu-

[57] *Ibid.*, p. 5; John Murray Forbes wrote Charles Sumner, "I only wish we had some anti-slavery officers of more experience than Wentworth Higginson!" He thought also that Higginson lacked discretion. Forbes to Sumner, January 17, 1863, Sumner MSS. I am indebted to Tilden G. Edelstein, who is now completing a biography of Higginson, for the suggestion that the colonel's identification with John Brown was an afterthought.

[58] Saxton to Stanton, November 12, 1862, *OR*, I, xiv, 189–191.

[59] Philbrick was as yet skeptical: Pearson (ed.), *Letters*, p. 102; Arthur Sumner wrote that the men were, "most of them, tall, fine-looking, manly fellows." Their "soldierly drill and bearing excites the respect of even their enemies here." Arthur Sumner to Joseph Clark, January 23, 1862, Arthur Sumner MSS. See also Billington (ed.), *Forten*, pp. 164, 176.

lar with the Negro recruits as with others of their race, volunteer teachers were needed to instruct them. As the regiment pinned down coastal districts, the Yankee teacher followed close behind with her primer. At the end of 1862 four hundred children in Florida were under instruction. Dr. Milton Hawks gave up his superintendency in order to join the regiment as surgeon. Gideon's Band, after all, thought of themselves as also belonging to "John Brown's Army."[60]

The white tents of Higginson's regiment were spread in orderly array on the grounds of the Smith plantation, located on a picturesque point about three miles south of Beaufort on the site where the French had built a fort in the sixteenth century. As the last few days of 1862 approached, the camp was a hive of activity, for General Saxton was planning a great celebration for the first day of January, when he expected some five thousand freed people and their missionary friends to visit the camp to hear the Emancipation Proclamation read. Great stores of molasses, hard bread, and tobacco were laid by for the guests, and a dozen oxen were roasted on spits.[61]

Saxton, as military governor, wished to mark with special cheer a day of so much significance for the people of the islands. Nowhere in all the occupied districts of the South could the document have had more meaning than in his Department. The Proclamation

[60] Higginson, *Army Life*, p. 34; Towne MS diary, December 31, 1862; Billington (ed.), *Forten*, note on p. 241; Arthur Sumner to Joseph Clark, January 23, 1863, Arthur Sumner MSS.

[61] Primary accounts of the Emancipation Day ceremonies at Camp Saxton are in substantial agreement and are found in the following sources: Higginson, *Army Life*, pp. 51–57; Holland (ed.), *Towne*, pp. 98–99; Pearson (ed.), *Letters*, pp. 128–134; Billington (ed.), *Forten*, pp. 153–157; Taylor, *Reminiscences*, p. 18; Port Royal *New South*, January 3, 1863; Tomlinson to McKim, January 16, 1863, McKim MSS; French to Chase, January 2, [1863, but misdated 1862], Chase MSS; The Charles Howard Family History, a manuscript collection privately reproduced and bound, pp. 105–107. Copies of this collection may be seen at the Southern Historical Collection in Chapel Hill and at The Johns Hopkins University Library.

had in general emancipated only the slaves *outside* the grasp of the
Federal armies and had gone to the lengths of specifically excluding from its liberating provisions the Negroes within the lines in
Virginia and Louisiana, leaving their situation dependent upon
whatever bearing the Second Confiscation Act could have upon
their case.[62] No such exclusion was made in the case of South
Carolina, so for the islanders and their friends there was no more
hopeful waiting, no more doubt. The great day had come.

Early in the morning of January 1 the general's little steamer,
the *Flora*, plied to and fro among the islands, bringing thousands
of freedmen to Camp Saxton. A cloudless sky, the blue river, and
the warm southern sun imparted a summertime atmosphere to the
lively assembly in the oak grove where the speakers' stand was
erected. The Negroes wore their holiday best. The gay kerchiefs
of the women and the scarlet trousers that the regiment was now
wearing made a lively scene. Many described the three-hour-long
service, but all agreed that it was quite *beyond* description. Only
those who had pursued the cause of liberty through the lean years
could really understand. Prayers, hymns, and speeches were the
substance of the program. A poetic evangel rendered an ode of his
own composing, which he joined a few friends in singing; but the
highlight of the ceremony was the reading of the President's
Proclamation by Dr. William H. Brisbane. A native Sea Island
planter turned abolitionist, Brisbane had freed his own slaves many
years before. The most touching moment of all came when the
freedmen broke into a spontaneous singing of "My Country, 'Tis
of Thee" at the very point in the exercises when Mr. French presented Colonel Higginson with a flag for the black regiment.
Everyone agreed that the freed people could never really have

---

[62] Referring to the "excepted" counties of Louisiana and Virginia, the
Proclamation states, ". . . and which parts are for the present, left precisely
as if this proclamation were not issued." No exceptions were made for the
occupied parts of Arkansas or the toeholds in Florida, Georgia, and North
Carolina, as well as South Carolina. Basler (ed.), *Lincoln*, VI, 29.

sung of "My Country" until that day, and Higginson said as much in his acceptance of the flag.[63]

Two Negro leaders in the regiment addressed the people, exhorting them to enlist and fight for their relatives and friends still in bondage. The soldiers sang the "John Brown" song and closed the ceremonies. In the words of Suzie King Taylor, the pretty little Negro laundress of the regiment, "it was a glorious day for us all . . . ," and she no doubt expressed the unanimous verdict in saying that the great barbecue provided "a fitting close and the crowning event."[64]

At his headquarters in the Heyward house in Beaufort, Saxton entertained his staff and a gathering of teachers at supper and a dance. The party was a great success, so much so that the general unbent to the extent of flirting ominously with several pretty young teachers. It did not escape the eagle eye of Laura Towne that in adorning Miss Matilda Thompson with his gold sash Saxton allowed her to rank all the rest.[65] John Brown's war in South Carolina was assuming a holiday and romantic aspect that the grim old man had never known in Kansas. There were times when fighting seemed remote from the Department of the South.

Matters of concern remained, but the less felicitous sidelights of the glorious day were reserved for private cogitation. Although the Proclamation could be regarded as heralding a revolution to come, in itself it was hardly a revolutionary document. Colonel Higginson was still "very anxious" about "the ultimate fate of these poor people," feared that the promises of the Proclamation would be broken, and remembered a fact of history: "that revolutions may go backward. . . ." That numbers of Negroes were still deeply suspicious of the good faith of their new friends was clear to William Gannett, who commented on the unwillingness of the

---

[63] Billington (ed.), *Forten*, p. 154; Pearson (ed.), *Letters*, p. 129.
[64] Taylor, *Reminiscences*, p. 18.
[65] Holland (ed.), *Towne*, p. 99.

colored people in his vicinity to go to the ceremony at the camp because they feared "a trap."[66]

The ugliest revelation of the day was enough to vindicate Negro skepticism. The superintendent in charge of the refreshments at the Smith plantation was shortly sent out of the Department in disgrace by Captain Hooper, Saxton's watchdog. He was charged with having dishonestly watered the government-supplied molasses provided for the feast. Even in the best of causes the right hand of fellowship sometimes strays into someone else's pocket, but nothing can so readily embarrass philanthropy. Years later, a fellow superintendent who remembered the "joyful occasion" thought that this transaction on the part of "a sanctimonious religionist" made the day a little less "sublime."[67]

But the most pressing cause for concern at the end of the year was a growing uncertainty about the future of the Port Royal experiment. The wheel of revolution that had brought so much satisfaction to the missionaries had also turned up a Congressional Act providing for the sale of properties within the Federal lines in South Carolina.[68] What would a property revolution do to the plans of the missionaries? With the impending sale came the sinister threat of speculators, land-hungry, nonphilanthropic purchasers, and a swarm of questions regarding the future welfare of the freed people.

[66] Higginson, *Army Life*, pp. 63–64; Gannett MS diary, January 1, 1863, Gannett MSS.

[67] Charles Howard Family [MS] History, pp. 105–107.

[68] French to Chase, January 2, [1863, misdated 1862], Chase MSS.

seven ⬦ CONFISCATION, PUBLICITY,
AND CLOSE CALCULATION

IN 1863 FANNY KEMBLE, THE FAMOUS ENGLISH ACTRESS, OBSERVED most truly that the course of emancipation in the United States would inevitably be complicated because of its relation to the war. She accurately predicted that the resolution of the issue of the Negro's place in postwar life would be, as a consequence of military exigencies, "one tremendous chapter of accidents, instead of a carefully considered and wisely prepared measure of government."[1] She understood better than most Americans how important a wise plan would be, for her personal experience on a St. Simon's Island plantation in the 1830's had served not only to deepen her hatred of slavery but also to inform her of the desperate needs of the people emerging from bondage.

The American Civil War was a typical nineteenth-century conflict in that it swept relentlessly toward political liberty. But if emancipation was decreed by the war, its course remained without concerted Federal direction. This was true despite the consistent pressure of interested people who went promptly to work, as soon as the Preliminary Emancipation Proclamation was announced, to promote a systematic approach to the great social question of the day. What place would the emancipated slave assume in the United States after the war was over? The dearest hopes of the friends of the Negro race misfired, as often as not, through lack of a coordinated plan conceived early enough to become an effective pattern for postwar reconstruction. The ambiv-

---

[1] Frances Anne Kemble, *Journal of a Residence on a Georgian Plantation in 1838–1839* (London, 1863), p. 423.

alence of the early steps toward liberty and the use of Negro troops illustrates this confusion, but in no question was the ambiguity of purpose more apparent than in the goal of making the freedman a freeholder on his native soil. Even at Port Royal, where the opportunity to win this goal was the greatest, where it first appeared, and the only place where it was at last in any measure achieved, the story is confused not only by amazingly out-of-phase operations of executive and legislative authority but also by sad conflicts in the ranks of the Negroes' best friends. The legal foundation that buttressed Negro landownership, strangely enough, was inspired not so much by radical pressures as by the simple requirements of war.

How certain fortunate freedmen at Port Royal eventually came to inherit their masters' domains is a tortuous story, and its ultimate origin lies, surprisingly enough, in the passage of a law that predated the occupation of the islands. On August 6, 1861, an Act of Congress levied a direct tax upon each and every state to raise revenue for the prosecution of the war. South Carolina was assessed a tax of $363,570.66, but the terms of the law made no provision for the collection of the funds within the insurrectionary states.[2] An Act of June 7, 1862, supplemented the previous legislation by lining out how the tax should be raised in states where the civil authority of the United States government was "obstructed." The procedure was simple enough. The President was authorized to appoint tax commissioners for each of these states as soon as the military authority was established in any portion of the state. These commissioners were to determine according to the property evaluation of 1861 the proportion of the state tax owed by each estate within the Federal lines, give sixty days' notice of the delinquent tax, and then offer the land for public sale to the highest bidder. A 50 per cent penalty for nonpayment was added to the amount of the tax in each case, and the land was not to be released for less than the sum of the tax plus the penalty.

[2] *United States Statutes*, XII, 294–295.

The properties were to be sold in lots not exceeding 320 acres, to "loyal citizens" or servicemen who had the privilege of paying one-quarter down and taking three years to pay. The certificate of sale the commissioners could offer conveyed a title in fee simple.[3]

Written in the guise of a tax law, the Act of June 7, 1862, was in its practical effect a measure of confiscation exceeding in its alienation of property even the Second Confiscation Act, passed later in the same year, whereby property could be seized for treason, but only during the lifetime of the owner.[4]

However satisfactory the confiscatory aspects of the June 7 law were to the radical missionaries, full of anger at the absent rebels, it was difficult for them to see how the law as it stood could serve the interests of *Negroes*. The provision that the lands were to be sold in lots so large as 320 acres was in itself a prohibiting factor, and the competition at an open sale would all but exclude the impecunious freedmen. There was no assurance whatever that the prospective purchasers would have the interests of the laborers in mind. It was therefore with some trepidation that the Gideonites saw the arrival of three tax commissioners at Beaufort in late October of 1862.[5] The interpretation these men placed on their instructions would be of great consequence to the Port Royal experiment.

A closer acquaintance with the commissioners partially reassured Captain Hooper, who wrote to Edward Atkinson that they were "nearly, if not quite all Southern men, and yet extreme emancipationists, and very bitter against the slave-holding aristo-

[3] *Ibid.*, pp. 422–426.

[4] See James G. Randall, *Constitutional Problems Under Lincoln* (New York, 1926), p. 320. The surplus above the tax and penalty was also turned into the U.S. Treasury. It will be recalled that pressure from President Lincoln caused the bill of attainder feature to be dropped from the July 17, 1862, Confiscation Act. See Basler (ed.), *Lincoln*, V, 328–331, especially the note on p. 329.

[5] Towne MS diary, October 30, 1862; Pearson (ed.), *Letters*, p. 109.

crats who have brought on the war."[6] The commissioners had good antislavery credentials. The most colorful member was Dr. William Henry Brisbane, a native son of South Carolina who had abandoned his state in the 1830's on a point of freedom of speech, moving to Ohio. After a conversion to emancipationism he had returned, bought back his slaves, and carried them North to freedom. A second member, Judge Abram D. Smith of Wisconsin, had gained friendly notice with abolitionists by a decision that the Fugitive Slave Law was unconstitutional. The third member, Dr. William E. Wording, was a less colorful man who fell from the beginning under the influence of Brisbane and acted with him in all the business of the commission.[7]

They lost no time but immediately looked up the town records and ascertained that all of St. Helena Parish and most of St. Luke's were within the Federal lines. They began proceedings.[8] The vehicles for the advertisement of the land sales were two small weeklies that had been launched in the Department in the summer and fall of 1862. The Port Royal *New South* catered largely to military affairs and circulated primarily among the soldiers and officers at the post. Adam Badeau was the first editor, and to him goes the credit for originating the term "New South," which enjoyed such large currency in the postreconstruction years. The *Free South*, published at Beaufort, was at the beginning under the auspices of the tax commissioners themselves. Reporting freedmen's affairs at length, as well as military events, the paper was probably launched to provide an organ for advertising the sales,

[6] Edward Hooper to [Edward Atkinson], n.d., but probably November, 1862, Atkinson MSS.

[7] Billington (ed.), *Forten*, pp. 177–178; Allen MS diary, January 17, 1864, p. 98, typescript copy; Minutes of the U.S. Direct Tax Commission for South Carolina, Treasury Department Archives. Wording almost always voted with Brisbane, the chairman of the commission. See also Boston *Commonwealth*, March 18, 1864.

[8] Report of the Direct Tax Commissioners, January 1, 1863, *Senate Executive Documents*, No. 26, 37th Congress, 3rd session, serial 1149. The estates are listed in the *New South*, January 31, 1863.

in conformity with the law. The early issues demonstrated that the commission would be likely to agree with the missionaries in residence.[9] Mansfield French wrote, "We trust the paper will be a powerful organ for freedom." The estates to be sold, with the names of the former owners, were listed and described. The sales were set for February 11, 1863.[10]

The consternation of the missionaries was understandable. Just as the social experiment was demonstrating possibilities of success, its foundation was about to be destroyed. Although there were solid accomplishments, pridefully noted, few evangels wanted a final verdict to rest upon the record as it stood in 1863. The educational work had been the most successful branch of the experiment. Approximately 2,500 children were being taught in the department, and many more adults were gaining a rudimentary English education through formally organized classes or by private arrangement with the generous teachers.[11]

Unfortunately, however, the agricultural and industrial wing of the experiment was at best inconclusive. The first year's work had certainly shown that the Negroes were capable of supporting themselves from the soil. Labor statistics compiled in September of 1862 indicate that on the principal islands of Hilton Head, Port Royal, and St. Helena, 3,817 "effective" laborers had planted 6,444 acres of corn and 1,407 acres of potatoes.[12] This was thought to be sufficient to feed the population. That supplies for the Ne-

[9] Richard H. Edmonds, *Facts about the South*, pamphlet (Baltimore, 1894), p. 1. Badeau was shortly succeeded by Joseph Sears as editor of the small journal; E. W. Hooper to [Edward Atkinson], n.d., probably early November, 1862, Atkinson MSS.

[10] Mansfield French to Governor Andrew, November 22, 1862, Andrew MSS; Edward Hooper to [Edward Atkinson], n.d., probably early November, 1862.

[11] Towne MS diary, December 31, 1862.

[12] Port Royal *New South*, September 6, 1862. Pierce gives the figure 4,429 as the number of workers in his "The Freedmen at Port Royal," *Atlantic Monthly*, XII (September, 1863), 299. He probably includes the Negroes evacuated from Edisto.

groes had to be rationed again in the spring was owing to Army depredations and requisitions and to the abandonment of the crops put in on Edisto, not to lack of planning or work. The grander aim, however, of the Olmsted-Atkinson-Philbrick school, to prove that free labor could grow more cotton more cheaply than slave labor, was far from having been demonstrated.

Nobody could claim that the 1862 cotton crop had been even a moderate success. Only 3,384 acres had been planted on the islands named above, and the ginned product weighed, at the highest estimate, only 90,000 pounds, giving an average of less than 26 pounds of lint cotton per acre. Even though long-staple cotton never produced per acre the weight a short-staple producer could expect, this was an appallingly low yield. Eighteen years of ante-bellum cotton planting on an Edisto Island plantation had given an average lint cotton yield of 137 pounds per acre.[13]

The result was a heavy disappointment to the planter missionaries, but they were well aware that the outcome of the crop was not a definitive commentary on the industry of the labor force. The two-month delay in planting had laid a good part of the crop open to the ravages of cutworm, caterpillar, and frost. The good seed, the essence of numberless years of careful selection, had been lost as a result of ginning the 1861 crop in New York; it was axiomatic that the selection of seed was one of the most important factors in long-staple cotton success. The Negroes had had small inducement to faithful husbandry. The activities of the first cot-

[13] See the *New South*, September 6, 1862; Pierce estimated that the crop turned out 65,000 pounds, but he probably made the estimate before the crop was all in. See his "Freedmen at Port Royal," p. 299. I have used Edward Hooper's estimate, in his letter to William Gannett, October 25, 1864, Gannett MSS. He was in the best position to know the final result. For ante-bellum expectations on long-staple cotton, see Lewis Cecil Gray, *History of Agriculture in the Southern United States to 1860* (Washington, 1933), II, 737. One year on St. Helena before the war, the average yield was 130 pounds per acre. See William Allen MS diary, February 29, 1864, p. 141, typescript copy.

ton agents, the uncertainty of pay, and the arbitrary and erratic course pursued on Negro conscription had done nothing to establish confidence in the Northerners. Many of the most enterprising workers had gone to the army posts, where pay was better and more certain. Most people on the spot understood these matters very well, and few made such acid comments as Arthur Sumner's, that "the caterpillar got into the cotton; and the Negroes didn't." Edward Philbrick said of the people that it was "wonderful how much they have done and in what an excellent state they are, under these discouraging circumstances."[14]

The real cause for concern as Philbrick and others saw it was that "the Government will look too much to the material results of the year's occupation for the success of free labor among the slaves."[15] If this should be the unhappy result, the gloomy prognostications of disaffected abolitionists that the Port Royalists would do more harm than good would, after all, be clothed in the substance of reality.

Fortunately, there was a ready means of obscuring the fact that the government had lost, in the first year's undertaking, somewhere between $50,000 and $75,000.[16] When the House of Representatives became inquisitive about "the amount expended . . . in the employment and sustenance of slaves in disloyal states" and instructed Secretary Chase to produce the figures, he calmly lumped the 1862 return with that of the great planter's crop of 1861 and came up with $501,278.76 to the credit of the Port Royal enterprise. Chase said blandly that he welcomed the opportunity "of rectifying false impressions, industriously propagated that the collection of cotton and the care of plantations and laborers on the

[14] Arthur Sumner to Nina Hartshorn, November 22, 1862, Arthur Sumner MSS; Pearson (ed.), *Letters*, p. 99.

[15] *Ibid.*, p. 98.

[16] E. W. Hooper to William C. Gannett, October 25, 1864, Gannett MSS. Hooper reports that the crop sold for less than $1.00 per pound, which was low considering the scarcity of cotton.

sea islands of South Carolina had been attended with great cost to the government."[17] Other published accounts of the year's work followed Chase's formula. Edward Atkinson, in an open letter to English friends of the Port Royal movement, said the enterprise had raised "sufficient cotton to pay expenses," and the New York Freedmen's Aid Society followed Chase's figures exactly in its statement of income. The method of accounting was certainly deficient from the standpoint of business, but the legerdemain was not without merit in the sense of strict justice. Without the aid of the Negroes the bumper 1861 crop could not have been collected, and they had been woefully underpaid and abused for their pains.[18] But the disappointment over the 1862 crop was keen indeed, even for those who knew very well how to account for it. The missionaries did not like the prospect of giving up the government's free-labor experiment in favor of assorted private speculators before it had a fair chance to succeed.

There was also reason to believe that the Port Royal area was becoming, in early 1863, just such a showcase for freedom as its originators had envisioned; it was gaining, through publicity, an opportunity to influence public policy. In January the Emancipation League of Boston, a radical group especially organized to advance emancipation as a major war aim, had sent a questionnaire to officials and teachers on the islands and had published the findings in a pamphlet for popular distribution. Captain Edward Hooper had the chance to testify that the freedmen "would readily become industrious and productive laborers" under any fair

[17] *House Executive Documents*, No. 72, 37th Congress, 3rd session, serial 1163, pp. 1–3.
[18] Edward Atkinson to the Reverend John Curwen, May 18, 1863, in *The Freed-Man's Aid Society* [n.d., n.p.], pamphlet in the Edward Atkinson MSS; *Annual Report of the New York National Freedmen's Aid Society of New York, with a Sketch of its Early History* (New York, 1866). White labor, including cotton agents, collectors, and superintendents, was paid $82,747.70, while colored labor received only $34,527.21. *House Exec. Docs.*, No. 72, 37th Congress, 3rd session, p. 2. The figures are given here for the period from February, 1862, to January, 1863.

system of employment and that it was the conclusion of teachers in the field that Negro children learned their letters "as quickly as white children." Hooper soothed Northern nerves about two old bugbears. No, the Negroes were not of a mind to emigrate to the *North*, nor was there any detectable spirit of revenge against their old masters. While entering a reservation that the Negroes' religion was revealed "in faith, rather than practice," leaving them with "the common habit of lying and stealing," Hooper thought that freedom and a diffusion of "the 'pernicious doctrines' of liberal Christianity" would promptly remedy these faults. It is not probable that Hooper anticipated a mass flocking to the Unitarian standard, but rather that he expected Yankee homilies on thrift and honesty to bear early fruit.[19]

But the land sales seemed about to dash an even more promising opportunity for Port Royal to influence national policy. From the time the Preliminary Emancipation Proclamation was announced, a number of Northeastern friends of the Port Royal movement had seen the need for a more systematic approach to emancipation. Negroes were by this time collecting in every sector occupied by Federal troops, and their numbers were expected to increase rapidly after the announcement of the Emancipation Proclamation. No regular pattern for meeting the situation had yet evolved. As early as November 15, 1862, F. W. Bird, a radical Massachusetts Republican, was urging Governor Andrew to see what could be done toward getting a Bureau of Emancipation established. Soon afterward, another Bay State radical of John Brown fame was asking that a commission be formed to study the large literature that had accumulated in Europe "concerning

[19] *Facts Concerning the Freedmen, Their Capacity and Their Destiny, Collected and Published by the Emancipation League* (Boston, 1863), p. 4. Richard Soule testified grumpily that "White laborers would have earned more in the same time. The pay of twenty-five cents a day is really for about five hours' work." *Ibid.*, p. 11. For the aims of the Emancipation League, see Edith Ellen Ware, "Political Opinion in Massachusetts During the Civil War and Reconstruction," in Columbia University *Studies in History, Economics, and Public Law*, LXXIV (New York, 1916), 93.

negro labor in slavery and in freedom. . . ." Frank Sanborn thought that "without some such proposition, we shall approach the matter with great ignorance, and shall certainly make great mistakes." Andrew appealed to Charles Sumner to work for the establishment of a commission to study "the main question—to which all others are tributary . . . how to establish . . . just and normal relations between the labor of so many poor men without capital and so much capital needing laborers to render it productive." Andrew referred Sumner to a recent visit of Dr. LeBaron Russell, a prominent officer of the Boston Educational Commission, to investigate the condition of the freedmen in the Fortress Monroe area. He wished a committee could be sent to Port Royal to study the situation there. Andrew thought an executive committee would be "more efficacious than a legislative one."[20] In the meantime James Miller McKim was pressing Sumner in the same direction, the only difference between his plan and Andrew's being that he thought the committee should be made up of congressmen, for the measures that must at last be taken would be "largely of a legislative character. It seems to me," he wrote, "that the decencies of legislation, in a matter so important, demand official inquiry." Sumner sounded Secretaries Chase and Stanton. Chase seemed hesitant, but the Secretary of War promised his support and, favoring an executive committee, promised to organize it at once.[21] The Freedmen's Inquiry Commission, which was responsible for the report that had been aptly labeled "The Blueprint for Radical Reconstruction," was thus formed on March 16, 1863. It had authority "to investigate the condition of the colored population emancipated by acts of Congress and the President's proclamation of January 1, 1863, and to report what measures will best contribute to their protection and improvement, so that they may

[20] F. W. Bird to Andrew, November 15, 1862, Andrew MSS; Frank Sanborn to John Andrew, December 8, 1862; John Andrew to Charles Sumner, December 10, 1862, and December 25, 1862, Sumner MSS.

[21] McKim to Sumner, December 24, 1862, Sumner MSS; William Morris Davis to J. Miller McKim, December 23, 1862, McKim MSS.

protect and defend themselves; and also how they can be most usefully employed in the service of the Government for the suppression of the rebellion."[22]

In these instructions Stanton fingered the dual goals which accounted for the haphazard approach to all questions related to the full liberation of the Negro that Miss Kemble had predicted. He wanted to know, essentially, how the nation could help the black man help himself, and how the black man could help the nation survive. The logic of the historical situation demanded the two goals, and perhaps most thinking Americans could have agreed upon the merits of both; certainly good abolitionists knew that the second aspiration could serve to commit the nation to the first. But men have far more trouble in establishing an ordering of values than in agreeing upon what things are good and right. At last the nation ranked the second good above the first commitment, and the failure of Reconstruction to provide the freedmen with real opportunities for education and economic freedom was the final result. It was the great moral failure of the nation.

In the meantime Stanton's idea of what had to be learned about the emancipated people took hold, and he selected men for the Freedmen's Inquiry Commission who would view the problem with sympathy. Robert Dale Owen, Samuel Gridley Howe, and Colonel James McKaye were all antislavery men.[23] Their plans and recommendations would be given careful consideration by radical Republican congressmen and at the same time strengthen the hands of these politicians in planning for the Negro and for the reconstruction of the Southern economy. It was clear that the Port Royal Negro community would be one of the most significant areas of investigation and that it might in time profit from the recommendations of the Commission. The complete turning over of the estates to private ownership could very possibly wreck

[22] John G. Sproat, "Blueprint for Radical Reconstruction," *Journal of Southern History*, XXIII (February, 1957), 25; *OR*, III, iii, 73.

[23] Both Howe and McKaye were involved in prewar abolition activities. See Sproat, "Blueprint," p. 34.

both the opportunity and the probable efficacious results of the inquiry.

In addition to these reasons for objecting to the prompt sale of the lands, the missionaries had private and perhaps only half-recognized motives for resisting a change. By spring of 1863 the town of Beaufort and the outlying plantations had begun to seem a little bit like home to the immigrant Yankee population. The whole enterprise was unmistakably settling in, and after emancipation South Carolina did not seem a bad place in which to live. Riding through the sun-dappled shade of the live-oak forests, or driving makeshift buggies over the sandy roads and through the vast open cotton fields, or picnicking on the palmetto-lined shores of Hunting Island, the Northerners began to feel the infinite attractions of a beautiful and languorous, if admittedly dangerous, climate. The colored people themselves, if dependent, were grateful, and if frequently provoking, were also endearing; caring for their needs and teaching them gave as their daily boon a deeply rewarding sense of purpose. For those who had survived the harassments of the first year a thousand frustrations could not offset the sense of well-being that came with doing good. They could exult with their wittiest member, "I am well and happy. I have a fine school of little niggers, whom I love well and cheerily. I have a delightful house-mate, . . . neighbors enough; a good train of vassals; (meaning, cook, boy, hostler, and huntsman) a very fine horse, all to myself; good health (that is, so so), and a clear sense of duty toward all mankind." If there was in this some self-conscious jesting about his role in life, Arthur Sumner's satisfaction was evident. All told, Sumner thought, "This is a great time to live in! . . . I am filled with the heartiest satisfaction at the close of each day's work."[24]

A letter from William Gannett affords the strongest sign that the roots were going down. He wrote, "The wives are multiply-

[24] Arthur Sumner to Joseph Clark, January 23, 1863, Arthur Sumner MSS.

ing on St. Helena. . . . Brave youth,—in these times! One man has
brought his sister and established her as the beauty of the island;
one his mother; and one an older sister, a perfect New England
housekeeper, who makes his home the paradise of mince pies and
family bread." By early 1863 the first Gideonite baby was already
expected. In March, when the yellow jessamine and the blossoms
of flowering fruit trees suffused the spring air with sweetness,
General Saxton took Miss Matilda Thompson, the afore-acknowl-
edged "beauty of the island," down the aisle of old St. Helena
Church in Beaufort. Almost before the sensation excited by the
romantic match had subsided, Miss Nelly Winsor accepted the
hand of Josiah Fairfield, a neighboring superintendent.[25] These
were but the first of the missionary matches. The deepest associations of family-building with time and place were forming in the
transplanted community.

But the main objection to the land sales continued to be the fact
that the future security of the plantation Negroes was in danger.
Most missionaries felt that the freedmen were entitled to some
preference in the disposition of the lands whereon they had toiled
so long without recompense. As early as February 10, 1862, Rufus
Saxton had expressed his opinion that "it would be well to parcel
out the fertile lands of these islands among the different families
in lots large enough for their subsistence." This was also the recom-
mendation of Commissioner A. D. Smith, and it was warmly seconded by Secretary Chase.[26] All through the winter the friends
of Port Royal had been at work to get a modification in the law
making a provision for the Negroes, but as the date of the sale

[25] Pearson (ed.), *Letters*, pp. 115–116. Laura Towne records in her
manuscript diary the birth of a child to Mr. and Mrs. George Wells on
August 27, 1863, the Saxton–Thompson wedding on March 11, 1863, and
the Fairfield–Winsor wedding on May 7, 1863. See Billington (ed.), *Forten*,
entry for March 10, 1863, p. 173, for the flowers of March.

[26] Saxton to Mansfield French, February 10, 1862, in *New York Times*,
March 2, 1862; Report of the Direct Tax Commissioners of South Carolina,
Senate Executive Documents, No. 26, 37th Congress, serial 1149.

drew near it began to appear that Congressional action, if it should come, might be too late.[27]

One day in late January, when General Saxton was dining at The Oaks and expressing his apprehension about the impending sales, the resourceful Laura Towne deftly suggested that General Hunter might intervene. As Supreme Commander in the Department, he could halt the sales on grounds of military necessity. Saxton pounced upon the idea eagerly and found the intrepid Hunter more than willing to cooperate. On February 7 Hunter took the position that the needs of the army and the colored population required the retention of the land within the lines, pointed to the Congressional "legislation now pending," and by a General Order stopped the sales until the views of the government could fully be known in the Department.[28]

Most of the missionaries heard this news with relief, and when the word reached Port Royal that Congress had on February 6 amended the Tax Law and empowered the President to instruct the tax commissioners to bid off and reserve certain lands for government use and charitable purposes, there was general jubilation.[29]

The satisfaction was not universal, however. Edward Philbrick and a group of superintendents who had associated closely with him had already devised an alternate plan that seemed on the point of being blocked by the new development. Conceived originally as a defensive action, the Philbrick plan had become more and

[27] Pearson (ed.), *Letters*, p. 147; John Murray Forbes to Saxton, January 16, 1863, copy, and Forbes to Charles Sumner, January 17, 1863, Sumner MSS; Minutes of the General Committee of the New England Freedmen's Aid Society, December 4, 1862, and January 1, 1863. The records form a part of the Sturgis-Hooper Papers in the Massachusetts Historical Society.

[28] Holland (ed.), *Towne*, p. 103; Beaufort, *Free South*, February 14, 1863. The news of Hunter's intention to suspend the sales was known by the second of February. See Towne MS diary, February 2, 1863.

[29] Holland (ed.), *Towne*, p. 103; *United States Statutes*, XII, 640.

more attractive. As the ablest businessman on the islands, Philbrick had shown, despite the multitude of difficulties, a small but perceptible margin of profit on his crop; he had concluded that the greatest problems he had encountered had resulted directly or indirectly from government control. The worst drawback had been the slow pay. He was convinced that there would be many advantages to private ownership if there were some assurance that the new owners would not be selfishly motivated.[30] Philbrick had accordingly persuaded John Murray Forbes and fourteen other businessmen, all but one of them Bostonians, to join him in a plan to buy a large number of plantations. The purpose would be to continue the free-labor experiment under private auspices. The final arrangements provided that Philbrick should buy the land in his name and assume full responsibility for its management. The subscribers were to be entitled to 6 per cent interest. Philbrick would receive one-fourth of the net profits after the deduction of the interest, was to be liable for all losses, and would have no right to call upon the subscribers for further contributions. The net proceeds were to be divided pro rata at the time the business was closed; no member could withdraw his funds until such time as Philbrick gave up its management.[31]

John Murray Forbes, who organized the combination, thought that, although there should be provision for the Negroes to get homesteads, it would be an advantage to them to have "land around them owned by individuals, who can pay them wages and furnish supplies without the intervention of an U.S. Quartermaster." He explained to General Saxton that he was not expecting to make a profit from the concern but felt that the danger of "speculators" could best be averted by such "combinations of liberal men at the North, whose chief concern would be to give

[30] Pearson (ed.), *Letters*, pp. 117–118, 135; E. S. Philbrick to Dr. LeBaron Russell, June 15, 1863, Atkinson MSS; Towne MS diary, February 2, 1863.

[31] Pearson (ed.), *Letters*, p. 140, note on pp. 140–141.

the experiment a fair trial under the system of both free labor and the stimulus of individual interest." Philbrick planned to use a number of "first-rate men among the superintendents" to carry on the work.[32] These superintendents were by the terms eventually determined upon to receive one-half the net proceeds of the crop after the deduction of the necessary costs of operation.[33]

Having matured a plan of action, and being well aware that the crucial weeks for beginning work on the new crop were passing, Philbrick and his associates were frustrated when the sale was suspended.[34] They promptly petitioned that it be resumed. In the meantime President Lincoln had made Generals Saxton and Hunter a part of a commission of five, including the three tax commissioners, to determine the size and location of the lands to be reserved for government use and for "charitable, Educational or police purposes." A significant part of the land that the commission reserved was for the purpose of making provision for the Negroes the following year.[35] After taking the action, the commission was free to proceed with the sales.

On March 9, 1863, exactly one year after the arrival of the Gideonites at Beaufort, the first land sales took place. The office of the commissioners was crowded with superintendents, teachers, and army sutlers, but everyone was relieved to observe that there were no suspicious Southern agents or unsavory land sharks. Of the 76,775 acres put up for sale, the commissioners struck off to the government by far the greater part, 60,296 acres. Individuals

[32] J. M. Forbes to Charles Sumner, January 17, 1863, and Forbes to Saxton, January 16, 1863, a copy, in the Charles Sumner MSS; Pearson (ed.), *Letters,* p. 118.

[33] Contract between Philbrick and William C. Gannett, January 1, 1863, Box XXXVIII, Gannett MSS. The contract was drawn up and signed June 19, 1863, but predated to the first of the year.

[34] Towne MS diary, February 3, 1863.

[35] Abraham Lincoln to David Hunter, Rufus Saxton, and the Direct Tax Commissioners, February 10, 1863, Basler (ed.), *Lincoln,* VI, 98; Pearson (ed.), *Letters,* p. 171.

bought 16,479 acres at an average price of $1.00 per acre, a ridiculously low figure and a distinct comment upon the lack of competition and, most probably, the lack of faith in the legality of the sale.[36] Several plantations, about 2,000 acres of land, were purchased cooperatively by the Negroes, who by pooling their small savings were able to preserve their right to live and work on their own places. Presumably, for purposes of the sale, the freedmen were regarded as "citizens," as their right to buy does not appear to have been questioned.[37] Some land went to people with no connection with the missionary work, but the largest unit of land passing into private ownership went to Philbrick for the Boston joint-stock company. For a piddling $7,000 the company bought eleven fine cotton plantations, comprising 8,000 acres, and leased two others from the government, thus gaining possession of one-third of St. Helena Island and indirect control over nearly a thousand people who lived upon the land.[38]

Philbrick and the superintendents who joined him in the new private enterprise wing of the experiment did not escape charges of self-interest. Reuben Tomlinson referred sarcastically to "E. S. Philbrick, 'the Philanthropist,' " who had "bought thirteen plantations" in order to work them "for his own profit." Laura Towne was also slightly skeptical, and recorded thoughtfully and deliberately in her diary that Philbrick "says he will sell again to the people as soon as he finds it for their interest. He says he will sell

[36] Beaufort *Free South*, March 11, 1864. The figures given as the average sale price vary from 90 cents to $1.25 per acre. William Gannett stated that the lands brought approximately $1.00 per acre. See William H. Pease, "Three Years among the Freedmen: William C. Gannett and the Port Royal Experiment," *Journal of Negro History*, XLII (April, 1957), 106–107.

[37] *First Annual Report of the Boston Educational Commission, May, 1863* (Boston, 1863), p. 9.

[38] Pearson (ed.), *Letters*, p. 172; *First Annual Report of the Educational Commission*, p. 8; E[dward] A[tkinson] in the *Freedmen's Record*, I (May, 1865), 85.

at cost."[39] For many of his fellows Philbrick was, with his brisk manners and lack of sentiment, a missionary they would never understand. One thing was certain; whatever he did would be closely watched.

Toward Philbrick and his enterprise Edward Pierce was far more charitable. He wrote of the young engineer that, "combining a fine humanity with honest sagacity and close calculation, no man is so well fitted to try the experiment." Perhaps Pierce had forgotten his former opinion that "not even the best of men . . . should be put in a position where there would be a conflict between his humanity and his self-interest. . . ."[40] From this period onward, on part of the island territory, the free-labor experiment would be carried forward on terms more properly comparable to those of the old masters, with the necessity to balance the books a constant factor. Only time could tell if it was possible to marry philanthropy to the profit motive; whether, in short, "a fine humanity" could long remain on genial terms with "close calculation."

[39] Reuben Tomlinson to James Miller McKim, March 19, 1863, McKim MSS; Holland (ed.), *Towne*, pp. 101, 106–107. It also seems to have been Atkinson's understanding that Philbrick intended to sell "a large portion" of the land to the Negroes at cost. *First Annual Report of the Educational Commission*, p. 9.

[40] Pierce, "The Freedmen at Port Royal," p. 308.

eight ❈ THE CORNERSTONES
OF CIVIL SOCIETY

AFTER THE TAX SALE OF 1863 AND THE TRANSFER OF PART OF THE
Port Royal plantations into private ownership, the fundamentally
differing goals among Gideon's Band shifted abruptly into sharper
focus. Outside the Boston group, who looked to Philbrick and
Edward Atkinson for leadership, the free-labor thesis was little
emphasized. With large numbers of the missionaries cotton-
growing had always run a very poor second to preaching moral
habits, faithful domestic life, and cleanliness; many of these men
were miserable failures as planters. "The great work," declared
W. J. Richardson, the Beaufort representative of the American
Missionary Association, "is to *unlearn* them and learn them *from*,
the vices, habits and associations of their former lives." This was
"the tug and toil" of the mission and could not be left undone if
the evangels were to succeed in their effort to "elevate this people."[1] The deeply religious nature of the freedmen seemed to
afford the best foundation for advancing such goals, and there was
much sermonizing. The preaching missionaries were inclined to
dwell upon the debt society owed the Negroes because of their
accumulated wrongs as slaves, while their detractors made spurious comments about their sentimental attitudes. The representative figures among them wanted the freedmen to become
freeholders at the earliest possible moment, either by gift from

---

[1] W. J. Richardson to George Whipple, May 21, 1864, uncatalogued
box labeled "1862—A–J," AMA MSS.

the government or at minimal cost. They believed the Negro was entitled to considerable assistance on the road to a free and independent status. Paradoxical though it may appear, the preaching evangels frequently espoused the most radical program for the freedmen.

Mansfield French stated clearly the goals of these missionaries, who were little influenced by the relatively recently accepted laissez-faire notions. French stated his credo at a date earlier than many missionaries would have followed him. It was inspired by religion, not economics. "God's programme," he wrote, "involves *freedom in its largest sense—Free soil, free schools,—free ballot boxes, free representation in state and national*" governments. He saw that all these things must come and that "No power on earth save a *wicked* one can prevent it." But the people would need help. They required "teachers, helpers, men who can grasp the destiny and mission of this people. Men who are not ashamed to bear the cross of the black man. Men who can quarry in the mountains, and bring the tall cedars from the forests, are fitted for this work." Men must have "heart power" as well as "brain power."[2] This was French's Biblical lyricism at its best, and there was more than a grain of truth in what he thought the circumstances required at Port Royal.

As we shall see, the Philbrick school thought that such assistance was not only unnecessary but also harmful. Although these differences were far from clean-cut among the groups, the majority of those believing in maximum assistance came from the New York National Freedmen's Aid Society, which had been from its inception an offshoot of the American Missionary Association. The latter organization had also sent its own representatives directly into the field by 1863, and these two groups comprised a strong evangelical strain that frequently came into conflict with the

---

[2] Mansfield French to Simeon Jocelyn and George Whipple, December 2, 1863, in uncatalogued box labeled "1862—A–J," AMA MSS.

business-minded Boston superintendents.[3] The major problem for the preaching missionaries was a disease endemic to organized religion—sectarian disputes. Sometimes they quarreled ignominiously among themselves as they took sides in the freedmen's church disputes, each attempting to spread his own sect or to enlarge his following.[4] A kindly gentleman who joined the work under the misapprehension that "he should find peace and zeal down here—a band of fellow workers living in harmony and working with combined effort," confessed to Laura Towne that he was sadly disappointed. He had found friction in every quarter—military, religious, and political.[5] The representatives of the Pennsylvania Freedmen's Aid Society are more difficult to categorize. Such outstanding individualists as Reuben Tomlinson, Laura Towne, and James Thompson could be relied upon to oppose at once the incipient sectarianism of the preaching missionaries, as well as Philbrick's restricted business point of view.

There were fewer ministers among the Bostonians, and of those

[3] Mansfield French, though an officer in the New York National Freedmen's Aid Society, made reports from the beginning of the Port Royal work to George Whipple, an officer of the AMA. See French to Whipple, March 8, 1863, in uncatalogued box labeled "1862–A–J," AMA MSS. Two letters of December 12 and 28, 1863, from W. J. Richardson to George Whipple, make it clear that the separate AMA work was by then well organized. See box labeled "Letters from South Carolina," AMA MSS.

[4] W. J. Richardson's letters of the spring of 1864 reveal a struggle between a group of "Free-Will" or open-communion Baptists, sponsored by Richardson, and the Reverend Dr. Solomon Peck, who led the "Old" or "closed Communion" Baptists. The focus of the trouble was control of a "Praise House," but it also involved the character of the Negro elder who was leading Richardson's secession movement. See Richardson to Whipple, March 25, and April 5 and 11, in box labeled "Letters from South Carolina, 1862–1865," AMA MSS. Another dispute involving use of a church building is recorded in Holland (ed.), *Towne*, pp. 118–119; see further Towne diary February 7 and March 14, 1864; see also W. J. Eaton to Whipple, July 28, 1864, in "Letters from S. C.," AMA MSS.

[5] Towne diary, March 18, 1864.

few not many actually took positions as preachers to the people; rather, they went directly into plantation work. With a preponderance of handsomely educated Unitarians among them, they felt a species of contempt for such poor preachers as gave "stones, not bread," as they said, by way of a Sunday sermon to the people.[6] What was perhaps worse, the enthusiasm of the fervent brethren was embarrassing. Several years passed before Mrs. French's emotional behavior upon her arrival at Hilton Head was forgotten, and her published account of the Port Royal mission was referred to by one of Philbrick's employees as "one of the most ridiculous books I ever looked into." Captain Edward Hooper was bitter in his criticism of "hungry missionaries" who took salary from the societies sending them, took pay, rations, and free house-rent from the government as superintendents, and then asked the Negroes of their churches for a thousand-dollar annual stipend for preaching.[7]

Sometimes such "hangers-on of Missionary Societies," sent to Port Royal because they were "fit for nothing else," got into worse trouble. Caught selling at a steep mark-up certain supplies earmarked for distribution to the freedmen at cost, and pocketing the difference, they were summarily packed out of the Department. Sometimes the embarrassment at these transactions dissolved into amusement. This was the case when missionary James A. McCrae was "condemned to walk up and down the Main Street in Beaufort for seven days with a placard hung to his neck—'I sold whiskey to a private soldier'—then to pay a fine of $500 or be imprisoned at hard labor for six months and finally to be sent out of the department."[8]

6 Harriet Ware's opinion, in letter of February 8, 1863, in Pearson (ed.), *Letters*, p. 153.

7 Allen MS diary, January 10, 1864, p. 88, typescript; Arthur Sumner to Nina Hartshorn, August 8, 1864, Arthur Sumner MSS. Of such ministers, Laura Towne wrote, "It is gouge, gouge, these people. White people asking for something all the time." Towne MS diary, October 18, 1863.

8 Allen MS diary, November 28, 1863, pp. 36–37, and March 27, 1864,

The Boston people referred indiscriminately to evangels who got into this sort of predicament as "one of the *French* set," by this means firmly attaching the most influential of their opponents to the largest cluster of rotten apples in the enterprise.[9] Thomas Howard, General Superintendent on Hilton Head Island, who had been sent out from Boston, characterized French unpleasantly as a hypocrite, "a man of rotund form, oily address, and assumption of authority" who could furnish "a good illustration for one of Dickens's Pecksniffs." Howard was understandably annoyed with French because he thought the preacher had attempted to trick him into employing the Reverend Mr. Hyde, a man already dismissed from the Department for having unduly watered the molasses for the freedmen's Emancipation Day celebration. French remained to the last an enigma; but all his enemies acknowledged that his manner of addressing the Negroes was superb. He was vastly influential.[10]

The friction between the evangelical and Unitarian persuasions found its grinding edge high in the councils of General Saxton, in the persons of Chaplain French and Captain Hooper. That there were a number of incompetent, dishonest, or at best extremely foolish missionaries sent into the Department is beyond question.[11] In his determination to root out these individuals, Hooper some-

---

p. 161, typescript copy. See a letter from Tomlinson to McKim, January 16, 1863, McKim MSS, for three superintendents discharged for fraud and cruelty.

[9] Allen MS diary, March 27, 1864, p. 161, typescript. The Boston people nicknamed French "Mendax." *Ibid.*, February 13, 1864, p. 126 of the typescript.

[10] "Charles Howard [MS] Family History," pp. 105–106.

[11] "It is very sad to have persons come from the north with the pretense of being *teachers* of *good* to this people, and then turn and serve the Devil themselves and seek to do all in their power to lead them *down to hell!*" W. J. Richardson to George Whipple, June 24, 1865. See also Carrie A. Hamblin to Mrs. E. A. Lane, April 29, 1865. These letters are in "Letters from South Carolina, 1862–1865," AMA MSS; see also Tomlinson to McKim, October 17, 1862, and January 16, 1863, McKim MSS.

times found French attempting to subvert his purpose, and the Chaplain became his "pet aversion." Captain Hooper undoubtedly scored a point in November of 1863, when General Saxton separated the regular teaching from religious instruction and ruled against ministers' taking on the superintendency of plantations. The evangelists, on their side, laid their troubles to the disproportionate influence of the Unitarians, who were too strong "to come into open conflict with . . . under the present state of things," but were best to be managed "in faith and prayer." W. J. Richardson of the American Missionary Association protested that "Brother Root," a fellow AMA representative who had been banished for fraud, "had not intended to do wrong in these things" but had merely "acted unwisely" in antagonizing the Unitarians.[12]

The growing factionalism was a straw in a wind that had nearly reached the dimensions of a gale already; the Bostonians were justifiably alarmed at the evidences all around of incompetence and denominational jealousy. They themselves could have used, nonetheless, a little more of the enthusiasm, patience, and wholehearted abolitionism that the best of the evangelicals had at command; a goodly stock of all these would be needed as the miniature social revolution on the islands entered its later stages. It would also be seen, at the end of the race, that the organized churches had the virtue of staying-power as well as a strong penchant for proselyting. But, for the time being, the special care taken by the New England Freedmen's Aid Society to select competent individuals for Port Royal had kept their ranks free of corrupt evangels and mediocrities. The Bostonians had sometimes been regarded as lukewarm in their antislavery convictions, but until Philbrick and his colleagues withdrew to operate on a free enterprise basis the charge of self-interest was not flung at them.

From that time forward, however, Philbrick's wages and man-

[12] Allen MS diary, January 10, 1864, p. 88, typescript; W. J. Richardson to S. S. Jocelyn, February 22, 1864, in "Letters from S. C., 1862–1865," AMA MSS; H. Hyde to George Whipple, March 6, 1863, and French to "Dear Brethren of the AMA," November 19, 1863, in box labeled "1862–A–J," AMA MSS; "Charles Howard [MS] Family History," pp. 105–106.

agement came under searching criticism from his fellows, some of whom felt that his philanthropy languished to the nutriment of his profits. In fairness to Philbrick and to those who wished "to try what private enterprise can do in this field," it must be said that they saw no conflict of interest. True believers in the laissez-faire principle, they understood that the path of enlightened self-interest was the surest way toward industrial development. "Negro labor has got to be employed, if at all," wrote Philbrick, "because it is *profitable*, and it has got to come into the market like every-thing else, subject to the supply and demand. . . ." Philanthropy could not protect it long, and Negro labor could "afford to *lose* some of the Methodism now bestowed upon it at Beaufort." These men recommended an early abandonment of large-scale assistance. "Let all the laws of labor, wages, competition, etc., come into play, —and the sooner will habits of responsibility, industry, self-dependence, and manliness be developed," wrote William Gannett. "Very little, very little, should be given them; now in their first moment of freedom is the time to influence their notion of it." Gannett believed it would be "*Most unwise and injurious*" to give the Negroes free lands, because doing so would remove the bene-fits accruing to the people from the struggle to obtain them.[13]

A corollary to the principle was that gifts of land or a too-rapid rise in wages would enable the Negroes, accustomed to a very low standard of living, to achieve their simple wants with a minimum of effort and would thus encourage idleness and improvidence. "You will remember," wrote Atkinson to Forbes, "that in all my cotton documents, I have pointed out the danger to the Negro, to be too high wages." Proponents of this stern doctrine were not without a bleak sympathy for those freedmen who would fall by the wayside in the rugged, competitive world. "I pity some of them very much," wrote Gannett, "for I see that nothing will rouse and maintain their energy but suffering."[14]

[13] E. S. Philbrick to LeBaron Russell, June 15, 1863, Atkinson MSS; Pearson (ed.), *Letters*, pp. 221, 148.

[14] Atkinson to [Forbes], August 30, 1865, Forbes MSS; Pearson (ed.), *Letters*, p. 148.

The ambiguities of the commercial-philanthropic venture were more readily apparent to those who stood outside the Philbrick concern than to those involved. William A. Park, who had given up being a Port Royal evangel after the first summer, wanted to know of his friend Gannett, "if you consider yourself now as a missionary or a raiser of cotton." He thought his friend was placing himself "in a situation where you will be very likely to be drawn into a business life, for I think the emancipation business must grow in a commercial character." History would verify young Park's intuition, but for the economic liberals at Port Royal there were no ambiguities. It was a compliment to the freedmen to be regarded as ready and able to fend for themselves. "Strike the fetters off at a blow and let them jump, or lie down, as they please, in the first impulse of freedom, and let them at once see the natural effects of jumping and lying down."[15]

After fifteen months of plantation experience, Philbrick had lost some of his original optimism about the *prompt* establishment of his labor theories and was ready to admit that it might be some years after the war before the agricultural output of the islands returned to its "former standard." But he felt that it would eventually do so and might even surpass ante-bellum production, "when the ordinary laws of trade and the competition of private enterprise shall be relieved from the restraints of martial law and the needs of an all-absorbing war."[16]

The labor system that had been inaugurated in late 1862 was based on the experience of the first year and was applied on all the plantations, both those owned by individuals and those held by the government. The Negroes themselves, it will be recalled, had forced Philbrick to an early abandonment of the "gang" system, and he believed that this accounted for his successful management of the first year's crop as compared to that of the missionaries who had stubbornly maintained the old system the first year. It had

[15] William E. Park to William Gannett, July 9, 1863, Gannett MSS; Pearson (ed.), *Letters*, p. 179.
[16] Philbrick to LeBaron Russell, June 15, 1863, Atkinson MSS.

been largely at Philbrick's insistence that a system based more completely on individual interest was adopted. The cotton lands on all plantations were allotted to the separate families on the basis of the amount they were likely to be able to cultivate successfully. The wages were paid by the day's work according to the daily "task" requirement of the old masters, which could usually be completed by an able and energetic hand before noon. Those who accomplished more were paid accordingly. The basic wage was twenty-five cents per day, admittedly low. The low pay served the purpose of securing faithful cultivation of the crop through the entire season; when the crop was in, the workers received two-and-a-half cents per pound for all the cotton they picked. This was considered high for picking, but it had the effect of providing a bonus on the total result.[17]

Individual families received an assignment of corn land in amounts corresponding to their needs, and they were expected to grow their own provision crops. A small tax paid in corn was collected from the freed people to support the livestock on the plantations and such superannuated Negroes as could not work. Draft animals and farm equipment were supplied by the government or the private owners. The government superintendents, and of course private owners, were empowered to turn people who would not cooperate off their places. Although frequently used as a threat, this power was seldom exercised. Those freedmen who preferred independent pursuits such as truck farming or fishing for the Hilton Head market were obliged to pay a rent of two dollars per month for their little houses and garden plots, which cost cotton hands nothing.[18]

[17] Pearson (ed.), *Letters*, text and note, p. 177; Philbrick to Russell, June 15, 1863, Atkinson MSS; Allen MS diary, January 14, 1864, pp. 94, 94a typescript; Gannett MS diary, March 17, 1863, Gannett MSS; Boston *Commonwealth*, December 4, 1863.

[18] Charles Nordhoff, *The Freedmen of South Carolina* (New York, 1863), p. 14; Allen MS diary, January 14, 1864, pp. 94–94a typescript; Boston *Commonwealth*, December 4, 1863.

In their complete devotion to King Cotton, the planter-missionaries were as loyal as ever the former slave-masters had been. This was the largest blind spot in the thinking of the Atkinson free-labor school. That many Negro farmers preferred to raise vegetables and fish for the soldiers in the camps and to gain more income by this means was in the strictest accord with the Manchestrian "laws" that these men were so fond of quoting. Frederick Law Olmsted, whose conclusions about Southern slavery were otherwise very influential with the Atkinson-Philbrick group, was himself convinced of the need for "more objects of industry, more varied enterprises . . ." in the South. On this point Edward Atkinson apparently abandoned Olmsted's reasoning; he argued that it was economically better for the free Negro laborer to stick to cotton and buy Western grains. That the light sandy island soil was eminently suitable to truck farming has been amply demonstrated by the recent agricultural history of the area.[19] Almost always, however, the superintendents objected that economic enterprises other than the cultivation of cotton and the essential provision crops were conducive to idle and thriftless habits.[20]

It is this exclusive preoccupation with cotton that has given

[19] Atkinson quoted Olmsted in an approving context in his "The Reign of King Cotton," in the *Atlantic Monthly*, VII (April, 1861), 462, but by 1865 he spoke for a concentration on cotton. See Atkinson in the *Freedmen's Record*, May, 1865, p. 85. Today truck produce is the most important agricultural enterprise for Sea Island farmers, and cotton is a vanished crop. For the transition see T. J. Woofter, Jr., *Black Yeomanry* (New York, 1930), pp. 116–117. "This region can be profitably occupied in the culture first of the great variety of early fruits vegetables, etc, which has been a large business around the cities of Savannah, Charleston and Norfolk, filling the semi-weekly steamers to New York on their return trips during the spring and early summer months." Saml H. Terry to S. P. Chace [sic], December 18, 1861, item 22, PRC.

[20] Philbrick wrote of one 'Siah's plan to seine for the market, "I don't believe it will do him any good to spend his time a-fishing. It has a sort of excitement, like gold-digging, which unfits a man for steady, plodding industry, witness Limus." Pearson (ed.), *Letters*, p. 221. Limus had previously been held up as a good example by Gannett.

most support to the idea that the planter-missionaries were pure economic imperialists, forerunners of an uglier breed of a later day. Their vision of the freed people as agricultural peasants devoted to a single-crop economy and educated to a taste for consumer goods supplied by Northern factories fulfills the classic pattern of tributary economies the world over. It is important to remember that at this early time there seemed nothing conspiratorial about this. Behold Harriet Ware on horseback going from cabin to cabin teaching the Negro women of Coffin Point the fine art of making bread with yeast—and wheat flour. Northern-milled flour, calico frocks, clocks, candles to read by, and thousands of bars of soap would "civilize" the imbruted slave and keep the Northern mills humming.[21] But what was there to be ashamed of in that?

The argument for the Negro as a consumer that J. Miller Mc-Kim had referred to as throwing "incidental light" on the question of emancipation, in the days before emancipation had become government policy, now became a thoroughly expounded topic. Charles Nordhoff, who explored the islands a year after McKim's visit, posited that "the day which sees the introduction on these islands of the itinerant Yankee peddlar will be an important one. If he is only moderately honest, and quick-witted, he will be a valuable helper in advancing civilization here."[22]

A pious supporter of the Pennsylvania Freedmen's Aid Society expanded upon the subject of the large trade done by the Philadelphia Store sponsored on St. Helena Island by his organization.

[21] Pearson (ed.), *Letters*, pp. 144–145; Edward Atkinson gave a detailed account of the goods demanded by the laborers on Philbrick's plantations in May, 1864. Nine hundred and thirty-three people had called for supplies worth $6,879.58. The greatest sales were in drygoods, flour and corn, and molasses. Tobacco, bacon, and hardware were also significant items. See the *Freedmen's Record*, May, 1865, p. 85, and April, 1865, p. 54, where the correspondent states that "In one year there was sold to the negroes at St. Helena Island, West-Indian dry goods, iron and wooden ware to the amount of $50,000." See also the Boston *Advertiser*, July 20, 1863.

[22] Nordhoff, "The Freedmen," p. 18.

Clearly, he said, here was an argument for emancipation "which addresses itself to the pecuniary sense of the people"—and he asked with feeling, "If a mere fraction of freedmen be such valuable customers for our Northern products and Northern merchandise, what will 4,000,000 be? Answer: 'Godliness hath the promise of the life that now is as well as that which is to come.' "[23]

It had indeed.

Baldly stated, the pronouncements of the laissez-faire evangels ring a harsh and stupid note in the middle of the twentieth century. Trumpeting a free-labor system that masked wage slavery and foreign markets that resulted in exploitation, the missionary-planters thought they could see a time when the normal selfishness John Murray Forbes valued so highly would automatically result in enlightenment and prosperity. Because a hundred years has shown how deluded they were, it is now far easier to suspect their motives than to acknowledge that they ever had a dream of a better world for any but themselves. Because their ideas formed the economic justification for the Victorian imperialism that the Western world blushes to recollect, it would be soothing to detect some faint consciousness of guilt among the evangels who interested themselves in cotton and Southern markets. One finds instead only naïve recommendations of hard work as the universal panacea, and such an unabashed optimism that one is forced to the unwilling conclusion that not all the "Godly" talk was hypocrisy.

A man like Edward Atkinson was obliged to believe in the efficacy of hard work, for he himself had risen, with scant formal education, from the lowly position of office boy in the Boston firm of Read and Chadwick at the age of fifteen to that of treasurer of Ogden Mills before he was twenty-five.[24] In prewar America such success stories were not uncommon. In the assessment of Edward Philbrick's motives, it is fair to remember that he backed his belief in Negro advancement with a free-will gift of a thousand

---

[23] Philadelphia *Freedmen's Bulletin* (February, 1865).

[24] Harold Francis Williamson, *Edward Atkinson; The Biography of an American Liberal* (Boston, 1934), pp. 2–3.

dollars before there was any thought of land-buying or private enterprise. While laying plans to show a good profit on cotton, he also included the provision that the Boston concern should pay for schoolteachers on his plantations.[25] The children were working as of yore in the cotton field, but they would also acquire a rude English education.

It is at last their unbounded faith in education that alone removes the stigma of cynicism from the projects of the planter-missionaries. "The tutelary goddess of American liberty," wrote Edward Atkinson in 1861, "should be the pure marble image of the Professor's Yankee school-mistress. Education is the fundamental support of our system. It was education which made us free, progressive, and conservative; and it is education alone which can keep us so." The Yankee schoolmarm had come South, and her plan was to build there a new New England, replete with Yankee institutions. One of Philbrick's employees recalled "John Adams' maxim, that civil society must be built up on the four corner-stones of the church, the school-house, the militia, and the town-meeting. . . ." Whatever was to be done "in the great work of the admission of the four million negroes in our civil society, and the establishment of their social rights," would fail unless "all four of the essential rights of religion, education, self-defense, and self-government are provided for."[26]

Self-government had to await the last turning of the wheel of revolution, but the Port Royal evangels were busily laying the other three cornerstones, even if they did quarrel among themselves over their course on religion and even over the use of Negro soldiers. They were as one on the question of education; this gift seemingly had no strings attached.

Teaching the Negro children to read and write continued to

[25] Philbrick to Alpheus Hardy, December 28, 1863, *Fourth Series of Extracts* (Boston, 1864), p. 14.

[26] Atkinson, "The Reign of King Cotton," p. 454; [Gannett and Hale], "The Education of the Freedmen," *North American Review*, CI (October, 1865), 528.

be the most satisfying of tasks. By the end of 1862 more than 1,700 children were attending school on St. Helena, Ladies, and Port Royal Islands alone. There were 400 children receiving instruction in Florida and probably another 500 on Hilton Head and Paris Islands. Conceived originally as a means of gaining the confidence of the colored people, teaching became an exciting goal in its own right, and the readiness and eagerness of the Negroes to learn to read was the subject of endless comment.[27] Most teachers agreed that on the lower levels of learning, involving in those days primarily rote memory of letters and numbers, the children acquitted themselves exceptionally well. A long heritage of oral communication of folk customs, songs, and stories perhaps prepared the children to shine in these exercises. William Gannett decided that his pupils made better relative progress in spelling and writing than in reading, and he had the wit to realize that this was readily accounted for by the total unfamiliarity of the children with most of the words found in the Northern primers then in use. Another teacher pointed out that the scholars could write well from dictation, as "their eyes and ears were seldom at fault; —but when writing themselves they made sad havoc with the English language."[28]

The teachers and superintendents were often shy in stating a full belief in the equality of all races in ability to learn. The very assumption of a supposed inequality underlies many of their statements on the subject of Negro education. Some teachers predicted trouble in the more advanced levels of study, where reason and application were more directly involved. "It is more than prob-

[27] Towne MS diary, December 31, 1862; [Gannett and Hale], "The Education of the Freedmen," p. 533; Billington (ed.), *Forten*, p. 129.

[28] Pierce wrote, "The memory is susceptible in them,—too much so, perhaps[,] as it is ahead of the reasoning faculty." See Pierce, "The Freedmen," p. 307. One teacher reported that her scholars "know the numbers by sight as far as 100 . . . and show I think a marvelous quickness at it." Teacher's Report of May 21, 1863, in Atkinson MSS; Botume, *First Days*, p. 283; [Gannett and Hale], "The Freedmen," p. 3.

able that the untrained mind of generations will reveal its weakness just where the higher faculties begin to come into existence," was the opinion of William Gannett. Charlotte Forten, from Philadelphia, found the children "so entirely unused to intellectual concentration" that "keeping their minds from wandering" was more of a problem than with Northern children. Although one teacher, who came early to Port Royal, could not detect a "difference in ability between the blacks and mulattoes," he thought "it would be interesting to build up a theory on the subject."[29]

The teachers who noted these supposed inequalities, however, attributed them to the relatively higher *development* of the whites and were optimistic about the ultimate achievements to be made by Negroes. The institution of slavery had retarded the development of the colored people, and it was now the responsibility of Christianity to assist them to further progress. At this early stage these thoughtful people were relatively free of contemporary notions about *inherent* superiority and inferiority of races. The most universal standard of comparison was the immigrant Irish population of New England, and it must be said that most teachers were more charitable toward the Negroes. But the constant references to "degraded" races of men, unpleasant and inaccurate as these assessments were, implied, whether the missionaries spoke of the Negroes or of the Irish, that these people had fallen, through the operation of economic and social restraints, from an original state of natural equality.[30]

Nearly all the Negro children came to study under disadvantageous circumstances, getting in their lessons between chores and field work. An Edisto Island teacher described the problems of her young student Hector, approximately thirteen years old, who had to bring his younger brother and a baby to school, along with the bucket of rice that was to provide the noon meal for all. After

[29] *Ibid.*, p. 4; Forten, "Life on the Sea-Islands," *Atlantic Monthly*, XIII (May, 1864), 307; Teacher's Report of May 21, 1863, Atkinson MSS; Pierce, "The Freedmen," p. 307.

[30] Pearson (ed.), *Letters*, pp. 11, 15, 18, 22, 56, 75.

depositing the older child and the rice on the floor, Hector "most maternally" held the baby, who kept his peace for a while, absorbed in the novelty of his situation. When the baby began to show signs of crying, Hector rocked him to and fro, "at the same time crowding in the rice as if to force back the coming cry, and the child as if in compassion for his beseeching look, is quiet a little longer, and Hector asks for a book. All is quiet for a few moments, and then [comes] the cry again. . . ." Hector had to leave.[31]

In refreshing contrast to the prevailing docility and earnest endeavor that the teachers tirelessly praised, there were youngsters who showed a healthy tendency toward restlessness and mischief-making. A visiting army officer was called in to punish some naughty boys who had made trouble in "the first day of the reign of Miss Norwood. The chief culprit's chief sin was throwing a live cat into the school-room. . . ." Sometimes, when the children were provoking, the teachers resorted to the venerable expedient of spanking. Arthur Sumner said he had been obliged to give a boy a whipping "for protracted sulkiness and disobedience" and had "locked up two girls for fighting." But the most knowing teachers regarded these spontaneous outbursts of mischief as indications of a happy falling away of slavish servility.[32]

The best teachers managed disciplinary problems as they have always been most successfully met, by keeping the children busy. This was difficult with large classes. At the Brick Church on St. Helena, where several teachers held classes together, the situation as Laura Towne described it was so bad that nobody could understand who had not been obliged "to make herself heard over three

[31] Ellen Kemper's letter of June 3, 1865, to the *Freedmen's Record*, I (August, 1865), 133. See also Forten, "Life on the Sea-Islands," p. 592; Towne to "R," December 18, 1864, Towne MS letters; Teacher's Report of May 21, 1863, in Atkinson MSS.

[32] Thomas Wentworth Higginson to his mother [n.d., but probably late 1862], Higginson MSS; Arthur Sumner to Joseph Clark, postscript to letter of July 8, 1862, Arthur Sumner MSS; Pearson (ed.), *Letters*, pp. 208–209.

other classes reciting in concert, and to discover talkers and idlers among fifty scholars while one hundred and fifty more are shouting lessons and three other teachers bawling admonitions, instructions and reproofs." Then the babies cried "from a disinclination to remain five hours foodless," and because their small nurses were "rather careless of infant comfort in their zeal for knowledge." It was a great day for Miss Towne when the bounty of Philadelphia sent her a small prefabricated schoolhouse of two rooms. Soon an impressive bell swung from its little tower and gave the children for miles around the classic American summons to learning.[33]

The organizing zeal of the teachers was astounding. At the Adams School on St. Helena, the teacher established a typical New England School Committee among the Negro elders. The fact that the committeemen were illiterate seemed a small matter compared with the advantage of having these people address directly the charitable sensibilities of the New England Freedmen's Aid Society. "Uncle Robert" Chaplin, the aged chairman, spoke with pride of the progress the children had made and explained that the duties of his committee were "to visit the school and see that everything go regular among the children" and to assist "the teacher so far as our understanding goes. All books and property that belong to the school is in our charge. . . ." He spoke with gratitude of "the good friends of the North," who "through the assistance of God, are helping us to drop the scales from our eyes. . . . Even I, Robert L. Chaplin, myself 73 years old, had feel within myself that it was impossible for the slavery bound" ever to "see light in this world, until the good friends send us a good friend. . . ."[34]

We may be sure that Boston benevolence did not neglect the

[33] Towne to "R," December 18, 1864; Holland (ed.), *Towne*, pp. 144, 147.

[34] A. D. Milne to [Edward Atkinson], May 9, 1863, Atkinson MSS. All the committeemen signed with an "x" the letter from which the quotations from Chaplin are taken. See *Fourth Series of Extracts from Letters* (Boston, 1864), pp. 5–6.

needs of the Adams School. "Uncle Robert," as he was called in the days when he had invested such serious occasions as weddings and funerals on the T. B. Chaplin plantation with some of his own personal dignity, had seen many welcome changes and would live to see more.[35] Only time would tell whether or not such a unique grafting as a New England School Committee could flourish on the stubborn palmetto; the cultural roots of the South Carolina Negroes went far back in time, and theirs was indeed a latitude different from that of Boston.

But the formal exercises comprised only a part of the offerings of the Yankee teacher. The adult Negroes who came in the evening to get a reading lesson were especially gratifying. These older people were "fighting with their letters" so as not to be "made ashamed" by their children, and also because they sensed the advantages they would derive from learning.[36] Often these ambitious people came from the class of natural leaders among the slaves, the plantation drivers. Limus Anders, approximately fifty years old, came regularly to Harriet Ware for instruction, and she pronounced him "very smart," although she had ample reservations about his morals. "He has a wife here and grown children, and another on another plantation, the rascal." Limus was approvingly called "a black Yankee" by William Gannett, who said, "without a drop of white blood in him, he has the energy and *cuteness* and big eye for his own advantage of a born New Englander." Anders immediately set his fellows an example in enterprise by fencing in and planting a garden for growing vegetables to sell to the soldiers. Hunting and fishing during the appropriate seasons and raising pigs and poultry, he soon had sufficient produce to keep his "express" boat for Hilton Head amply supplied. Limus undertook to plant and cultivate twice as much cotton acreage as others and was soon prepared to employ additional labor at eight dollars per month. Gannett relates that Limus, "not to leave the luxuries behind . . . rigs up a kind of sulky and bows

[35] Chapter 4, p. 138, and Chapter 13, p. 361.
[36] EHP in *Third Series of Extracts from Letters* (Boston, 1863).

to the white men from his carriage." It was the young teacher's confident expectation that Limus would in ten years be "a tolerably rich man."[37]

But Limus was exceptional, and it is doubtful whether most of the evangels at Port Royal expected or even desired the affirmation of liberty to take such an energetic form among the great multitude. The limited goal of a free peasantry was, for good or ill, the most common ideal among the missionaries. Any independent streaking off to Hilton Head for better wages was, as we have seen, not usually smiled upon. Arthur Sumner noted approvingly that if General Saxton would forbid the Negroes to visit Hilton Head and Beaufort, "we shall have as happy and contented a peasantry as the most ardent abolitionist could desire." The pattern sought after was that of industrious and self-reliant families working the cotton through the week and enjoying their Sunday holiday in clean clothes, with happy shining faces. Elizabeth Hyde Botume said, "We were convinced . . . [that] needles and thread and soap and decent clothing were the best educators, and would civilize them sooner than book knowledge."[38] It was perhaps this philosophy that disposed the teachers to accept the plan of having the schoolchildren work at field labor until noon and spend only half the day in the classroom. No one

[37] Pearson (ed.), *Letters*, text and note, pp. 37–38.

[38] Arthur Sumner to Joseph Clark, July 7, 1862, Arthur Sumner MSS; Botume, *First Days*, p. 236; "The instruction most needed by the blacks was not in the knowledge of school books, but in that which should lead them to appreciate the advantages of civilized life, to relinquish many of the habits and customs of slavery, and to learn the duties and responsibilities of free men." *First Annual Report of the Educational Commission,* May, 1863 (Boston, 1863), p. 11; "The teachers have been taught . . . that the work of education proposed was the education of savages into self-governing men; that books . . . were of use so far as they tended toward this aid." [Gannett and Hale], "The Education of the Freedmen," p. 529. The Northern supporters of the aid work consistently assigned the Negroes a lower spot on their imaginary scale of "civilization" than did the evangels in the field, who came to appreciate in time the Negroes' common-sense approach to problems.

seemed to protest the arrangement or to think that perhaps the value of labor would have been enhanced by a reduction of the labor force to include only adult males.

One of the more important extracurricular activities of the missionary teachers was the effort to regularize Negro family life, to make it conform to the accepted pattern. Parson French was the foremost advocate of matrimony. Saxton appointed him to take special charge of this work through a General Order of August 22, 1862. Negroes having more than one "wife" were now obliged to make a choice. Any lawful marriage had to be honored, but in the absence of a ceremony in any case, the man had to select the wife who was the mother of his children, be married legally, and live with her only. Some missionaries felt that the women should withdraw from field work immediately and devote themselves entirely to housekeeping duties. Austa French was of this opinion, and she vigorously condemned the superintendents, who were acting on "present expediency" in working women in the fields without distinction from the men. Edward Pierce, however, was presenting the prevailing point of view when he said, "Better a woman with the hoe than without it, when she is not yet fitted for the needle or the book."[39] The women teachers were especially influential in pushing forward the program of uplift, enjoining the copious use of soap and water, whitewash, and truth. They were amply rewarded by many protestations of affection and an unending supply of fresh eggs.

Meanwhile, in the six months following the Emancipation Proclamation, sagacious people of the North could at last see clearly that the nation was in the throes of a great social revolution. The Union could never be restored in its old shape. Many people of more conservative views than those of General Benjamin Butler would have been obliged to agree with the radical

[39] General Order No. 7, August 22, 1862, published in the Beaufort *Free South*, October 17, 1863; French, *Slavery in S.C.*, pp. 105–106; Pierce, "The Freedmen," p. 309.

general in thinking that "we can have a better union next time. It was good enough if it had been left alone. The old house was good enough for me, but as they have pulled down the L part, I propose, when we build it up, to build it up with all the modern improvements." Thoughtful men were turning more and more to a consideration of how far the "modern improvements" ought to go and what they would cost.[40]

Since the nature of the human building material would be of critical importance in the renovation of the Union, there was increasing interest in the behavior of the Negroes as free laborers and as soldiers. Port Royal was by far the best place to observe black men in their new roles. So it came to pass that the Department of the South became a mecca for assorted planners, reporters, and radical thinkers coming South to work, observe, collect information, and make recommendations to the government. Edward Pierce returned in a new capacity. Ironically, he was reinstated in the Department in the unlikely role of cotton agent extraordinary, with full powers from Chase "to regulate commercial intercourse and to take charge of captured and abandoned property." In answers to inquiries from Charles Sumner about his having taken a mere "money" place, Pierce said he thought he could make his new job serve the radical cause in ways that did not appear on the surface. This he did by writing an able and laudatory article on the progress of the Port Royal work for the *Atlantic Monthly*. He also served as an unofficial watchdog for Secretary Chase and as a strong advocate for General Saxton with Sumner himself.[41] Harriet Tubman, the famous black "Moses"

[40] B. F. Butler, *Character and Results of the War* (Philadelphia, 1863), p. 17.

[41] Pierce to David Hunter, June 9, 1863, and Pierce to Chase, September 7, 1863, in "Letters Sent by E. L. Pierce," Fifth Special Agency, Treasury Department Archives; Chase to Pierce, May 1, 1863, "Letters Sent to E. L. Pierce," *ibid*.; Pierce to Charles Sumner, May 1, 1863, and June 18, 1863, Sumner MSS; Pierce, "The Freedmen at Port Royal," *Atlantic Monthly*, XII (September, 1863), 291-315.

who had led so many slaves to freedom in the years before the war, arrived in Beaufort. She was not long in finding a new and astonishing avenue of usefulness as a Union spy among the Negroes of the interior. Charles Nordhoff did a comprehensive job of reporting the condition of the freed people under the governorship of "General Saxby," as the freedmen called him. Soon the methods used in the Department were being imitated in other areas where refugees had to be dealt with in large numbers.[42]

By far the most influential visitor to the islands in the summer of 1863 was Colonel James McKaye, who arrived in mid-June to study the Port Royal situation for the Freedmen's Inquiry Commission. He sent for the teachers to come into Beaufort, where he questioned them at length about the capabilities of the freedmen, and a shorthand reporter took down every word. The conduct of the Negroes as soldiers was of especial interest. Colonel Higginson testified that the discipline of military life was of "unspeakable value" to the freedmen, and Judge Smith, one of the tax commissioners, assured McKaye that service in the army "makes men of them at once." Captain Hooper said that the Negroes were ready and willing to work for wages. Saxton again adverted to the Northern fears of a Negro inundation, when he told the commission that the Negroes did not desire to leave the islands.[43]

The district was of especial significance in the study of the commission, for it was here, it decided, that "the system of Negro slavery seems to have reached its furthest development with the least contact with external civilization." Slavery had here "run

[42] Billington (ed.), *Forten*, pp. 161–162; Earl Conrad, *Harriet Tubman* (Washington, 1943), pp. 165–166, 171; Charles Nordhoff, *The Freedmen of South Carolina: Some Account of Their Appearance, Character, Condition and Peculiar Customs* (New York, 1863); John D. Eaton, *Grant, Lincoln, and the Freedmen* (New York, 1907), p. 47.

[43] *OR*, III, iii, 435; Holland (ed.), *Towne*, entry June 11, 1863, p. 111; Thomas Wentworth Higginson to his mother, June 10, 1863, Higginson MSS.

out nearer to its logical consequences" than in any other sector the commissioners visited. The disintegration of Negro family life was cited as the most striking result of the severity of the system. Surely methods that were succeeding in helping the islanders to an independent existence would be adequate in other regions.[44]

The Preliminary Report of the Freedmen's Inquiry Commission was broad in scope, and its specific recommendations covered the entire field of social and economic reconstruction so thoroughly that it formed a basic text for radical legislation of a later day.[45] It is interesting to note a basic assumption of the commission that Reconstruction was a proper function of Congress rather than of the executive branch. The single most important proposal was that a Bureau of Emancipation be created within the War Department, an idea that had already been proposed by such friends of Port Royal as Charles Sumner and Governor Andrew. This Bureau should be endowed with authority to control freedmen's affairs, act in a friendly and advisory capacity to the Negroes in their new condition, and coordinate the work of the benevolent societies. The underlying presumption of the commission was that the Negroes would require temporary assistance but that they should be encouraged to assume an independent status as soon as possible and discouraged from a sustained attitude of dependence upon charitable efforts. Landownership could help them on their way, and the commissioners recommended that they be given every opportunity to buy confiscated estates in the South. Specifically, they proposed that freedmen be assisted toward this goal financially through the use of funds accruing from the sale of confiscated cotton and other property. They had doubtless been pleased to observe the steps being taken at Port Royal to

[44] *OR*, III, iii, 435–436. The commission said a greater danger to the North from a large influx of Negroes would result if they were remanded to slavery. *Ibid.*, pp. 437, 433.

[45] The text of the Preliminary Report is found in *OR*, III, iii, 430–454. It is ably analyzed in James G. Sproat, "Blueprint for Radical Reconstruction," *Journal of Southern History*, pp. 36–38.

provide the Negroes with land at minimum cost, from the estates set aside for "charitable purposes" before the 1863 land sale.

The commission also took notice of the most formidable of all obstacles to the development of serious plans for the future of the freed people, the abiding prejudice of many Northerners against the Negro. "Every aggression, every act of injustice committed by a Northern man against unoffending refugees from despotism, every insult . . . is not only a breach of humanity, an offense against civilization, but also an act which gives aid and comfort to the enemy."[46]

Violent examples of race hatred could be found wherever Northern troops came into contact with numbers of freedmen. Even at Port Royal, where Saxton's benevolent protectorate should have deterred overt demonstrations, there were appalling clashes. As late as February of 1863 unruly parties from several regiments, including the 9th New Jersey, the 100th New York, known as "Les Enfants Perdus," and the 24th Massachusetts, went berserk and terrorized St. Helena Island. They killed and stole livestock, took money from the Negroes, and culminated their outrages in burning all the Negro cabins on the Daniel Jenkins plantations. They beat Negro men and attempted to rape the women, and when the superintendents intervened the soldiers threatened to shoot them. Superintendent Hammond wept helplessly when he told Saxton and Hunter "what had been done under his very eyes on his own plantations." "For three whole days and far into the night," wrote Gannett, "I did nothing but chase soldiers and ride about to protect the people." Harriet Ware said the whole affair was "beyond description," that the soldiers had behaved "like marauders in an enemy's territory," and that "the loss of confidence in Yankees is an incalculable injury." Laura Towne's faithful cook, Rina, told her that the colored peo-

---

[46] Preliminary Report of the Freedmen's Inquiry Commission, *OR*, III, iii, 451.

ple were saying "they would be glad if all the white people would go away and let them live by themselves."[47]

The warnings of the commission were seasonable and reasonable when such barbarities could be perpetrated under the very noses of such devoted radicals as Generals Hunter and Saxton. They only gave point to an inescapable fact, that while thoughtful men were trying to determine the course of the revolution, to work out the details of the future of the Negro as a free man, and to make his future secure, numbers of people were still loath to accept the idea that the Negro ought to be free at all.

There were always the two questions, for the Inquiry Commission and for the nation at large: How could the Negro help the Union, and how could the Union help the Negro to his freedom? Two questions, two answers, and two commitments. The time was near at hand when the black man's *right* to freedom could no longer be challenged by rational men. By midsummer, 1863, the military colony at Port Royal was astir with great plans for an assault upon the symbolic heart of the rebellion, the city of Charleston. Forever afterward, the most solemn obligations of the Northern people would be bound to the cause of freedom by the blood of Negro soldiers who fought and died under the flag of the Union in that renowned action.

[47] Pearson (ed.), *Letters*, pp. 155–156; Towne MS diary, February 15, 1863; Holland (ed.), *Towne*, pp 102–103; Gannett MS diary, February 12, 1863, Gannett MSS; Boston *Commonwealth*, March 6, 1863.

nine ❦ "FROM A CHATTEL
TO A PERSON"

IN SUMMER ON SEA ISLANDS, THE OCEAN IS A BOON. THE SAME Atlantic that may in autumn hurl destruction upon the weathered shores can in June provide sustaining breezes and a time-out-of-mind haze that conjure up dreams and friendly spirits. If it is true, as is sometimes claimed, that spirits of departed men may visit their favorite haunts before their eternal rest, surely old-times' sake and immortal curiosity drew James L. Petigru and William Elliott back to Beaufort.

The two staunch old Union-loving Whigs had died in early spring of 1863, and it is easy to imagine them on a fine day in June walking the oak-vaulted streets, arm-in-arm, surveying such Yankee improvements as the new pier on Bay Street and the reduction of the ancient street names to letters of the alphabet and ordinal numbers, after the plan of Washington, D.C. The ironies were abundant. How the shades must have smiled to observe that the U.S. Direct Tax Commissioners, sent South to carve up and retail South Carolina, were quartered, of all places, in the Edmund Rhett house.[1] They probably agreed that the gasconading,

[1] William Elliott died in February, and James Petigru died on March 3. James Petigru Carson (ed.), *Life, Letters and Speeches of James Louis Petigru* (Washington, D. C., 1920), pp. 469, 472. Elliott was converted to secession late in the day, and Petigru never was; The William G. Reed Photograph Album, in the Beaufort Township Library, identifies the Rhett house as the tax commissioners' headquarters. For the "Yankee improvements," see the Beaufort *Free South*, June 18, 1864, and Charlotte Forten, "Life on the Sea Islands," *Atlantic Monthly* (May, 1864), p. 587.

fire-eating Rhetts had deserved no better. Since Petigru and Elliott had never in life seen precisely eye-to-eye on the touchy question of slavery, Petigru possibly forebore reminding his old friend of his own stubbornly maintained principle: "So much am I a disciple of Locke and Montesquieu that my mind does not balance between freedom and slavery." In Beaufort, now a "Negro's Heaven," freedom was clearly in the ascendant, and Elliott may have shaken his head to recall how he had himself waggled a finger at its nullifying citizens thirty years before and warned them that once a revolution is let loose men can hardly prescribe its course. Petigru had seen it all. When South Carolina had fired upon the *Star of the West* in pre-Sumter days, he had said, "I never believed that slavery would last a hundred years; now I know it won't last five."[2]

June 3, 1863, would have been just the day for Elliott and Petigru to visit Beaufort. The signal events of that day in that particular town transcended in their inward meaning their allotted space in time. Such days are riddles that may be read forward or backward. Three vessels slipped up to the pier in the clear early morning, and if the shady denizens of the past had joined the throng that quickly formed in Bay Street, they could have seen an amazing and informative sight. How William Elliott would have stared at the 727 Negroes, men, women, and children, who crowded the vessels to the gunwales. These "genuine contrabands," still wearing "their field suits of dirty gray," had only yesterday dropped their hoes where they worked along the banks of the Combahee, in the country where the Elliott clan had owned acres and men for generations. Now they appeared in Beaufort, according to reporter James Thompson, "with every lineament beaming with that intelligence, which is inseparable with plantation negroes enjoying their freedom."[3]

[2] Carson (ed.), *Petigru*, p. 348; see Chapter 1, p 9.

[3] Beaufort *Free South*, June 6, 1863. We know that June 3 was a flawless summer day from the account of Charlotte Forten, who went that day on an excursion to Edisto Island. See Billington (ed.), *Forten*, pp. 187–188.

The 250 black soldiers who had convoyed them out of enemy territory belonged to the newly formed 2nd South Carolina Volunteers, and the tall, weather-bronzed white man who disembarked with them was their new colonel. James Montgomery, a veteran guerrilla of the Kansas wars, was inaugurating his own kind of fighting in the spit-and-polish Department of the South. With him came a gnomelike, beturbaned little black woman, evidently in a position of authority, who shepherded the tatterdemalion human cargo ashore. John Brown had called her "General"; the hundreds of slaves she had delivered to Canada in antebellum days knew her as "Moses"; but to everyone else she was Harriet Tubman. This oddly assorted pair had left Beaufort two days before to raid the rich rice plantations on the Combahee River. Harriet had gleaned, with the assistance of a number of hand-picked Negro scouts familiar with the interior, considerable knowledge as to the location of supplies and the disposition of the Negroes in the region. The whole expedition had come off without a hitch.[4]

The slaves had looked up "like startled deer," as Harriet said, wavered, and then streamed to the boats en masse. Where there was time, the slaves collected a few favorite belongings. Women had come with small children hanging to their skirts, sometimes also carrying a steaming pot of hominy. The summer air was rent with the confusion of children crying and of the squealing pigs and squawking chickens the Negroes brought aboard. As the gunboats moved rapidly from point to point, the Confederate resistance was disorganized, feeble, and always too late. "The enemy seems to have been well posted as to the character and capacity of our troops and their small chance of encountering opposition, and

[4] Boston *Commonwealth*, July 10, 1863. The best description of Montgomery is found in "Letters of Dr. Seth Rogers, 1862, 1863," in *Massachusetts Historical Society Proceedings*, XLII (Boston, 1910), 367; for Harriet Tubman, see Benjamin Quarles, *The Negro in the Civil War* (Boston, 1953), p. 226, and Earl Conrad, *Harriet Tubman* (Washington, D.C., 1943), pp. 72, 165–166, 171, 179.

to have been well guided by persons thoroughly acquainted with the river and the country," concluded the Confederate officer who investigated the raid. "Their success was complete."[5]

By June of 1863 there was nothing exactly new about coastal raiding with Negro troops. In late January Colonel Higginson had taken the 1st South Carolina Volunteers up the St. Mary's River, between Georgia and Florida, where he had captured valuable supplies of lumber, bricks, and iron, much needed in the Department. In March, on a raid up the St. John's River, Higginson's men held the town of Jacksonville for ten days. Although General Hunter had suddenly called off the expedition to make ready for a projected assault on Charleston, the soldierly qualities of the one-time slaves had already been demonstrated. Higginson's men had behaved well in stand-up fights, and they could take pride in their accomplishment. When Private "Abram," of The Oaks plantation, came back home to visit, he told Laura Towne that he had always been afraid of white men until he had seen how afraid *they* were of black soldiers.[6] Higginson's own vivid reports of the exploits of the 1st South Carolina Volunteers did much to publicize the outfit and the cause of Negro troops.

The author-colonel spoke later of being under "pretty heavy bonds to tell the truth" because his regiment had "lived for months in a glare of publicity, such as tests any regiment severely. . . ." Camp Saxton had "attracted a continuous stream of visitors, military and civil."[7] Although Higginson considered his men very

[5] *Ibid.*, pp. 174–175; *OR*, I, xiv, 290–308. The quotations are from the official report of John F. Lay, Confederate Assistant Adjutant-General, p. 306.

[6] *OR*, I, iv, 195–198, contains Colonel Higginson's account of the St. Mary's raid. See *Ibid.*, pp. 226–229, for the Jacksonville occupation. An able secondary account of these raids is found in Dudley Taylor Cornish, *The Sable Arm; Negro Troops in the Union Army, 1861–1865* (New York, 1956), pp. 134–142; Towne MS diary, February 5, 1863.

[7] Thomas Wentworth Higginson, *Army Life in a Black Regiment* (Cambridge, 1900), p. 6.

docile and childlike in their attitude toward their officers, they underwent, he said, an "amazing" transformation in combat. "Their fire and fury appear more like the old Berserker madness of the Northmen than anything more modern; while their local knowledge gives them a sagacity like that of the Indians. The only difficulty is to coerce them into prudence." Hold them in check he had. When a part of Jacksonville was burned upon evacuation, the Northern newspapers saved Higginson the trouble of explaining that the deed was done by white reinforcements.[8]

No, there was nothing new about Colonel Montgomery's raiding the coast with Negro troops, or even about evacuating the slaves, though the Kansan had brought them off in unusual numbers. What was new was what the Jayhawker had left behind him. Where Higginson's raids had been conceived primarily as a means of recruiting Negro soldiers and gathering supplies, Montgomery's progress up the Combahee had been a massive assault upon property. Numbers of "large mansions, known to belong to notorious rebels, with all their rich furniture and rare works of art, were burned to the ground. Nothing but smouldering ruins and parched and crisp skeletons of once magnificent old live oak and palmetto groves now remain of these delightful country seats." James Thompson of the *Free South* was exuberant. He told how Montgomery's men had burned rice houses, Negro quarters, "everything inflammable." "Sluices were opened, plantations flooded, and broad ponds and lakes made where, but a few hours before, luxuriant crops of rice and corn were putting forth their leaves." The property damage was estimated at two million dollars, not to speak of the loss of the slaves themselves, who had flocked to the river banks in droves at the shrill piping of the gunboat whistles despite mortal threats from their overseers and drivers.[9]

[8] Higginson to Edward Atkinson, February 2, 1863, Atkinson MSS; Cornish, *Sable Arm*, p. 141.

[9] Beaufort *Free South*, June 6, 1863; Port Royal *New South*, June 6, 1863.

After their debarkation at Beaufort, the Combahee contrabands were temporarily lodged in a church, where Montgomery addressed them "in strains of thrilling eloquence." The people responded with a spiritual to the effect that "*There is a white robe for thee.*" Harriet Tubman then "created a great sensation" with a homespun speech of "sound sense and real native eloquence." All the able-bodied men were then promptly inducted into Montgomery's regiment.[10] The *Free South* pronounced the raid "brilliant and entirely successful," and the Boston *Commonwealth* said "it was a glorious consummation." Colonel Higginson called it "a most brilliant success" but added grudgingly that he personally did not subscribe to "burning private houses."[11] Although he joined Montgomery in hearkening to the soul of John Brown, the two colonels had seen the old man in life from opposite directions: East and West. Higginson's support of John Brown stemmed from a transcendental and romantic dedication to the concept of freedom. Montgomery had been out on the Kansas front, fighting a bloody and partisan war from which Higginson and his Boston friends had been safely insulated. Now that Higginson saw it, he was not sure he liked what he saw. The colonel of the 1st South Carolina Volunteers was a romantic who idealized his cause, took a paternal attitude toward his "childlike" troops, and was extremely careful of their good reputation. Deeply sympathetic to the mystical elements of the Negro religious life, he called his men "a Gospel Army" and undoubtedly agreed with his friend, Surgeon Seth Rogers of his regiment, who said of the Negroes, "They are all natural Transcendentalists."[12]

Montgomery idealized nothing. His grim dedication to bringing the war home to the civilian population would be seen again

[10] Boston *Commonwealth*, July 10, 1863; Port Royal *New South*, June 6, 1863.

[11] Beaufort *New South*, June 6, 1863; Port Royal *New South*, June 6, 1863; Boston *Commonwealth*, July 10, 1863; Thomas Wentworth Higginson to his mother, June 5, 1863, Higginson MSS.

[12] Higginson, *Army Life*, p. 73.

in the face of General William T. Sherman. It was the attitude of the future, when men grew tired of parades and flag-waving and wanted victory and peace enough to pick up the ultimate weapon to win the war. All this was far from clear, however, just after the Combahee raid. Whether public approval of the use of Negro troops was sufficiently firm to withstand a possible reaction to using them in guerrilla fighting was a ponderable factor. Higginson quietly voiced his objection in a private letter to his mother, but in the North even the Boston *Commonwealth*, ever friendly to Negro troops, seemed to approve burning "lordly dwellings and striking terror to the heart of rebeldom."[13] The incipient differences between the two colonels awaited the advent of a third factor for clarification.

On the very day Montgomery returned from the Combahee, the first regiment of free Northern Negroes arrived in Beaufort. The famous 54th Regiment of Massachusetts had enjoyed a few days earlier the most spectacular sendoff the city of Boston could afford, and Beaufort did her best to give the men an appropriate welcome. Detachments of the 1st Massachusetts Cavalry came careening down Bay Street, officers' wives and lady schoolteachers emerged from the waterfront mansions in their best crinolines, and knots of white soldiers and Negroes gathered at the pier as the vessel moved up the river. The bands played and the crowds sang and cheered as the officers and men came ashore. Except perhaps for the restless shades of Petigru and Elliott, the populace expressed the most hearty satisfaction, for by June of 1863 there were probably more abolitionists in proportion to the population in Beaufort than in Boston.[14]

The 54th could hardly have been sent to a more suitable theater

[13] Boston *Commonwealth*, July 10, 1863.

[14] Beaufort *Free South*, June 6, 1863. On the Beaufort reception of the 54th, I believe Luis F. Emilio's memory to be at fault and have used Thompson's *Free South* account. Cf. Emilio, *History of the 54th Regiment of Massachusetts Volunteer Infantry* (Boston, 1891), p. 37. For Boston's sendoff, see Cornish, *Sable Arm*, p. 148.

of war, for the arming of the regiment had been the enthusiastic labor of the same radical Bostonians who had agitated incessantly for every advancing step of the Port Royal movement. Governor John Andrew had been the generating force. "If Southern slavery should fall," wrote Andrew, "and colored men should have no hand and play no conspicuous part in the task, the result would leave the colored man a mere helot." Negroes would be in the bad case of having "lost their masters, but not found a country." The Governor had descended upon President Lincoln with a host of Massachusetts radicals in January and had won authorization to raise the 54th. Among the men who had painstakingly recruited the regiment were such familiar Port Royal supporters as John Murray Forbes, Dr. LeBaron Russell, William I. Bowditch, Francis George Shaw, and Dr. Samuel Gridley Howe.[15] All New England and the old Northwest had been scoured for suitable recruits, and much was expected of the pioneer Northern Negro regiment. Governor Andrew wanted it to be "a model for all future Colored Regiments." As Andrew knew, the success or failure of the organization would "go far to elevate or depress the estimation in which the character of the Colored Americans will be held throughout the World."[16]

The men chosen to lead the 54th were the very distillation of New England education, culture, and class distinction. Andrew sought these officers from "those circles of educated Anti-Slavery Society, which next to the colored race itself have the greatest interest in the success of this experiment." They would be, of course, "gentlemen of the very highest tone and honor." Their abolitionism, however, was not of the John Brown variety. Robert Gould Shaw, whose father, Francis George Shaw, was a prominent figure in the New York National Freedmen's Aid Society,

[15] Andrew to Lewis Hayden, December 4, 1863, quoted in Henry Greenleaf Pearson, *The Life of John A. Andrew* (Boston, 1904), II, 70; Cornish, *Sable Arm*, pp. 105, 108.

[16] John Andrew to Francis G. Shaw, January 30, 1863, quoted in Pearson, *Andrew*, II, 75.

became colonel of the Regiment. "Bob Shaw is not a fanatic," wrote a friend. This gallant young man, who courted ridicule and special dangers at the head of a Negro regiment, was slight of frame, with a gentle, almost schoolgirlish charm that inspired affectionate admiration and caused women to think how proud his mother must be.[17] Sarah Shaw was proud indeed. When her son had at first declined the regimental command, she wrote Andrew that it was "the bitterest disappointment" of her life and that she would have died satisfied to hear of his acceptance. Her maternal pride was to be vindicated amply. Second-in-command was Norwood P. Hallowell of Boston, and the adjutant was Garth Wilkinson James, whose brothers Henry and William would in the future distinguish their family and America in letters and philosophy. Colonel Higginson pronounced the officers "the best style of Boston." General Hunter, in reporting the arrival of the regiment, told Andrew that "from the appearance of the men I doubt not that this command will yet win a reputation and place in history deserving of the patronage you have given them." He promised that the regiment should "soon be profitably and honorably employed."[18]

A fitting climax to the exciting events of June 3 in Beaufort was the presentation of a handsome regimental flag made by a patriotic lady of Norwich, Connecticut, for the 2nd South Carolina Volunteers. With the exception of an interpolation of tired verse, which poetic evangels were apt to produce on such occasions, the speeches were vigorous. General Saxton addressed the regiment and its visiting missionary friends in terms of revolutionary enthusiasm. "I can see in the times hope for your race written all

[17] *Ibid.*, p. 74; Charles Russell Lowell, writing to his mother, [?] February, 1863, quoted in Cornish, *Sable Arm*, p. 107; Billington (ed.), *Forten*, pp. 191, 193.

[18] Sarah Shaw to John Andrew, February 6, 1863, in Pearson, *Andrew*, II, 77; Emilio, *History of the 54th*, p. 34; Higginson to his mother, June 5, 1863, Higginson MSS; David Hunter to John Andrew, June 3, 1863, in *OR*, I, xiv, 462.

round in letters of light." When the nation was ready to see "her cherished flag, . . . hallowed by the blood of her bravest and her best, waving at the head of a regiment of South Carolina freedmen," there was reason to trust the future. Saxton then, in a graceful tribute to Massachusetts, "the nursery of truth, justice, and liberty," spoke of the "regiment of black men" sent by the Bay State "to help you get your liberty." General Montgomery, his "hazel eyes of destiny" focused on the future, accepted the flag for his men and assured them that "it means that you have a country and a home." The bearded Jayhawker showed that he had absorbed the radical goals of Gideon's Band when he promised his soldiers, "The ground over which you march, the fields on which you fight are to be your own." The flag would protect their rights. "You are to be as free as the winds of Heaven that now kiss these ample folds. But," he added grimly, "all depends upon your courage, your obedience to orders, and your constancy in the work of crushing this rebellion."[19]

On such a crashing note the ghosts of Petigru and Elliott would have been well advised to surrender the town to the Yankees. Colonel Montgomery knew how to make a stirring speech quite as well as Colonel Higginson, and their goals were precisely the same. They might, however, differ quite sharply as to the means.

The first news of the Combahee raid had struck General David Hunter altogether favorably. He had referred happily to the expedition as "but the initial step of a system of operations which will rapidly compel the rebels to either lay down their arms . . . or to withdraw their slaves to the interior, thus leaving desolate the most fertile and productive of their counties along the Atlantic seaboard." When the full details came to the commanding general's notice, however, he wrote Montgomery in some haste, sending him a copy of the rules of warfare and calling his atten-

---

[19] Beaufort *Free South*, June 6, 1863. The phrase describing Montgomery's eyes comes from Surgeon Seth Rogers' incomparable vignette, *Massachusetts Historical Society Proceedings*, XLIII, 367.

tion to the accepted regulations. He warned Montgomery to spare "household furniture, libraries, churches, and hospitals," and hoped that the Colonel would not destroy crops growing in the ground "without mature consideration."[20]

Whether Montgomery received the admonition before his next foray is questionable. The very day it was written, Colonel Shaw reported with his regiment to Montgomery on St. Simon's Island. The men of the 54th had hardly pitched their tents before they were pressed into service.[21]

On June 10 Montgomery and Shaw, accompanied by the 2nd South Carolina Volunteers as well as by the 54th, steamed up the Altamaha River toward the pretty little town of Darien, Georgia. After shelling the site, the troops landed unopposed. They found the town deserted, and Montgomery set the soldiers to looting the houses. "After the town was pretty thoroughly disembowelled," Shaw reported that Montgomery informed him quietly, with "a sweet smile," that he intended to burn it. Over the protests of Colonel Shaw, the deed was done. James Thompson of the *Free South* described the conflagration. "Ere the sacking was done, the curling volumes of flame half enveloped in a black smoke, rising in a strong southern breeze, proclaimed that the demon destruction riots and holds high court on every soil cursed by war." The gunboats then fell back toward the Sound, barely escaping the searing flames. The Southerners ought to know, explained the thin-lipped Montgomery, that the war was real, and that they were "to be swept away by the hand of God like the Jews of old."[22]

Shaw did not stand meekly by. What Montgomery did with his "contraband" troops was his own affair; but placing at the ugly work of pillage and destruction Shaw's own "model" Negro regi-

[20] David Hunter to John Andrew, June 3, 1863, and Hunter to James Montgomery, June 9, 1863; *OR*, I, xiv, 426 and 466–467, respectively.
[21] Cornish, *Sable Arm*, p. 148; Emilio, *History of the 54th*, p. 39.
[22] *Ibid.*, pp. 41–43; Beaufort *Free South*, June 20, 1863.

ment, which bore the highest aspirations of Northern radicals, angered the young colonel very much. He investigated what limitations Hunter had placed on Montgomery's methods and complained directly to Governor Andrew that his men had been sent South to fight the enemy, not to burn private homes. Friends in the Department picked up the quarrel. Edward Pierce told Senator Sumner of the dispute and said he thought Higginson and Shaw would be unable to work with Montgomery in an advance movement. They feared that Montgomery's methods would "bring dishonor" to the Negro troops. Colonel Higginson wrote to Sumner in the same vein, exonerating the Negro soldiers from any responsibility for Montgomery's "brigand habits." "These I utterly repudiate. This indiscriminate burning and pillaging is savage warfare . . . and demoralizes the soldiers—and must produce a reaction against arming the Negroes." The Northern press proved the truth of the charge. Greeley of the *Tribune* called for an explanation; even the Boston *Commonwealth* reversed itself. "What harping there has been upon the 'horrors of servile war,' all men know. And now the very first act of the government, or at any rate, of those whom the troops must obey, seems studiously calculated to give the colors of truth to this malicious falsehood." Even James Thompson of the *Free South* admitted that Montgomery's "irregular proceedings" had had a bad effect upon the reputation of black troops.[23]

Montgomery's personal relations with his troops also came in for a share of criticism. He was a stern disciplinarian and soon acquired a reputation for harshness. When plagued with desertions he promptly closed the issue by making an example of an offender. He had him shot. There was no formal inquiry and,

[23] Shaw to Charles Halpine, A.A.G., June 14, 1863, quoted in Emilio, *History of the 54th*, pp. 43–44; Pierce to Charles Sumner, June 18, 1863, and Higginson to Sumner, June 20, 1863, Sumner MSS; New York *Tribune*, June 24, 1863, and the Beaufort *Free South*, July 18, 1863, quoting and commenting upon the protests of the Boston *Commonwealth* of July 3, 1863.

beyond Montgomery's own questioning of the man, no further hearing.[24] A young Massachusetts officer said Montgomery was "cordially detested" in the Department as "an Abolitionist of the Western type . . . who hates slavery because it is an institution belonging to his neighbors over the border with whom he has always been carrying on a barbarous and bloody partisan warfare."[25] While Higginson wanted the war to advance the cause of freedom, Montgomery wanted freedom to win the war and hasten the defeat of a hated slaveocracy. While the two propositions were not precisely antithetical, the difference in their emphases was pregnant with meaning. The implications were far wider than the relatively small question of the proper disposition of Negro troops. As long as the war lasted, neither goal could be obtained without a commitment to the other. But one could only ask if the nation would recall its obligation to freedom after the fighting subsided, or recall what the colored troops had done for the Union. Higginson had once been worried about the tendency of revolutions to roll backward.

In the meantime, Colonel Shaw was eager for some great action that would erase the memory of Darien. At last there were promising signs of a serious military engagement in the Department of the South. It was none too soon. To soldiers coming south from Virginia the life seemed easy and gay, the soldierly routine almost nonexistent, and the prospects of actual fighting rather dim. The Department was gaining a reputation as a "military picnic."[26] Excepting the unsuccessful attempt to occupy Florida and an

[24] Emilio, *History of the 54th*, p. 48; Towne MS diary, June 29, 1863.

[25] John C. Gray to Elizabeth Gray, October 15, 1863, in John Chipman Gray and John Codman Ropes, *War Letters, 1862–1865* (Boston and New York, 1927), p. 232.

[26] Pearson (ed.), *Letters*, text and note, p. 154; Richard Skinner (a staff officer to General Hunter) to [William Woolsey Johnson], March 24, 1863, in Richard Skinner MSS, Southern Historical Collection, Chapel Hill. The Skinner MSS consist of only several items.

abortive attack on Charleston Harbor in the spring, there had been no serious undertakings on the mainland. But now, in midsummer, the rapid build-up of troops in the usually neglected Department and a change in commanding officers revealed that Charleston was in for more hot work. General Quincy A. Gillmore, who had earned recognition as a capable engineer and artillerist, arrived to replace Hunter. Gillmore's plan was to grasp control of the outlying batteries on James and Morris Islands, to the south of Fort Sumter, and from this vantage point to reduce the famous fortress commanding the harbor's entrance. Robert Gould Shaw pleaded that the 54th have a part.[27]

He won his point. On July 8 Shaw received the command to ready his regiment, and in two days the first action on James Island began. The main objective of the Union forces was the reduction of Battery Wagner, located on the harbor end of Morris Island, long and fingerlike, pointing northeastward from James Island, which was nearer Charleston and to the west of Morris. The Confederates had to be deceived into regarding James Island as the main objective so that the defenses of Wagner would be reduced to meet the onslaught. As a part of this diversionary action, the 54th acquitted itself well. In an exposed position on the right flank, the black soldiers held their lines firmly and won warm praise from Commanding General Alfred H. Terry. It was their first taste of "honorable" soldiering.[28] The 54th then withdrew to the base of operations on Folly Island, whence they received orders to go immediately to Morris Island to join the main attack on Wagner. Because of the marshy terrain and the shortage of transportation, this transfer from James to Folly and then to Morris Island took two awful days, in which the men had no sleep, no rations, and very little water except for the rain. Cold, tired, and wet, they would have had every reason to decline the

---

[27] OR, I, xiv, 464–465, 469; Emilio, *History of the 54th*, p. 49.
[28] *Ibid.*, pp. 51–52, 63.

foremost position in the assault on Wagner when they at last reported.[29] But such opportunities had as yet come seldom to black soldiers, and Shaw would not say no to such an irrefragable test of Negro manhood.

There was some hope of success. The fortress, which stood three-quarters of a mile away at the end of a narrow corridor of sand, had been under naval bombardment all day, but as the last paints of sunset faded in the west Wagner surely looked formidable to the weary black soldiers as they formed their columns. "I guess they kind of 'spec's we're coming!" remarked one young soldier sagely to another. Colonel Shaw took his place at the front of his regiment and told his men that the hour of destiny had come. The world would know what they did that night. "Now I want you to prove yourselves men," he said. Pale, but purposeful and graceful as becomes a gentleman born, he took his place at the center and front of his regiment. He wore the handsome uniform of a colonel of volunteers, with close-fitting navy jacket and light blue trousers. With his silver eagles upon his shoulders, his fine silk sash about his waist, and an ancient ring upon his finger, Sarah Shaw's son was groomed for the sacrifice. He had earlier handed his personal effects to Edward Pierce, who had come from Beaufort to report the engagement. Shaw said to his friend Lieutenant Colonel Hallowell: "We shall take the fort or die there!"[30]

At the signal, the lines moved forward in the gathering dark.[31] The ominous stillness of the long march up the beach was disturbed only by fitful bursts of fire from the forts and the restless wash of the Atlantic, as each returning wave obliged the companies on the right flank to walk in water to their knees. At a point two hundred yards from the fort, the easterly extension of marshland constricted the regiment into a narrow defile of sand. Press-

---

[29] *Ibid.*, pp. 64–65.

[30] *Ibid.*, pp. 76–78.

[31] *Ibid.*, pp. 79–85; George W. Williams, *A History of Negro Troops in the War of the Rebellion* (New York, 1888), pp. 195–200.

ing forward, now in almost total darkness, the soldiers attempted to hold their lines on the narrow bar. At this critical moment the guns of Wagner exhaled a blistering fire. The black soldiers advanced at double-quick, men falling on all sides, and at last gained the partial protection of the high parapet of the fort. They then slipped down into the water-filled ditch that defended the outer works. Those who emerged clawed their way to the ramparts, bearing the national and state colors to the parapet and defending them there. Those who gained the interior contended with bayonet and clubbed rifle in a vain effort to subdue the garrison. Colonel Shaw himself stood for a timeless moment upon the parapet with his sword held high, waving his men into the carnage, and then fell. The first furious onslaught failed for lack of timely reinforcement, but in the space between the parapet and the ditch the black soldiers swept the heights with rifle fire to prevent the service of the guns. At last, as their numbers were so reduced as to make even this work impossible, it became abundantly clear that reinforcements could never arrive in time. The assault had failed.

Painfully retreating through a hail of musketry, the decimated regiment had cause to reflect upon the poor generalship that had entailed the costly expenditure of life both in their own regiment and in those sent up too late to save the day. But allocating the fault, even resolving the question whether the white Union soldiers who had fired into their ranks were motivated by malice or simply confused, all this was beside the point. The black men had done enough. Of a regiment at the strength of only 600 men, they had lost as killed, wounded, or missing 270 enlisted men and officers.[32] In great causes immolation is often exacted. The Negro could gain nothing in destroying property on the Combahee and

[32] Emilio, *History of the 54th*, pp. 75, 91. The relatively small number listed as actually killed in E. N. Hallowell's report is misleading, for numbers of the seriously wounded men died subsequently in Beaufort hospitals, both of their injuries and of the fevers, which were unusually severe in the summer of 1863.

at Darien. At Battery Wagner he had gained, by the rigorous standard of aggressive America, his full right to manhood. A Negro historian writing more than twenty years later remembered what service in the war had meant to colored troops: "It was midnight and noonday without a space between; from the Egyptian darkness of bondage to the lurid glare of civil war; from passive submission . . . to the brilliant aggressiveness of a free soldier; from a chattel to a person. . . ."[33]

Morris Island was not the first engagement in which Negro soldiers had stood up manfully against the armed Confederacy. In the West at Milliken's Bend, and more recently at Port Hudson, Negroes had fought bravely. But it was at Battery Wagner that the tide of public opinion was fully turned on the question of arming the Negro. Conservative newspapers, which previously had viewed the matter with contempt or caution, now responded warmly to the revolutionary idea. After July 18 the arming of Negroes accelerated to a remarkable degree, and by the end of the year sixty colored regiments were being organized.[34]

Battery Wagner was definitive. There was a powerful symbolism of sacrifice in the story. Young Shaw's body was stripped of his uniform by a company of Confederate thieves; they took his gold watch and chain and all other appurtenances of wealth and distinction, leaving his remains in the undeniable democracy of underwear. The nation was shocked at the reports that filtered out of the fort in the days which followed. When General Johnson Hagood, the Confederate commander, regarded the corpse of the young colonel, whom he had respected in other years, he thought to cover it with shame by ordering it buried in the com-

[33] Williams, *A History of Negro Troops*, p. xiii.

[34] Cornish, *Sable Arm*, p. 156; Quarles, *The Negro in the Civil War*, p. 20, and Allen Nevins, *War Becomes Revolution, 1862–1863* (New York, 1960), pp. 527–528; see also Pearson, *Andrew*, II, 86, 90. It is significant, as Pearson states on p. 86, that it was only after Wagner that Lincoln took the step of threatening retaliation upon Confederate prisoners for failure to treat Negro prisoners as regular prisoners of war.

mon trench with the black soldiers. At a later date, when the Union forces regained the fort, Francis George Shaw squelched a plan for the recovery of his son's body. "We hold that a soldier's most appropriate burial-place is on the field where he has fallen." Privately, to Edward Pierce, he wrote, "We can imagine no holier place than that in which he is, among his brave and devoted followers, nor wish for him better company— . . . what a bodyguard he has!"[35]

The nation was deeply moved. The story was told and told again. Poets sang Shaw's death and its meaning for antislavery men and women everywhere:

> "They buried him with his niggers!"
>   A wide grave should it be.
> They buried more in that shallow trench
>   Than human eye could see.
> Ay, all the shames and sorrows
>   Of more than a hundred years
> Lie under the weight of that Southern soil
>   Despite those cruel sneers.[36]

There were better poems written for Shaw, but none expressed better the aspect of expiation. Abolitionist New England had an easier conscience after Battery Wagner. The accumulated shame of national complicity in the sin of slavery was on its way to being exorcised. Maria Weston Chapman, antislavery for thirty years,

[35] Francis George Shaw to Quincy Gillmore, August 24, 1863, in Emilio, *History of the 54th*, pp. 102–103; Francis Shaw to E. L. Pierce, July 31, 1863, E. L. Pierce MSS. Hagood denied specific malevolent intent with regard to Shaw's burial in a letter to Higginson, dated September 21, 1881. The account of Assistant-Surgeon John T. Luck, U.S.N., captured on the morning of the day after the battle, is the popularly accepted version. The omission of the ordinary protocol was enough to give Luck's account the benefit of the doubt. Both statements are in Emilio, *History of the 54th*, pp. 99–100.

[36] Williams, *A History of Negro Troops*, p. 204.

performed her rites by framing the hero's portrait in pine cones and chestnut wood. Finally, St. Gaudens created a monument to Shaw and the famous 54th; the young Anglo-Saxon Colonel leads his swarthy troops forever under the elms of Boston Common.[37]

While the nation felt a sense of exaltation over what was after all a Pyrrhic victory, Gillmore's army set to work by slower methods of siege to win control of Charleston Harbor. The remnants of the 54th joined with other outfits for further duty. They probably had little time for thought. The case was far different for the scores of wounded sent to Beaufort hospitals for long weeks of slow recovery or possible death. Their reflections come to us filtered through the hearts and minds of the Port Royal evangels, who went into action as nurses and doctors under the emergency existing in the little town.

Charlotte Forten and Laura Towne observed that uppermost in the minds of the men was their concern for Colonel Shaw and their grief at his death. The men bore their troubles with a good heart, and Mansfield French said that he saw "with devout thankfulness, that many of them read, in their very sufferings, a promise of good in the future." There was surely reason for deep thankfulness that their untried regiment had behaved as very brave men of any color behave in extreme circumstances. There was surely a profound gratitude for the kind favors rendered the sufferers by the sympathetic teachers who wrote letters home, ten-

[37] Maria Weston Chapman to E. B. Chapman, January 17 [1864], Weston MSS; Vol. 6, item 92; James Freeman Clarke wrote, "But he has done a noble work in dying. . . ." Clarke to E. L. Pierce, August 8, 1863, Pierce MSS. James Russell Lowell's inscription for the Shaw monument reads:

"Right in the van of the red rampart's slippery swell
  With heart that beat a charge he fell
        Foeward as fits a man.
  But the high soul burns on to light men's feet
  Where death for noble ends makes dying sweet."

derly mended the riddled uniforms, and concocted tempting dishes for the ailing. The island people sent gifts of fresh melons and produce by the cartload to the soldiers "wounded for we," as they said.[38] But if gratitude was not mixed with some bitterness at the irony of their new role as wounded heroes, the black soldiers were more than human, or somewhat less.

After all, these men had come from a regiment that had been subjected to intolerable insult only a few weeks before. Recruited with the promise of the regular pay of volunteers, they had been offered upon their first payday in the Department of the South the customary salary of the "contraband" regiments. Rather than $13 per month, they had been offered $10, $3 of which could be paid in clothing; the men had refused it. They were reported to have been almost mutinous in the weeks just before Wagner. Even the offer of Governor Andrew to make up the difference from the State Treasury was refused, for the men objected to being represented "as holding out for *money* and not from principle. . . ." So it came about that the Massachusetts regiment fought for eighteen months with no pay but the initial bounty of $50, waiting for a stubborn Congress to make good on the promises made at enlistment. Those among the sick and wounded who went back to their regiment before September 30, little more than two months after Wagner, would have arrived in time to hear James Montgomery, who succeeded for a time to Shaw's command, urge the men to accept their insulting pay. "You must remember you have not proved yourselves soldiers. You must take notice that the Government has virtually paid you a thousand dollars apiece for setting you free." Montgomery was clearly forgetting that he was speaking to men who had been free before the war. Nor were his urgings without personal insult: "Any one listening to your shouting and singing can see how

[38] French to George Whipple, July 30, 1863, AMA MSS, uncatalogued box labeled "1862–A–J"; Holland (ed.), *Towne*, pp. 114–115; Billington (ed.), *Forten*, pp. 194–195.

grotesquely ignorant you are." In their refusal to accept their pay, which was all they were "legally entitled to," Montgomery declared, they were "guilty of insubordination and mutiny" and could be "tried and shot by court-martial."[39]

Even more crushing to Negro soldiers must have been the ugly news from New York. At the very time the 54th had been fighting doggedly about Charleston harbor, a furious mob, angered over the draft policy of the government, had vented its spleen on the hapless Negroes of the city. Ugly indeed was the thought that while they had been fighting at the front, black people were being lynched in the North, and that a Negro orphanage had been burned. Abused mercilessly and undercut in pay by their own government, the soldiers also had to reflect upon the possible fate of their comrades taken within the fort at Wagner. The Confederate government had cast them beyond the pale of civilized warfare, and the captives were subject to death or sale into servitude. They would not know for some time that their captured friends were saved from slavery by the fortitude of an unsung Charleston lawyer of Union convictions who successfully defended the men before a South Carolina court.[40]

However, the missionaries who nursed the soldiers detected no spirit of bitterness but rather, as Mansfield French observed, "a subdued feeling—a chastened submission to the will of God." If, as the chaplain thought, "a spiritual vision seems to be coming over the army," it was not without cause. By the end of July it

[39] Pearson, *Andrew*, II, 104, quoting a letter from the camp of the 54th Massachusetts Volunteers, first appearing in a communication from Theodore Tilton to the Boston *Journal*, and dated December 12, 1863; for Montgomery's address to the 54th on pay, see Emilio's *History of the 54th*, pp. 130, 137, 227; Gannett MS diary, June 19, 1863; Milton Hawks to Esther Hawks, September 28, 1863; the struggle for equal pay is told well in Cornish, *Sable Arm*, pp. 181–196. The men of the 54th received justice in equal pay, with arrears, in October of 1864. It was March of 1865 before the "contraband" regiments of the islands received the same. *Ibid.*, pp. 193–194.

[40] Williams, *A History of Negro Troops*, pp. 174–175; Emilio, *History of the 54th*, p. 97.

seemed very much as though the Almighty had at last joined the Union side. A man of French's convictions would see this as a result of the growing acceptance of "God's plan of mercy, of freedom—of purity for the nation. . . ."[41]

Although much hard fighting lay yet ahead, by the end of July the great military crises of the war were past. On the rolling Pennsylvania hills near Gettysburg the Union forces had defeated the formidable army of Robert E. Lee and placed it on the defensive; it would never recover fully. On July 4, the same day that saw Lee's retreat to the Potomac, General Ulysses S. Grant received the surrender of the besieged city of Vicksburg; and within four more days, Port Hudson, Louisiana, fell, and the Union forces controlled the whole length of the Mississippi. The Confederacy was divided, and it was about to be divided again. In September the Army of the Cumberland took Chattanooga, thus opening from this key point a route southward and eastward to the vital center of the Confederacy.

The Department of the South was destined to have no part in the fierce onslaughts that ended the war. Except for the numbers of Confederate troops rendered inactive by the very presence of the armies at Hilton Head and the usefulness of the base to the blockade, little was accomplished. Gillmore was able to plant his big guns, and the *Swamp Angel* on Morris Island hurled cannon at Sumter with devastating effect until nearly the end of the fighting. But the fort did not surrender, nor was Charleston evacuated until the end was in sight.

The last major assault on the mainland from the Department of the South took place in early 1864, when a full-scale attack was launched in northern Florida with the purpose of separating that state from the Confederacy and setting up a "reconstructed" government. In a bloody battle at Olustee the Northern forces were disastrously defeated. In this engagement Negro troops again

[41] French to George Whipple, July 30, 1863, AMA MSS, uncatalogued box labeled "1862—A–J."

played a major part, and it was no fault of the black soldiers, those recruited in the slave states as well as the Massachusetts 54th, that the expedition ended ignominiously.[42] There simply never was in the Department of the South a military leader of the stature of Grant or Sherman.

In the realm of ideas, however, and in the rapid integration of the expanding goals for Negro freedom and equality with military exigencies, no other Department was quite so significant. In this context, Battery Wagner may be regarded as a turning point, not only for the nation's felt obligations to the American Negro but also for the Port Royal experiment. The acceleration of military developments and the rapid evolution of the full program for arming the Negro were warmly supported by most of the missionaries. Numbers had recognized from the beginning that the results of their social experiment would pale, historically speaking, in comparison to the gains the Negro would make as a soldier in the Union army. By mid-1863 those of the evangels who had at first doubted that soldiers could be made of the late slave population were convinced of their error.[43] These were creditable attitudes in view of the abundant difficulties thrown upon them by the work of recruitment.

The withdrawal of able-bodied males from the plantations was the most obvious problem. In any comparison with ante-bellum agricultural output this factor would be a paramount consideration. The expeditions of Higginson and Montgomery contributed to this abnormal situation by bringing into the Department thousands of dependents. Settlements of hundreds of freed people in the environs of Beaufort memorialized their liberators in their

[42] An account of the Olustee debacle may be found in Emilio, *History of the 54th*, pp. 148–185.

[43] Harriet Ware, of the Philbrick group on St. Helena, wrote in March, 1863, "We did not think a year ago that these people would make soldiers, though it might be a wise measure to organize them for garrison duty. . . . Now it is a matter of fact . . . that they will fight in open warfare. . . ." Pearson (ed.), *Letters*, p. 164.

names: Higginsonville and Montgomery's Hill. The men customarily went into the army, but the children, the women, the aged, and the infirm had to be provided for as quickly as possible on the plantations.[44]

The larger problem remained, however, one of morale. William Channing Gannett stated the problem succinctly when he admitted that "The truth must be owned that the Port Royalists have shown great apathy in sacrificing anything to secure their liberty. The real volunteers have been comparatively few. By far the greater part of the native regiments have been filled by wholesale conscription, and in several instances shooting down fugitives." It was all too true. The habits and attitudes of generations of slavery died hard. When William Allen tried to induce a student named "Billy" to enlist, he was met with the response that Billy "would rather be a slave all his life than fight" but that if he had to do so, he'd fight "with a stick, but not with a gun." The old story that the Yankees wanted to carry them to Cuba for sale still continued to have some currency among the plantation Negroes. Unwilling to accept this skepticism as genuine, the military authorities continued to blame their poor luck in recruiting on the supposed reluctance of plantation superintendents to give up their best hands.[45]

This accusation was true only to the extent that the missionary-superintendents sometimes winked at the ruses of the freedmen to elude the draft, which was carried on in a manner calculated to antagonize anyone regarding the Negroes as a part of the human

[44] Laura Towne describes the reunion of Negro families resulting from the arrival of new "refugees" brought in by Higginson and their relocation on the plantations. Towne MS diary, July 12, 13, 1863; see also Boston *Commonwealth*, December 4, 1863; Beaufort *Free South*, September 19, 1863.

[45] [Gannett and Hale], "The Freedmen at Port Royal," *North American Review*, CI (July, 1865), 27; Allen MS diary, February 24, 1864, typescript, pp. 138–139; Towne MS diary, May 2, 1863; Port Royal *New South*, March 7, 1863; Pearson (ed.), *Letters*, p. 189.

race. On the other hand, the teachers and superintendents tried persuasion and attempted to arouse in the Negroes a sense of duty to their race and some notion of patriotism. Because this method was largely ineffectual, they were often disappointed in the apathetic attitude of their charges. "I wish sincerely," wrote William Allen, "that something would turn up to make these men more willing to fight for their freedom—they have got it altogether too easily. But forcing them into the ranks at the point of the bayonet is only driving them away."[46]

That was the crux of the matter. From the time of Hunter's abortive draft of 1862 straight through the war, military authorities treated the islanders as suited their convenience, with utter disregard for the claims of humanity. Nor did they ever once allow drafting policy to be influenced by any understanding of the simplicity of a people who had hardly known a world existed beyond their islands until the Yankees started teaching them geography. The colored people did understand *promises*, however, and they understood that the Yankees were not keeping faith. General Saxton had assured them at the time he began recruiting on an authorized basis that no man would be taken against his will.[47]

But as soon as the induction of freed slaves into the army became public policy Hunter resumed operations, and Saxton was powerless to impede his precipitate commander. With a customary lack of foresight, Hunter waited to begin forcible drafting in the spring of 1863 until the people had put in their crops. Naturally, the Negroes did not fully exculpate the missionaries who rounded them up to explain the new developments. "Old Rachel" told William Gannett, "I tho't Mr. G. you were a gentleman and had feeling but now I see you have none."[48]

[46] Allen MS diary, February 24, 1864, typescript, p. 75.
[47] Pearson (ed.), *Letters*, pp. 167, 172.
[48] Gannett MS diary, March 20, 1863, Gannett MSS; Tomlinson to McKim, March 16, 1863, McKim MSS.

Hunter's own action of the year before had left a legacy of suspicion that would never be eradicated. "Robin," of the Fripp place, expressed it quite well. "Look here, sir," he said to Willian Allen, "I poor man, wid large famerly—my wife Rinah she can't work . . . can't work wid de hoe for more'n twenty year.— Dey took me an' kep me tree mont' an' nebber pay me, not one cent. My wife hab notting to eat—mus' starve."[49] The missionaries who were trying to teach the Negro fathers to assume family responsibilities were bound to see Robin's point.

When the people did not come voluntarily, squads of soldiers forcibly herded them into the camps. Surprise encirclements by day and sudden seizures in the night became ordinary occurrences. People were taken indiscriminately to Beaufort, without a chance to tell their families where they were, and sometimes kept for days, even when they held exemption certificates in their pockets. Much of this impressment was done by black soldiers already in the "contraband" regiments. They were not overly nice in their methods and shot at random, to the consternation of livestock and frequent injury to the people. Being for the most part illiterate, they distrusted and disregarded exemption papers; one man legally exempt was killed by a Negro press-gang that attempted to bring him in against his will. For these operations the white officers were of course fully responsible. The colored people did not take it like sheep. On one place the field women attacked the black soldiers with their hoes and were in turn fired upon. They shouted that the white men were afraid to fight and only wanted the Negroes to do their work.[50]

Those who were lucky enough to elude the first forays took to the swamps, living the life of maroons just as they would have done in slavery times under unendurable circumstances. The ap-

[49] Allen MS diary, January 31, 1863, typescript, p. 116.
[50] Charles Nordhoff, *The Freedmen of South Carolina* (New York, 1863), p. 3; Towne MS diary, March 25, 30, April 14, 20, 26, May 18, September 21, 22, 1863; Gannett MS diary, April 14, March 23, 25, 1863; Pearson (ed.), *Letters*, pp. 183–189; Port Royal *New South*, June 13, 1863.

pearance of a pair of epaulets was enough to break up a church service, send the schoolchildren scurrying away, or cause the men to drop their hoes in the field and make for the woods.[51]

Once in uniform, the reluctant Sea Island soldiers could anticipate an inconceivably poor and inexperienced set of officers, except for a few of the highest rank; their only common trait was a belief in the use of Negro soldiers to fight the war. Some of the best men in Higginson's regiment mutinied against the leadership of an inept officer who took a contingent of the 1st South Carolina on an ill-fated raid into Georgia. The courts-martial arising out of this and similar cases caused General Gillmore to rap the officers' knuckles quite smartly, accusing them of being more responsible for the troubles than the men. He blandly pointed out that the people ought not to be unusually hard to discipline, in view of their former condition, but that their officers were on the one hand guilty of "unofficer-like familiarity" and, on the other, of "extreme harshness." He was far from alone in his judgment.[52]

It is hardly surprising that men brought into the army and held there under such conditions would take the first opportunity to desert. As a result, the plantation routine was plagued until the end of the war by sporadic details of soldiers sent to bring in deserters, even during periods when no draft was in effect.[53]

[51] "Not a man sleeps at night in the houses, except those too old to be taken. They have made a camp somewhere and mean never to be caught." Pearson (ed.), Letters, p. 177.

[52] Quincy A. Gillmore's General Order No. 10, published in the Port Royal New South, January 23, 1864; Port Royal New South, June 13, 1863; Thomas Wentworth Higginson to his wife, June 10, 1863, Higginson MSS; Towne MS diary, June 29, 1863; Pearson (ed.), Letters, p. 189; John C. Gray, Jr., to John C. Ropes, September 28, 1863, Gray and Ropes, War Letters, p. 218.

[53] Allen MS diary, December 27, 28, 1863, typescript copy, pp. 73–75; Pearson (ed.), Letters, pp. 239–240. Philbrick describes a particularly ruthless scouting party, sent without white officers, which shot three deserters on sight. "One is badly wounded and may not recover, but the others probably will." Ibid., p. 236.

The authorities seemed to regard the islands as an inexhaustible source of manpower. After three regiments of South Carolina "Volunteers" were raised, few fully eligible males remained on the plantations, but the drafts continued. In July, 1864, after much hesitation, Congress yielded at last to overwhelming pressure and authorized state governments to fill out their draft quotas in occupied areas of the South.[54] Officials, armed with the power to offer bounties to the Negroes they could "persuade" to enlist, descended upon the islands like the plagues of Egypt, seized men at random, and as often as not pocketed the bounty money themselves. Laura Towne wrote that on the Frogmore plantation two men were shot, one killed outright and another mortally wounded. She wrote that Secretary Stanton, when he at last made a personal investigation, found that these procedures were "not uncommon, but that men were seized, their bounty appropriated and themselves sent to Morris Island without being allowed to return to tell their families where they were going." A Treasury official completely unconnected with the missionary work wrote Governor Andrew, attempting to dissuade him from supporting state recruiting on the islands. He wrote that "The poor negroes are hunted like wild beasts. . . . There is a perfect panic throughout all these islands. Old men and invalids have taken to the bush through fear of the conscription. . . ." He could "conceive of no greater terror and distress on the coast of Africa after a slave hunt" than he had witnessed. "They have been pursued and fired at by cavalry." He had heard of one "d—d black-hearted, black-coated pseudo Chaplain turned negro broker" who had tried "to procure blood-hounds wherewith to hunt contrabands."[55]

A young Massachusetts officer in a white regiment blushed to think of "this traffic of New England towns in the bodies of wretched negroes, bidding against each other for these miserable beings who are deluded, and if some of the affidavits I have in

[54] Pearson, *Andrew*, II, 143, note on p. 144.
[55] Laura Towne to "R," January 21, 1863, Towne MSS; Pearson, *Andrew*, II, note on pp. 144–145.

my office are true, tortured into military service." It formed "too good a justification of all that is said against the Yankees." Anyway, it was a very poor system. In four months of state recruiting in the South, it took 1,045 men to raise 2,831 Negro soldiers.[56] These mercenary officials cared little that many a disabled Negro would have to be discharged promptly for ill health, so long as they received their pay. The Civil War abounded in ironies, but none was stranger than the fact that in the role of soldier the Negro at once made his most secure step toward ultimate independence and was subject to the most ruthless exploitation.

Whatever else may be said of this wartime experience with Yankee recruiters, one thing is certain. The islanders had met in the flesh the heralds of the most unscrupulous elements of postwar carpetbaggery. Either the Negro would learn to discriminate among his Yankee friends, or he would take the more comprehensive plan of distrusting them all. Experience, especially for unlettered people, tells for something. Charles Ware, superintendent, said he was always met by the remark, "We are a year older than we was last year, sir."[57]

But experience is, after all, a slow road to knowledge. And events were moving very rapidly. When the war was over, Northern people would not make nice discriminations about which Negroes had done what, or how willingly, or who had been abused. The historical fact remained that yesteryear's slave had served honorably in the Union army. This fact, as Governor Andrew had fully foreseen, would more than any other fix the status of the Negro as a free man.

As a free man the Negro would enjoy advantages and disadvantages. Benevolent protection might be withdrawn at an overly-rapid rate, subjecting the freedmen to use and abuse. On the other

[56] John C. Gray, Jr., to his mother, January 30, 1865, in Gray and Ropes, *War Letters*, pp. 449–450; Pearson, citing the report of the United States Provost-Marshal-General, in *Andrew*, II, 145.

[57] Pearson (ed.), *Letters*, p. 174.

hand, in the national mind the conception of freedom was inseparable from self-support. When John Adams stated his idea that
civil society was based on the church, the schoolhouse, the militia,
and the town meeting, he made no mention of land or of self-
support. It was merely an oversight, for deep in the national sense
of the fitness of things, so deep perhaps as to require no statement,
was the idea that a free farmer ought to have sufficient land on
which to support himself.

ten ❧ "SQUATTER RIGHTS," OR "CHARITABLE PURPOSES"?

PARSON FRENCH HAD SELECTED HIS TEXT. ON A FINE OCTOBER Sunday, just outside a little church near the center of Port Royal Island, he was speaking to a throng of freedmen, Negro soldiers, and their missionary friends. Fond as French was of the rich imagery of the Old Testament, no subject in all the ancient books could have had quite the appeal for the evangelist as the words of Moses to the Children of Israel: "Behold the Lord thy God hath set the land before thee; go up and possess it, as the Lord God of thy fathers hath said unto thee; fear not, neither be discouraged."[1]

A few weeks before, in his instructions of September 16, 1863, to the Direct Tax Commissioners of South Carolina, President Lincoln had outlined the plans of the government for the disposition of the 60,000 acres of land that the commission had bid in for the United States at the sale of the preceding March. At an auction scheduled for early in 1864, the property was to be offered at public sale in lots not exceeding 320 acres, with the important exception of certain lands retained for naval, military, educational, and charitable purposes. Within the last category came the special provision reserving for "heads of families of the African race" certain specifically named plantations, which were to be subdivided into small twenty-acre lots and sold at a preferred rate of $1.25 per acre. The intention of the government had been under-

---

[1] *Report of the Proceedings of a Meeting Held at Concert Hall, Philadelphia, on Tuesday Evening, November 3, 1863* (Philadelphia, 1863), p. 21.

stood in the islands for some time, and the commissioners, with the cooperation of Saxton's chief carpenter, D. C. Wilson, had been surveying the lands and erecting small houses on the lots designed for freedmen. Now that the word was official, the missionaries lost no time in telling the people of their advantages.[2]

The Negroes who met to hear the news on Port Royal Island opened their services with the ringing spiritual:

> *Children of a Heavenly King,*
> *As we journey, let us sing, ...*

After Mr. French delivered a stirring sermon about Moses and the promised land, General Saxton explained the President's instructions and also explained to the colored people why they ought to own a little land to secure their future. In the Western tradition of "squatter rights," the freedmen agreed upon plans for claiming the land, framed a few rules for their future government, and pledged allegiance to the United States. Sergeant Prince Rivers, Colonel Higginson's able and tireless recruiting officer, seized the occasion to make a speech in favor of enlistment, emphasizing the especially generous provision for soldiers to own land. He made the most of the manly and independent feelings of a freedman who became a soldier for the Union and ended by exhorting the "cowards" who would not join the army to be at least fair with the old men and women in the competition that would inevitably ensue for the best land. Afterward, the Negroes were invited to inspect a rude little model house that was brought out for the occasion. Approximately 16 by 20 feet, the cabin was made of poles and planks ingeniously put together without benefit of nails. The cost of the prospective landowners who would erect the cabins on their tiny freeholds was $25.[3]

[2] "Instructions to the Tax Commissioners in South Carolina," September 16, 1863, in Basler (ed.), *Lincoln*, VI, 453–459; Beaufort *Free South*, September 19, 1863; Towne MS diary, April 22, 1863.

[3] *Report of the Proceedings at Concert Hall*, pp. 21–23.

On November 3 Saxton formally issued his instructions in a circular published in the *Free South*, telling the people to deposit their money, together with an accurate description of the land they wanted to own, at his headquarters. Captain Hooper would take charge, and "at the sale, *if possible*, bid in the land for the person who has filed the claim. . . ."[4]

There was one signal element of mystification. There was surely no need to wait upon the auction to purchase the plantations specifically reserved for Negro sales. That would be done at the office of the tax commissioners, and they as yet had not even determined upon the form of the certificate to be issued to prospective Negro purchasers. While Saxton was at pains to point out the specific plantations reserved for Negro sales at $1.25 per acre, he referred also, in general terms, to *all* the lands. His suggestion was oblique: "The theory of selection proposed is, to divide up as nearly as possible every alternate quarter section among the Freedmen, leaving the other alternate quarter section to such other persons as may wish to buy. . . ." If a man built his cabin upon this land and proposed to live there, he would "be considered as having a pre-emption right in equity to the soil." Saxton thought it "highly probable that no person would feel disposed to interfere with this right." Of course he could not be *sure*, although he did not say so.[5]

General Saxton and Parson French had launched themselves upon a doubtful course of circumventing the President's instructions. Disappointed that only "alternate quarter sections" of the Port Royal lands were set aside for Negro settlement, Governor Saxton was encouraging the freedmen to build their cabins upon the public lands of their own choice in the hope of establishing a subsequent clear claim. While appearing to *implement* the instructions, he was, in fact, seizing the initiative in the tax commis-

[4] Beaufort *Free South*, November 14, 1863. Italics mine.
[5] *Ibid.*; Minute Book, entry for December 4, 1863, in Records of the United States Direct Tax Commission for South Carolina, National Archives. Hereafter cited as U.S. Dir. Tax Com., S.C.

sioners' own bailiwick. The commissioners understood at once.[6]

The President's instructions of September, 1863, had encompassed the plans of the majority of the commission, and they clearly did not envision a wholesale surrender of the rich island districts to "charitable purposes" at $1.25 per acre. The plantations specifically indicated for Negro sales under the instructions comprised only 16,000 of the 60,000 acres open for sale.[7] In the eyes of most observers keenly interested in the future of the Negroes, the plan was unfair and inadequate to the needs of the freedmen.[8] Saxton's ambiguous instructions assume, in the light of subsequent developments, all the earmarks of deliberate obfuscation in a worthy cause. If the freedmen happily and innocently struck their claims hither and yon over the islands, was there not a good chance that the commissioners would be obliged to have the instructions changed to suit the status quo? Would not *all* the lands in this way eventually fall to the black people who had so justly earned them through years of unrequited toil?

[6] William E. Wording to Joseph Lewis, Commissioner of Internal Revenue, November 10, 1863, Records U.S. Dir. Tax Com., S.C. Wording phrased the action of Saxton and French as "an attempt to get up among the Negroes a sort of 'squatter sovereignty' to have them stake out their lands which they want, and then make a public opinion which will frown down a bidder over a certain sum."

[7] Lincoln's instructions (Basler [ed.], *Lincoln*, VI, 456–457) did not give specific acreages, but named the plantations by their ante-bellum designations. Two fairly detailed summaries, however, give the allotment for "Heads of Families" at preferred purchase for Negroes as 16,629 acres. See *Free South*, March 11, 1864; F. J. Williams to Salmon P. Chase, February 27, 1864, in Records U.S. Dir. Tax Com., S.C. Commissioners Brisbane and Wording insisted that the lands that were suitable for agriculture had been evenly divided between "Heads of Families" and the open sale, and that 20,000 acres fell within each category. Since they used round figures throughout, it seems likely that the 16,629 figure is more accurate. See Brisbane to Joseph Lewis, January 21, 1864, in *ibid*.

[8] F. J. Williams to Chase, February 27, 1864, *ibid*.; Boston *Commonwealth*, March 18, 1864; F. J. Childs to Edward Atkinson, March 4, 1864, Atkinson MSS.

Such seems to have been the reasoning implicit in Saxton's instructions of November 3, in which he voiced his hopeful opinion that if a Negro struck his claim and was prepared to pay "the government price" he "should have an acknowledged right to purchase."[9]

Commissioner Brisbane was upset. There was nothing to do with "pre-emption" in his instructions. At a conference in Washington during the summer, he had reached an agreement with the Commissioner of Internal Revenue that the rich Sea Islands could not be disposed of on the same basis as the virgin lands of the West. A general pre-emption plan was not appropriate for the "improved" agricultural lands of the South.[10] According to the instructions of September 16, "charitable purposes" constituted a mere embellishment to the main point, raising revenue. The implication is plain enough that there was no expectation that all the Port Royal freedmen would be provided with land at $1.25 per acre. The commissioners had authority to issue "certificates" to the small lots to such heads of Negro families as applied, "preferring such as by their good conduct, meritorious services or exemplary character, will be examples of moral propriety and industry" to their race. The idea of elimination of some applicants was implicit. In a hasty letter to Washington, Commissioner Brisbane and Commissioner William Wording protested that the mass meetings Saxton and French were promoting were stirring up a troublesome spirit. They accused the pair, accurately enough, of giving the people the notion that "squatter sovereignty" in the land would be acknowledged.[11]

The commissioners had their hands full, for Saxton had become an extremely difficult man to criticize directly. The general,

[9] Beaufort Free South, November 14, 1863.

[10] Brisbane to Joseph Lewis, February 25, 1864, Records U. S. Dir. Tax Com., S. C.

[11] Basler (ed.), Lincoln, VI, 457; William E. Wording to Joseph Lewis, January 30, 1864, Records U.S. Dir. Tax Com., S.C. See also Brisbane to Lewis, January 16, 1863, in ibid.

though perhaps not a profound or original thinker, was a man who appeared to be even more guileless than he actually was. A doubt of his sincere devotion to the welfare of his islanders could never be entertained seriously in any quarter. As is the universal practice in such cases, the general's advisers bore the brunt of criticism whenever Saxton's policies were questioned. The worst the commissioners dared to assert against the general was that he was "ambitious in his sphere" and "very much" under the influence of Chaplain French. The minister was dressed out in the robes of Machiavelli in the correspondence of the commissioners, who denounced him as a subtle intriguer and an unsound "theorizer."[12] Playing the power behind Good King Saxton's throne was a role French gladly accepted. When asked about his part in these proceedings, French insisted that he had been the "prime mover" who had "obtained *at last*" General Saxton's consent to an overt challenge of the instructions of September 16. The whole success of the attempt would rest upon the extent of French's influence with Secretary Chase, and General Saxton does not appear to have been alone in the assumption that that was considerable. Again and again the Secretary had followed French's recommendations in Port Royal matters.[13] But French and Saxton did not constitute the full extent of the commissioners' problem. Of the two newspapers published on the islands, the *Free South* was by far the abler journal. James G. Thompson, the editor, had given up his job as a plantation superintendent to conduct the small weekly, which concerned itself primarily with freedmen's affairs and the microscopic politics of Port Royal. Thompson supported the plan of General Saxton, who was at once his good friend and his brother-in-law; as a talented journalist, armed with a stinging and clever style, Thompson was a formidable enemy of the tax commission.

[12] Wording to Lewis, January 30, 1864, *ibid*. See also Brisbane to Lewis, January 21, 1864, *ibid*.

[13] William B. Lucas, a statement to Brisbane, January 30, 1864, and Brisbane to Lewis, January 16, 1864, *ibid*.

While giving Saxton's instructions the fullest possible circulation, the *Free South* muffled the extent to which they differed from the official policy.[14] That point would not be developed until the timing was right.

The worst problem for the commissioners, however, was an internal division between Brisbane and W. E. Wording on the one hand and Commissioner Abram D. Smith on the other. Smith had made common cause with Saxton and French to obtain pre-emptions for the freedmen; he joined them in the desire to see *all* the land thrown open to the Negroes at the preferred rate of $1.25 per acre. Much to the ire of his fellow commissioners, Smith had graced the Saxton-French mass meetings with his official presence.[15] Although this cleavage on principle had appeared early in the correspondence of the commission, it was recognized from the beginning by few people. French caught it and referred to the divergence of views as early as February 7, 1863, when he wrote Secretary Chase of the "broad, and most unfortunate gulf" on the commission, which he thought could *"never be bridged."* He hoped God would give the Secretary the "wisdom to discern which parties have been true to their trust," but French did not wish to leave too much to providential interference. He added promptly, "I must say, what you will be rejoiced to hear, that Judge Smith is as true to his trust, and to the freedmen, as were Caleb and Joshua, to the charge to them by Moses."[16]

In truth, everybody wanted the leading part in conducting the freedmen to the promised land, and Commissioners Wording and Brisbane would not readily admit that Commissioner Smith, or

---

[14] Beaufort *Free South*, November 14, 1863; Wording called Thompson "a most unblushing scoundrel" whose real-estate interests prompted his interest in getting the pre-emption plan adopted, so he and others like him could "make a fine speculation buying up soldiers and Negro claims." Wording to Senator J. R. Doolittle, February 25, 1864, Records U.S. Dir. Tax Com., S.C.

[15] Brisbane to Lewis, December 12, 1863, *ibid*.

[16] French to Chase, February 7, 1863, Chase Papers.

Governor Saxton and Chaplain French, for that matter, were better Calebs and Joshuas than they were. The essential problem was that the disputing parties had differing perspectives on the new Canaan. Each saw a vision, and each party regarded the other as impractical—and visionary. On one point they were in absolute agreement: The steps taken at Port Royal would provide a pattern for the future agricultural reconstruction of the South. The breaking-up of the great estates was an essential feature. Both parties were contending for a far wider application of their theories than the Sea Islands alone.[17]

The majority of the tax commissioners envisioned a mixed settlement of Negroes and whites covering the islands with farms of widely varying sizes. They believed that the ownership of small acreages of from five to twenty acres would provide the freedmen with sufficient independence to release them from the threat of peonage to the prospective white Northern owners who would presumably purchase the larger farms contiguous to the "alternate quarter sections" of Negro settlements. This would, they believed, enhance the value of the Negro farms and also convey certain other benefits. The larger owners would be able to organize agricultural activities on their land and to provide employment for landless Negroes and those with limited acreages.[18] Although the commissioners did not line it out, assuming that Sea-Island cotton would continue to be the primary staple was to grant their plan a number of salient points. Community use of the

---

[17] The proponents of pre-emption thought it would "establish as the foundations of a New South, principles broad and equitable." Beaufort *New South*, January 23, 1864. Senator Doolittle wrote of the plan as originally outlined in the law of June 7, 1863, without pre-emptions, that it would "put some money in the Treasury, break up the great estates of the rebels and be a most efficient means of reconstruction of society upon what society at bottom must rest, *upon the land itself.*" Doolittle to Chase, February 6, 1864, Records U.S. Dir. Tax Com., S.C.

[18] Brisbane to Joseph Lewis, December 12, 1863, and January 21, 1864, in *ibid.*; Boston *Commonwealth*, December 4, 1863.

marsh meadows, woodlands, livestock, and farm equipment would be a distinct advantage to numbers of freedmen who might otherwise be unable to undertake independent operations on a farm consisting of a single plot of arable land. It is interesting to note that this fact did not escape the consideration of certain freedmen who had not been engaged in farming all their lives for nothing.[19] The other significant point is best phrased as a question: Could small owners surmount the natural hazards of the Sea-Island cotton farming or withstand the financial shocks of a risky crop that might easily fail for several years before producing a rich return?

It may be further stressed that under the plan of the commission Negroes who had managed to accumulate the capital were entirely free to compete at the general auction, if they could fix upon a farm of a size within their means; some farms slated for public sale were as small as forty and eighty acres. Negroes were also free to pool their funds and buy their own plantations. This had been done successfully in some instances as early as the original sale of March, 1863. Yet another means whereby the freedmen could gain land on generous terms was through the special provision that soldiers could purchase with only one quarter of the price as down payment and three years to pay.[20]

The commissioners had been busy for months working out their blueprint for the future of the Sea Island district. According to their plan, education for all was to be provided through the income from leasing reserved "School Farms." Dr. Brisbane had a special interest in the regeneration of his native state, and the old gentleman must have enjoyed working out the provisions for its commercial future. Many observers before and since have thought it more than passing strange that the best deep-water port on the South Atlantic coastline should be of no account commercially,

[19] Pearson (ed.), *Letters*, p. 246.
[20] Lincoln's instructions, in Basler (ed.), *Lincoln*, VI, 454; Brisbane to Joseph Lewis, January 21, 1864, Records U.S. Dir. Tax Com., S.C.

and Brisbane was sure that after the war a great future in trade was waiting. He drew up detailed plans for two "cities of commerce," one at Land's End on St. Helena Island and the other where the small village of Port Royal stands today, near the southern tip of the island of that name.[21] Few white people at Port Royal in those days were without a vision.

There was certainly an aura of unreality in Brisbane's plans, set forth in neat charts of cities yet unborn, replete with town greens and college campuses. The element, however, that was most open to the charge of impracticality was the provision for a completely new survey of the whole region. The new lines cut across the islands at ruthless right angles, completely disregarding the ancient plantation markers, the winding creeks and inlets, and the time-honored task divisions in the great cotton fields. These fields were usually square to the roads, but the roads did not run true to north-southerly or east-westerly directions. The result was that after the new surveys the old task markings were useless, and odd triangular sections of land were left on all sides of all the plantations. The fact that numbers of plantations had already passed into private hands as plantation units in the 1863 sale compounded the difficulty.[22] The survey system used in the West was simply impractical in a settled region. Such an overturning of the old divisions would doubtless serve as a double guarantee against a possible attempt to restore the lands after the war, but it was a time-consuming and expensive operation and an unnecessary precaution, as time would prove.

The delays resulting from these extensive surveys had almost as much to do with Saxton's determination to challenge the instructions as did his basically different attitude toward the disposition of the land. No work would go forward for the 1864 crop on the

[21] Brisbane to Lewis, February 2, 1864, in *ibid.*, and Brisbane to Quincy A. Gillmore, March 28, 1865, in Letters Sent, *ibid.*

[22] Allen MS diary, January 24, 1864, pp. 105–106, typescript; Richard Soule to A. B. Cooley, May 13, 1864, Records U.S. Dir. Tax Com., S.C.

plantations being offered at public auction until after the new owners were in possession, and the interim posed some difficulties for Saxton, who had to provide employment for the people.[23]

The main point at issue, however, was the conviction of the Governor, Commissioner Smith, French, and numbers of other missionaries that the commission had not made sufficient provision for Negro landownership. While the commissioners looked to revenue as well as "charitable purposes," their opponents wanted all the Port Royal lands for the freedmen, not as a special benefit but as a natural right.[24] The specter of the profiteering landlord again loomed large in their minds.

While still underplaying the internal differences among the authorities, Saxton continued to promote meetings among the people, encouraging them to select lands and educating them on the advantages of owning property. This knowledge was by no means intuitive. Harriet Ware reported that "some of the most ignorant of our people thought they should be obliged to buy land, and came to C[harles] in distress at leaving the plantation." William F. Allen discovered that the Negroes in his district felt "that they have a sort of right to live upon their own plantations" and were reluctant to buy elsewhere. One "intelligent and trusty" man expressed the idea that it would be "as bad as slavery if they had to leave their old homes."[25] The constricted life under slavery

[23] Correspondent "N," to Boston *Commonwealth*, January 22, 1864; Judge A. D. Smith to Lewis, February 7, 1864, Records U.S. Dir. Tax Com., S.C. Smith claims this problem was the main reason for Saxton's challenge to the Commission.

[24] French was quoted as saying he wanted no Northern and Western people to buy the lands and was trying to prevent it. William B. Lucas to [Brisbane], January 30, 1864, *ibid*. The Boston *Commonwealth* charged that Brisbane, though a man of good intentions, could not rid himself of "the prejudices of his first forty years" as a Southerner and was not ready to "recognize the negro as a man. He doesn't talk of rights, he talks of benefits." *Commonwealth*, March 18, 1864.

[25] Pearson (ed.), *Letters*, p. 230; Allen MS diary, November 25, 1863, p. 32, typescript.

and the great isolation of the islands had encouraged an attachment to home that the urbane Notherners were slow to understand but could not fail to recognize.

Saxton had his most impressive audience on New Year's Day of 1864. A bitter east wind rose with the dawn, and the overcast skies provided an inauspicious setting for the great celebration the Governor had organized to commemorate the first anniversary of emancipation. But the weather could not expunge the spirit of revolutionary hope and enthusiasm of the day. In accepting a presentation sword from the freed people, Saxton made a speech that conveyed his personal vision of their future. He recalled the "destitution and ignorance" of two years before and complimented the swift progress of the people, which had exceeded his "most sanguine expectations." He urged them forward on the "career of improvement." In a grand peroration he depicted an agrarian idyl where the people would live together in peace and happiness; it was the typical abolitionist dream of a free peasantry:

. . . Ere two . . . [more] years be added to the great record of the past, we may see these islands covered with neat cottages, each the centre of a happy home, little farms well tilled, school houses built and teachers hired to instruct your children. These islands are as fertile as any upon which the sun shines, the rivers and bays swarming with the finest fish: the necessaries and luxuries of life are produced here in rare abundance and excellence.

For the rest, the great cotton staple would provide "an endless source of wealth" to the people. Whether the cold and shivering freedmen also envisioned this we do not know, but they must surely have sensed that the revolution was in full swing by the general tenor of the events of the day. Above the speakers' stand the names of John Brown and Toussaint l'Ouverture were emblazoned alongside those of Washington, Lincoln, and Robert Gould Shaw. Lest the significance be lost upon his audience, Colonel Charles Van Wyck spoke to the theme of "servile insurrection," which *he* would no more stop, he said, than any other act of the Almighty that might be inflicted upon the rebels. In a highly dubious compliment to the orderly and sensible people who had come to celebrate the day, he flung out, "If unchaining the fiend will work our deliverance, then let the fiend be unchained."[26]

Many of the island notables spoke on the occasion, but one familiar face was not seen. Chaplain French was in Washington, and nobody could have been more concerned about the outcome of his visit than General Saxton.[27] Under the conviction that no amount of persuasion could induce the tax commission, as it was constituted, to approve pre-emption rights for the freedmen, the Chaplain had gone to Washington to bring his persuasive personality again to bear upon the Secretary of the Treasury. Precisely what occurred is not on record, but presumably French emphasized the inadequacy of the amount of land set aside for the freedmen and the essential justice of providing all with an opportunity to purchase at preferred rates. He enlisted the aid of Senator Sumner and presumably stressed the point that one member of the commission agreed with him about pre-emptions. Whether French "tricked" Chase, as was later charged, is impossible to say. His subsequent behavior does indicate an unseemly haste to carry out the completely revised plans that he brought triumphantly back to Beaufort in early January.[28] But his conscience never showed a sign of malaise.

James Thompson was exuberant. The *Free South* praised French's successful exertions "to procure a just provision" for the

[26] *First Anniversary of the Proclamation of Freedom in South Carolina, Held at Beaufort, S.C., January 1, 1864* (Beaufort, S.C., 1864), pp. 4–5, 9, 11. The weather was so bitter that two small colored children froze to death in the steamer returning from Beaufort to St. Helena Island. See Towne MS diary, January 2, 1864, and Allen MS diary, January 4, 1864, p. 81, typescript.

[27] Brisbane to Lewis, January 16, 1864, Records U.S. Dir. Tax Com., S.C.

[28] F. J. Childs to Edward Atkinson, March 4, 1864, Atkinson MSS; Allen MS diary, February 13, 1864, p. 126, typescript.

freedmen. "Few men have a larger claim upon the gratitude of the black man, despite the slurs of those who have no *real* sympathy with the cause."[29]

By terms of the new instructions of December 31, 1863, all the lands owned by the government on the islands not reserved for military or educational purposes were thrown open to pre-emption at the rate of $1.25 per acre. Only two-fifths of the price was due upon pre-emption, and the remainder, at the receipt of the deed. The pre-emptor could be "any loyal person" of twenty-one years of age or more who had since the time of the Federal occupation resided for six months within the Department or was in residence at the time of the issuance of the instructions. Such loyal persons could pre-empt twenty- or forty-acre tracts. In this provision lay the genesis of the famous postwar expectation of the freed slaves that the government would provide them with forty acres of land. Under the second clause, soldiers and sailors could pre-empt twenty acres if single and forty if married, under precisely the same arrangements as for other "loyal persons."[30]

General Saxton went to work promptly and, armed now with full authority, he urged the Negroes to take up their lands, instructing the superintendents to assist them. The general and the chaplain cleverly refused to allow the commissioners themselves to see the new instructions until after the departure of the vessel that had brought French back to Port Royal. The commissioners could not protest something they did not know about, and as a consequence pre-emption was well on its way to being made a reality before Brisbane and Wording found out the extent of the new instructions. Only Commissioner Smith was in on the secret.[31]

A typical meeting was held on St. Helena on the seventeenth of January. The Brick Church was filled to overflowing with freedmen and missionaries who came to hear Saxton, French, and Judge

[29] Beaufort *Free South*, January 16, 1864.
[30] Basler (ed.), *Lincoln*, VII, 98–99.
[31] Brisbane to Lewis, January 16, 1864, Records U.S. Dir. Tax Com., S.C.

Smith explain, as James Thompson phrased it, "those measures whose operation will reorganize the whole system of Southern Society." After the religious exercises, French read the instructions of the President, and nearly everyone of any consequence had an opportunity to make a speech. All afternoon the oratory droned on, until the patience of certain evangels was exhausted. William Allen described the emotion of Judge Smith on the momentous occasion with slight sympathy:

Judge Smith ascended the pupit, and, looking around at the audience, asked why—why—when hearts were bursting with joy, and tongues were silent, and manly faces bathed in tears. As everybody was looking straight at him, and nobody was shedding any tears except himself (he occasionally wiped his eyes with a dirty pocket-handkerchief) there didn't seem to be any occasion to answer his question, so nobody did. He then relieved himself of a very large mouthful of tobacco, wiped the tears from his eyes, and went on to say that there were two kinds of joy, and this was t'other kind.[32]

After the Judge explained at length the Latin roots of the word "pre-emption" and retired, the freedmen sang a few favorite songs: one to the tune of "John Brown" and another that demonstrated an affecting trust in Providence. "Jehoviah hallalujah, de lord will perwide—de foxes hab holes and de birdies hab nests, but de son ob man hab nowhere to lay his weary head." General Saxton urged the people "not to sleep till they had staked out their claims," but Chaplain French, remembering that it was the Sabbath, suggested they wait till Monday. He exhorted the freedmen not to be selfish and not to approach the land with "horns" and "sharp elbows."[33]

Within a few days the commissioners were literally swamped

[32] Allen MS diary, January 17, 1864, pp. 97–100, typescript. For Thompson's account, see Beaufort *Free South*, January 23, 1864.

[33] Pearson (ed.), *Letters*, p. 244; Allen MS diary, January 19, 1864, p. 102, typescript.

with pre-emption claims from all over the islands, most of them patiently worked out by the superintendents and carefully marked with the "x" of the pre-emptor. Sometimes, the shaky penciled signature of the claimant proclaimed the proud state of new literacy, but either way the little slips of paper represented the happy anticipation of the Negro farmer to own a bit of the "home place." Today packet after packet of these musty little papers may be found among the records of the tax commission, brittle and dry as the broken hopes to which they are the mute witnesses. For the pre-emption plan failed.[34]

It was not the first or the last time that the interests of the freedmen were sacrificed in the conflicts of men who meant to help. General Saxton had stolen a march on the commission by acting promptly, but Brisbane and Wording were not without defenses. On January 15, after a strategic five-day delay, the new instructions were revealed to the commission; but even before the instructions were presented, Commissioner Smith had introduced a resolution obliging them to carry out President Lincoln's wishes.

Brisbane and Smith naturally voted it down and then began an infuriating campaign of passive resistance. They simply sat on their hands—after firing off a letter to Washington presenting their side of the argument and asking for further explanations. The advertisement for the public land sale continued to appear in the papers at the same time the pre-emption claims were pouring into the commissioners' headquarters at the Rhett house. Brisbane ignored them and would accept no money.[35]

But he must have *read* at least a few of the pre-emptions. For among the claimants he found a significant number filed by white men in the Department, who were in point of law as free to pre-empt as the freedmen. The Reverend Dr. Solomon Peck, for instance, had taken up 160 acres by manipulating the possibilities of

[34] Large box marked "Pre-emption Claims," Records U.S. Dir. Tax Com., S.C.

[35] Brisbane to Lewis, January 16, 1864, *ibid.*; Minute Book, entry January 10, 1864, in *ibid.*

his numerous family to the best advantage. The John Hunn family at "Seaside" had also laid claim to a large amount of property, including the great plantation house of Edgar Fripp.[36] While there was no massive onslaught upon the public lands by abolitionists-in-residence, there was plainly enough action to stiffen, if not to justify, Brisbane's claim that the more intelligent and greedy white people of the Department were gobbling up the lands at the expense of the freedmen.[37]

In a rigorous analysis of the June 7, 1862, law and of the ways in which the December pre-emption instructions conflicted with it, Judge Brisbane's legal mind showed to good effect. In a telling series of fifteen questions he laid bare the basic disparity. How could lands be pre-empted when no houses had been erected upon them? How could the "charitable" lands allocated under law be diverted from their purpose except by re-entry for public sale? Was the residence requirement for pre-emption under the December instructions to be construed to cover Northern citizens living on the plantations? The law of June 7 required soldiers to pay one-fourth down, and the instructions required two-fifths. How could this be resolved? And so on.[38] The new instructions were, in actuality, poorly rooted in law, and perhaps in the long view of history and the postwar legal history of the land question, it is well that the Negro land claims did not rest upon so weak a foundation. But at the time many people regarded Brisbane's triumph as one of legalism and wickedness.

Another salient point in Brisbane's belief was his prediction

---

[36] Box labeled "Pre-emption Claims" in Records U.S. Dir. Tax Com., S.C. I have also located the pre-emption claims of missionaries H. G. Judd and his family to 110 acres and Josiah Fairfield to land on Wassa Island, in *ibid.*; see Towne MS diary, January 20, 1864. For John Hunn's abolition career, see Chapter 3, p. 78.

[37] Brisbane to Lewis, January 16, 1864, in Records U.S. Dir. Tax Com., S.C. A number of missionary pre-emptions are cited in this letter, with details, but no names.

[38] Brisbane to Lewis, January 21, 1864, *ibid.*

that the Negroes would be thrown into utter confusion and hopeless conflict over the pre-emptions.[39] Supporters of the commission appear to have blown this out of proportion, for on Port Royal Island, and generally in areas where the freedmen could pre-empt their own home plantations, there was little trouble. Matters did not proceed so smoothly, however, on the eastern end of St. Helena Island, where the large holdings of Edward Philbrick's Boston concern made it impossible for the Negroes to pre-empt the "home place." They thought it hard that they could not own land on their own plantations. When Negroes ambitious to own land proceeded to stake out their claims on the government-owned plantations in their neighborhood, "they met the stubborn hostility of the people already living there. These people considered, logically enough, that their own claims were stronger, and they pulled up the stakes planted by the outsiders.[40] Considerable bickering resulted. It was abundantly clear that since the Negroes were human, they were individuals, and some of them had "horns and sharp elbows." Such noisy conflict was no more than Brisbane had expected, or quite possibly no more than the old gentleman wanted to hear, since he had predicted it.

While stubbornly refusing to acknowledge the pre-emptions, Brisbane and Wording were building up their own brief. All the while, they were subjected to the most steady public pressure. Seemingly, nearly everyone in the Department interested in the freedmen opposed their course. A meeting of Beaufort citizens who wished to prod them into action called out a stubborn statement from Brisbane that it was "utterly impossible" to give out information on how pre-emptions could be made. The vigorous old man stoutly maintained that the "questions involved" were

[39] Brisbane to Lewis, January 16, 1864, *ibid.*

[40] Boston *Commonwealth*, February 12, 1864; Allen MS diary, January 11, 1864, p. 90, typescript. Allen reports that the St. Helena Islanders "were quarreling furiously about their claims, and almost coming to blows." He was working in the district where large tracts were owned by the Philbrick concern. See *ibid.*, January 19, 1864, pp. 101–102 of typescript.

"very grave and weighty" but that the citizens who had framed the resolutions he had received "could not possibly desire more than we do, to promote the welfare of the 'colored people,' " or of other loyal citizens for that matter. James Thompson's small weekly quivered with indignation at the "cruel and contumacious" course of the commission and at the "shuffling insincerity" of its response. He accused its members of merely wishing to "perpetuate their own offices." "What," cried Thompson, "but a determination to disobey at all hazards a positive order of the President actuates them in refusing to withdraw the advertisement of a public sale which they know cannot take place?"[41] A group of the most influential Northerners, civil and military, signed a petition on January 22, expressing to Chase their sorrow at "the failure of the U.S. Direct Tax Commissioners to carry out, in good faith, the wise and humane orders" of the President. Saxton, Higginson, Colonel Van Wyck, Thompson, and numerous other prominent residents joined the appeal, but it was in vain.[42]

In early February the news came that Chase had reversed himself, had withdrawn the December pre-emption instructions, and wanted the public sale to go forward.[43] Now the Negroes could only apply for the limited amount of land set aside for "charitable purposes." It was a triumph for paternalism. It is difficult to de-

[41] See resolutions of the January 17 meeting and Brisbane's response, in the Beaufort *Free South*, January 23, 1864, together with editor Thompson's angry reaction. W. J. Richardson of the AMA was an exception to the general rule, declaring that the commission was "seeking the good of the freedmen with *far less selfishness* than Mr. French." He thought the Negroes would secure half the land under the commissioner's plan, and seemingly he considered that enough. Richardson to Simeon Jocelyn, March 3, 1864. "Letters from South Carolina (1862–1865)" in AMA MSS.

[42] Petition to Chase, January 22, 1864, Records U.S. Dir. Tax Com., S.C.

[43] As early as February 4, 1864, Brisbane was assuring a prospective buyer from Massachusetts that pre-emptions had not been allowed, and within the week it was common knowledge in the department. I was unable to locate the letter rescinding the December instruction. Brisbane to Thomas Roberts, February 4, 1864, Letters Sent, Records U.S. Dir. Tax Com., S.C.; Towne MS diary, February 11, 13, 1864.

termine which of the many arguments Brisbane and Wording advanced was decisive. Their charges against the greedy white people and the wracking confusion among the freed people undoubtedly carried weight. More fundamental, perhaps, was the dubious legal standing of the pre-emption plan. Sorting and weighing the charges and countercharges emanating weekly from the Port Royal Islands must have provided Chase with a severe headache. In defending the Secretary from Laura Towne's charge of vacillation, Edward Pierce explained to her that it was impossible "for one not personally versed with affairs at Port Royal, to find out what should be done, as the officials and others there disagree so much among themselves." He felt that Saxton's word ought to be law in every matter but that Saxton had not stood his ground well and even in the matter of enlistments of soldiers had let Hunter "run over him." And then, he added, Saxton "sends French to Washington as his messenger, and people judge one very much by his representatives."[44] French was clearly not the winner he had once been.

It is just possible that the political implications of yet another personality factor may have been more important than all the 'legal arguments the commissioners made against the pre-emption plan. For the conflicts on the board were not limited purely to matters of land policy and the future economic security of the freedmen. While Brisbane and Wording may have been, as was freely charged, more solicitous of the United States Treasury than of the freedmen's security, they at least had no outstanding personal vices to discredit their influence. Even the missionaries who supported him knew that *their* man on the commission was a heavy drinker. It was too bad, as Judge Smith was pronounced a "judicious" man when sober. Superintendent H. G. Judd, who actively pushed Smith's plan, said ironically, "if you catch him before ten, you will find him sober and clear; but then he doesn't get up till quarter of ten."[45] Brisbane and Wording had been peppering

[44] Pierce to Laura Towne, April 18, 1864, Towne MS letters.
[45] Allen, quoting H. G. Judd, in Allen MS diary, January 17, 1864.

Chase and Commissioner of Internal Revenue Joseph J. Lewis for several months with complaints of Smith's frequent intoxication, and he was already in bad grace when the crisis over pre-emption came into focus. They had also complained to Senator James Doolittle of Wisconsin, the man whose political influence had been responsible for the appointment of all three men. The Senator wrote Chase on the sixth of February to advise Smith's removal. He had been sadly disappointed in Judge Smith's failure to *reform* "in spite of his promises to me to abstain from intoxicating drinks. . . ."[46] An abstemious man, Salmon P. Chase did not suffer drunkards gladly. Smith's fall from official favor coincides roughly with retraction of the pre-emption instructions.

As early as February 4 Brisbane was assuring a prospective land investor in Lynn, Massachusetts, that it was now quite safe to buy lands in South Carolina and that the pre-emptions were not being allowed. He predicted comfortably that the Negroes would work for the Northern buyers once they recovered from the ill effects "of some professed friends of the blacks discouraging them from working for the whites."[47]

Father French, as his fellow evangels called him, had enough faith to live by, and he was resourceful. He gently and mournfully protested to Chase that "The willows bend again under the weight of broken harps. The voice of joy and thanksgiving has given place to mourning." Chase had made a mistake that he would understand some day, and French said he could forgo the Secretary's confidence "*in time*, so I have it *through all eternity*." He had one little request. Could not the pre-emptions made under the December instructions, and before their retraction, be acknowledged? Even thus he could have won the game, for as Thompson pointed out in the *Free South* (a fact Chase probably did not know), "Before the order of suspension reached the com-

---

[46] Wording and Brisbane to Chase, September 5, 1864, and J. R. Doolittle to Chase, September 5, 1864, in Records U.S. Dir. Tax Com., S.C.

[47] Brisbane to Thomas Roberts, February 4, 1864, in "Letters Sent," *ibid.*

missioners, more than a thousand persons had secured [by preemption] the right to purchase, at $1.25 per acre, from twenty to eighty acres each; and to-day the United States has not eighty contiguous acres of tillable land to offer at public sale."[48] But no soothing word came from the federal treasury.

French had signed his despondent note to Chase "Yours for the *truth* and *justice* even to the *bottom of the crucible*." But his air of patient resignation was not quite real. Now he took up the cudgels in earnest and followed a course some regarded as "jesuitical," dangerous, and even treasonable.[49] At every church service, even at funerals, he seized the occasion to tell the freedmen of their wrongs. He exhorted them to take the land they needed and stay there, defending it if need be, even with their hoe handles. He told them to give the prospective buyers as much trouble as possible in dispossessing them and urged them "to plant for themselves instead of others." Pointing to the white purchasers of the year before, Philbrick in particular, French declared that they were "getting rich" on black labor and that the Negroes "were no richer at the end of the year than they were at the beginning."[50]

[48] French to Chase, February 13, 1864, Chase Papers; Beaufort *Free South*, February 20, 1864.

[49] William Allen said French was "alleged" to be "unscrupulous and jesuitical" in his methods but that he personally believed him sincere in the freedmen's cause. Allen MS diary, July 5, 1864, p. 226, typescript. The severest critics were Tax Commissioners Brisbane and Wording, who asked that French be removed from the Department. See Brisbane to Lewis, February 15, 1864, Records U.S. Dir. Tax Com., S.C.

[50] Towne MS diary, February 21, 1864. Even Laura Towne thought French had gone too far; two missionaries, the Reverend Dr. Solomon Peck and Josiah Fairfield, wrote letters to Brisbane complaining that French had on February 14 converted a funeral into a political affair, urging the Negroes to hang on to their land. The two thought this in very bad taste and highly insurgent. Fairfield to Brisbane, February 15, 1864, and Peck to Brisbane, February 15, 1864. The letters were used by Brisbane to urge French's removal. Brisbane to Lewis, February 15, 1864, all in Records U.S. Dir. Tax Com., S.C.

Neither side had really accepted defeat, and the struggle broke into the open on February 18 as the crowds of buyers, pre-emptors, freedmen, and missionaries gathered before the Rhett house for the land auction. Brisbane and Smith locked horns, as the question recurred again and again whether a given plot of land was pre-empted or not. Brisbane always said it was not and Smith always said it was; little land changed hands. There were probably few persons present who had sufficient detachment to appreciate any possible humorous aspects, for most people agreed that Sergeant Prince Rivers, from Higginson's regiment, said the only sensible words of the day. He made an indignant speech attacking the government's shambling and ambivalent policies on the land question.[51]

When the sale was resumed the following week, the indefatigable Brisbane wore Smith down, and the latter retired from the conflict "in disgust." The lands then sold at prices that created considerable astonishment in the Department. The tax commission was pleased to report that the lands had on an average sold for more than $11 an acre and added smugly in their account to Revenue Commissioner Joseph Lewis, "You will readily see therefore what an imposition upon the government it would have been to have had these lands pre-empted at $1.25 an acre."[52] Philbrick's astonished superintendents, recalling that their lands had been procured for less than a dollar an acre the year before, chalked it all up to inflation. They predicted that the new buyers would find they had paid too much in going so high and would not be able to make planting pay, especially on plantations where the people were "chagrined at being deceived as to the pre-emptions," for it was "not at all likely that they will work well—if at all—for the purchasers."[53]

[51] Beaufort *Free South*, February 20, 1864; Allen MS diary, February 18, 21, 1864, pp. 129, 132–133, typescript.

[52] *Ibid.*, February 29, 1864, p. 140, typescript; Brisbane to Lewis, February 23, 1864, Records U.S. Dir. Tax Com., S.C.

[53] Allen MS diary, February 21, 1864, pp. 132–133, typescript.

There were ample signs of impending trouble. A group of superintendents returning to St. Helena from the sale of February 26 were met near Land's End by a crowd of freed people, who surrounded them clamoring for information and "complaining that their land—that they had pre-empted—had been sold away from them, and declaring that they wouldn't work for the purchaser." They protested they would have paid as much for the land as anyone. The people of Redwood Point, Laura Towne reported, also had refused to work for the new owner, and would not permit their pre-emption money to be returned.[54] All around were increasing signs that the freedmen were becoming fully awake to their economic needs.

The action of the Negroes on Wassa Island and on the Marion Chaplin plantation indicated a road around the pre-emption suspension that French and Saxton had not seen or had been too stubborn to accept. On these places the people had pooled their funds and bought their own lands, intending to work them in common.[55] If the superintendents had taken lively action after the suspension was known this might have been done on a larger scale; but their clinging to a forlorn hope had deprived the Negroes of leadership and had left the black people with a sense of frustration and bitterness toward the government that was deeper than it had been since the Federal occupation. Few white men were now exempt from their profound distrust. There had perhaps been a grain of truth in William Gannett's idea that only suffering would arouse the people, and 1864 was a bad year.

An unusually severe season of disease in the winter had lowered morale, and the senseless government recruiting policy of the spring had depressed the freedmen even more.[56] It is a profound

[54] *Ibid.*, February 29, 1864, p. 140, typescript; Towne MS diary, March 15, 1864.

[55] Allen MS diary, February 29, 1864, p. 140, typescript.

[56] Laura Towne's diary contains numerous references to the bad smallpox epidemic of early 1864. See entries of January 3, 4, 5, 15, 1864; Pearson (ed.), *Letters*, pp. 251–252.

commentary on the integrity and consistency of Federal policy during the war that on the land question the freedmen were regarded paternalistically and given an opportunity to buy small "charitable" allocations of land, while they were at the same time ruthlessly exploited for military service in a manner far from paternal. Nevertheless, the plan of the tax commissioners, limited and faulty as it was, did represent a minor commitment to the idea that the government had some responsibility toward launching the newly-released slaves on the road toward economic independence. It also represented some constructive thinking about postwar economic and social problems, which had already been allowed to drift too long. But the shuffling, struggling contradictions and delay had embittered the people, who regarded the betrayal of their hopes to inherit the land as the last straw. A deep and sullen anger developed which the Northerners understood but did not view with sufficient sympathy. Small wonder it was that smallpox, the ancient plague, was by March known as the "Government lump."[57]

Even after the sales of the spring of 1864, however, vast acreages still remained in government hands, and the question of the right of the freedmen to possess them at minimum cost would remain alive for a long time.[58] The profound social question of the place of the freedmen in the post-bellum economic structure would be increasingly agitated.

[57] Those who had the "lump" were "Union," and those who didn't were "Secesh."! *Ibid.*; the commentaries on the distress of the freedmen in the period following the sales are too numerous for individual citation, but typical observations are in the following sources: Pearson (ed.), *Letters*, pp. 254–255; Allen MS diary, March 15, 1864, p. 150; typescript; Towne MS diary, March 16, 1864.

[58] Brisbane to Lewis, April 21, 1864, Records U.S. Dir. Tax Com., S.C.

eleven ❈ *"THE RIGHTEOUS RAIL*
AGAINST US"

SOME THERE WERE AMONG THE MISSIONARIES WHO APPARENTLY
had only the foggiest notion of the far-reaching social implications
of the land controversy. George W. Sisson of the American Missionary Association, for instance, may have been an adequate
religious leader, but he patently failed to grasp the main question.
If he did grasp it, he underestimated its importance. When he
found his little flock "burdened and troubled" after the sale of
the lands, he solemnly exhorted them, from the 55th Psalm, to
cast their burdens on the Lord. "As their trouble seemed to come
from an over-anxiety to secure riches," he wrote, "I referred them
to the rich man and Lazarus."[1] Sisson convinced the freedmen
that it would be better to be Lazarus in the Judgment Day, and
to grant his presumptions was to grant him a point. But the fatuity
of likening a desire for a twenty-acre homestead to "an over-
anxiety to secure riches" throws Mansfield French's Jacobinical
talk into pleasant relief.

Few superintendents demonstrated so vast a disparity between
concern for the afterlife of the Negroes and concern for their
temporal welfare, or so naïve an attitude toward the land question. But there were several among the most sophisticated social
thinkers at Port Royal who had opposed the pre-emption system

[1] George W. Sisson to George Whipple, February 24, 1864, "Letters
from South Carolina," AMA MSS. Sisson's letter is altogether concerned
with his evangelical triumphs on Seabrook plantation, and his postscript
advises us, "If any of the above should be desired for publication it is at
your service."

and had felt from the beginning that the Brisbane plan of mixed white and black ownership (with the accent on white) was the superior system. Their only complaint after the smoke cleared was that the effect of the crisis had been to make the Negroes dissatisfied.

Most of this thinking was restricted to Edward Philbrick and his superintendents, who were in 1864 entering their second successful year of cotton planting on a free-enterprise basis. Philbrick's statements on free labor continued to be predicated on the assumption that white management, offering prompt and fair wages for labor, was the smoothest road toward industrial progress. Although never opposing directly the attempts of industrious and active freedmen to obtain land, the Bostonian thought that the majority of Negroes needed the moral example of industrious Northern laborers and managers before them, either as landowners or as fellow farmers.[2]

Until early 1864 and the land crisis, the so-called Boston Concern was apparently bringing the blessings of profit to its investors and contentment to its laborers. Another such halcyon year would not come again for the Bostonians; after the land controversy of early 1864, Negro labor asked more questions, showed more bargaining power, and demonstrated more independence. Philbrick's success, his profits alone, raised so great a howl among others interested in the freedmen's future as perhaps to embitter the complete satisfaction he might have felt at having demonstrated conclusively the economic feasibility of free labor. Young William Gannett wrote sadly about the criticism he and Philbrick's coadjutors incurred from other well-meaning people. "Did you know we had long ceased to be philanthropists or even Gideonites? We are nothing now but speculators, and the righteous

[2] This idea is implicit in all Philbrick's writings and is clearly stated in his letter to William Gannett of July 8, 1864, in Pearson (ed.), *Letters*, p. 273. Edward Atkinson, in a letter to [John Murray Forbes] of August 30, 1865, reported that Philbrick felt that "the diffusion of Northern labor should be the rule and not concentration," and Atkinson added, "I must admit I agree with him." Forbes MSS.

rail against us. A great crowd of our brethren have just come down to be present at the late sales."[3] An examination of the Philbrick operation may explain why he and his fellow superintendents opposed land distributions below market price for the freedmen, and why they also sometimes came into conflict with other Port Royalists on the subject of the rate of wages.

In early November of 1863, when young William Allen had driven across St. Helena Island for the first time, in a rickety wagon, to assume his position as a teacher for Philbrick's laborers at the John Fripp plantation, he observed all along the way that cotton fields had grown up in weeds, until he entered the Philbrick lands. Laura Towne, ever suspicious of Philbrick's intentions, admitted that, of all the white purchasers in 1863, only Philbrick had managed well for the prosperity of the Negroes.[4] By mid-January of 1864, the New Englander was in a position to assess the financial aspects of his work and to publish his findings. He was sending to market 73,000 pounds of ginned cotton, and he reported that labor costs had been approximately $20,000. Labor had been his only large expense, and Philbrick calculated that his cost for producing a pound of ginned long-staple cotton fell within the cost of producing the same unit in antebellum times. He cited *DeBow's Review*, where the cost is given as averaging between thirty and forty cents, considerably greater than the expense of raising a pound of short-staple cotton but rewarded by a correspondingly higher market price.[5]

Philbrick emphasized the great disadvantages under which he had labored—the absence of the best field hands, who were in the army; the fact that he had procured the plantations somewhat

[3] Pearson (ed.), *Letters*, p. 254.

[4] Allen MS diary, November 10, 1863, p. 10, typescript; Towne to "R," February 7, 1864, Towne MS letters.

[5] Philbrick circulated the figures on his 1863 crop widely, but I have found his letter to Tax Commissioner W. E. Wording of January 14, 1864, most useful and complete, and I believe it to have been least influenced by considerations of publicity. It is in the Records of the U.S. Dir. Tax Com., S.C.

later than the crops should have been planted; the dearth of live-stock; the distraction of the camps; and the prejudice of the freed-men against working cotton. One significant drawback Philbrick touched upon very lightly. "It must be remembered," he said, "that we worked with little or no manure. . . ."[6] The saline content of marsh mud and grass was of prime importance in growing long-staple cotton and was as near as the grassy flats that bordered the plantations. Digging it, however, and bringing it onto the fields had been an unpopular task in slavery, and the freedmen were ex-tremely reluctant to undertake the task as a part of the ordinary farm routine.[7]

Philbrick replied to charges that he paid less for Negro labor than he would have been obliged to pay for Northern farm labor with the argument that the Negroes did not apply themselves as regularly and that the daily wage was actually based upon a half-day's work. Philbrick paid twenty-five cents per daily "task" at the outset in 1863, but by early 1864 he was giving fifty-five cents.[8] Although he did not disparage free Negro labor, the Bos-tonian was convinced that the habits and attitudes of slavery would have to undergo considerable modification before the

[6] *Ibid.*; for other accounts of Philbrick's great crop, see E[dward] A[tkinson's] report in the *Freedmen's Record*, Vol. I, no. 5, (May, 1865), p. 85; Philbrick to Alpheus Hardy, December 28, 1863, in *Fourth Series of Extracts from Letters of Teachers* (Boston, 1864). This letter to Hardy received wide circulation in the Northern press. See Pearson (ed.), *Letters*, p. 248.

[7] For the reluctance of the freedmen to dig marsh, see [Gannett and Hale], "The Freedmen," p. 19, and the special reports of the Southern correspondent to *The Nation*, November 17, and December 14, 1865. See also Pearson (ed.), *Letters*, p. 297.

[8] Pierce, "The Freedmen at Port Royal," *Atlantic Monthly*, XII (Sep-tember, 1863), 398; Allen MS diary, May 28, 1864, p. 198, typescript; Beau-fort *Free South*, March 26, 1864; Pearson (ed.), *Letters*, p. 266. In a letter to the New York *Independent* Philbrick referred to himself as a common-sense Yankee and not a philanthropist, although he thought there might be a lot of philanthropy in a common-sense approach. *Independent*, May 5, 1864.

freedmen would perform on a level with Northern labor. He thought the desired changes would come about through a process of education and example, with the incentive of new opportunities. He therefore supported schools at an annual expense of $3,000 from the profits of the cotton and offered in his non-profit plantation stores a wide variety of household and personal articles that he expected the Negroes to desire to purchase. This stimulated industry, according to the Philbrick thesis, by increasing the number of "civilized" wants and needs of the people. On the other hand, Philbrick felt that a rapid rise in wages would enable the Negroes to secure these goods with a minimum effort, thus defeating the purpose. He contended that the advantageous prices at which he offered merchandise in his plantation stores more than compensated for the difference between the pay he offered for a daily "task" and that paid on certain other privately-owned plantations in the district. He obviously considered his wages adequate, for they were based, he said, "upon the enormous prices paid now for the necessaries of life by the Negroes."[9] Whether he reasoned correctly or incorrectly, it will be seen that Philbrick was thinking on a deeper level concerning the problems of social change than that attained by most of his contemporaries on the islands.[10]

In order to present Philbrick's accomplishments in proper perspective, it is necessary to recapitulate briefly for a statement of what the laissez-faire liberals had hoped to prove at Port Royal. As free men, Negroes would be a better working force than they had been as slaves. A planter would be able to raise more cotton

[9] "The negro is motivated by the same motives as other men, and we must appeal to the *human nature* and make it appear for his interest to work and then he *will* work. With a view to multiply their simple wants and stimulate industry, I have placed within their reach by purchase a great variety of new food, articles of useful domestic ware, clothing adapted to their wants and tastes, etc. etc." Philbrick to Wording, January 14, 1864, Records U.S. Dir. Tax Com., S.C.; Pearson (ed.), *Letters*, p. 264.

[10] See Philbrick to William Gannett, July 8, 1864, in Pearson (ed.), *Letters*, pp. 272–278.

more cheaply with free men than with slaves. Fundamental to these hopes were the beliefs that slavery was wasteful as well as immoral and, even more important, that enlightened self-interest was a greater galvanizing force for the energies of men than compulsion. Philbrick believed that his great 1863 crop had demonstrated these points, even while he entertained reservations on the current effectiveness of Negro laborers as compared with Yankee farmers.

For purposes of measuring the industry of free men as opposed to that of slaves, which was after all the fundamental question, only one figure was at all meaningful. The average poundage of ginned cotton raised per acre under cultivation provides a crude index of productivity. Although Philbrick had tripled the output of the skeleton crop of 1862, he had still raised only 90 pounds of ginned cotton per acre; the ante-bellum average had been 135.[11] But the figure was not really so damning of free labor as it might at first appear. If one bears in mind that the best field hands were in the army, as well as the very important fact that the art of fine seed selection was lost with the old planters who understood it, it will be seen that despite the propitious weather conditions 1863 had not been, after all, a year properly comparable to ante-bellum times. The inexperience of even so good a manager as Edward Philbrick was a significant factor bearing upon the general productivity of the land and labor. Counterbalancing these factors, and restoring some validity to the ginned cotton ratio, are two considerations: Philbrick had not undertaken to plant as many acres per hand as had been the ante-bellum practice; and one might consequently expect a slightly higher productivity from the acres planted to result.[12] In addition, the older people on the

[11] Philbrick to Wording, January 14, 1864, Records U.S. Dir. Tax Com., S.C.; see p. 204.

[12] Allen MS diary, February 29, 1864, p. 141, typescript. In referring to this matter in his letter to Wording (see note 11, above) Philbrick speaks of having planted four acres to the hand, but obviously he includes the provision crops in the figure.

Distributing clothes and supplies in the earliest days of the Port Royal Experiment.

The Whitehall ferry landing in Beaufort, with General Saxton's headquarters in the foreground. Formerly the Heyward home, this mansion commanded a lordly six-mile view down the Beaufort River toward Port Royal Sound.

Above: The Brick Church on St. Helena Island, where Chaplain French told the freedmen to defend their land with their hoe handles. Built in 1855 by the Baptist planters of the island, the church doubled as an effective New England town meeting during the Civil War. Below: In 1864 the Penn School was sent to St. Helena Island in prefabricated sections by the Pennsylvania Freedmen's Relief Association. Its bell called children from more than three miles around.

plantation and the women had turned in a remarkably good account of themselves. In many cases they had outproduced the men and the younger people; and in this fact the missionaries found one more argument for free labor.[13] What a cynic might have seen as a commentary on the slave-master's generosity in turning the older people into pasture too soon, or perhaps as the preference of the aged for hard work over abject poverty, the missionaries viewed more optimistically. In positive terms they concluded that the stimulus of wages provided new incentives for the aging.

When the vitiating factors are weighed, it appears that the ginned cotton ratio does show that the freedmen were less effective in raising cotton than they had been as slaves. This is not to say that the freedmen were not working as hard. They simply regarded their provision crops as more important than cotton. Bread was more significant than cash in hand. The food they raised above their own needs found a ready market at Hilton Head, and it is most probable that the Negroes felt a greater sense of personal satisfaction in their garden crops than in cotton, and for a sound reason. Provision crops had been their own individual projects even under slavery. An even more significant consideration must be taken into account: The freedman now had other interests and pursuits. Whether learning to read, cultivating a better family life, developing a talent for driving a bargain, or simply recreating himself, he had entered a life of greater variety than he had known as a slave. The only decent requirement that could have been imposed was that the freedmen support themselves. They were demonstrating that capacity at Port Royal.

[13] *Freedmen's Record*, I (April, 1865), 53; *ibid.* (May, 1865), 85; William Allen reports that a great-grandmother "cultivated three acres of cotton (a full man's task in old times . . .) besides three of corn and one of potatoes; and did probably half the work on her worthless grandson's land. She thanked the Lord fervently for living to see this day. . . ." Allen MS diary, December 27, 1863, pp. 74–75, typescript. Such accounts occur frequently in the missionaries' letters.

Philbrick had assisted them by organizing his plantations well, but he had not shown that free men would produce *more* cotton than slaves were made to do or that they would produce it more *cheaply*.

It would have been extremely difficult for Philbrick to acknowledge that he had not conclusively demonstrated his main point, for his enterprise had been extremely profitable. His gains did not really affect the main theoretical question of free labor versus slave labor because of two considerations, which the Bostonian in one case did not understand and in the other largely ignored. Philbrick, despite his abolitionist background, or possibly because of it, did not comprehend the efficiency of slavery as a system of extractive labor, nor did he realize how important the element of compulsion could be when exercised at crucial points in the planting and harvest seasons. Philbrick had compensated for this advantage that the old masters had held in the case of the cotton picking by his bonus system, but he had devised no method of obliging the freedmen to gather marsh mud. Over a period of years the neglect of this particular would have the distinct effect of deteriorating the land for cotton production. Philbrick simply had no way of knowing how much profit a slave-master could have made in a year when the weather had been so favorable as it was in 1863.

A second factor that makes Philbrick's profit a poor indication of the superior productivity of free labor is that he consistently underplayed the advantages that he had enjoyed. He always assumed that his drawbacks had surpassed his special assets; therefore, he concluded from his experience that when the war was over and more normal conditions prevailed, "any just and equitable man can raise cotton or any other product here at far less cost than under any system of compulsory labor."[14] Philbrick may have been right; he may have been wrong; but his own find-

14 Philbrick to Wording, January 14, 1864, Records of the U.S. Dir. Tax Com., S.C.

ings did not justify so bold an assertion. A definitive test of free labor, in the case of a risky staple like Sea-Island cotton, could not rest upon the outcome of one year's crop. The variable factors between Philbrick's situation and that of Thomas Aston Coffin, the man he had displaced, were far too numerous; some of these factors were in the Bostonian's favor.

Philbrick might well have asked himself, for instance, if the day had ever been, or, when the war was over, if it would ever come again, when long-staple cotton sold in Liverpool for $2.00 per pound.[15] He had purchased the plantations at a fraction of their actual worth, making interest on land a negligible factor, and the livestock and equipment left on the plantations were used through the season without cost. All plantation buildings and barns had been quite literally "thrown in" with the land. But the greatest advantage of all was the enormous price of cotton in late 1863 and early 1864, when the crop went to market. Most accurate of all Philbrick's statements about his "experiment" was that there truly was no excuse for not making money in cotton when the market was so favorable.[16] While having no direct bearing on the cost of raising the cotton, it had the most emphatic influence upon the profits.

At last an even more fundamental question must be raised. Philbrick thought he was testing free labor, and it is surely justifiable to inquire if the approximately five hundred hands who worked on his plantations through the year for $20,000 were unequivocally *free*. Although the legal status of slavery is absolute,

[15] Edward Hooper wrote that the best cotton raised in 1863 brought $2.00 and more a pound. It is clear that if any planters on the island got such prices Philbrick was among them. Hooper to Gannett, October 25, 1864, Gannett MSS, Box I. In April of 1864 a steamer carrying a large part of Philbrick's crop went down. "The cotton was insured," wrote Philbrick, "for $1.50 a pound, but would have brought more in the market." Pearson (ed.), *Letters*, note on p. 264.

[16] New York *Independent*, May 5, 1864; Allen MS diary, February 21, 1864, pp. 132–133, typescript; Pearson (ed.), *Letters*, p. 255.

freedom, on the other hand, admits of degrees. While Philbrick had, as he said, "no paupers" on his places, it is arithmetically clear that the Negroes had shared only a minute part of the wealth produced on the Boston-owned plantations.[17]

The "Concern" had netted for an investment of approximately $40,000 a clear profit of more than $80,000.[18] This told but half the story, for the truly great profiteers had not been John Murray Forbes and his philanthropic friends in Boston but Philbrick himself (entitled by the contract to one-fourth of the clear profit) and the idealistic young superintendents who had joined him to try "an experiment in American emancipation." The stay-at-home Bostonians, after all, were receiving only 6 per cent interest until such time as Philbrick closed business, when there would be a pro-rata distribution of the profit. In fact, despite the large return of the 1863 crop, after Philbrick had deducted the superintendents' huge salaries and, presumably, his own, he decided against a dividend for the stockholders, on the ground that he had only sufficient funds to meet the expenses of the 1864 crop.[19]

But the astonished young superintendents received promptly as commission one-half the amount each had cleared on his crop. The figure probably amounted in each case to not less than $6,000 or more than $7,500.[20] It was quite a windfall for missionaries who had come to Port Royal expecting to earn $50 a month.

[17] In his letter to Alpheus Hardy of December 28, 1863 (*Fourth Series of Extracts from Letters of Teachers*, Boston, 1864), Philbrick estimated that he had 500 laborers. His letter of January 14, 1864, to Wording, two weeks later, gives it as approximately 400. He was probably attempting to arrive at a figure accounting for a considerable number of old or young people regarded as only partially employed. Records of the U.S. Dir. Tax Com., S.C.

[18] See Appendix.

[19] Pearson (ed.), *Letters*, p. 149; the terms of the contract with the investors are summarized in *ibid.*, note on pp. 140–141, pp. 256–257.

[20] Philbrick had employed six superintendents, and on the assumption that they produced approximately the same amount of cotton within each division, each received $6,666.66 as his part of the clear profit. Their

William Gannett was embarrassed to find philanthropy paying so well. He squirmed over his "ridiculously large" profits and said he had "rather not have it told about when known."[21] For him there would be no second kiss of fortune; he caused his contract with Philbrick for the 1864 crop to be rewritten with the stipulation that he would earn no less than $1,000 nor more than $4,000. In the best tradition of New England stewardship, he formed a "Pine Grove Fund" with his money and spent the proceeds keeping a teacher on St. Helena Island for many years after the war.[22]

Philbrick felt no such embarrassment. The Boston enterprise had been taken up in the first place with considerable risk, as the hesitant statements of the principals and the terms of the contract demonstrate. Now that it had been successful, Philbrick considered that he had done a good service to the nation in proving to Northern investors the safety of Southern agriculture.[23] He circulated the results of the 1863 crop widely during the spring of 1864, both by private correspondence and in the newspapers. He met the voluminous criticism in the abolition and radical

---

expectations were soaring by mid-December, when they anticipated receiving $4000; but if the letter of their contract was followed, they received a much higher figure. See Arthur Sumner to Nina Hartshorn, December 19, 1863, Arthur Sumner MSS.

[21] Pease, "Three Years Among the Freedmen," p. 109.

[22] *Ibid.*; Gannett's contract may be found, dated May 29, 1864, in the Gannett MSS, Box XXXVIII. Laura Towne in a letter to a sister, April 8, 1877, reports that "There are few as faithful friends to the freedmen as Mr. Gannett has proved to be." He had paid $350 annually for six or eight years to keep a teacher on St. Helena. Late in life, Gannett referred to his efforts in a letter to Mrs. Louis Craig Cornish, November 5, 1911. Both are in the Laura Towne MS letters. His record of the "Pine Grove Fund" expenditures are in a notebook in the Gannett MSS.

[23] All Philbrick's published letters seem dedicated in the last analysis to demonstrating this point. See especially his letter to the *Independent*, May 5, 1864. A number of free-labor enterprises based upon his own were started in the West during the 1864 season but were by no means so successful as his had been. See the *National Freedman*, I (April, 1865), 105–106.

journals with a firm restatement of his laissez-faire principles, some of them pleasing to radicals and others far from satisfactory. He was sure that "no restrictions" could advantageously be placed on Negro labor, which "must be *entirely voluntary*. Any half-way system of pupilage or apprenticeship will fail, as compared with a perfectly free intercourse between employer and employed." On the other hand, Philbrick solidly opposed on the same principle any discrimination in favor of the freedmen in disposing of the government lands. The administration had been misguided in its plan to offer homesteads to the freedmen on a pre-emption basis, but he felt—and only because good faith had become involved—that the pre-emptions ought to have been carried through.[24]

Perhaps the criticism of Philbrick on the score of his profits would have been less bitter if his public statements had not coincided with the uproar over the land sales. James Thompson summed up the connection, as well as a whole body of dissatisfaction expressed elsewhere, by a neat query in the *Free South*:

Mr. Philbrick says in his letter to the Evening Post on raising cotton by free labor, that negroes would be demoralized by obtaining land at $1.25 per acre. We ask, has Mr. Philbrick been demoralized by obtaining land at that price? Also in what time would a negro be able to buy a farm at $25 per acre if he worked for Mr. Philbrick at 55 cents per working day?[25]

It was a good question. The realization that Philbrick had no intention of selling his own lands to the freedmen at cost came as a shock to others keenly interested in the welfare of the freedmen. Laura Towne recalled her own understanding of Philbrick's original philanthropic intent to sell at cost and roundly con-

[24] Philbrick to Wording, January 14, 1864, Records U.S. Dir. Tax Com., S.C.; Pearson (ed.), *Letters*, p. 266.
[25] Beaufort *Free South*, March 26, 1864.

demned his "excuses" for retaining the land. "It will not be well for them, he says, to make money so fast on their cotton and land as they would now." For herself she thought these profits would be "just the encouragement" the Negroes needed. "I wonder," she asked sarcastically and appropriately, "if it is good for him to be getting rich so fast?"[26]

Philbrick always maintained that he had never made a commitment as to how he would dispose of his land. He was perhaps sincere in his belief that he was not selfishly motivated in his plans for selling the land he had bought under exceptional circumstances for $1.00 an acre to both Negroes and white men at its enhanced market value. In explanation, he wrote to William Gannett:

As to price, I never considered the question of profit to myself or those I represent as of consequence in fixing the price. It is no doubt an expression of this kind which gave rise to the general belief, claimed by some whites as well as blacks, that I would sell at cost, 'was bound' to do so, etc. It did not occur to those who so believed that I could have any good or disinterested reasons for selling for more than cost. It may be difficult to fathom one's own motives in such cases, but I can say honestly that I do not believe in the success of a system of selling to any people any property whatever for less than its market value, with a view to confer a lasting benefit upon them.

He reverted to his morbid fear that such easy gains would "beget idleness and unthrifty habits," that the Negroes as "recipients of charity" would not be taught the true feelings of independence.[27] Many businessmen before and since would agree with him, but numbers of missionaries at Port Royal did not, nor did many abolitionists in the North. Neither did the freedmen. For them it was Edward Philbrick who had been "demoralized," and

[26] Towne MS diary, May 28, 1864.
[27] Letter of Philbrick to Gannett, July 7, 1864, in Pearson (ed.), *Letters*, pp. 276–277.

he remained the embodiment of a man whose good motives had been corrupted by good fortune.

Aside from the problem of "fathoming his own motives," Philbrick had other valid considerations as he squirmed over the proper disposal of the acres he held. He especially feared the "terrible and disastrous confusion" likely to arise when the small freeholds secured by the freedmen were divided and subdivided among heirs. It made his "orderly bones ache," he declared, "to think of a time when, after some men now purchasing land shall die, leaving two or three sets of children, some born under wedlock and some not," there would be disputes, with everyone "claiming a slice of the deceased man's land, and of course all claiming the best." The "stake and stones" method of land division on the islands would make the problem worse. What was even more to be regretted, in Philbrick's estimation, was the collapse of large-scale organization of labor that would ensue. He recalled the "minute subdivision of land among the French peasantry," where the units of land were so small as to make profitable organization of agriculture difficult. While toying with the notion of life-leases rather than fee simple as a means of surmounting the problem, Philbrick was balked by the thought that the Negroes ought to have the incentive of providing a secure future for their families. Striving to own land to bequeath to one's heirs was "one of the best stimulants to good order and civilization."[28] Philbrick's ideal revolution was an *orderly* one.

Philbrick retained the land until the fall of 1865, when he sold in fee simple, according to his convictions—some to white men and more to Negroes, to whom he conveyed land at $5.00 an acre, five times what he had paid but less than market price, after all. Neither the 1864 crop nor that of 1865 was really profitable.[29] The cotton market fell, and the cost of labor steadily increased.

[28] *Ibid.*, pp. 273–275.
[29] *Ibid.*, note on p. 277, pp. 295–296, 310.

A spirit of restlessness and striving had overtaken the formerly placid freedmen.

Before the land sale crisis, Harriet Ware recorded a happy payday at Coffin Point, with the Negroes waiting their turn to receive their money. Her brother Charles summoned an elderly woman named Nancy and asked her if she knew how much she had earned. Nancy replied, " 'Me dunno, Massa, you knows.' As much as ten dollars? 'Oh yes! Massa, I tink you gib me more nor dat.' Fifteen, perhaps? Five for you, Doll, and Peg, each? 'Yes, Massa, I tink so.' And it was pleasant to see the corners of her mouth go as he counted out $48—which she took in perfect quietness and with a sober face, a curtsey and 'Tank 'ee, Massa.' " Nancy's friend Sinnet was more demonstrative, "lifting up hands and eyes, and ending with 'Tank de Lord; I mus' go praise.' "[30]

After the tax sale crisis, such unquestioning thankfulness would no longer be the rule at Coffin Point or anywhere else. As early as February 9 a group of farm hands, including the "best people" at Coffin Point, came to Philbrick to complain that their pay was too low. Harriet Ware said it was "a thing which had never happened before and shows the influence of very injudicious outside talk, which has poisoned their minds against their truest friends." The protests about low wages and Philbrick's refusal to sell land to the Negroes increased in intensity throughout the 1864 season. By a petition of March 1, 1864, the complaints of fifteen Negroes were carried to Washington, and the investigator whom Chase sent south to look into the squabbles on the tax commission was also instructed to sift out the true situation on Philbrick's lands.[31]

The investigator, Judge Austin Smith, made a series of recom-

[30] *Ibid.*, p. 222.

[31] *Ibid.*, p. 250. The petition of John Major and fourteen other freedmen was dated March 1, 1864, and may be seen in the Records of the U.S. Dir. Tax Com., S.C. See also Pearson (ed.), *Letters*, p. 258.

mendations on both matters that helped to bring a cautious truce. He asked that the lands still unsold be added to the Negro allotments under the tax commission's "Heads of Families" certificate plan. This would greatly enlarge the chances of the freedmen to gain land at preferred rates under the "charitable purposes" provision of the instructions of September 1863.[32] Judge Smith also conducted an informal hearing at Coffin Point, and the petitioning Negroes were invited to state their case. Even Harriet Ware, whose brother Charles was particularly complained of, appreciated the significance of seeing 'Siah and Pompey, "intelligent, hardworking, and honest . . . men whom we all respect, . . . only two years out of slavery, respectfully but decidedly standing up for what they thought their rights in a room full of white people." Their chief complaints were of low wages and Philbrick's refusal to sell the land at cost. The chief spokesman, a man named John Major, created an unfavorable impression, however, and the cause of the whole petition was weakened because Major did not himself work for Philbrick and because the charges in at least one particular, whether the Wares knew it or not, "had so overshot the mark" as to strain belief.[33] Who would believe that Charles Ware, "adorned with the inevitable goodness of Wares" so well known in New England, had bared a pregnant Negro woman and placed her over a barrel for a strapping? If he had done so, the missionary community would have been as inflamed as it was over other instances of missionary cruelty. The investigation also brought out the fact that some of the signers, including the reliable Pompey and 'Siah, had not even known all the charges on the petition marked with their "X." The document bore the signs of having been framed by an unknown white person who did not sign his

[32] Judge Austin Smith's proposals on the tax commissioners' difficulties are directed to Chase, dated April 26, 1864. Records of the U.S. Dir. Tax Com., S.C.

[33] The hearing is recorded by Harriet Ware, April 21, 1864, in Pearson (ed.), *Letters*, pp. 259–263.

name. Nevertheless, Judge Smith wisely and privately advised Philbrick to raise wages, and Philbrick did so.[34]

But concessions did not allay discontent, and the freedmen were, as Harriet Ware said, "silenced, but not convinced." They signed a contract with Philbrick for the next year but continued to press for better wages and for ultimate ownership of the land. The mass meetings of French and Saxton, though failing in their main purpose, were bearing fruit in arousing the Negroes to reflect on their future prospects. Desires that had been unknown before were now manifest, and increasing suspicions of white men's motives developed in all directions. The Negroes could only regard the retraction of the pre-emptions as a betrayal, and the violence accompanying military conscription in 1864 further embittered them. It was indeed hard for the missionaries to see these signs of restlessness as the imprimatur of freedom. The Negroes protested on the Coffin Point lands by planting their corn in the cotton fields, and they refused to pull it out. When William Allen scolded the freedmen about thus appropriating Mr. Philbrick's property, he drew out a vigorous response: "Man! don't talk 'bout Mr. Philbrick lan'. Mr. Philbrick no right to de lan'." Unable to get the colored people to pull up the corn, young Gannett at last was forced to pull it out himself, incurring the wrath of those who had planted it. In all his troubles, Philbrick maintained steadily that "the amount of cotton planted will always be a pretty sure index of the state of industry of the people, and their industry will always be the best measure of their improvement." He made a blazing admission, however, when he told William Gannett

[34] *Ibid.* The description of the Wares is from Thomas Wentworth Higginson's letter to his mother, January 2, 1863, Higginson MSS. The charge against Charles Ware appears only once in the whole literature, on the petition itself, signed by Major and the other freedmen, dated March 1, 1864, Records U.S. Dir. Tax Com., S.C. 'Siah actually had never signed the document with his mark, which led Miss Ware to conclude the work might have been a forgery. Pearson (ed.), *Letters*, pp. 260–261. See also Allen MS diary, May 26, 1864, p. 198, typescript.

that he could not agree with him that the people of the islands were unnaturally *dependent*. "I don't see any people on the face of the earth of their rank in civilization who are so independent as they are." Missionaries were apt to chalk up the new independence to ignorance and ingratitude.[35]

The freedmen did not consult the opinions of white people so carefully as they once had. Certain lessors and superintendents found it practically impossible to hire hands because they had unfortunate personalities or bad heads for business. Josiah Fairfield had trouble on this score, and a colored man explained to William Allen, in the muscular language missionaries were beginning to understand, that Mr. Fairfield had a "ractified mind," meaning poor judgment and a hot temper. These qualities no longer had to be suffered gladly, and the freedmen had had two years in which to study Josiah Fairfield.[36]

The Negroes began also to see examples of leadership and success among their own race, with a corresponding increase in self-confidence. In Beaufort, a number of freedmen had bought at the auctions the town houses of the late white residents. Robert Smalls had purchased the Prince Street house of Henry McKee, where he had spent his own childhood as a spoiled houseboy, and he was running a store on Bay Street. Harry MacMillan had borrowed money in 1863 to buy a plantation on Ladies Island and had raised a successful crop there that first year with the labor of

[35] Pearson (ed.), *Letters*, p. 262; Allen MS diary, June 1 and 13, 1864, pp. 203, 210, typescript, respectively; Philbrick to Gannett, July 8, 1864, in Pearson (ed.), *Letters*, p. 275. Gannett acknowledged the aspect of growing freedom in a backhanded compliment when he wrote of the petition incident, "One of my plantations is decidedly ahead of the others in intelligence and energy. They were so energetic about March 1 as to get a petition sent up to President Lincoln, praying for redress against their various oppressions." *Ibid.*, p. 263.

[36] Allen MS diary, January 14, 1864, pp. 93–94. The freedmen were probably right about Fairfield. See Towne MS diary, December 6, and June 21, 23, 1863.

his own family. In 1864 he planted sixty-five acres of cotton and carried on independent operations with twenty-one hired field hands. The Negroes who had bought small plots at the land sales also were doing very well with their crops. A Port Royal Island plantation called Edgerly was bought collectively in 1863 by the Negroes who lived on the land, and it was worked successfully in common, entirely without white direction. "Its prosperity was the envy of others."[37]

One forum of leadership known to Negroes even in slavery had been the church. It is therefore significant that it was during the tax sale agitation that they began to wish for less white interference in religious matters. Elder Demus was undoubtedly expressing more than his private opinion when he said he wished all the white people would go to worship at the Episcopal "White Church" and leave the Brick (Baptist) Church to the Negroes alone. The freedmen were especially fearful that the white people would draw them into some denomination other than Baptist, and they made up their own minds about what minister they would call, firmly resisting the counsel of the interested white minority. A Negro minister on Port Royal Island was already worried that some of his Baptists were "dodging about under the umbrellas and parasols of other denominations." When the congregation at the St. Helena Brick Church decided to raise a choir, they went about it without consulting the whites.[38]

[37] For the Edgerly arrangements, see A. B. Plimpton's letter of August 8, 1863, in *Fourth Series of Extracts from Letters* (Boston, 1863), p. 6. For Smalls, and Negro purchasers at the Beaufort sales, see Beaufort *Free South*, January 23, 1864, and Boston *Commonwealth*, February 12, 1864. For Harry MacMillan and other Negroes successful at farming independently, see Reuben Tomlinson's letter of April 10, 1864, in *ibid.*, May 20, 1864, and the Allen MS diary, June 19 and July 5, 1864, pp. 216 and 226, typescript.

[38] For the "parasols and umbrellas," see Botume, *First Days*, p. 264. For further details on the churches, see Towne MS diary, February 12, 13, 1864, and W. J. Richardson to George Whipple, March 9, 1864, "Letters from South Carolina," AMA MSS.

The spring of 1864 also saw the first feeble entry of Negroes into national politics. Some politically-minded Port Royalist conceived the ambitious scheme of sending from the islands a full contingent of delegates from the State of South Carolina to the Republican National Convention. On May 18, 1864, a rally in Beaufort elected sixteen delegates and numerous alternates; and among them were four Negro leaders, including Robert Smalls and Prince Rivers. There was some tension at this meeting, which was attended equally by Negroes and whites, and for a time "white paired off against black."[39] Order returned with a timely speech by Reuben Tomlinson, who routed an extremist Assistant-Surgeon named T. P. Knox, accused of stirring up Negro opposition to white leaders.[40]

Some observers laughed at the presumption of the Port Royal citizens who yearned for political recognition; they satirically referred to the delegation to the Baltimore convention as "three or four army sutlers sandwiched between contrabands."[41] William Gannett, although he was hopeful that the delegates would be, recognized, complained that the "whole affair [was] premature and foolish" and that there were hardly thirty-two "decent" white men in the whole Department. Many, he said, had taken

[39] "It is probably the first time that the slaves—contrabands—freedmen—have asserted themselves our fellow-countrymen by claiming the right of voting." Gannett in Pearson (ed.), *Letters*, pp. 267–268.

[40] Gannett MS diary, May 19 [1864]. The entry is mistakenly entered under 1863. Assistant-Surgeon Knox was eventually sent from the Department at the order of Saxton. Knox subsequently attempted to interpret his dismissal as resulting from his political action with regard to sending Negro delegates to the convention. His charges against the missionaries and against the Department in general appeared in a pamphlet entitled *Startling Revelations from the Department of South Carolina, and Exposé of the So Called National Freedmen's Relief Association* (Boston, 1864). Bound with the pamphlet is a refutation of Knox's charges by Thomas Wentworth Higginson.

[41] Beaufort *Free South*, July 2, 1864, referring to pejorative statements of others regarding the delegation.

part in the proceedings with no intention of remaining after the war as permanent citizens.[42] Gannett was mistaken on several counts. Although the delegation may have been "premature," it was not without significance. The South Carolina flag flying from Guy's Hotel created a small sensation in Baltimore, and James G. Thompson, a delegate himself, reported that "many distinguished citizens from all sections of the Union called upon different members of our delegation, and great interest was manifested in the work of reorganization in progress in South Carolina." The members received seats on the floor of the convention, but they were denied official representation and were not acknowledged by the chairman. All efforts to bring the question of Negro suffrage onto the floor were adroitly circumvented. "All were ready to have the negroes fight for the Union, die for it, but were hardly ready to let him vote for it." Thompson concluded philosophically, "Well, we could afford to wait." He correctly predicted that South Carolina would have a far more important role by the time of the election of 1868.[43]

Taking advantage of their proximity to Washington, the delegates also brought to the attention of appropriate officials there the need for civil courts in Beaufort and asked that the trade restrictions still in effect be lifted. The Northern citizens were definitely interested in the economic future of the town, and many clearly meant to stay. These pioneering "carpetbaggers" of South Carolina were by mid-1864 well established. At the sale of town property in January, Northern residents had come into actual possession of a large part of Beaufort, and they began to feel a proprietary interest in the old-fashioned resort town. "The impetus given to private enterprise by the transfer of the public property in this town to citizens, is evident in every street." Business was flourishing; erstwhile army sutlers had opened spacious new stores; a "first-class" restaurant was serving hungry diners

[42] Gannett MS diary, May 19, [1864]; Pearson (ed.), *Letters,* p. 268.
[43] Beaufort *Free South,* July 2, 1864.

on Bay Street; and the Magnolia Hotel was receiving guests. For those who wished to give the Northern home-folks a view of the sights of the town and its environs, Photographer S. A. Cooley had for sale a full series of pictures "equal as works of art to any taken by Brady." The Yankeefied outpost happily celebrated the Fourth of July in 1864 in the classic New England manner, with a parade of the fire department, band music, and patriotic speeches. "It was one of the most splendid turn outs South Carolina ever saw, reminding one of similar demonstrations in the North."[44]

There was, however, one omnipresent reminder that this was indeed the South, that a war was being fought, and that the revolutionary social implications of that war were not even yet fully revealed. Every vessel putting in to Hilton Head or Beaufort contributed new increments to the colored population. From "up country" or "down South," the fugitives from bondage fled to the island lodestar, where men worked for wages and where rumor had it that a twenty- or forty-acre farm could be had by any man who would work.[45] These wanderers represented only an initial installment. Before the end of July, General William T. Sherman had forced Confederate General John Bell Hood within the entrenchments of Atlanta, close to the geographical heart of the original Confederacy. The city was evacuated in September, and before many weeks passed the great march southeastward to the sea began. In the early morning of November 16 the Union army moved out of Atlanta, which lay smoldering beneath a pall of smoke. A practical soldier, keenly attuned to the morale of his men, General W. T. Sherman thrilled to the army's spirited ren-

---

[44] *Ibid.*, July 2, April 2, 9, January 16, July 9, 1864; There is an excellent set of Cooley's stereopticon views in the Beaufort Township Library. See the Photographic Album of William G. Reed, also in the Library at Beaufort. For a list of licensed trade stores in the area, see Daybook of Captured and Abandoned Property, Fifth Special Agency, Treasury Department Archives.

[45] Botume, *First Days*, p. 33.

dition of the exalted and ferocious "Battle Hymn of the Republic."[46]

With an army sixty thousand strong, Sherman cut off his lines of communication and burned across Georgia the avenue to his fame among the great generals of modern times. Behind his army followed an ever-growing throng of liberated Negroes, seeking freedom and security somewhere beyond the confines of the home plantation, perhaps on the coastal islands, waiting quietly in the declining autumn sunlight.

[46] William T. Sherman, *Memoirs of William T. Sherman* (New York, 1875), II, 179.

twelve "*RECONSTRUCTION IS EASY . . .*"

GENERAL SHERMAN HAD MADE ABRAHAM LINCOLN VERY HAPPY. On Christmas Eve the President received exciting news from Georgia: "I beg to present you as a Christmas gift," wired the General, "the city of Savannah, with one hundred and fifty guns and plenty of ammunition, also about twenty-five thousand bales of cotton."[1] The thrilling news brought a Christmas joy unknown in the North for four long years.

On this same Christmas Day, on St. Helena Island, Laura Towne entertained two Negro teachers at her holiday board. Examining her conscience with satisfaction, she wrote that the dinner had seemed to her "the most natural thing in the world"; the conversation had flowed without constraint. Since the great news of the Department was the arrival of Sherman's army on the coast, it doubtless formed the substance of the table talk, for Miss Towne recorded later in the evening her impression that the evacuation of Savannah by the white people would be a wonderful thing "if it leaves the country as this has been left, for freedmen under Northern influence. I wish," she wrote, "the Southerners would evacuate their whole territory."[2]

Where they should go Miss Towne did not suggest. But the destination of the fugitive colored population was as clear as the polar star. General Sherman's Christmas gift to Rufus Saxton ar-

[1] William T. Sherman, *Memoirs* (New York, 1875), II, 231.

[2] Towne to "T," December 25, 1864, Towne MS letters; Holland (ed.), *Towne*, p. 146. Actually, only about two hundred inhabitants of Savannah left. See Sherman, *Memoirs*, II, 234.

rived late in the day. On Christmas night seven hundred cold, shivering, and hungry freedmen of all ages came into Beaufort, consigned to "General Saxby" and in the direst need of every human requirement. These homeless ones were "in a state of misery which would have moved . . . a heart of stone" and, sadly enough, were "but the advance of a host no less destitute."[3] Exhausted, ill, and hungry, the people bore terrible memories as well. One woman's legs bore the marks of her master's shackles, applied to prevent her running away. Sherman's foragers had found her, but she had been half-dragged and half-carried for miles before the means to sever the chains had been found. There were cruel stories of mothers who had been driven to destroy their children when the hope for saving all the family had given out. One family of twelve had managed to stick together by means of tying the children along the length of a rope. But they had stubbornly followed the army, despite all General Sherman's efforts to dissuade them.[4]

Upwards of a thousand Negroes shortly arrived at St. Helena Village, where they were made welcome by the local inhabitants, who generously shared their own meager comforts. Bringing the strangers into their homes and to their own "chimblys," the Edisto people living at the Village reminded the downcast refugees of their own plight of just two years before.[5] To the Georgians who had begun to regret leaving the old plantation and half to fear the new life of responsibility, their hosts replied cheerily, "Look 'o we," and pointed to their own comparative comfort. "We come here wi' noffin at all," but now they had "money for cotton and

---

[3] *National Freedman*, I (February, 1865), 18.

[4] Botume, *First Days*, p. 140; Pearson (ed.), *Letters*, pp. 293–294; Sherman had early attempted to discourage the old, the very young, and the disabled from following his army, although he was ready to absorb young and able-bodied men into the army as "pioneers." Sherman, *Memoirs*, II, 181.

[5] Holland (ed.), *Towne*, p. 148. "A 'chimbly' here is a man's castle, and the privileges of this coveted convenience are held sacred."

all the tater and hominy we can eat." One generous Negro woman was proud and glad to have "striven and got enough to give *seven* gowns to these poor folk."[6]

Absorbing the initial refugees was hard, for the Negro population had already swelled from less than ten thousand at the time of the Federal occupation to more than fifteen thousand, even before any Sherman refugees arrived.[7] Finding employment and housing, food, clothes, and medicine for the flow of refugees into the Department was almost impossible. The month of January, which saw the arrival of thousands, was both wet and cold; ice did not melt all day. The harsh weather aggravated every problem, and at St. Helenaville victims of malnutrition and pulmonary disease died at the rate of three to four daily. "The poor Negroes die as fast as ever," wrote the worried Miss Towne, who was trying to cure them. "The children are all emaciated to the last degree and have such violent coughs and dysenteries that few survive. It is frightful to see such suffering among children."[8]

The freedmen kept coming. Nearly ten thousand had reached the coast by the second week in March, and they were still arriving at the rate of nearly a hundred each day.[9]

The presence of the army of liberation was no asset in the mammoth task of resettling the wanderers. Through the month of

[6] Pearson (ed.), *Letters*, p. 294.

[7] Saxton refers in a letter to Stanton, of February 7, 1864, to having 15,000 freedmen in the Department. *OR*, III, iv, 119.

[8] Holland (ed.), *Towne*, pp. 153–154; Botume, *First Days*, p. 135; W. J. Richardson to George Whipple, in a postscript dated February 8 to a letter of February 7, 1865, in "Letters from South Carolina, 1862–1865," AMA MSS. See also a letter of Arthur Sumner to the New England Freedmen's Aid Society, dated January 21, 1865, summarized and quoted in the Daily Records of the society. Further reference to these records, which are located in the Massachusetts Historical Society as a part of the Sturgis-Hooper collection, will be to the NEFAS MSS.

[9] Letter of March 12, quoted in the *National Freedman*, I (April, 1865), 89.

January a large part of Sherman's army passed through Beaufort on the way to resume its march through the mainland of South Carolina. The abuse of the freedmen that had always occurred whenever new troops came into the island district was vigorously reenacted. Some soldiers cheated the Negroes by selling them horses they did not own, and others behaved "like barbarians, shooting pigs, chickens, and destroying other property." Negroes who attempted to defend their belongings were "very roughly" handled. Most of the soldiers spoke scornfully of "niggers" and would not listen to teachers who stoutly maintained that their scholars had ability equal to that of whites.[10] General Saxton was at last obliged to place Beaufort out of bounds to freedmen, for their own protection. The "ragged-looking heroes" had literally taken over the town, "our little town," as an evangel of the American Missionary Association said, bristling with indignation. The denizens of Beaufort reacted to Sherman's army with envious admiration, some pride, and a quantum of alarm.[11]

The missionaries and the spit-and-polish Eastern regiments stationed at Port Royal were looking at an army the like of which they had never seen before. While ferociously disparaging "niggers," the Westerners were inconceivably democratic among themselves. "The officers and men are on terms of perfect social equality," marveled Arthur Sumner. "Off duty they drink together, go arm in arm about the town, [and] call each other by the first name in a way that startles the Eastern man." One civilian agent gasped to hear a private address a brigadier general as "Jake." Accustomed to the protocol of an Eastern post, the residents of Beaufort could hardly believe their eyes when a general took off

---

[10] G[aynor] H[eacock] in a letter published in the *Pennsylvania Freedmen's Bulletin*, I (February, 1865), 6–7; Pearson (ed.), *Letters*, pp. 301–302.

[11] Arthur Sumner to Nina Hartshorn [? February, 1865], Arthur Sumner MSS; W. J. Richardson to M. E. Strieby, January 31, 1865, "Letters from South Carolina, 1862–1865," AMA MSS; Botume, *First Days*, p. 133.

his coat and worked on the wharf, elbow to elbow with his men, unloading barrels.[12] The brotherhood of the Western army stopped abruptly, however, at the color line. The Western soldier was appalled by the free manners of the missionaries with Negroes. The sight of "a beautiful white woman driving in a wagon with a coal-black negro man" so shocked one soldier that he subsequently declared he would have shot her on the spot, "if she had been anything to me." Seeing the Negro regiments was also a revelation. Private Theodore Upson confessed that they made "pretty good looking soldiers" but added, "our boys dont think much of them. They still say this is a *White Man's War*." "Sherman and his men," explained Arthur Sumner to a Northern friend, "are impatient of darkies, and annoyed to see them so pampered, petted, and spoiled, as they have been here."[13]

It was disturbing to the civilians to be mistaken, in the first place, for converted rebels, snugly ensconced within the Union lines. Before Sherman's men got the matter straight, they made free use of all property "lying around loose" and burned great stores of lumber to keep the "moveable army" warm.[14] The soldiers bought out the stores in a flash, paying cash when they had it for items ranging from dictionaries to harmonicas but gaily instructing the shopkeepers, when the funds were gone, to look for their pay on the next battlefield. "Strange, rough-looking, unshaven, and badly dressed," they seemed to one young teacher, "like a gang of coal-heavers, when compared with the trim and snug fellows here, who have nothing to do but guard-duty with white gloves." The rugged and victorious army came "trooping

[12] Arthur Sumner to Nina Hartshorn, [? February, 1865], Arthur Sumner MSS.

[13] Isabella D. Martin and Myrta Lockett Avary (eds.), *A Diary from Dixie, as Written by Mary Boykin Chesnut* (New York, 1905), p. 386; Oscar Osburn Winther (ed.), *With Sherman to the Sea, the Civil War Letters, Diaries, and Reminiscences of Theodore F. Upson*, p. 149; Arthur Sumner to Nina Hartshorn [? February, 1865], Arthur Sumner MSS.

[14] Pearson (ed.), *Letters*, pp. 297, 305; Botume, *First Days*, p. 133.

through the streets, roaring out songs and jokes, making sharp comments about all the tidy civilians, and over-flowing with merriment and good-nature. Their clothes were patched like Scripture-Joseph's. Hats without brims, hats without crowns," and some with no hats at all. "One man had a live cock on his knapsack—the bird had been with him twenty-two months—all the way from Wisconsin. It was a treat, I assure you, to see some real soldiers, who had won battles."[15]

The morale of the Western troops was high because they had made the slaveholding aristocrats of Georgia feel the force of their élan. They could hardly wait to get to South Carolina.[16] The goal of Negro emancipation would continue to play for the "ragged heroes" a poor second to the preservation of the Union and the destruction of treason. Officers and men had shown plainly in Beaufort that they were little concerned with the abolition element there or for the ultimate goal of Negro political equality that was slowly and surely gaining ground in the island community. Sherman was thought "foolish in his political opinions" by a teacher who resented his crusty remark that "Massachusetts and South Carolina had brought on the war, and that he should like to see them cut off from the rest of the continent, and hauled out to sea together."[17]

Impatient to be on the march again, Sherman was extremely irritated with the delays keeping his army in the Massachusetts-occupied district. The most formidable obstacle to a hurried dumping of the thousands of refugees and a rapid departure for the interior appeared in Savannah on January 11 in the shape of the Secretary of War. Stanton complained a great deal of his

[15] Arthur Sumner to Nina Hartshorn, [? February, 1865], Arthur Sumner MSS.

[16] Sherman, *Memoirs*, II, 252, 254; Gray and Ropes, *War Letters*, p. 428; Sherman to Halleck, December 13, 1864, "The whole army is crazy to be turned loose in South Carolina." *OR*, I, xliv, 701–702.

[17] Arthur Sumner to Nina Hartshorn, [? February, 1865], Arthur Sumner MSS.

health, although Sherman thought cynically that he looked "robust and strong." The dyspeptic Secretary promptly antagonized a good part of the military establishment. A young officer wrote a friend that Stanton was "bearish and boorish, as is his nature, and it will be a relief to everyone to have him out of the way."[18] While declaring that he had come South to get a rest from the turmoil in Washington, Stanton obviously had practical matters on his mind. He wanted to know how much truth there was in the reports he had received about the bad treatment of the Negro refugees by Sherman's officers and to sift to the bottom the charges against the state recruiting officers at Beaufort. He had to come to some decision about what should be done with the thousands of refugees.[19]

Stanton began by talking with Sherman and other officials and then made known his desire to speak directly with representatives of the freedmen. On January 12, 1865, he met twenty Negro leaders at Sherman's headquarters and asked their opinion on a dozen problems involving their welfare. Among these leaders were ministers, barbers, pilots, sailors, and former overseers of cotton and rice plantations. Their answers were sound in understanding and their judgments were careful. In the opinion of General O. O. Howard, later head of the Freedmen's Bureau, "it would have been wise if our statesmen could have received, digested and acted upon the answers these men gave to their questions."[20] They understood their status as free men and the way in which the Emancipation Proclamation had come to be issued. They advised Stanton that the state recruiters should be promptly withdrawn from the district, sagely pointing out that Negro soldiers recruited in this system merely served to replace Northern white men who would otherwise be drafted to fill state quotas.

[18] Sherman, *Memoirs*, II, 242; John C. Gray, Jr., to Elizabeth Gray, January 14, 1865, Gray and Ropes, *War Letters*, p. 442.

[19] Sherman, *Memoirs*, II, 243–246; Holland (ed.), *Towne*, pp. 150–151.

[20] Oliver Otis Howard, *Autobiography of Oliver Otis Howard* (New York, 1908), II, 189–190.

They said what they well knew, that their ministers could do a better job of persuading young men to enlist than could mercenary bounty agents.

Stanton asked, quite significantly, whether they would prefer living scattered in communities of mixed white and black settlements or in an area restricted to Negroes entirely. With the exception of one Northern missionary, the Reverend James Lynch, the Negroes agreed that they preferred to live by themselves, "for there is a prejudice against us in the South that it will take years to get over. . . ."[21] Whether their judgment was wise from the vantage point of a hundred years of hindsight is at least open to question, but in the context of 1865 it is understandable.

At last Secretary Stanton vexed Sherman by signaling his desire to query the Negroes privately on another matter. Sherman's adversaries in the North had charged him with "an almost *criminal* dislike" of colored people and with frustrating the Negroes cruelly in their attempts to follow the army from the interior. "It certainly was a strange fact," complained Sherman, ten years later, "that the great War Secretary should have catechized negroes concerning the character of a general who had commanded a hundred thousand men in battle, had captured cities, conducted sixty-five thousand men successfully across four hundred miles of hostile territory, and had just brought tens of thousands of freedmen to a place of security. . . ." Sherman was indignant, but he had no cause for worry. The Negro counsellors gave him an excellent rating, saying that the freedmen regarded General Sherman with "inexpressible gratitude" and that the general could hardly have been more courteous to Stanton himself than he had been to them.[22]

This conference and Stanton's other investigations resulted in the issuance, on January 16, with the full concurrence of the Secretary of War, of Sherman's famous Special Field Order Number

[21] *Ibid.*; Sherman, *Memoirs*, II, 145–147.
[22] *Ibid.*, pp. 247–248.

15. The whole Sea Island region, from Charleston southward to the St. John's River, and the coastal lands thirty miles to the interior, were designated for exclusive Negro settlement. Rights to property that had already been established through the operations of the Direct Tax Law were not affected, but all other "abandoned" property could be taken up by the Negro refugees from the interior in tracts not exceeding forty acres. The Negroes were to receive "possessory" titles to these lands and were to be protected in their occupation of them "until such time as they can protect themselves, or until Congress shall regulate their title." Being absent for military service could not affect a Negro's claim. As Inspector of Settlements and Plantations, Rufus Saxton was in full charge of a mammoth plan for colonizing Sherman's refugees.[23] Saxton may well have asked himself if he was again in full command of a lost cause.

He probably did so, for there are ample indications that he did not accept the new assignment cheerfully. He reported later that he had been most reluctant to undertake the settlement of the Negroes on the islands, for fear that they would later be dispossessed. Coming up to Beaufort on a steamer with Stanton, he had asked most particularly whether the freedmen would be maintained in possession, and the Secretary had most heartily reassured him.[24]

Saxton's statement is entirely consistent with the facts as they stood at the end of 1864 and with his own mood as he pulled away from his defeat on the pre-emption plan. On December 30, 1864, he had written a bitter letter to Stanton, reviewing the long series of frustrations he had endured in his Sea Island work. Over and over he had been the unwitting agent of the erection of false hopes among the freedmen. In the matter of recruiting he had assured the people that no man would be taken against his will,

---

[23] *OR*, I, xlvii, Part II, 60–62.
[24] Testimony, "Impeachment of the President," *House Reports*, No. 7, 40th Congress, 1st session, serial 1314, p. 116.

but he had been undone by General Hunter in the first place, by General Quincy Gillmore in the second place, and at last by General John G. Foster, who in 1864 resumed wholesale recruiting "of every able-bodied male in the department." The atrocious impressment of boys of fourteen and responsible men with large dependent families, and the shooting down of Negroes who resisted, were all common occurrences. The Negroes who had been enlisted were promised the same pay as other soldiers. They had received it for a time, "but at length it was reduced, and they received but little more than one-half what was promised. The question of the meaning and conflicts of statutes which justified this reduction could not be made intelligible to them," wrote Saxton. For the Negroes "it was simply a breach of faith." The reversal of the pre-emption policy had perhaps been the bitterest of Saxton's disappointments, for he had again been the instrument of high-raised hopes most cruelly dashed. He asserted that "not the least noticeable result is the uncertainty in the minds of the freedmen, induced by previous occurrence and increased by the proceedings, as to our ultimate purposes toward them." Saxton did not despair of free labor. "The experiment with the freedmen in this department is a success," he wrote firmly, for "amid all their obstructions, . . . they have made constant progress and proved their right to be received into the full company of free men." Rufus Saxton was nevertheless sufficiently embittered to offer his resignation.[25]

General Saxton had especially resented the manner in which his ostensibly independent command had been subordinated on point after point to the local military commanders. "My authority has been questioned by the department commanders, explanations of my official acts have been demanded, those acts annulled, and subordinate officers sustained and encouraged in preventing the execution of my orders." On these grounds Saxton offered his resignation, feeling that the "frequent disappointments" of the

[25] *OR*, III, lv, 1022–1031, especially pp. 1028–1031.

Negroes had weakened their confidence in him and impaired his further usefulness.[26]

After this letter it is impossible to disbelieve Saxton's subsequent assertion that he should never have accepted the assignment to carry out Sherman's Field Order without the fullest assurance that the arrangement would be permanent. He withdrew his resignation, received an advance in rank to Brevet Major General, and was firmly saddled with responsibility for freedmen's affairs from Florida to Charleston. By the middle of 1865 he had settled forty thousand freedmen on the coastal lands.[27]

Sherman was at last free to bring the war home to South Carolina. In late January he crossed to the mainland. A young officer, sent to catch up with Sherman to deliver a despatch and reaching him at nightfall, described the famous army on the march:

It was a beautiful sight to see the long lines of camp fires in the woods; with one or two exceptions all the buildings and fences on the road were burned, and it was a curious sight to see how the flames gradually died out, from the bright red flames pouring forth from house and cotton gin in the immediate rear of his army to the utter blackness near Pocotaligo where the army had been two days before.[28]

South Carolina would never have cause to complain of neglect in comparison with Georgia.

With the Western army out of the way, serious operations for the resettlement of the freedmen began immediately. Saxton and Chaplain French organized mass meetings in Savannah, explaining the opportunities before the freedmen and answering their questions.[29] A Northern observer remarked that the freedmen made "plain, straight-forward," and shrewd inquiries. They

[26] *Ibid.*, pp. 1030–1031.
[27] Testimony, "Impeachment of the President," p. 116; *Freedmen's Record*, I (August, 1865), 28–29.
[28] John C. Gray, Jr., to John C. Ropes, February 8, 1865, in Gray and Ropes, *War Letters*, pp. 455–456.
[29] *OR*, I, xlvii, Part II, 187, 424.

wanted to know the nature of the titles the government could give them and "what assurance they could have that . . . [the land] would be theirs after they had improved it." Considering the condition of the neglected fields and the ruined economy of the islands, this question was significant indeed. A heavy initial outlay of time and money would be required to restore these acres to fruitfulness. Presumably, the assurances were effective, for Saxton had no dearth of applicants. Within one day alone five thousand acres were assigned, and the movement gathered force.[30]

The Negroes organized themselves and, armed with rudimentary farming tools and seeds, flocked to the islands to begin spring planting. The Edisto people left St. Helena promptly, eager to return to their old homes as landowners. Other groups joined them from Georgia. "We shall build our cabins, and organize our town government for the maintenance of order and the settlement of all difficulties," said the Reverend Mr. Ulysses Houston, a Negro minister of Savannah, to an interested Northern correspondent. He was conducting a large party of Negroes to Skidaway Island and had laid his plans carefully. "He and his fellow-colonists selected their lots, laid out a village, numbered their lots, put the numbers in a hat, and drew them out." The reporter was thrilled. "It was Plymouth colony repeating itself. They agreed if any others came to join them, they should have equal privileges. So blooms the Mayflower on the South Atlantic coast."[31]

Saxton was roundly criticized by his adversaries for these "mass meetings," which the military officers regarded as demoralizing to the Negroes and the white citizens of Savannah alike.[32] Saxton had begun none too soon, however, for the numbers of fugitives entering the Department mounted steadily. By April hundreds more freedmen were being sent there from the flanks of Sherman's army as it passed through the Carolinas.

[30] *National Freedman*, I (April, 1865), 82–83.
[31] *Ibid.*; see also a letter of Ellen Murray, February 16, 1865, in *Pennsylvania Freedmen's Bulletin*, I (April, 1865), 33.
[32] *OR*, I, xlvii, Part II, 187.

The temporary encampments on the docks at Hilton Head and Savannah were death traps for many enfeebled refugees. Sleeping without bedding on straw-covered floors, with inadequate and unsanitary clothing, they were in tragic circumstances.[33] William Gannett, who had gone to Savannah to assist in the resettlement program, described the condition of several hundred people sent back from Sherman's army:

> One half of the number had to be helped up the plank; they would drop half way from weakness. Four men only were strong enough to carry up those who could not lift a limb. Long, bony, and still, they lay along the decks, the flies swarming around them, as if they lit upon the dead. The silence of four *was* that of death; and, before I had them all landed, the four were six. And yet their case has been that of thousands.

These debilitated human beings often went out to farm the islands, and they frequently died soon after from smallpox and diarrhea. Gannett wrote that "freedom means death to many. . . ."[34]

Wherever the freedmen went to farm, the Northern teachers and organizers followed and attempted to establish schools. It was difficult, because the luxury of an education for any but the smallest children was out of the question. Every hand capable of swinging a hoe was needed to raise a crop and stave off starvation. But the teachers went, and the Northern aid societies redoubled their efforts to meet the crisis of the overwhelming needs for medicine and clothing as well as for education. It is a significant fact that the interested officials in Beaufort made their first vigorous appeals in the crisis, as early as January 6, not to the government but to the freedmen's aid societies.[35] The assistance of volunteer groups could be expected to meet an emergency more rapidly than the overburdened and cumbersome bureaucracy of

[33] *Freedmen's Record*, I (April, 1865), 62–63.
[34] William Gannett, in a letter from Savannah, dated April 28, 1865, in *ibid.*, I (June, 1865), 93.
[35] *Ibid.*, I (July, 1865), 111. The text of the appeal was printed in several freedmen's aid publications. See *ibid.*, I (February, 1865), 26.

an administration that had been consistently late in meeting every crisis involving the Negroes.

From their relatively weak beginnings in the spring of 1862, when they had first organized for the benefit of the Port Royal "contrabands," the societies had grown steadily in numbers, size, and financial stability. The increasing numbers of freedmen coming within the lines throughout the war years had stimulated this growth, but the arrival of Sherman's pitiful refugees on the coast of South Carolina had created an unprecedented call upon the charitable impulses of the nation. James Miller McKim estimated that the combined income of all the aid societies would reach a million dollars for 1865. The records of the associations indicate that McKim was not overly sanguine. The New York society quadrupled the number of teachers it was supporting in the South during the year after the war, maintaining 206 teachers by the spring of 1866. The New England Freedmen's Aid Society, formerly the Boston Educational Commission, did proportionally well and sent 180 teachers in the spring of 1866. The Philadelphia society was supporting 60 teachers. Vigorous new societies had grown up in Cincinnati and Chicago, supporting 130 teachers in the year after the war, and Baltimore's new society financed approximately 50. The American Missionary Association, stronger than any individual society but not so strong as the combined force of all of them, was maintaining, during the winter after the war, not less than 327 Northern schoolteachers.[36] The charitable work of uplift for the freedmen had grown beyond the highest

[36] McKim's estimate is found in an undated note entitled "American Freedmen's Associations" in the McKim MSS. The other facts I have included, as well as further information on the freedmen's societies at the close of the war, are found in the following: Synopses of School Reports, I, 329–331, 341, Educational Division, BRFAL; *Annual Report of the New York National Freedmen's Aid Society of New York, with a Sketch of its Early History* (New York, 1866), pp. 11, 18; *National Freedman*, I (July, 1865), 185, and II (February, 1866), 48; Richard Bryant Drake, "The American Missionary Association and the Southern Negro, 1861–1888" (unpublished doctoral dissertation, Emory University, 1957), pp. 13–14; *Freedmen's Record*, I (April, 1865), 49, and I (November, 1865), 185–186.

hopes of Pierce's backers in 1862, when they had first set out "to plant the Northern pine." Unfortunately, the broader work for the whole South was afflicted with the same internal ailments that had plagued the experiment at Port Royal. The chief of these was, of course, rivalry over the place of evangelism in the freedmen's schools.

The nonsectarian and nonevangelical associations early felt the need of close organization in order to retain the support of contributors who might otherwise allocate their charitable funds to the American Missionary Association and other denominational organizations. The outlines of the old division between the Garrisonian and evangelical wings of the abolition movement were still clearly evident.[37] The union of the secular groups was difficult for yet another reason. The New England and Pennsylvania societies followed a form of expansion that was based upon smaller "branch" units in the towns. Each branch supported a teacher approved by the society, by paying her salary and corresponding with her. This kept interest alive and reduced administrative costs. The New York society, on the other hand, sent paid lecturers hither and yon, frequently into New England and Pennsylvania, to raise funds. This practice seemed to the rival societies very much like a raid on their own charitable bailiwicks, and it was hotly resented. The large contributions from England also became a source of rivalry and friction.[38]

Although the three larger societies had attempted cooperation from the early beginnings at Port Royal, a real union was slow in

[37] Drake, "The American Missionary Association," p. 15.

[38] Annual Report of the Teachers Committee, in *Freedmen's Record*, I (April, 1865), 54–55. Teachers were also "adopted" by towns in the Pennsylvania society's method of operation. See Synopses of School Reports, I, 332, Education Division, BRFAL: George C. Ward to J. Miller McKim, July 10, 1865, McKim–Maloney–Garrison MSS, New York Public Library. For the year 1865-1866, the English contributions made through the New York society amounted to $40,000, as opposed to $99,000 raised in this country by the same society. *National Freedman*, II (February, 1866), 48.

An 1862 photograph of the slave quarters, or "street," on an Edisto Island plantation. The man in the foreground wears a Union uniform, and the children have campaign hats.

Emancipated plantation workers gather to hear the terms of a free labor contract. This is probably Josiah Fairfield, reading to the laborers at The Oaks.

Wash day on Edisto Island.

Going to the field. The heavy cotton hoe was on most ante-bellum Sea Island plantations the sole means of cultivation, for plows were rarely employed.

coming. The New Englanders took an attitude of superiority, maintaining that their teachers were far better qualified than those of other groups. There was some justification for this, for Ednah Cheney, as head of the Teachers' Committee, was an extremely critical judge of good teachers. But the New Englanders were also fond of deprecating the large amounts other societies expended for the alleviation of physical wants, maintaining their own funds as exclusively as possible for educational purposes.[39] At last the fear of an evangelical victory overcame outstanding differences.

The movement for union began in the spring of 1865. A general meeting for the exchange of views took place in Washington in February, but no real constitutional union was accomplished until representatives of the Baltimore, New England, and Pennsylvania societies formed the American Freedmen's Aid Union on March 16, 1865. The mutual goal was to train the freed Negro of the South "for the duties of his new condition, and to fit him for all the franchises of unconditional freedom," to aid "in adjusting, on a better basis, the civil, social, and industrial relations of Southern society."[40] The Negro was free, and now he ought to be able to *vote*.

New York held aloof until the last minute. On May 9, at a meeting of the new union at Cooper Institute in New York City, certain members of the New York National Freedmen's Aid Society informed the officers that their organization had voted to join the union. Soon afterward, the Pennsylvanians and New Englanders were gratified to learn that New York had voted also to withdraw its collecting agents from Massachusetts and Pennsylvania. At the May 9, 1865, meeting, the delegates thrilled to

[39] *Freedmen's Record*, I (August, 1865), 129. The New England society did not wish to relieve the Negroes "from the salutary pressure of want, . . . Entertaining this view, we have not always been able to sympathize with the efforts made by some of our friends in other places." *Ibid.*, I (July, 1865), 107.

[40] *Pennsylvania Freedmen's Bulletin*, I (April, 1865), 38; *Freedmen's Record*, I (April, 1865), 66.

the eloquence of such tried and true abolitionists as John Jay of New York, Frederick Douglass, and William Lloyd Garrison. It was resolved by an almost unanimous vote to support Negro suffrage.[41] The movement would no longer have to suffer silently charges that some abolitionists had held themselves aloof, that the freedmen's work was weak in its demands for full equality for Negroes. With the accession of all the major secular societies to the Freedmen's Aid Union, no further unification could be attained. The movement was now neatly divided into two camps, making mutual action easier in the immediate view but preparing the ground for a long struggle over the place of evangelism in the schools of the South.

The point may be argued that by May of 1865 the aid societies, acting independently but cooperatively, had already accomplished their most important work. For they had served as gadflies to awaken the Administration and Congress to belated action to meet the impending social crisis. They had provided at Port Royal an example that deserved more study than it received but that was at least considered in the shaping of such inadequate and tardy plans as the Administration adopted. Negroes had been tried at Port Royal in nearly every capacity that ordinary citizens are called upon to fill, and they had acquitted themselves remarkably well. Port Royal had become, in the words of one historian, "an important element in Radical propaganda and a model for subsequent efforts by the War Department." In the words of another, Port Royal was an "official laboratory" for testing the freedmen's qualifications for freedom. "Rarely in our history has a social experiment been conducted on such a scale, rarely has one been conducted on such a crucial topic."[42]

[41] *Ibid.*, I (June, 1865), 89–90.
[42] James G. Sproat, "Blue Print for Radical Reconstruction," *Journal of Southern History*, XXIII (February, 1957), 29; Edwin D. Hoffman, "From Slavery to Self-Reliance," *Journal of Negro History*, LVI (January, 1956), 10.

But the supporters of the freedmen's movement had done more. They had been largely responsible for the creation of the Freedmen's Inquiry Commission. The reports of this commission formed an able reference for the last and most radical phase of the reconstruction process, even if its enactment was in 1865 as yet several years distant. The friends of the freedmen had regarded the commission as an agency for studying the whole scope of postwar adjustments but had foreseen from the beginning that national *action* must promptly follow national *study*. It had seemed exasperatingly slow in coming.

As early as December 1, 1863, an attitude of desperation had been evident in a letter to Lincoln, signed by prominent officers of the freedmen's aid societies. They asked for government help. "It is the magnitude of the work, not the nature of the work, that appalls us, and drives us to the government for aid and support." They pointed to matters that their experience had made clear. "We have found freedom very easy to manage, beyond our best hopes. . . ." They had demonstrated at Port Royal that the Negro was "willing and able to fight as a soldier; willing and able to work as a laborer; willing and able to learn as a pupil." They now wanted a *national* Bureau of Emancipation. The delegates came away from their conversations at this time with Stanton, Chase, and Secretary of State Seward with the feeling that they had accomplished their object.[43]

The struggle for a national freedmen's agency dates from the winter of 1863–1864 and resulted in the passage, on March 3, 1865, of the Freedmen's Bureau Act. The Port Royal experience was considered in the framing of the bill, and the reports of the Freedmen's Inquiry Commission were influential. But it was Sherman's land directive in South Carolina that provided the

[43] Letter to Lincoln, *Senate Exec. Docs.*, 38th Congress, 1st session, serial 1176, p. 2; see also a letter from Atkinson to Forbes, November 24, 1863, and from Atkinson to his wife, Mary, December 2, 1863, Atkinson MSS.

needed impetus to prompt passage of the compromise version of the bill in the closing hours of the Congressional session. Although the freedmen's associations had exerted a strong influence to save the bill, certain of its provisions were not altogether attractive. The protective element, that of military supervision to secure justice to the Negro, was criticized. At a large annual meeting of the National Freedmen's Aid Society held in the House of Representatives, statements were made opposing the supervisory aspects of the bill, which granted considerable power to a single head. The bill included, however, one overriding compensation: its provision for opening Southern lands for the cultivation of the freedmen.[44] In this Gideon's Band had ever seen the greatest security for the Negro.

The land provision of the first Freedmen's Bureau Act was the governmental response to the fundamental question concerning the way in which the slave laborer could be transformed into a free farmer. It constituted, in the eyes of the scholar who has studied it most carefully, a "promise" of land to the freed Negroes. An earlier historian also regarded the Act as legalizing the military action taken by Sherman on the Sea Islands.[45] The land clause said that "every male citizen, whether refugee or freedman," should be granted occupation of forty acres of land at rental for three years. He could then purchase the land from the government with "such title as it could convey." The Act was so written as not to place the national domain in the Southern states under his provision, but only "abandoned and confiscated" lands. Well aware that governmental ownership under the Direct Tax Law and the Confiscation Acts was open to legal challenge, Congress undoubtedly hoped that the Supreme Court would act

[44] LaWanda Cox, "The Promise of Land for the Freedmen," *Mississippi Valley Historical Review*, XLV (December, 1958), 413–440, especially 422–431.

[45] Cox, in "The Promise of Land," cites Walter L. Fleming as interpreting the Act as legalizing the Sherman claims. *Ibid.*, pp. 413, 430.

to clear government titles and that the great estates of rich rebels would be divided among the slaves.[46]

With the approval of the Thirteenth Amendment, Congress had put its blessing on the free status of Negro Americans; the land provision of the Bureau Act was the natural response of a nation of small farmers to set the black man on the road to economic freedom. The purpose of the Bureau itself was to assure a reasonable and temporary protection for the Negro as he passed into his new condition.

Three days after the Cooper Institute meeting, during which the freedmen's aid societies formed their union, Edwin Stanton received into his office General Oliver Otis Howard, whom the Secretary had named to head the newly created Freedmen's Bureau. The grumpy Stanton was for once in a playful mood; he held out to the general, in both hands, a large oblong bushel basket loaded with papers, saying, "Here, General, *here's your Bureau!*" He was playful but not very tactful; perhaps he had forgotten for the moment that Howard had lost his right arm at Fair Oaks.[47]

Although he was by no means a radical by reputation, Howard had been advanced to his post by the influence of such formidable exponents of radical Southern reconstruction as Stanton himself, General Saxton, and Henry Ward Beecher. He was only thirty-four, malleable perhaps, and he was not handicapped with the abolitionist label. He was also pious, and sympathetic toward the cause of the freedman. Howard had had relatively little experience to prepare himself for his position; he had perhaps seen more of Negro schools and the whole reconstruction problem during his brief stay in Savannah and Port Royal with Sherman's army than at any other time. Saxton had escorted him about his

[46] *U. S. Statutes at Large*, XIII, 507–509; Cox, "The Promise of Land," pp. 432–433.

[47] Howard, *Autobiography*, II, 208.

little kingdom and had obviously been pleased with General Howard's reaction. The evangels at Port Royal also liked the general. One of his visits had been to Laura Towne's school on St. Helena, where Howard had talked to the youngsters and where his empty sleeve had made "quite an impression" on the scholars.[48]

From the beginning Howard showed the greatest sympathy with the educational work of the societies. He promptly assured them that the Bureau under his supervision would assist their work as much as possible and would in no way supersede it. The societies warmly approved the choice of Howard and anticipated a period of hearty cooperation. The Bureau would, they believed, take over the work of physical relief and agricultural reorganization and leave all voluntary funds free for the special purpose of education.[49]

In any event the societies and their missionaries in the Port Royal area fortunately had not waited for the erection of a federal agency to meet the crisis. The work of resettlement on the islands went forward briskly under Saxton's management, and from the nucleus of experienced men and women on the central islands General Howard found leaders to send out to Edisto and the other islands being resettled. Within a few weeks the Port Royal veterans were widely dispersed.[50]

By March 3, 1865, and the passage of the Bureau bill, South Carolina was, to all practical purposes, a completely defeated state. By the middle of February Sherman's army had reached the capitol at Columbia, and on the night of February 17 the better part of the city shot up in flames. On the same night the Confederate

---

[48] Pearson (ed.), *Letters*, pp. 298–299; Bentley, *Freedmen's Bureau*, pp. 53, 55, 56.

[49] Howard's Circular No. 2, May 19, 1865, in *Freedmen's Record*, I (May, 1865), 135; see also p. 81.

[50] Towne to "R," January 21, 1865, Towne MS letters; letter of Arthur Sumner, January 21, 1865, copied into the Daily Record, NEFAS MSS; Holland (ed.), *Towne*, p. 155; Towne letter of March 19, 1865, in *Pennsylvania Freedmen's Bulletin*, I (April, 1865), 31–32.

forces and most of the citizens withdrew from Charleston, now considered untenable; the city that had embodied so much of the spirit of Southern resistance was at last in Union hands.

Within two weeks a large company of Northern officials connected with the freedmen's work came up to Charleston from Beaufort aboard Robert Smalls's little steamer, making its highly significant return to the city with Smalls himself, now owner as well as skipper of the *Planter*, at the helm. On March 4, the day following the enactment of the Freedmen's Bureau bill, the freedmen's schools opened in Charleston. "Of course," wrote James Redpath, who was in charge, "I received all white, black, and yellow children alike. . . ." He had enrolled fifteen hundred children, three hundred of them white. The Northern teachers began to establish an orderly routine against almost insuperable odds, for with the masses of freedmen passing through the city on their way to the islands, there was much irregularity of registration, and many were dropping out.[51] Despite all, however, the system was begun, and it was pushed forward with much faith as the one sure way to convert the South to the ideals of New England public education.

On the fourteenth of April Charleston was the dramatic setting of a ritual celebration of the close of hostilities. General Robert E. Lee had surrendered his army at Appomattox five days before, and General Joseph Johnston was warning Jefferson Davis that further resistance was in his own case hopeless. Within two weeks Johnston would surrender his forces to Sherman. Exactly four years and one day after the surrender of Fort Sumter, a host of Northern abolitionists, politicians, teachers, missionaries, and freedmen converged on Charleston to witness the raising of the old flag over the battered fortress in the harbor.[52]

[51] James Redpath, in a letter of March 9, 1865, in *Freedmen's Record*, I (April, 1865), 61.

[52] [Justus Clement French], *The Trip of the Steamer Oceanus to Fort Sumter and Charleston, S.C., Comprising the Incidents of the Excursion, the Appearance, at that Time, of the City, and the Entire Programme of*

The beauty of springtime in South Carolina put a brave face on the ruin of the city, but nothing could conceal from the curious eyes of the alien sightseers that she had fallen upon very hard times. Years of bombardment and desultory fires had told upon Charleston's elegance, and the rattling emptiness of her deserted mansions published her desolation. The army had confiscated the rich furnishings from all homes not taken over by the civilian and military establishments or held by the old residents who stood their ground and shuttered their windows.[53]

In Charleston private dwellings offer their anonymous sides to the street, reserving for the cool privacy of their walled gardens the impressive front of verandah and column. Now the exclusive gates of these gardens swung open by military order, and in tramped the Northern visitors to gape, pick flowers, and gather souvenirs. Nature lovers were enthralled by "the most luxuriant growth of trees and shrubs—the orange, the mock-orange, the magnolia, the lilac, the hawthorne, the jasmine, roses and vines of every variety," and came away with the "floral trophies" of South Carolina. The experience of being in Charleston at such a time was almost too much for William Lloyd Garrison, for upon hearing "John Brown's Body" played by a regimental band, he burst into tears and exclaimed, "Only listen to that in Charleston's streets!" Laura Towne, who had come up from Beaufort with a steamer full of Northern missionaries and freedmen, took special pains to look up the workhouse, of which she had heard so many terrible stories in times past. A Negro woman passing by assured her that she was indeed looking at "the old sugar house" but added significantly, "it's all played out now." The few white citizens who had remained were "as full of spite as they can be," Miss Towne wrote. She had overheard one woman say aloud, "See those nasty yankees," and another say, "I wish I had their winding

---

the Exercises of Re-raising the Flag over the Ruins of Fort Sumter (Brooklyn, 1865).
[53] Ibid., pp. 34–35.

sheets to make when the yellow fever comes."[54] These were novel experiences for Laura Towne.

The ceremonies within the fort did not quite match the lively anticipations of the throng. One visitor noted distrustfully that the *Planter* "with its load of contrabands, for some as yet unexplained reason, had not been permitted to land and witness the exercises. . . ." Major Anderson's speech was not so enthusiastic as Laura Towne thought it should have been, and Henry Ward Beecher, the famous orator of the day, "spoke very much by note, and quite without fire."[55] With the stiff ocean wind whipping his iron-gray locks, Beecher promptly discovered that the only way to control the situation was to clap his hat upon his head and hold his address with both hands. Hearers familiar with the Beecher style were disappointed that he "*read* his entire oration" but praised the substance of his "carefully composed" remarks as suitable to the serious occasion. It was a satisfaction to know that the eminent divine held the secessionist aristocrats fully responsible for the war. These "polished, cultured, exceedingly capable and wholly unprincipled" men had "shed this ocean of blood." Vividly and at length Beecher described the fate of "these guiltiest and most remorseless traitors" on the Judgment Day. Confronted and condemned by their victims, "caught up in black clouds, full of voices of vengeance and lurid with punishment, [they] shall be whirled aloft and plunged downward forever and forever in endless retribution. . . ." For other Southerners, less guilty of treason, Beecher spoke of forgiveness and of the right hand of fellowship. That the sheep might not be easy to separate from the goats in later days did not occur to the speaker; nor that there might not be, after all, very many sheep.[56]

The missionaries present were most interested in hearing what so famous a man had to say about their burning issue, Reconstruc-

[54] *Ibid.*, pp. 34–35, 119; Towne to "S," April 23, 1865, Towne MS letters.
[55] *Ibid.*; [French], *Steamer Oceanus*, p. 81.
[56] Towne to "S," April 23, 1865, Towne MS letters; [French], *Steamer Oceanus*, pp. 65, 67, 68–69.

tion. After a rest and a glass of water he told them. The laboring man of the South had to be educated, but who should foot the bill Beecher did not suggest. In an oblique reference that probably indicated Negro suffrage, he asked of the freedmen, "Since they have vindicated the Government, and cemented its foundation with their blood, may they not offer the tribute of their support to maintain its laws and its policy?" Further he did not go.[57]

Beecher's saddest mistake of the day was to underestimate the problem of Reconstruction. The conditions of peace in the South were simply acceptance of the Constitution, its laws, and the national government. *"One nation, under one government, without slavery,* has been ordained, and shall stand. There can be peace on no other basis. On this base reconstruction is easy, and needs neither architect nor engineer."[58] The Port Royal veterans probably wondered where Beecher ever got an idea like that. If the Northern public should take Beecher's stand, the problems of social and economic reconstruction might never be met.

There was another signal point of confusion. Beecher's address was aimed at the citizens of Charleston—white ones. Had he been deceived, back in his Brooklyn study, into thinking these proud and freshly humiliated people would turn out to hear him tell them how they ought to behave? Laura Towne thought that there "were not a dozen" local white people among the whole throng.[59]

But the error did serve to remind the teachers sitting on the front row that now the Southern white people would provide a new and probably troublesome element of Reconstruction. The Southern whites were not going "to evacuate their whole territory" or leave the freedmen entirely "under Northern influence" in order to simplify Reconstruction. The task had seemed serious enough before the return of those individuals "full of spite" who referred to evangels as "nasty yankees."[60]

[57] *Ibid.*, p. 75.
[58] *Ibid.*, p. 58.
[59] Towne to "S," April 23, 1865, Towne MS letters.
[60] *Ibid.*

The Charleston celebrants had hardly reached home before they heard most distressing news. While they had been trumpeting Northern victory at gay parties in Charleston on the night of April 14, Abraham Lincoln had been shot in Ford's Theater in Washington, a victim of one Southern fanatic who would never be reconstructed. The President had died the next morning.

thirteen ❖ "PLANTATION BITTERS"

IN THE MONTHS FOLLOWING THE CLOSE OF HOSTILITIES, THE FREED people of the Sea Islands were watchful and quiet, waiting expectantly for something to happen, although they were not really sure for what. "Every movement of their white friends was to them full of significance, and often regarded with distrust," wrote Elizabeth Botume. Edwin Ruggles, superintendent on St. Helena, wrote that the death of Lincoln had been "an awful blow" to the freedmen. They were asking, "Uncle Sam is dead, isn't he?" or "the Government is dead, isn't it? You have got to go North and Secesh come back, haven't you? We going to be slaves again?" Laura Towne reported that the freedmen would not believe that Lincoln was dead, that they prayed for him in church "as wounded but still alive and said that he was their Savior—that Christ saved them from sin and he from Secesh. . . ."[1]

In all their trials the freedmen had maintained a steady confidence in the President's intentions toward them. Slow and reluctant as it had been, the Lincoln Administration had arrived, by the close of the war, at a loose series of commitments that were advantageous to freedmen. Would President Andrew Johnson regard these commitments as binding? Now the freedmen saw their masters returning to the islands, and one cold fact was clear to all: Reconciling the interests of the late landowners with the Negroes' claims to consideration in the land was impossible.

[1] Botume, *First Days*, p. 176; Pearson (ed.), *Letters*, pp. 310–311; Towne to "S," April 23, 1865, Towne MS letters.

In late spring of 1865 the first of the dispossessed planters came drifting back to their old island homes, and, as their numbers increased late in the summer, Laura Towne complained that "Secesh are coming back thick." "They are crawlingly civil as yet, but will soon feel their oats." Dr. Clarence Fripp was living in the house next door to Miss Towne, who was now the owner of Fripp's old home. A Northern reporter who met Dr. Fripp at a hotel on Hilton Head described him as sitting there calmly, smoking and freely discussing his present poverty and his plans for the future. Dressed in the characteristic Southern manner, with gray clothes and "a display of crumpled linen at the collar and cuffs," the doctor explained that it was as well for him "to starve in Beaufort as any strange place." He hoped to get a little medical practice and eke out a living on fish and oysters if it proved necessary. Ever a popular man with his slaves, Dr. Fripp was soon assisted by the colored people with a little ready cash, and he took up the struggle to survive.[2]

The transformation of Beaufort and the islands was overwhelming to men whose hereditary roots in the once quiet little backwater had been wrenched away by the war. Thomas Elliott returned to his plantation on Hilton Head and reported in astonishment, "Hilton Head is a Town, I was lost in wonder at the vast buildings, the wharf is 1,400 feet long and cost $300,000." He could not yet bring his family back, however, for "it is impossible to take them to Beaufort at present. The town is not fit for a white Lady to stay in, Yankees and negroes are all the rage." Elliott was able to report that the former slaves of his family had treated him "with universal politeness" and had inquired kindly for the rest of the family.[3] His kinsman, Stephen Elliott, also met with kindness from his late servants. "They were delighted to see me, and treated me with overflowing affection. They waited on

[2] Holland (ed.), *Towne*, p. 167; Pearson (ed.), *Letters*, p. 319; New York *Nation*, November 30, 1865.

[3] Thos. R. S. Elliott to Emily Elliott, December 19, 1865, Elliott–Gonzales MSS.

me as before, gave me beautiful breakfasts and splendid dinners"; but he added, "they firmly and respectfully informed me: 'We own this land now. Put it out of your head that it will ever be yours again.' "[4]

A Northern reporter saw that the Negroes were in many cases truly sorry for the poverty of their former masters and "surprisingly free from a vulgar contempt for these men merely because of their sudden poverty and the shifts and straits to which they see them reduced. . . ." The Negroes advanced little loans and performed the kind deeds within their power to alleviate the distress of the indigent planters. Miss Botume wrote of talking with a handsome young colored woman who was overtaken in the act of doing a favor for her old mistress. "Us going to well fur water fur the lady what bring we up, an' was like a muther to we." She had come back "awful poor an' sick," said the young woman, and her former servants couldn't "stan' seein' her workin' fur herself, bringin' water, an' sich-like, fur she bin very kind to we." Defensively, the young woman went on to say that the old master and her own mother had been "babies togedder," and "us mus' help them now." Duly reassured that Miss Botume admired her spirit, the young woman left, "very happy, singing as she went on her way."[5]

The veterans of slavery, however, understood well the sources of power; it was one thing to *volunteer* loans and kind deeds, but quite another to hire as labor to men who had once owned slaves. One Northerner was surprised that the "genuine commiseration" should be so general, for he came to the conclusion that the Negroes as a whole "fear and dislike the slave-holders, both as a class and individually. The probable return of their former owners to the island, the possibility that they may sometime be compelled to work for them and be governed by them, seem to excite the

---

[4] Ben Ames Williams (ed.), *A Diary from Dixie by Mary Boykin Chesnut* (Sentry Edition; Boston, 1961), p. 540.

[5] New York *Nation*, November 30, 1865; Botume, *First Days*, p. 142.

liveliest apprehensions and very strong expressions of hostility."[6]

A relative of Dr. Richard Fuller returned to the family property on St. Helena and began to lay plans for putting in a crop. Enlisting the aid of his former driver "to persuade" his late slaves to work for him, Fuller called the freedmen up, requesting "those who were willing to stay with him another year to step over to his left hand." His disillusionment began with the driver, for "Old Gib" turned away himself and went toward the quarters. Fuller called, " 'Why Gib, you will stay, won't you?' 'No, Sir.' Then he went through the whole list, and every one marched straight home . . . much to his disgust."[7]

Laura Towne was unwilling to believe that the generosity of the Negroes toward their whilom owners had any foundation in old affections. "The people receive the rebels better than we expected," she wrote, "but the reason is that they believe Johnson is going to put them in their old masters' hands again, and they feel they must conciliate or be crushed."[8] While her assessment revealed an inadequate understanding of the highly complex human relationships under slavery, Miss Towne had fingered the main point. The freedmen were deeply troubled.

The planters expressed a disturbing assurance about the probable restoration of their property, and it was not without foundation. President Johnson, in his haste to resolve the conflicts of the war and to protect the letter of the Constitution, had been far more conciliatory toward the late rebels than Congressional radicals had hoped. Apparently, President Johnson's view of Reconstruction was similar to the one Henry Ward Beecher had referred to as "easy"; all the returning Confederates had to do was to accept the laws, acknowledge the end of slavery, and submit to the Federal authority. As early as May 29 the new President had granted amnesty to all participants in the rebellion, "with restitu-

[6] New York *Nation*, November 30, 1865.
[7] Pearson (ed.), *Letters*, p. 315.
[8] Holland, *Towne*, p. 167.

tion of all rights to property, except as to slaves." Although several categories were excepted from the general provisions, the persons who fell within the excepted categories were entitled to make individual applications for pardon and amnesty. By fall of 1865 the President was evincing a marvelous generosity.[9] The bearing of the proclamation on lands that had been at no time seized as "abandoned" was quite clear; the pardoned owners were in full possession. Confiscation would form no part of the President's plan for Reconstruction of the South. On the coastal islands, however, nearly all real estate was in some state of legal process, and those interested in the Negroes' security in their small estates waited anxiously for the evolution of the President's policy on details.

Lands "abandoned" by their owners were of two general classes. Within the first of these were the properties that the United States Direct Tax Commissioners had seized and condemned for failure to pay the war tax. Much of this land had already been sold to third parties, some to Negroes in small lots and much more to Northern investors. The commissioners still held much town property in Beaufort, however, and large tracts that had been bid in at the sales for government use. The islands most affected were those which the Federal forces had occupied longest—Port Royal, St. Helena, Ladies, and Paris. Within the second and larger category came the islands closer to Charleston and Savannah, more recently occupied, and the low coastal lands on the mainland. These were the estates being used for the resettlement of the Negroes who had gained "possessory titles" under Sherman's Field Order 15.[10]

---

[9] Eric L. McKitrick, *Andrew Johnson and Reconstruction* (Chicago, 1960), pp. 49, 146–147. In a letter of June 18, 1865, Laura Towne referred to the "cool assurance" of planters expecting restoration. See *Pennsylvania Freedmen's Record*, I (August, 1865), 41; see also Richard DeTreville to Mrs. Ann Elliott, November 9, 1865, Elliott–Gonzales MSS.

[10] George R. Bentley, *A History of the Freedmen's Bureau* (Philadelphia, 1955), pp. 91–93.

During the summer of 1865 it was far from clear whether a pardoned Confederate could regain lands that had fallen into either of these categories. Some of those who returned to their homes on the coast optimistically came away disappointed. "For months past," wrote Ralph Elliott from the up-country town of Greenville, "young men of my acquaintance have been selling their little valuables, and going to Charleston and the coast—most of them have obtained transportation from the enemy, or begged money from their slaves, and returned to the up country—being unable to recover their homes or to make their bread in the City."[11] They had applied in vain to the Freedmen's Bureau for the land.

Hoping that he could commit the government to a land policy for freedmen and present President Johnson with an accomplished fact, General Howard had worked industriously to distribute as much land as possible before the President's policy crystallized. He refused all applications for restoration of property in the districts where the Sherman Field Order applied. Johnson's plans became increasingly clear, however, as the complaints of pardoned owners came into his office. All lands that had not been *sold outright* by the Direct Tax Commission could be retrieved by the owners if they paid the tax, took the oath of allegiance, and obtained the President's pardon.[12] Since their lands were not affected, such Northern investors as Philbrick, as well as the freedmen who had bought at the government sales, could now breathe a sigh of relief, but General Howard and Rufus Saxton were in an impossible position. They were caught squarely between the President's orders and their own commitment under the Freedmen's Bureau Act to carry out the resettlement program on the coastal islands. Without the income from the abandoned lands, the Freedmen's Bureau would be without funds, and the dream

[11] Ralph Elliott to Emily Elliott, October 15, 1865, Elliott–Gonzales MSS.

[12] Bentley, *Freedmen's Bureau*, pp. 92–93, 95.

of the Port Royal veterans and radical reconstructionists everywhere—that the Negro should come to his freedom with some
economic independence—would be gone a-glimmering.[13]

Their only remaining hope lay in stalling the restoration of the
land until Congress convened in December, when radical Republicans might be able to succeed in validating the Sherman "possessory" titles. In their policy of procrastination Howard and Saxton
could rely upon the support of Secretary of War Stanton, but
they had to fly in the face of a very stubborn man when they
attempted to circumvent the will of Andrew Johnson. Saxton
most reluctantly complied with the President's order to restore
lands that were unoccupied. At the same time, he stoutly resisted
efforts of old owners to regain their property in districts where
the freedmen had been assigned their forty-acre lots under the
Sherman order.[14] He returned all such petitions to General
Howard with the reminder that the freedmen had been promised
protection in their possession of the land. "In my view, this order
of General Sherman is as binding as a statute."[15]

On September 23, 1865, a number of the former residents of
Edisto Island petitioned President Johnson for their lands, explaining that their old homes were the only place they had to go
to.[16] Colonel William Whaley, who represented his fellow planters, had been trying unsuccessfully to get the Freedmen's Bureau
to release the property. Appealing directly to the President turned
the key. Johnson ordered Howard to go to Edisto and meet with

[13] *Ibid.*, p. 96. For the best account of the provision for Negro landownership in the Freedmen's Bureau Act of March 3, 1865, under which
Howard was operating, see LaWanda Cox, "The Promise of Land for the
Freedmen," *Mississippi Valley Historical Review*, XLV (December, 1958),
413–440.

[14] Bentley, *Freedmen's Bureau*, p. 98.

[15] New York *Nation*, October 26, 1865.

[16] Petition to Andrew Johnson, September 23, 1865, Edward Stoeber
Papers, South Caroliniana Library, Columbia. Stoeber was Saxton's aide-
de-camp.

the freedmen and the interested planters to try to find a "mutually satisfactory" arrangement. His meaning was clear.[17]

The freedmen had got wind of trouble, and when General Howard arrived on Edisto in late October the Negroes were in a state of panic. Accompanied by Whaley, another planter, and several military officers, the general went to meet the freedmen at a large Episcopal church near the center of the island. The auditorium and galleries were jammed with sad and angry Negroes who were in no mood to come to order. Howard reported that he could make "no progress" until "a sweet-voiced negro woman began the hymn 'Nobody knows the trouble I feel—Nobody knows but Jesus.' " As the crowd joined in the song the audience at last grew quiet enough to listen to Howard's reluctant message. "My address, however kind in manner I rendered it," wrote Howard afterward, "met with no apparent favor." The people cried "no, no!" and their eyes "flashed unpleasantly." A strong man called out from the gallery, "Why, General Howard, why do you take away our lands? You take them from us who have always been true, always true to the Government! You give them to our all-time enemies! That is not right!"[18]

Howard finally persuaded the freedmen to select three representatives from their number to meet with three men from the Freedmen's Bureau and three representatives of the planters. After elucidating the legal complications as fully as possible and explaining that the titles they held were not "absolute," Howard advised the freedmen "to make the best terms they could" with those who held the *legal* titles to the land. The freedmen's committee could not have managed better than they did in telling the sympathetic general that they wanted to leave everything in his hands, for they gave him an idea to accompany their faith. They would not, they insisted, work for their old masters under overseers, but they would agree to *rent* the land. It might be impossible to effect a

[17] Bentley, *Freedmen's Bureau*, p. 98.
[18] Oliver Otis Howard, *Autobiography* (New York, 1908), I, 238–239.

"mutually satisfactory" arrangement after all, at least not until after Congress met. Howard received shortly after the meeting a letter from Secretary Stanton, who was cast down that General Howard had gone so far toward reinstating former owners on Edisto and said that he had not interpreted Johnson's orders to oblige Howard "to disturb the freedmen in possession at present, but only to ascertain whether a just mutual agreement can be made . . . , and if we can, then carry it into effect."[19]

In the plan Howard had set up the freedmen found a little room for argument. In order to have his land restored, a planter had to agree to leave the existing crop to those who had planted it, to let the Negroes stay on the land "so long as the responsible freedmen among them would contract *or lease*," and to permit the freedmen's schools to continue. Howard then appointed a Board of Supervisors, headed by Captain A. P. Ketchum, a veteran Port Royalist and a former leader of Negro troops. Ketchum was sympathetic to the cause of the freedmen and could be counted upon to move very slowly in the restoration of land. Howard then returned North.[20]

Much "torn in mind," the freedmen of Edisto expressed their indignation well. After the meeting with Howard and the planters, one of Colonel Whaley's former slaves told the teachers from Boston that despite the Colonel's protestations he remembered only that when he was a slave Whaley had not treated him well. "I talk no word with him." The freedmen expressed a determination "never to make contracts with, or work for, their former owners. . . ."[21] One freedman told Mary Ames that he could forgive his master past abuse, but he would not work for him. He had "lived all his life with a basket over his head, and now that it had been taken off he would not consent" to have it put on again. The night following the meeting at the church was spent in in-

[19] *Ibid.*, pp. 239–240.
[20] *Ibid.* Italics mine.
[21] *Freedmen's Record*, I (December, 1865), 199.

dignation rallies, which culminated in a poorly spelled but well reasoned letter to the President.[22]

Howard's visit, the freedmen said, had awakened "a grate many of the peple understanding what was said, . . . to stody for them Selves what part of this law would rest against us. . . ." The matter that they held to be "very opressing . . . [was that] wee freemen should work for wages for our former oners. . . ." It was unjust of the President, they felt, to expect the freedmen to ask "for bread or shelter or Comfortable for his wife and children" from men whom they had stood against "upon the feal of battle." They had, they said, no confidence in their late owners, and especially none in Colonel Whaley, who had refused, when asked, to sell even so much as an acre and a half to each family, declaring that he would not take a hundred dollars an acre. "That is a part of his union fealing. . . ."[23]

The letter did not induce the President to change his policy, but the stubborn resistance of the freedmen helped Howard immeasurably in his strategy of obstruction. He assured anxious Northern radicals that he did not believe much land would be restored on the islands until Congress met. A teacher reported that "if a white man appears here . . . [the freedmen] guard him with their guns until they are sure he is a Yankee, and not in the interest of the 'rebels.' "[24] The freedmen refused to accept contracts with the irate planters, who had small chance even to make them offers. One owner complained that Captain Ketchum "would not compel contracts . . . unless the owners are willing to lease or sell to the freedmen. . . ." It seemed to Richard De Treville of Beaufort that the Bureau was "carrying on a most extensive scheme of fraud. . . ." Another disgruntled old resident complained that "The yankees have instilled into the negroes minds

[22] Ames, *A New England Woman's Diary*, pp. 98, 101–102.
[23] *Ibid.*
[24] Bentley, *Freedmen's Bureau*, p. 99; *Freedmen's Record*, I (December, 1865), 199.

the belief that the Island country which they helped to conquer belongs to them and they throw every obstacle in the way of the planters revisiting their plantations."[25]

In the meantime the hopes of radicals rested with the bill before Congress to renew and extend the life of the Freedmen's Bureau and to enlarge its powers. Freighted with a number of cherished schemes for a stringent Reconstruction policy, the provision of special interest to Howard and Saxton was the validation of the Sherman land titles. Even before the bill reached the President's desk, however, the land provision was amended to give the freedmen possession for only three years. Johnson was not prepared to go this far, and after a consultation with General Sherman, who explained that he had never thought his titles conveyed any claim to ownership, the President marshalled his arguments against the entire bill, and on February 19 he vetoed it.[26] Johnson had now opened his public battle with the radicals, and the obstructions that Howard and Saxton had placed in his way had merely served to fan the President's resentment of the Freedmen's Bureau.

The President had not been idle, however, even while waiting for the Bureau bill to reach his desk. Laura Towne and Cornelia Hancock, who had gone to Washington in January to plead with the President and Secretary Stanton on behalf of the Sherman freedmen, understood at once: "I know now how they stand," wrote Miss Hancock, "the President has the power but not the will to do for the colored people. Stanton has the will and not the power to help." Stanton told the teachers that "it would be a thousand years before the rebels would repossess the land if he could have his way and that he had the highest regard for General Saxton." While they were in Washington, the teachers also heard

[25] Bentley, *Freedmen's Bureau*, p. 99; Richard DeTreville to Mrs. Ann Elliott, November 16, 1865; in Elliott–Gonzales MSS; [John Bachman] to Emily Elliott, February 1, 1866, *ibid*.

[26] Bentley, *Freedmen's Bureau*, pp. 118–119; McKitrick, *Andrew Johnson*, p. 12.

that Rufus Saxton was to be removed from his long association
with the freedmen of South Carolina.[27] Because of his steady
refusal to do what he regarded as again breaking faith with the
freedmen, General Saxton was being replaced by General R. K.
Scott. The action was a part of a move even more ominous. The
Bureau was now to be tied more firmly to the regular military
occupation forces and, in some important respects, made subordinate to them. All obstructions to the restoration of the Sherman
lands were now abruptly removed.[28] Congressional radicals had
not given up their struggle with the President, but whatever they
might gain would now come too late to help the freedmen establish
their Sea Island land claims.

In late February and early March the regular military forces
seized control of restoring the lands to their late owners, and the
freedmen who refused to make contracts were forced to leave.
Mary Ames reported seeing, one day in February, all the Negroes
on one plantation leaving the fields, "their hoes over their shoulders. They told us that the guard had ordered them to leave the
plantation if they would not work for the owners. . . . We could
only tell them to obey orders. After this many of the Sherman
Negroes left the island." Of those who chose to leave rather than
to make contracts, presumably most were originally refugees
from Georgia. Those who remained were now faced with the
necessity of making terms with their late owners. "Occasionally
they were glad to see their old masters," wrote Miss Ames, but
sometimes she saw the landlord's " 'How dy' and outstretched
hand rejected."[29] The necessities were apparent, however; the
island spring was at hand, and nature called men, white or black,
to plant or starve. Soon Miss Ellen Kempton reported that "The

[27] Henrietta Stratton Jaquette (ed.), *South after Gettysburg: Letters
of Cornelia Hancock, 1863–1868* (New York, 1957), pp. 191–192, 196.
[28] Bentley, *Freedmen's Bureau*, pp. 122–124.
[29] Ames, *A New England Woman's Diary*, pp. 121–122; *Freedmen's
Record*, II (January, 1866), 2.

people are becoming more willing to make contracts with their former masters, though they feel yet a want of confidence in them."[30]

Life would be easy for no one, hardly better for the old planters who regained their property than for the freedmen whose hopes for it had been betrayed. Five years of war had wrecked the highly organized agriculture of the low country. A Northern traveler in the region in the decade following the war saw again and again the ruined live-oak avenues leading through "a rank and noxious jungle of weeds" toward "the two blackened chimneys, like lonely unpropitiated ghosts" of a forsaken home. The fields were ruined; "acres upon acres of abandoned rice swamps are dank with weeds, or black with rotting . . . lilies. . . ."[31] At a time when every man who would plant a crop needed credit, it could only be obtained at "grinding" rates. Credit could cost a man as much as a 50 per cent lien on his crop. Some who took the chance lost their land; others regarded interest on money as prohibitive and decided, as John Fripp did, to give up planting for the season, "except for what we are doing ourselves on a small scale with very hard work [we] not being accustomed to it."[32]

Young William Elliott returned to Oak Lawn at nightfall one day in early March and looked down the live-oak avenue to his old home. He had heard that Oak Lawn had been burned, but in the twilight he believed for one tantalizing moment that his information had been false. "I could almost believe myself in a

[30] *Freedmen's Record*, II (March, 1866), 55.
[31] Stephen Powers, *Afoot and Alone: a Walk from Sea to Sea* (Hartford, 1872), p. 46.
[32] Ralph Elliott to Mrs. A. H. Elliott, February 8, 1866, Elliott–Gonzales MSS; John Edwin Fripp to [n.n., n.d.], III, 121–122, typescript copy, Fripp MSS; final entry of Thomas B. Chaplin MS diary, of January 1, 1866, in which Chaplin recapitulates his postwar experiences. See also John Jenkins' contract with C. M. Rose, of New York, January 27, 1869, Box 2 (legal documents) in John Jenkins MSS, South Caroliniana Library, Columbia.

dream," he wrote his mother, "for there stood a dwelling house at the other end—a kitchen and outhouse," where "a cheerful fire seemed to bid me welcome." The nearer view told Elliott that he only saw the outer shell of a blackened ruin. Jacob, an old family servant, came to meet the young man, and they looked over the grounds together, marking the damage, from the broken family china in the rubble to the ravaged flower gardens, the last shred of the horticulture that had been a hereditary hobby with Elliotts. Thirty-four years old and ill of tuberculosis, young Elliott wrote his mother that he had to plant or his life was useless.[33] Living in an outhouse with his father's late slaves, Elliott hired a few hands and put in a crop. Getting help was difficult, and the young man was soon blaming Jacob, who was not, he thought, trying hard enough to persuade prospective hands. Jacob was now, plainly enough, a free man, Elliott pronounced crossly, "eaten up with self-esteem and selfishness."[34]

The new order was severe, but the Elliotts had their land and something else besides, for whatever moral and spiritual comfort it was. The magnolia legend sprang up phoenix-like upon the ashes of the ante-bellum world. The family had managed to scrape together the money to send young Elliott Johnstone to Georgetown University, where he was doing credit to the family. "Oak Lawn in its ruin, as I have heard it described by you and Aunt Annie," he wrote to his Aunt Emily, "has furnished me the subject of several compositions of ruins and scenery . . . , and Oak Lawn helped me to the premium at the end of the session." In time the legend of the happiness of ante-bellum life would become unrealistic with the retelling. From a schoolboy's theme, the

[33] William Elliott to Mrs. Ann Elliott, March 13, 1866, Elliott–Gonzales MSS. Young Elliott died in January, 1867. T.R.S. Elliott to Ralph Elliott, January 22, 1867, *ibid*.

[34] "Jacob's six or seven relatives have not appeared, and he, I am compelled to think, is indifferent in the matter. He wishes to squat on the place and have [the] lion's share of everything he may make." William Elliott to Mrs. Ann Elliott, March 25, 1866, *ibid*.

pathos of the epic return of broken men like William Elliott was on the first step of a ladder that led down to a tired melodrama. For the time, however, the tragedy was real, and capable of evoking a sympathy from Northerners who could more readily identify themselves with Southern white people than with Negroes evicted from their lands. When friends in Boston heard of the tragic circumstances of the Elliotts, whom they had known well in better days, they raised a thousand dollars for relief of the family. "Yr. present privations and hardships, could not fail to wring the hearts of those who remembered the proud position, the charming attractions, and social advantages of yr. family," wrote one of the distinguished Amorys to Ann Elliott.[35]

Some there were who bore their trouble with a gallantry deserving of admiration. "It is hard to believe in our utter ruin," wrote widowed Mary Johnstone, who was taking in boarders, "and yet present difficulties tell us plainly enough what the future may be. I bless the hard work I have to do for making me weary enough at night to go at once to sleep—waking refreshed for the same routine. . . ." The Southern white people drew together, disregarding some of the old social distinctions that had marked their ante-bellum relations. Annie Stewart wrote from Beaufort that "a good deal of the stiffness and nonsense has been shaken out of us . . . and we are much more sociable, and sensible than we used to be. The lower ten are delighted at the change. . . ." The sociability did not extend to the Yankees, however, for, as Miss Stewart wrote, although they had "behaved with the greatest civility and consideration," she did not "love them a bit better" than she had before, and avoided them "as studiously as if they were as many rattlesnakes."[36] Well watered by Northern sympathy, the magnolia legend would flourish. The "lower ten" might even cling

[35] Elliott Johnstone to Emily Elliott, November 28, 1867, in *ibid.*; [W.] Amory to Ann Elliott, February 6, 1867, in *ibid.*

[36] Mary Johnstone to Mrs. Ann Elliott, September 5 [1865], and Annie Stewart to Emily Elliott, July 29, 1866, *ibid.*

to its lower branches, but Yankee intruders would be far outside its shade.

For the owners in the Beaufort District who returned to find their land already sold by the government to private individuals, Northerners and Negroes, the cup of bitterness was brimful. They faced a long legal battle of doubtful outcome and in the meantime could see their hereditary homes only "on a visit as strangers," in the words of Thomas Chaplin. The most galling dose of all was reserved for those who returned to the islands in time to stand in the crowds at the final tax auctions, too poor to compete with Northerners in the bidding for their old estates. "Long will that day be remembered in the Southern part of the community," wrote Mary Hamilton of Beaufort, "when their homes were bid up by different parties, in spite of the assertion by the real owners that they were homeless and wished to try to purchase or redeem these homes by paying the amount claimed by the Government."[37]

It may have been that among the greatest afflictions the Southern whites felt was the gnawing sense of having been supplanted in their relations to the black race. The Northerners resident had become the guiders of the black destiny, and Negroes preferred being employed by Yankees. Thomas Chaplin penciled into the margin of his ante-bellum diary a bitter reflection on his personal tragedy of 1845—his financial failure and the consequent sale of ten of his slaves. He ought not to have "felt bad about it," Chaplin decided after the war, "for in truth, the Negroes did not care as much about us as we did for them." He particularly resented the defection of the estimable "Robert," who was now assiduously avoiding him. Robert had appropriated a favorite oak chair, which he never offered to return. There was a distinct sense of personal loss involved that transcended the loss of slave property or even

[37] Final entry of Chaplin MS diary, January 1, 1886, a recapitulation of his life after the war; letter of Mary S. Hamilton in Katherine M. Jones (ed.), *Port Royal Under Six Flags* (New York, 1960), p. 300.

of the oak rocker.[38] Edward Pierce had written truly when he said that no man, "least of all the master," can know the mind of the slave.

It was surely an embarrassing experience for men who had held hundreds of Negroes in their service to be reduced to calling upon agents of the Freedmen's Bureau to persuade men to work for them in the fields. In a spontaneous reaction the whites began berating the Negroes and the social consequences of the war. "From all I can see of this free labor system," wrote John Edwin Fripp, "I am not pleased with it." He thought it now took three free Negroes to do the work of one slave. Another embittered man wrote, "The black thieves are rapidly dying out of smallpox and loathsome diseases," and he predicted that the Negroes were "doomed to perish in compliance with the infamous prejudices" of the Yankees who had freed them. In 1865 predictions of Negro extinction and race war were frequently heard by Northern reporters.[39]

"The hatred of some white people for the colored race amounted almost to a frenzy," wrote Elizabeth Botume; she added, significantly, that "It was by no means confined to the old Southerners, but was largely shared by Northern adventurers, a host of whom had followed the army." Nobody spoke "more contemptuously of 'the nigger and his school-ma'am'" than many of the Northern businessmen newly come South. The wisdom of the wariness and skepticism Miss Botume observed among the colored people at the close of the war was patent. They would need time "to find out who were their true friends."[40] No class, neither Northerners, Southerners, nor freedmen, could afford to evince

[38] See Chaplin's penciled comments by diary entries for May 3, 1845, January 28, 1852, January 14, 1854. Chaplin MS diary.

[39] John Edwin Fripp to [n.n., n.d.], Fripp MSS, III, 121–122, typescript copy; [John Bachman] to Emily Elliott, February 1, 1866, Elliott-Gonzales MSS; New York *Nation*, July 27, 1865.

[40] Botume, *First Days*, p. 177; *National Freedman*, I (November, 1865), 328.

real confidence in any other group. Not every Northerner who cheated the Negroes was precisely a speculator, or an "adventurer" either. Of a missionary who had deceived and cheated him, one colored man wrote that "He'll shuck han's wid his right han', an' fling a brick-bat at you wid his lef'." Another complained that the missionary *right* hand was apt to catch the pocketbook, and that some of those who came South to enlighten the Negroes forgot "about Christ and Him crucified" when "they see the cotton bag."[41]

There were probably only a few evangels throwing brickbats in 1865, but there were still fewer throwing bouquets to the freedmen. The coming of peace had precipitated a reaction that had been steadily developing since the crisis of the land question. While numbers of courageous people had escaped a numbing frustration, and others had quietly buried their disappointment in silence, a bitter accent entered the private correspondence of evangels who had expected social miracles to follow emancipation overnight. Charles P. Ware had written optimistically in 1862 that he had hoped "before the war is done we shall have furnished the Government with sufficient facts to enable them to form a policy for the . . . millions whom the conclusion of the war must throw on our hands. . . ." He was sure that the Freedmen's Inquiry Commission would, if its members came to Port Royal, have their ideas on "the 'Universal Nigger' much revised. . . ." He was sure, back in 1862, that "When more is known of their powers and capacity . . . more attention will be paid to the cultivation of free black labor." By 1864 Ware was complaining steadily of the "untrustworthiness" of the colored people, "their skill in lying, their great reticence, their habit of shielding one another" and "their invariable habit of taking a rod when you, after much persuasion, have been induced to grant an inch. . . ." He was think-

[41] Botume, *First Days*, p. 177; quoted in Francis Butler Simkins and Robert H. Woody, *South Carolina During Reconstruction* (Chapel Hill, 1932), p. 379.

ing by 1864 that "their freedom has been too easy for them" and that the evangels had "fair spoiled" the Negroes. Although Ware had always sought to cover an essentially idealistic approach with what he thought were realistic, or perhaps humorous, references to "niggers," there had been present in his early correspondence an unmistakable sense of personal satisfaction in his work and a real liking for Negroes as individuals. He had enjoyed writing home about his preferred standing with the freedmen, about how he had "passed through the Pine Grove 'nigger-house' one day and retired, after a distinguished ovation, incubating, like a hen, upon a sulky-box full of eggs."[42] The lighthearted touch had given way to cynicism by the end of the war.

The case of the disillusionment of Arthur Sumner is most instructive. He had been happy and successful as a teacher, chortling happily about his "little black-birds" who showed so much promise. He would be glad to see "universal and immediate emancipation," for he felt the Negroes were "qualified for freedom."[43] In order to retain his teaching position, he had been obliged to lease a plantation when the lands were sold on St. Helena Island. "He is now a landed proprietor, or planter," wrote Laura Towne, "and takes a planter's view of all things." She could no longer appreciate Sumner's famous sense of humor when it found its sarcastic butt in the freedmen. By fall of his first year as a planter Sumner was freely complaining that "the vexations of the planting season fostered a spirit of disgust toward the negro, in the minds of almost every planter in the Department. In this feeling I, and many of the most humane and benevolent of the proprietors, shared." The freedmen, he stated, "in spite of all the nonsense which has been written about them, are a very low and degraded class of beings." When winter came Sumner was glad to be out of the planting business, glad to be a full-time teacher again, glad to

[42] Pearson (ed.), *Letters*, pp. 75, 98, 115, 287.

[43] Arthur Sumner to Nina Hartshorn, November 22, 1862, Sumner to Joseph Clark, July 7, 1862, Arthur Sumner MSS.

have his "mind drawn away from contemplating the vices and meanness of the grown people." With the children, "Life among the Lowly" was again "good and worthy and profitable."[44] Sumner went to Charleston after the war and served successfully for many years in the freedmen's schools there, but he never undertook planting again.

In general, the teachers had been discouraged by their experiences far less than the superintendents had been, particularly those superintendents who were most interested in proving the free-labor thesis. Edward Philbrick, who had had much faith in the miraculous effects of freedom on the labor force, was writing in 1865: "Now, to tell the truth, I don't believe myself that the present generation of negroes will ever work as they were formerly obliged to, and therefore the race will not produce as much cotton in this generation as they did five years ago. The change is too great to be made in a day."[45] Dr. Joseph Parker, who visited the islands after the war, wrote that it was "instructive to observe the disappointment of some sanguine sentimentalists, philanthropists and other worshippers of mammon who had hoped to make a fortune in a single year." New England Unitarianism had sent "many of its advocates to plant a new paradise" on the islands, who were now disgusted that "the seed did not bring the harvest which those who sowed it had anticipated." Many men had given up hope, observed Parker, but he found some of the staunch lady teachers "who did not abate one jot of heart or hope. They fought on in the forlorn hope as though they had all the enlisted hosts by their side."[46]

After the war the missionaries began to think of returning to

[44] Towne to "R," October 23, 1864, Towne MS letters. See also November 17 and December 18, 1864, *ibid.*; Arthur Sumner to Nina Hartshorn, December 13, 1864, Arthur Sumner MSS.

[45] Pearson (ed.), *Letters*, p. 317.

[46] Manuscript memoirs of Dr. Joseph W. Parker, pp. 149, 182–183, typescript copy. The manuscript belongs to Mrs. Perce Bentley, Phillipsburg, New Jersey.

their old lives and the careers they had interrupted to come to Port Royal. For some the change was not dramatic, and they felt free to withdraw without the sense of having failed their principles. William Gannett went to Savannah from St. Helena to join in the work of resettling the Sherman refugees, and from there he began to think of returning North. "Prospects for Negro work," he reflected, were "very uncertain and unsatisfactory." After a European tour, Gannett went home to take up his interrupted divinity studies. Although he was free from the bitterness that characterized many of his fellow evangels, a change had taken place, for there had been a time when Gannett had anticipated making his life's work among the freedmen.[47] Some Gideonites harbored a notion that the wear and tear of life on the islands was destroying the very idealism that had sent them to the South. In a conversation about how they should like to stay on the islands and how hard it would be to leave, Charles Folsom said to Charles Ware, "But, after all, one must remember that one has an immortal soul." Of a fellow missionary who began to talk of leaving, a friend said, "I think Mr. Soule will be glad to get away from this 'Sodom.' He is too good a man to be worn down by the barbarians of this latitude." The superintendents referred to the "complaints, faithlessness, and general rascality of the 'poor negroes,' " as the "Plantation Bitters."[48]

The missionaries complained now frequently of the freedman's agricultural and social failings, with a significant emphasis on his ingratitude and faithlessness. The Negro continued to rate cotton culture distinctly second-place in his farming interests; he was reluctant to haul the "salt marsh" so necessary to its success, and after enough freedmen owned their own land to make detection difficult, he was also apt to steal it. John Hunn, the Quaker evangel

---

[47] William H. Pease, "William Channing Gannett" (unpublished doctoral dissertation, University of Rochester, 1955), pp. 88–89.

[48] Pearson (ed.), *Letters*, pp. 298, 310, 323–324.

of underground railroad fame, frankly told a reporter for the *Nation* that "as a friend of the colored people, he would . . . not wish a final judgment of them to be deduced from their present condition in the Sea Islands." "Father Hunn," as he was called, was operating at a loss, and his condemnation of a labor system that allowed the people living on the properties so much liberty was "unqualified." He complained to the reporter that "for every acre that his people planted for him for wages they planted precisely two acres for themselves, and it was hard to induce them to take up more cotton ground than would supply them with spending money."[49]

Richard Soule told the same reporter that he believed the faults of the Negroes "had been encouraged and confirmed rather than discouraged and removed, during the past four years." He was sure the Negroes would prove themselves worthy laborers under a system "which should leave the employer and the negroes perfectly free." All Soule needed was "the power over his laborers which a Northern farmer has over his hired hands. . . ."[50] Presumably the "Plantation Bitters" comprised not only the faults of the Negroes, but also the surveillance of contracts which Saxton had instituted on the islands and which the Freedmen's Bureau had continued. Mr. Soule undoubtedly resented "owning" property in which he had incomplete authority. His laissez-faire ideas fitted ill with a situation where the Negroes appeared to have manorial "rights" to their own plots, which they carefully tended at the expense of the main object—cotton. His objections to "free labor" as it was developing were very similar to those of the returning ante-bellum planters, much as Soule might differ with them as to the remedy.

The planter-missionaries complained that "stealing is very com-

---

[49] New York *Nation*, December 14, 1865. See also Pearson (ed.), *Letters*, pp. 311, 313, 315–316, 320–321, 322–324.

[50] New York *Nation*, December 14, 1865.

mon; cotton is pilfered on all sides, and sold to unprincipled dealers in Beaufort, who buy and ask no questions."[51] Cotton theft provided the plantation commissions that Saxton had instituted to try disputes with a great amount of legal business. A superintendent wrote of a drawn-out litigation involving the theft "of twelve hundred pounds of seed cotton," complaining that although there was "a cloud of witnesses" it was very hard "to discern in it any glimmering of truth." Nothing had done more, over the years at Port Royal, to exasperate even the most sincere friends of the freedmen, than service on the plantation commissions. Those with insight, although sorely tried, understood why this should be. "Till law is recognized as the strong power in society, the righteous man fears the consequences of his own virtue, fights baseness with its own weapon, and becomes a coward before a force stronger than his own," wrote William Gannett. A freedman, although a devout church member, "is not a moral hero or martyr, tells a lie even on the Bible, rather than send his friend to jail by his evidence, and live in plantation odium for six months afterward." Gannett concluded that there were few freedmen who could always be relied upon to tell the truth, but he saw that it was "in those circumstances . . . which are most akin to their old position, where they expect punishment, or distrust promises" that the Negroes were most likely to take "their old recourse," lying.[52]

As time passed, however, the evangels were less apt to recall how compelling the virtues of plantation loyalty and the protection of friends and family had been to the slave. Reuben Tomlinson had been a faithful friend to the freedmen, one who had been little discouraged in most matters, but his experience on the plantation commission made him, he thought, see the worst side of the Negroes. "It is frightful and disgusting, the way in which they

[51] *Ibid.*
[52] Pearson (ed.), *Letters*, p. 313; [Gannett and Hale], "The Freedmen at Port Royal," *North American Review*, CI (July, 1865), 26.

will lie about each other, their superintendents, or the owner of the place." To make their case good, the plaintiffs would "stick at nothing." This was true, Tomlinson grumbled, of people who were ordinarily "perfectly trustworthy."[53]

Arthur Sumner came to the heart of the matter when he explained that "The negro has always been oppressed by the white man, and knows that even now . . . [the white man] has it in his power to cheat him. Even the best of the young men sent down here by the benevolent societies at the North, have failed to gain their confidence. [The Negroes] . . . are stupid and ignorant, and therefore incapable of comprehending that a man who has it in his power to cheat them, should fail to do so." Even Sumner understood that there was some ground for mistrust. When Edward Philbrick introduced a new superintendent at Coffin Point, the Negroes thronged about, demanding promptly, "A dollar a task, A dollar a task!" Their spokesman, the ubiquitous John Major, told Philbrick he was sure he could afford it, for he had seen him "jamming the bills into that big iron cage (meaning . . . the safe at R[uggle]s) for six months, and there must be enough in it now to bust it." Major may have been right.[54]

The real problem was that many Gideonites could not recognize the signs of the growth of freedom. Harriet Ware reduced a host of peevish observations to a single sentence when she said that she was glad to see the Negroes losing some of their old *servility*, but sorry that they were no longer very *obedient*.[55] The freedmen's mounting protests were to many evangels simply signs of ingratitude. The wisest observers were looking for independent thought and action.

Laura Towne knew how to recognize the small gains. When she drove out with a Negro family to meet an aged grandmother

---

[53] Tomlinson to McKim, September 23, 1863, McKim MSS.

[54] Arthur Sumner to Nina Hartshorn, February [?], 1865, Arthur Sumner MSS; Pearson (ed.), *Letters*, pp. 300–301.

[55] Pearson (ed.), *Letters*, p. 218.

who had arrived with a band of refugees brought from the mainland by Higginson's regiment, she noticed a significant reaction. The old woman was amazed to see how freely the little grandchildren expressed their joy at the reunion in the presence of the "buckra" lady! One Northern observer of several years' experience on the islands saw that the freedmen were busy building homes in the spring after the war, as well as "cornhouses, fences, [and]carts." He thought the colored people were working harder than in any year since slavery, and that they were cultivating their crops better, concentrating on provision crops, especially vegetables. They were also learning to read and to conduct their own business affairs. The same observer commented that the freedmen were "rising in the scale of civilization, however much they may be traduced by those who only look at single specimens of their race, or who from mismanagement or fraud have failed to gain the respect, or good-will of the people."[56]

In the same summer that many Gideonites were experiencing so much difficulty with the freedmen as laborers, a Northern reporter for the *Nation* observed that in the Sea Island communities where Negroes were cultivating crops for themselves, the result was "highly encouraging." He saw large fields of corn under good cultivation and described a "crazy little steam flat, . . . crowded with colored people who were carrying their produce to market—tomatoes, okra, huckleberries, water melons, chickens, eggs, and bundles of kindling." The same reporter judged that the freedmen were perhaps not working "according to the Northern standard," but they were able to care for themselves, which was "all we have a right to require of any set of people. . . ." Dr. Richard Fuller, who toured the islands in the distinguished company of Salmon P. Chase in the summer following the war, was favorably impressed with the progress of the freedmen who had once been his slaves. He told Whitelaw Reid, who was reporting the tour, that St. Helena was thriving under the new order. "I never saw as much land there under cultivation—never saw the same general evidences of prosperity, and never saw the negroes themselves appearing so well or so contented."[57]

Elizabeth Botume wrote that "some of the finest cotton brought to market on the islands" in the year after the war was raised by a group of freedmen who "hired and bought land, and worked independent of any white superintendent." That was the main point. Joseph Parrish, who visited the islands in the spring of 1866, noticed a great difference between St. Helena Island, which was denominated "A Negro's Heaven" because the freedmen had by that time come into possession of most of the land there, and Port Royal Island, where much land was worked on a contract basis for superintendents or larger white owners. "Wherever the lands are held in fee by the people they work better."[58]

Dr. Parrish also witnessed a scene which showed that some of the freedmen knew how to make the most of their economic opportunities. He described the successes of John Hamilton of the Edgerly plantation, a landowner, and relates the first meeting of Hamilton with his old master. Hamilton had gone to town "dressed in his best" to attend to an affair of business:

For the first time, since the occupation of the island by our forces, the master and his family returned to the town the day before. John and his master met. Master inquired of John after all the people, and John described the division of the farm among the people, their success, etc., and told his master that he was in town to attend to *bank business*, and must be excused. Master looked with some surprise, and asked the privilege of getting a cart-load of wood from the plantation, as he was in need. "Certainly," said John, "I send you de wood, Mr. ——, wid pleasure; and if old Misses would like to have a few

[57] Letter of "Marcel," from Charleston, July 21, 1865, in New York *Nation*, August 10, 1865; Whitelaw Reid, *After the War: A Southern Tour* (Cincinnati, 1866), p. 113.

[58] Botume, *First Days*, p. 226; *Pennsylvania Freedmen's Bulletin and American Freedman*, I (June, 1866), 7–8.

blackberries, de boys will pick some and send you." Master consented, with gratitude, and John went off to attend to his *bank business*.[59]

The missionary least apt to be discouraged was the missionary who loved the particular work in which his days were spent. Divinity students from Harvard, Andover, and Yale eventually found themselves ill-fitted for cotton planting, whether they admitted their lack of true interest or not, and no matter how staunchly antislavery their principles. Laura Towne was by no means blind to the faults of the freedmen. She duly noted instances of stealing and roughly criticized a failing among them to which she was especially sensitive, cruelty to animals; but she continued to attribute the fault to the lessons learned in slavery, well after her fellows had begun to forget the real significance of "the old allegiance." The advantage she enjoyed was a true liking for schoolteaching.[60]

For Miss Towne the summit of annual exertions was reached with the gala closing of her school in early summer. Her description of these exercises in 1865 demonstrates her enthusiasm and her willingness to dedicate education to social causes (with a judicious mixture of propaganda), as well as an old-fashioned bondage to drill and rote memory. The Brick Church was decorated for the event with flags, oleander blossoms, and the holiday clothes of the children. The parents were present by *written* invitation to hear their youngsters recite. After the geography class had demonstrated that they understood that the earth was a planet and knew "what each country was famous for," there was a lively response to such questions as:

What was the wisest country of old times? "Egypt in *Africa*." What forms of government in the world? What form in our country? What a Republic is, and how its rulers are chosen? What are the people of the United States called? "American citizens." What are the

[59] *Ibid.*, pp. 4, 5.
[60] Towne MS diary, April 28 and May 4, 1862.

rights of an American citizen? "Life, liberty," etc. What are his duties? "To obey the laws, defend the country and vote for good men."[61]

Further questions drew out the children's information as to the duties of Congress and what the city of Philadelphia had done for *them*. The parents were amazed to see the children march to the blackboard, where they calculated "the price of two bales of cotton sold here at the market price per pound" and compared the price of the same two bales at New York, "deducting expenses, commissions, etc., and selling it at the market price there, to find the advantage or disadvantage of the two plans."[62] By this time Laura Towne's students were able to write compositions, knew all the parts of speech, and could construct sentences upon demand, as she said, using, "predicate, verb, and adverb." They had read a history of the United States and an easy book on physiology. The Penn School, in short, was a great success and, considering that it had been in existence for only three years, its standards were at once a tribute to the enthusiasm and talent of Miss Towne and Miss Murray and to the ability and exertions of the pupils. The teachers already regarded it as a high school, and they were soon training Negro teachers to go out through the state.[63] Of all the schools founded in the area by Northern teachers during the war, it is the only one that has maintained a continuous existence to the present time, and the good things it has brought to the Sea Islanders are beyond calculation.

The teachers with Laura Towne's zest for work were making an invaluable contribution to Southern Reconstruction, but they well knew that the sturdy institutions of New England that they wished to root required the soil of economic freedom as well as schoolbooks. There had been a few evangels who had demonstrated Edward Philbrick's aversion to cheap land, but the major-

[61] *Pennsylvania Freedmen's Bulletin*, I (December, 1865), 65–66.
[62] *Ibid.*
[63] Holland (ed.), *Towne*, p. 163.

ity had held the dream of a future when every freedman would find a small farm within his grasp, and a chance at a basic education as well. Agreeable as the new goal of suffrage had become, the missionaries had early put their faith in land and education as the most important, most practical, and most available means of social advancement. They anxiously waited through the turbulent year following the war for favorable developments, but the signs were inauspicious. It began to appear that the Congress regarded seizure of property, even the property of ex-Confederates, hopelessly radical; a massive assault upon illiteracy was hopelessly expensive.

President Johnson's veto of the Freedmen's Bureau Bill had been a heavy blow, and before the radicals gained strength in July, 1866, to pass it over the veto, the bill had been amended to the disadvantage of the freedmen in an important particular. The Negroes who had been ousted from the Sherman lands would get no more, it was now clear, than permission to lease twenty-acre lots in other government-owned lands, with a six-year option to buy.[64] Even while the heat of war animosities had not yet cooled, Congress had shown it would not undertake a radical land program for freedmen.

The prospects for education were slightly more promising. The Freedmen's Bureau had been authorized to spend five thousand dollars for the rent and repair of school buildings and hospitals.[65] The support and maintenance of teachers, however, was as dependent upon Northern charity as ever, and the field upon which the fund of good will had to be spread had become infinitely broader. Much would depend upon the ability of the American Freedmen's Commission to elicit popular enthusiasm. Expecting to cooperate closely with the Freedmen's Bureau, the Freedmen's Commission took an important step when it joined forces with the American Union Commission, organized for the benefit of white refugees in the South who had suffered because of their Union

[64] Bentley, *Freedmen's Bureau*, p. 134.
[65] *Ibid.*, p. 172.

sympathies. The step was made in order to simplify the cooperation of the aid societies with the Freedmen's Bureau, which was
involved in meeting the acute needs of both races. The new organization planned to ignore, in the words of J. Miller McKim, "all
distinctions of race or color." He explained to an English supporter that the American Freedmen's Union Commission would
be "broader and stronger" than the organization for slaves alone
had been, and that the freedmen's work would not suffer because
the illiterate whites of the South stood to benefit. "As we are
demanding our Government shall legislate, adjudicate, and admin-
ister its affairs without regard to color, we feel bound to make our
own course conformable to our demand."[66]

Many staunch old contributors to the freedmen's work objected
strenuously to including Southern whites in their beneficence. Dr.
William Furness, the old Philadelphia abolitionist whose sermons
had converted Laura Towne to the cause, was very unhappy about
it, as were many members of the New England branch of the
Freedmen's Union. Laura Towne said many people were con-
tributing directly to her school, placing their money where there
was no danger of a Southern white benefiting. Sensing that the
Freedmen's Bureau had already become a political football, Miss
Towne wrote McKim a barbed comment: "When you get this
great organization in working order, is it your intention to put
it under the patronage of the President: that is, merge it into a new
political power called an Educational Bureau?"[67]

The Freedmen's Bureau had thus early proved a disappointment to numbers of steadfast Port Royalists. They criticized the
new military personnel who now filled the Bureau positions,
claiming that they were more interested in securing order and in
making the freedmen work than in seeing that they went to work

[66] McKim to Joseph Simpson, February 16, 1866, letterbook copy,
McKim MSS.

[67] McKim to William Furness, March 30, 1866, letterbook copy, and
Laura Towne to McKim, March 26, 1866, McKim MSS.

under fair conditions. Chary with rations when the freedmen's need was real, an agent told Elizabeth Botume, when she complained, "Tell them to go to work." "This seemed hard," wrote the unhappy teacher, "when they were working day and night too."[68]

Unsatisfactory as it was, sensible evangels knew that without the Bureau their work would be much harder. How would they manage when it was gone? The Federal government, and even General Howard himself, seemed to regard the Bureau as a temporary institution.[69] Everything would rest, should the Bureau lapse, upon Northern charity, and few missionaries were sanguine enough to believe that it would last as long as the need.

E. S. Philbrick observed unfavorable trends in Boston as early as October, 1865. The freedmen's schools were "a laudable and noble work," he wrote, "but I fear it can't be sustained after the novelty is over. There seems to be a lethargy creeping over our community on this subject, which is very hard to shake off. The feeling is somewhat general that the negro must make the most of his chances to pick up his a,b,c's as he can."[70]

The freedmen of the South would be fortunate if Northern interest in their fate lasted even so long as that of the average Gideonite. From the beginning there had been two ways of looking at the Negro, two questions to ask: How could he be used to advance the cause of Union; and how could the war advance his freedom? The war was over, and the North would in time forget that the questions were ever asked.

Most evangels liked the imagery of the Old Testament. It is therefore hardly surprising that an excited observer of the meeting of freedmen to hear Mr. French and General Saxton explain

[68] Botume, *First Days*, p. 251; see also New York *Nation*, December 21, 1865, and Towne to "R," February 23, 1866, Towne MS letters.

[69] John Cox and LaWanda Cox, "General O. O. Howard and the 'Misrepresented Bureau,'" *Journal of Southern History*, XIX (November, 1953), 441.

[70] Pearson (ed.), *Letters*, pp. 317–318.

"squatter rights" and to make plans for their own local government was reminded of Ezekial's vision of "a wheel in a wheel." The Hebrew priest's vision had been equal in complexity to the difficulties of the Israelites, captive in the land of Babylon, but the reporter of the New York *Tribune* knew what *he* meant. Port Royal was "a little Republic . . . in our great Republic."[71] Through the chances of war the islands had assumed an importance far transcending their geographic size, and the Gideonites had run ahead of national sentiment on the future of the Negro in America every step of the way. Those same chances of war had enabled Port Royal to have more than a little influence on the development of that "chapter of accidents" Fanny Kemble had correctly predicted would be the story of Negro emancipation. If the Port Royal Experiment had been marred by foolish men who worked at cross-purposes, by pompous men who had the folly to identify their own economic advantage with the truest philanthropy, by bad men who cheated the Negroes to line their own pockets, and even by the government's own efforts, so halfhearted and inept as to earn it no credit, the enterprise had yet been at the very storm center of the Reconstruction process a-borning. All the goals, motives, and ironies first seen at Port Royal would be written large in the history of the turbulent years between 1865 and 1877. How would having had a dress rehearsal affect the islands in the main performance?

[71] A correspondent of the New York *Tribune*, quoted in *Report of the Proceedings of a Meeting Held at Concert Hall, Philadelphia, November 3rd, 1863* (Philadelphia, 1863), p. 21.

epilogue ✤ "REVOLUTIONS MAY GO BACKWARD . . ."

ON A PLEASANT FORENOON IN MID-DECEMBER, 1873, A CRACK RE-porter for *Scribner's Monthly Magazine* waited impatiently at Yemassee Junction, halfway between Charleston and Savannah, for the train to Beaufort. Edward King was on an extended tour of the South, to give Northern readers "an account of the material resources, and the present social and political conditions" of the former slave states. Doubtless, he looked forward with special interest to a Sea Island visit. After numerous delays, "which," concluded the journalist, "in the North would have been consid-ered disastrous," the train arrived, and King was whirled out toward the islands over the new railroad spur that was one patent manifestation of Yankee enterprise. Passing through rich wood-lands "where a startled doe, followed by her fawns, bounds across the track," past deserted fields, over "a wide arm of the sea," and into the swamps, where he caught a glimpse of a "mighty lagoon, lonely and grand," King arrived at Beaufort just at the siesta hour.[1]

Along Bay Street, the "only sign of life" appeared in the form of "a negro policeman, dressed in a shiny blue uniform, pacing languidly up and down." There was "not even a dog to arrest," and along the pier in front of the old Heyward mansion, formerly Saxton's headquarters but by now denominated the "Sea Island Hotel," several buzzards were sleeping peacefully. King wandered through the streets and noted the "remains of ancient beauty"

---

[1] Edward King, *The Southern States of North America* (Glasgow and Edinburgh, 1875), pp. v, 426.

sunk in the silence "of the grave." Some mansions were boarded up and had fallen into decay, and old St. Helena Church seemed to King "to have shut itself in from the encroachments of the revolution" between its high moss-grown walls. "The whole aspect of the place," reported King, "was that which I afterward found pervading all over South Carolina towns—that of complete prostration, dejection, stagnation."[2]

Well informed of the peculiar history of the region during the war, King thought he understood what he saw: "Here the revolution had penetrated to the quick." The colored population was in the ascendant, owning most of the land on the islands adjacent to the little town, and they were "too busy with politics to work." He noted that "City Hall is controlled by the blacks, and the magistrates, the police, and the representatives to the Legislature, are nearly all Africans." In Beaufort Negroes were in a ten-to-one majority; on Hilton Head Island there were thirty colored persons to every white; and on St. Helena there were only seventy white persons among six thousand Negroes. "They monopolize everything," wrote King, and were "in possession of a great deal" that they were unable to use. They had become "tools in the hands of the corrupt," were "immoral and irresponsible; emotional and unreliable...." The result was overwhelming, thought King. Here on the Sea Islands, "in a decade and a-half one of the most remarkable revolutions ever recorded in history had occurred. A wealthy and highly prosperous community has been reduced to beggary; its vassals have become its lords, and dispose of the present and pledge the future resources of the State."[3]

King was not the only Northern visitor who returned home in the early 1870's with a devastating assessment of the revolutionary developments in the South Carolina low country. A reporter for the Springfield *Republican* also was caustic. As a result of the persistent efforts of Northern capitalists resident in the

[2] *Ibid.*
[3] *Ibid.*, pp. 426–427.

region, direct oceangoing trade was established and maintained for a time at the "City of Port Royal," Commissioner Brisbane's visionary "New York of the South." The correspondent of the Springfield paper was derisive of the "commercial entrepot" consisting, in his words, of "a railway station and warehouse, with a dozen or so rude, unpainted houses, a preponderant population of the laziest blacks, and a hundred or more of the most scrawny breed of pigs," who wandered at will through the sandy streets. Beaufort was hardly better. "Utter stagnation marks its streets, and everything is flavored with decay." The natural beauty of the live-oaks, the singing of mocking-birds, "as if winter had no meaning for them," and the handsome architecture of the old mansions along the Bay could not remove the air of desertion that permeated the town. The houses were unkempt and indicated "only too sadly the prosperity that has fled from their owners. The merry tinkling of a piano that proceeds from the closed shutters of one of them seems altogether dissonant with their surroundings." To this reporter, the "lamentations of Jeremiah" seemed the only appropriate lyrics for the denizens of the Sea Islands.[4]

He was undoubtedly thinking of the famous jeremiad, "Servants have ruled over us: there is none that doth deliver us out of their hands," for he observed that there were "comparatively few whites" about the streets, and those were "mostly of the office-holding and carpet-bag persuasion. . . ." Negroes were everywhere, "in the greatest abundance," as were the "gaunt 'yaller' dogs and disgusting pigs." Writing contemptuously of the stores on Bay Street, the reporter saw "a woman's hat trimmed most gorgeously," with an eye to the "ebony belles," in a window display, surrounded "in picturesque confusion" by "cans of sardines, bottled pickles and a melange of tin ware and cooking utensils." He had a recollection of Beaufort "in the palmy ante war days" when it had been, the reporter recalled vaguely, "something of a

---

[4] Beaufort *Tribune*, February 24, 1875, quoting a recent issue of the Springfield, Massachusetts, *Republican*.

summer resort." He concluded that now "utter stagnation seems to be the only fate in store for it."[5] Just as Beaufort and Port Royal had been ten years before the embodiment of Northern hopes for a renovated South, they had now become symbols of the failure of radical Reconstruction and the final effects of a revolution the nation had disowned.

These criticisms were typical of Northern reports on the Carolina low country in the early 1870's. The bleak opinions were grounded, moreover, upon more tangible circumstances than the aura of dilapidation in the towns, and they had more justification than the irrational annoyance most Northern reporters betrayed at seeing the polls dominated by poor black folk. The area was indeed suffering. The amount of land under cultivation in Beaufort County had fallen from 259,543 acres in 1860 to 150,000 in 1870.[6] Some land was idle because of the cost of restoring the expensive system of dikes for flooding the rice lands, but other land was in disuse because many Northern investors had failed at cotton planting. Many old owners who had regained their land could afford to operate only with small acreages. In the three years before the war the Sea Island cotton crop had amounted to 54,904 bales; but in the three years between 1870 and 1873 the total output had only amounted to 23,307 bales.[7]

The true explanations, however, were far more complicated than the simple one most visitors gave, "the undoing of the old relations between the races." The national depression, the devastation of the low country through Montgomery's forays, the neglect of agriculture in many places for the entire duration of the war, the loss of the favorable marketing position which the old Carolina long-staple producers had enjoyed—all were responsible. In the ante-bellum period the planters had carelessly sold their fine seeds to growers in Egypt and in the Sandwich Islands, and they

[5] *Ibid.*

[6] South Carolina MS State Census, totals of the four parishes of Beaufort District, State Archives, Columbia; King, *Southern States*, p. 428.

[7] *Ibid.*

returned after the war to find that their own seed had been lost or had degenerated. The weather conditions also had been uniformly unfavorable in the years after the war.[8] Nevertheless, most visitors blamed the sad shape of agriculture in the region upon the intensity of the social revolution, underestimating the economic forces that were compelling adjustments of great scope if the region were again to become productive.

Edisto Island lands that had ranged in value from $75 to $100 an acre at the end of the war had gone down to less than $30 by 1867. The value of plantation land was only $6 or $7 in 1873, so low that James Thompson, who was now editing the Beaufort *Republican*, successor to his little wartime *Free South*, thought the old planters suing for restitution of their property would gain more by claiming the actual money the government had secured at the tax sales than by asking for the land itself. Although there were remarkable exceptions of farming success on a relatively large scale, most of the freedmen who had retained their little farms were living, in the years just after the war, on a subsistence basis, raising their own vegetable crops, with enough cotton to produce a little ready cash and pay the taxes.[9]

Depression and readjustments in agriculture were presenting hardships for both races, and the radical government at Columbia had hardly tackled the problem, much less corrected it. The constant efforts of Northerners to create a great commercial center on the islands, to give material reality to Commissioner Brisbane's dreams, had resulted in the building of a new railroad into the remote island region and in the establishment of direct overseas trade, but few of the promised blessings of progress had

[8] King, *Southern States*, p. 428; Francis B. Simkins and Robert H. Woody, *South Carolina During Reconstruction* (Chapel Hill, 1932), p. 10.

[9] Mansfield French to S. P. Chase, February 7, 1867, Chase MSS; Beaufort *Republican*, December 26, 1873; Botume, *First Days*, p. 228. Guion Griffis Johnson, *A Social History of the Sea Islands* (Chapel Hill, 1930), pp. 202–203.

followed. The charges of Northern critics that the local government of Beaufort was in the hands of Negroes and carpetbaggers
and that it was corrupt were true, and the evangels who had
heralded the social and political revolution in South Carolina with
so much enthusiasm were by 1873 placed on the defensive.[10]

James Thompson roared out at the corruption of the state legislature, which had cost $900,000 for its 1871–1872 session. "This
enormous swindle was participated in by nearly every member
of the House and Senate to a greater or less extent." He calculated
the eventualities well. "Let us glance at the promises and anticipations of four years ago, and then look to see how they have been
fulfilled." The young Republican party of 1868 had "resolved
upon a vigorous campaign against the abuses fostered by the pro-
slavery spirit which had so long ruled the State. It determined
upon an honest, economical but liberal government of the people
by the people. Education was to be encouraged; the children of
those kept in ignorance for the conservation of slavery were now
to be furnished with free schools," and so on. Thompson felt
that the Republican party had gained none of these goals and that
the freedmen were the greatest victims of the failure, for "in every
act of fraud, every waste of means, every increase of debt, every
job of extravagance and knavery, . . . [its enemies] see the weapons
to overturn all that has been secured to the emancipated race."[11]
Of the three elements in the electorate that shared responsibility,
the Negroes, the carpetbaggers, and the native South Carolinians
who had become Republicans ("scalawags" to the conservatives),
Thompson saw most virtue in the carpetbaggers and least in the
scalawags, and he did not hold the Negroes blameless. When a
book called *The Prostrate State* appeared, written by an embittered Republican who denounced in scornful language the
corruption of the South Carolina legislature, Thompson recom-

[10] Beaufort *Republican*, November 16, 1871.
[11] *Ibid.*, July 11, 1872, May 23, 1872.

mended it to "the attention of the intelligent colored men of the state."[12]

Laura Towne was also embarrassed. Writing a Northern supporter of her work, she confessed, "Sometimes it seems like work thrown away, especially just after reading the newspapers and seeing the estimation in which our State is held by the rest of the world, and not undeservedly." She could not find it in her heart, however, to hold the Negro leadership responsible. They were ignorant. "The colored members of the Legislation [sic] took bribes and did jobs because they looked eagerly to see *what* to do in their new circumstance, to their white brethren [sic], and as they saw, or were instructed so they did in imitation, and thought it the proper thing."[13]

Rufus Saxton was discouraged too. On the ninth anniversary of the Emancipation Proclamation, writing to Robert Smalls, who had become the most prominent political leader in the district, Saxton recalled January 1, 1863, on the Smith plantation. "Never in all his round did the glad sun shine down upon a scene of more dramatic power. . . . What a day of promise that was!" He recalled the emotions of the black soldiers and their friends when their "year of jubilee" had come. He reminded them solemnly, however, that freedom had brought responsibility as well, "freedom to be honest, industrious, temperate, true and pure," and that "the recording angel" would "note how faithfully its duties have been performed." General Saxton had "rejoiced when the right of suffrage came, and sorrowed when it was told that some had sold this precious birthright for a miserable mess of pottage." He did not believe all he heard but had concluded to send, along with his congratulations, "a few words of warning." He feared that "where there is so much smoke there must be some fire. . . ."[14]

[12] Port Royal *Commercial and Beaufort County Republican*, December 11, 1873. This journal was successor to the *Republican*.

[13] Towne to Francis R. Cope, July 12, 1874, Towne MSS.

[14] Rufus Saxton to Robert Smalls, December 25, 1871, in the Beaufort *Republican*, January 4, 1872.

What had gone wrong? The future had seemed so promising back in 1868 when the radical Republican government had begun its course. Part of the initial exhilaration had been sheer relief. All the fears for the freedmen associated with Saxton's last months in office, when he had tried manfully to block President Johnson's land restoration policy, were banished. The colored people had not been relegated to the tyranny of their late owners, and in the islands near Beaufort the freedmen had retained their land. President Johnson had been a poor politician and had understood little of the national sentiment in the year following the war; he had prescribed too mildly for the returning South. In the pivotal election of 1866, the radical reconstructionists had been returned to Congress in such strength that the meager alterations Johnson had conceived were swept from the board, and stern measures were promptly enforced. The radicals had, by a series of acts of 1867 and the enforcement of the Fourteenth Amendment, banished the old leading class from political power and "reconstructed" the South on the basis of an electorate composed, to all practical purposes, of enfranchised Negroes and Northerners in residence.

Back in 1864 James Thompson had written in passionate conviction of the great future in store for South Carolina with the overthrow of slavery. "To make another Massachusetts of South Carolina it is only necessary to give her freedom and education. To these ends we devote our best efforts."[15] For many idealists who converged on Columbia in 1868 to write a new constitution for the state, these words were as meaningful as they had been for young Thompson, a Gideonite. The radicals, who included among their number many of the missionaries sent South by the freedmen's aid societies, wrote an excellent constitution, based upon the most modern concepts of popular government. No good Gideonite could have asked for more. Every disability of race was demolished, and the legal foundation for a universal free system

[15] Beaufort *Free South*, January 2, 1864.

of public education was laid.[16] The evangels had approached their part in the Reconstruction with confidence.

Laura Towne wrote Edward Pierce of her feelings. She congratulated her old friend on a radical speech he had made in the fall elections and said she was sorry to be so far from the great events in the North, where men like Pierce were "moulding the destinies" of America. But she added, "We are doing a little moulding in a small way ourselves. Isn't South Carolina loyal, and are not the states where there are no 'Yankee school-marms' disloyal? Won't we grow in loyalty as the rising generations come up?" The satisfaction of most evangels regarding universal suffrage was strongly predicated upon the assumption that they would remain the controlling political influence among the freedmen. For as Reuben Tomlinson wrote, although he was "a universal suffrage man," he didn't "care a cent for it unless we can keep Northern influence here along with it." The Northern influence would remain, and the radicals would have their chance. E. L. Pierce was exultant. "How great [are] these days!" He thought he could see the end of the contest "concerning the African race in this country" and was confident that there had never been since Christian martyrdom or the Reformation the "opportunity for equal devotion—or like exhilaration of the moral sentiments." The Negroes of the South were "at last upon their feet provided with all the weapons of defense which any class or race can have."[17]

Pierce did not see the danger. The whole North seemingly joined him in thinking that, with the granting of suffrage, the slaves of a few years before were well "on their feet." By 1868,

[16] Simkins and Woody, *South Carolina During Reconstruction*, pp. 93–100.

[17] Laura Towne to E. L. Pierce, December 6, 1867, Pierce MSS; Reuben Tomlinson to J. M. McKim, December 4, 1866, and E. L. Pierce to McKim, April 20, 1867, McKim MSS.

when the radical government of South Carolina went into effect, the Freedmen's Bureau, except for two more years of assistance to education, had already finished its work.[18] The charitable organizations were left alone in the field, and their days were numbered. In fact, the great American Freedmen's Union Commission was hardly organized before it began to disintegrate. In early 1867 the Western branches at Chicago and Cincinnati forsook the non-sectarian commission and joined forces with the American Missionary Association. By fall of that year the American Freedmen's Union Commission was restating its goals in such modest terms that it was possible to claim that the commission had actually done what it had set out to do. It was a bad thing, thought the officers, to continue to press the cause of the black man before the public, because pressure might hasten a reaction against him. The triumph of the Republican party on President-elect Grant's "Let us have peace" slogan in the fall elections and the formation of reconstructed governments in the South were thought to have removed the necessity of Northern efforts for freedmen's schools. The organization had provided a model for the new state governments. "The skeleton of an educational system will be already there, waiting only to be filled up." At the close of its work the officers congratulated the organization mildly, and deceptively, on having "checked, if it has not altogether overcome, that spirit of denominationalism which endangered the whole movement."[19] Honesty should have compelled the officers to admit that the organized churches had triumphed and that nearly all that would be done in the future by the North for Negro education would come

[18] John Cox and LaWanda Cox, "General O. O. Howard and the 'Misrepresented Bureau,'" *Journal of Southern History*, XIX (November, 1953), 442.

[19] See the *American Freedman*, II (November, 1868), *passim*, and quotations from this issue of the *American Freedman* in the *Freedmen's Record*, IV (November, 1868), 169–170; Synopses of School Reports, I, 158, entry 158, Education Division, BRFAL MSS.

through the American Missionary Association and other denominational groups.[20]

Gone were the grand claims of making a new New England of
the South. What had happened in the North is much more clearly
seen in the statements of the officers of the New England branch
of the Commission, a branch that struggled on alone until 1874.
As early as the fall of 1866 the editors of its journal, the *Freedmen's Record*, were complaining of public indifference to the
cause: "were the tidings to come, as they did last year, that thousands were suffering from hunger, cold, and nakedness, the appeal would probably be responded to as generously as it was then.
The great mass of people do not as yet see that in the education
of . . . freedmen is to be found the solution of some of the weight-
iest public questions of the day." If the freedmen could not even
read a newspaper, would they not become political pawns, perhaps in the hands of their late masters?[21] The society rallied,
however, and spent an all-time high budget of nearly $76,000 for
Southern education in the year 1866–1867. The contributions
tumbled sharply in the succeeding winter, dwindling to approximately $29,000. The society again recovered some lost ground,
but not for long. Edward Hooper, the treasurer, was writing a
supporter in early 1873, in great complacency: "The New England Freedmen's Aid Society has had so much money from the
good people of Boston during the past ten years that it no longer
thinks it fair to urge its friends to continue their gifts. The Society has reduced its work very much, having turned over to the
local authorities in the South as many of its schools as they would
take." A year later, at the annual meeting, a letter was read concerning the transfer of the society's "Robert Gould Shaw

[20] Richard Bryant Drake, "The American Missionary Association and
the Southern Negro, 1861–1888" (unpublished doctoral dissertation,
Emory University, 1959), pp. 20–24; *A History of the American Missionary Association: Its Churches and Educational Institutions among the
Freedmen, Indians and Chinese* (New York, 1874), pp. 13–14.

[21] *Freedmen's Record*, II (November, 1866), 198.

Memorial School" to the city of Charleston. Then the question was put whether the society should disband. The first vote was to continue. The secretary then recorded, "These votes not seeming on the whole to reflect the exact feelings of the meeting[,] they were subsequently re-considered, and instead it was voted, to discontinue the Society in its present form." Adjournment followed, "*sine die.*"[22]

The North had plainly concluded that in granting the franchise the national obligation to the freedmen had been fulfilled. Edward King pointed out the folly of the federal government's granting voting rights without providing the means for national assistance to education, thrusting upon the impoverished South the responsibility for a public school system that it had not possessed in its flourishing days. By the time King came to South Carolina, the state had been on its own for five years, the state school system was simply one more tool in the hands of the corrupt, and Laura Towne was writing, "The need of education here seems to be greater than ever—the means less, friends fewer. . . ." Editor Thompson posited that "the fault of the North in its treatment of the South seems to us to be an indifference to it. This is a result of a reaction." The North was not completely oblivious of the South and its problems in the early 1870's, but there was an inclination to blame the sad state of affairs in the late Slave States on the ignorance of the electorate and on renegade Northerners who used them as tools. The North was not so much indifferent as tired, and the nation seized simple excuses that left the Northern conscience easier. Thompson, however, brought up the point of Northern indifference in order to scold Southern conservative white people who persisted in making no difference between Northerners of honesty and good will and those who were no credit to any section. The editor of the *Republican* was angry

[22] Financial statement in Synopses of School Reports, I, 341, Educational Division, BRFAL MSS; Edward Hooper to Miss M. G. Chapman, March 10, 1873, Weston MSS; Minutes of the New England Freedmen's Aid Society, March 20, 1874, NEFAS MSS, Sturgis–Hooper Papers.

because the conservatives had failed to come to the polls to help put in a reform Republican government in South Carolina in 1872. Thompson advised them "to give up looking for extraneous aid. . . . Quit sitting at home, thanking God that you were born between the Pedee and the Savannah, grumbling over the present and sighing for the past. No one cares for a self-made martyr."[23]

What had happened to bring James Thompson to such a pass that he cried out to the old planter class to aid Gideon's Band? He was smarting from the results of the failure in 1872 to elect his old friend Reuben Tomlinson to the governorship on a reform ticket. The results of the election, at least in Beaufort County, had made a certain matter completely clear, one that should have been foreseen by the Gideonites long ago. Northern "evangels," however high-minded, could not control the Negro vote. Robert Smalls had become the greatest political force in the region; and he had swung the colored vote for the "regular" Republicans, galvanizing the opposition to Tomlinson and his own opponent for the state senatorship, a Northern Negro lawyer named W. J. Whipper, with cries that the freedmen could not trust outsiders, that they should vote for none but Southern men.[24] It had worked. If Tomlinson had been known anywhere in South Carolina as a just and honorable man it would have been at Port Royal, where he had worked with the freedmen since 1862 with much credit and universal acclaim among his fellow evangels. He had received in Beaufort County a meager vote of 1,445 to 4,995

[23] Towne to F. R. Cope, April 9, 1873, Towne MSS; Beaufort *Republican*, November 21, 1872; King, *Southern States*, p. 602.

[24] Beaufort *Republican*, July 11, August 1, 1872; Simkins and Woody, *South Carolina During Reconstruction*, pp. 466–467. The authors list Smalls as among the bolters from the party, but on the local level he worked to defeat the movement, perhaps because his own opponent, Whipper, associated himself more closely with the reformers, and the carpetbag element was, as Thompson put it, "the heart of the reform movement. . . ." Beaufort *Republican*, August 22, 1872, and September 26, 1872.

for Franklin J. Moses, as blatant a swindler as ever sat in any gubernatorial chair, and a native white Southerner. In the "Brick Church" precinct, near his old headquarters as General Superintendent under Saxton, Tomlinson received only 62 votes, to 631 for Moses. Editor Thompson saw that the votes had been divided between the two men largely on the basis of color, with the white people voting for Tomlinson and the colored voters, following Smalls, voting for Moses.[25] Smalls had called for reform too, and in the murky waters of Reconstruction it was impossible sometimes for even well-educated men to differentiate between the degrees of corrupt associations that clouded the reputations of nearly all politicians. To the Negro electorate Smalls was a hero, the brave skipper of the *Planter* and "the smartest *cullud* man in Souf Car'lina."[26] If a Yankee missionary named Reuben Tomlinson, Gideonite, was remembered at all, it was not very distinctly.

It is also impossible to say that the instincts of the Republican majorities were completely wrong. Still being for the most part illiterate, they probably never read the aspersions of Editor Thompson against Smalls in the *Republican*. In truth, although Smalls was identified with the regular Republicans rather than with the reformers, he emerged from the Reconstruction era convicted of only one serious charge, that he had bribed the clerks of the House and Senate to state that a claim of his for $2,250 had been passed and approved. Smalls, self-educated, had become a self-possessed speaker; he was a man of undoubted intelligence and ready wit. The radical politician may well have been as deeply involved as most of his fellows in the depressing round of graft that characterized the government at Columbia; his conduct of the printing committee was at once politically successful and morally blameworthy. To the Sea Islanders, however, it was thrilling to have a leader who spoke to them in their own Gullah dialect, a

[25] *Ibid.*, October 24, 1872.
[26] [Justus Clement French], *Steamer Oceanus*, p. 86.

powerful man who was known to the conservative editor of the
Charleston *News* as the "King" of Beaufort County.[27]

On the other hand, the so-called reform wing of the party included in its ranks numerous unsavory characters. In actuality,
Tomlinson himself was connected strategically with an extremely
lucrative swindle. One of the most outstanding grafts of the era
was the Greenville and Columbia Railroad operation. Although
Tomlinson emerged in the odor of sanctity, he had been State
Attorney General and at the same time Treasurer of the Railroad
Company when the crucial transactions that so depressed the
credit of the state were made. He had been either a great fool or
subject to a serious moral lapse. Back home in Pennsylvania Tomlinson had been a bank clerk, and he ought to have been able to
read ledgers. The regular Republicans charged also that Tomlinson had bribed the legislature as freely as any "regular" had done
when he wanted the body to grant a franchise to a phosphate company that he was promoting. Whether it was true or not, the state
gained little from the franchises granted to such companies.[28]

The truth was simple: The voters of Beaufort had less confidence in the white people than in Negroes. Ten years of exposure
to the social and political ideas of Northern radicals had not made
them more confident of the ultimate intentions of their teachers.
Just as the immigrant population of New England in a later day
would follow on faith the city "boss" who understood them, so
Port Royalists accepted the leadership of their own people who

[27] Simkins and Woody, *South Carolina During Reconstruction*, pp. 133,
476, 543; [French], *Steamer Oceanus*, p. 86; George B. Tindall, *South
Carolina Negroes 1877–1900* (Columbia, South Carolina, 1952), pp. 54–55;
Beaufort *Tribune*, May 12, 1875, quoting the *News*. The printing swindles
were not exposed until after the election of 1872. Smalls was chairman of
the printing committee. See Beaufort *Republican*, December 5, 1872, and
Port Royal *Commercial*, April 9, 1874.

[28] Simkins and Woody, *South Carolina During Reconstruction*, pp.
204–206; John S. Reynolds, *Reconstruction in South Carolina* (Columbia,
1905), pp. 126, 223.

won power. Perhaps nothing illustrates better the naïveté of certain evangels than their failure to foresee this eventuality.

When the Republican party organized on St. Helena Island in 1867, Laura Towne reported that at a meeting of Negroes, with only a handful of whites present, one man rose to say "he wanted no white man on their platform." He was talked down by his more generous fellows, who said, according to Miss Towne, "What difference does skin make, my bredren. *I* would stand side by side with a *white* man if he acted right," and pleaded that the Negroes not be prejudiced "against their color." Another said, "If dere skins *is* white, dey may have principle."[29]

Laura Towne found it amusing. It was more significant than she imagined. The colored people were speaking the language of New England liberals, but the resentment of the member who "wanted no white man" was more widespread than the generous Miss Towne had reason to know. She had simply assumed that the whites would lead.[30]

The one man who might have challenged Robert Smalls successfully, the most popular of all the evangels with the Sea Islanders, had been Mansfield French. The minister, however, had returned North in 1872, "philanthropy being more his line than politics," in the words of his son, W. M. French, who remained on the islands to edit the Beaufort *Tribune*. It had not always been so, and in 1868 French had been much excited at the prospect of becoming United States Senator from South Carolina. He had written Chief Justice Chase that his friends regarded his "chances of success" as being "*very good.*" The minister's political hopes were bolstered by a formidable array of national radicals, who had petitioned him to run in the contest. By the time the radicals attained power in the state, however, French's reputation was under a black cloud. He had attended land sales in the low country

[29] Holland (ed.), *Towne*, p. 182.
[30] Letter of Laura Towne of June 7, 1867, in *Pennsylvania Freedmen's Bulletin*, III (October, 1867), 8.

regularly and seems to have been at the head of an attempt to buy up lapsed soldiers' claims and other cheap property to resell to Negroes. He had the backing of Chase and banker Jay Cooke.[31] There is no good evidence that French did not manage his part with integrity, but many people did not think that he had done so. A reporter for the *New York Times* charged that "in almost all cases the certificates ultimately found their way into Father French's pockets." The reporter venomously labeled French the "Tycoon of all the robbers" and charged that he had gotten thousands of Negroes in debt to him "on account of his lofty charges for meal and Attleborough jewelry." The reporter of the *Times* was clearly jaundiced, but he was not the only observer who held these opinions. Many schoolteachers in Beaufort thought him dishonest; in the words of Arthur Sumner, "a liar, scoundrel, thief, and hypocrite." It seems most unlikely that the overt charges of fraud had any basis in fact, and it is probable that certain of French's accusers confused the minister with his son, W. M. French, who had remained on the islands as a newspaper editor and was involved in numerous real estate ventures. If French's defenders are correct, the circulation of these charges at the time French was ambitious to become the first radical Senator from South Carolina was a calculated strategem on the part of his rival, and slander was the real cause of the minister's failure to be elected. French was not without friends, however, and Reuben Tomlinson, who had never liked French's methods, was writing to McKim in 1867 that "with all his eccentricities, . . . [French] is true to the colored man, and to the country."[32]

[31] Obituary of French, Beaufort *Tribune*, March 22, 1876; French to Chase, June 8, 1868, and same to same, February 7, 1867, Chase MSS.

[32] *New York Times*, July 23, 1866; Arthur Sumner to Nina Hartshorn, August 8, 1864, Sumner MSS; Mansfield Joseph French, *Ancestors and Descendants of Samuel French the Joiner* (privately printed, Ann Arbor, 1940), pp. 88–92. Tomlinson to McKim, February 19, 1867, McKim MSS. A Union soldier reported that French was not respected or admired by the officers stationed at Port Royal, who called him "Holy Joe" and "Aaron." Henry Hitchcock's diary, *Marching With Sherman* (New Haven, 1927), pp. 227–228, edited by M. A. DeWolfe Howe.

When even Gideonites could not with certainty identify virtue among candidates and good policy among the parties and factions, it is not astonishing that the largely uninformed Negro electorate was at a loss. In an age when corruption was rampant in nearly every state legislature and when "Grantism" came to signify demoralization in the national administration, the Southern states under Reconstruction drew a disproportionate degree of criticism. The opportunities for plunder afforded by the new and rapid growth of capitalism left the reputations of few public figures a decent covering. The voters of South Carolina were hardly more responsible for the chicanery of the Greenville and Columbia Railroad ring than were the voters of New York State at a time when Jim Fiske and Jay Gould could arrive at Albany and buy the legislature to do the will of the Erie Railroad ring.

The colored voters of Beaufort County did have the real issues placed before them in the spirited contests between 1868 and 1877, and if they could not determine precisely what occurred at Columbia after the successful candidates took office, they were little more confused than the mass of voters over the nation. The three most persistent local issues on the Sea Islands were discussed at nearly every meeting. They were corruption on state and local levels, exorbitant taxes, and the still unresolved controversy over the lands seized and sold under the Direct Tax Laws. On the head of corruption, the voters frequently heard charges flung directly at opposing candidates at political rallies, and staunch "regulars" warned the electorate just as freely as did the "reformers" not to send bad men to the legislature, on the ground that they "might steal." Of such a meeting Editor Thompson fulminated, "No allusion was made to the present splendid financial condition of the State, and no doubt many a hearer went away from the meeting with the impression that everything was going on as smoothly as possible in our State. . . ."[33] The voters of Beaufort County threaded their way through the confusion by trusting the skipper of the *Planter* to recognize the scoundrels, and they regularly

[33] Beaufort *Republican*, July 11, 1872.

returned the men he backed to the state offices. On the local level, the town and county offices usually went to carpetbaggers who managed with indifferent success. John Hunn and H. G. Judd, both of Gideon's Band, were local officers who managed badly but were apparently honest. The town went in and out of bankruptcy, and George Holmes, not of Gideon's Band, was certainly guilty of withholding teachers' salaries under the pretext of low funds and profiting from buying up teachers' pay certificates at a discount.[34]

The problems of taxation and land were closely related, and in this particular the small Negro landowners of Beaufort were in the frustrating position of finding their own interests at cross-purposes with those of most of the colored people in the state. At a Fourth of July political rally in 1872, a politician told the voters that "the object of the [high] tax law and the general legislation" of the previous session "was to take the lands out of the possession of the white people and place them in the hands of the colored people." Editor Thompson lined out the paradox: "We ask our delegation if this is so, [because] if so the tax law has utterly failed of its object, for two-thirds of the lands sold at the tax sales has been the property of colored people. Their little farms have been sold from them, and they are left destitute and homeless. Think of this, you owners of ten and twenty acre lots." Thompson did not exaggerate. Whatever the tax law did for landowners in the state at large, the Beaufort papers were lined with lists of small farms delinquent in taxes. With due warning most Negro farmers did scrape up the tax money, however, no matter what the sacrifice, for they well understood the basis of their security.[35]

The incessant litigation over the status of the Direct Tax lands troubled Negroes and whites alike. Throughout the Reconstruc-

[34] Beaufort *Tribune*, June 14, 1876, and February 3, 1875; Sworn affidavit of D. H. Hyatt, March 20, 1875, Education Petitions, State Archives, Columbia; Beaufort *Republican*, November 14, 1872.

[35] Beaufort *Republican*, July 11, 1872. See listing of delinquent properties, *ibid.*, February 22, 1872.

tion period the dispossessed whites worked under the leadership of Richard DeTreville to break the tax laws under which the confiscation of their estates had been effected. Using the house in Beaufort in which Robert Smalls had been reared as a slave and which the Negro leader had bought at the government tax sales, DeTreville fought the case through the state courts and lost. When the claim on the Prince Street house came into the possession of William DeTreville upon the death of Richard DeTreville, the case at last, in 1878, reached the Supreme Court, where it was defeated. The freedmen and Northerners who had benefited from the tax sales retained their land, and Port Royal became, in respect of landownership, very much what the Gideonites had hoped it would become. By 1890 Elizabeth Botume reported that three-fourths of the land in Beaufort County was owned by Negroes.[36]

As years passed, the animosities of war cooled, at least as far as the victors were concerned. In Beaufort County nothing demonstrated the mellowing attitude better than the growing sense among many resident Northerners that the local Southern white people had, in the loss of their property, suffered an unfair amount of punishment. In January of 1872 Editor James Thompson was still reminding them that there had been a certain "poetic justice" in the fact that "the hot-bed of rebellion" had "received the worst punishment" and that the former owners had no claim to the restoration of their lands. But he was already speaking of a possible money compensation.[37]

As a representative of those who wished to develop the commercial possibilities of the region, Thompson was especially concerned about the depression of property values that had resulted from the continuation of "occupance [sic] of lands and town

---

[36] *DeTreville* v. *Smalls,* 98 U.S.; *First Mohonk Conference on the Negro Question, June 4, 5, 6* (Boston, 1890), p. 24. The records of the Direct Tax Commission include a notebook that outlines the tangled legal history of the Direct Tax lands. Records of the Fifth Special Agency, United States Archives.

[37] Beaufort *Republican,* January 11, 1872.

property by the United States," which he pronounced an "unmiti-
gated nuisance." The sales of government property had been
halted in 1866, and the neglected town houses had become eye-
sores that appalled visitors like Edward King. "No improvements
can be made upon adjoining property because of the filthy condition of the government ruins, the disgusting character of their
inhabitants and the danger from fire." Insurance was expensive
and frequently unobtainable at any price. The wreck of Commissioner Brisbane's dream of a property revolution had become
an embarrassment; Thompson was glad when a plan was effected
whereby the old owners were allowed to redeem by paying the
tax those parts of their property that had not been sold, and he explained just how they ought to go about making their claims.
Afterward, the government would be free to sell what remained
of the property, and Thompson joined the clamor for a financial
settlement for those whose property had been sold outright before
the end of hostilities.[38]

There were other signs of peaceful coexistence. Indigent
Southern whites accepted positions teaching in the Negro schools.
Within the county, of the nineteen teachers reporting in 1870 all
but five Negro teachers and two Northern whites were Southern
whites. Thomas Chaplin came back to St. Helena; living in an
overseers' house on a plantation neighboring his own old home,
he taught "a large school for Negro children."[39] The signs of
peace were even more pronounced in the religious life of the community. As early as the spring of 1867, the Reverend Mr. Elliott,
son of the General Stephen Elliott who had held Fort Sumter for
so long against Gillmore's guns, came to St. Helena Episcopal
Church and spoke peace to "a crowded house, with about an equal

[38] *Ibid.*, July 24, 1873, and June 6, 1872; Jan. 25, 1872. W. M. French,
editor of the Beaufort *Tribune*, took the same view. See the *Tribune*, May
19, 1875.

[39] Teachers' Monthly School Reports, State Archives, Columbia. Chaplin MS diary, final entry, January 1, 1886, relating the salient events of
Chaplin's life during Reconstruction.

number from each section," North and South. Northerners began to hear that Southerners were ready to "let 'bygones be bygones.' " An ominous sign developed when the Northern white people of St. Helena Island began to go to the "White Church," apart from the Brick Church of the freedmen, the scene of so many exciting meetings during the war. Much as such a move was resented by so strong an integrationist as Laura Towne, who castigated whilom "army sutlers and low camp followers" for becoming "too uppish" to associate with the Negroes, the signs that the Northerners resident were beginning to conciliate the "native" whites were abundant.[40] Editor Thompson began to regret "the loss during the war, of the names by which the respective streets in the town of Beaufort had been previously designated" and concluded that the "temporary system" had "subserved" its original purpose. The old names were restored. In 1873 Thompson ran a series of articles in his paper written by an old white resident who outlined, presumably for the benefit of the newcomers, the history of the region and the plight and sentiments of the dispossessed "natives." He ended on a note of brotherhood.[41]

Not every white resident shared the amicable spirit; a young Southern white woman wrote in 1876 that spring had come to Beaufort—"Drumfish is scarce, but Yankees abundant. . . ." She had "not the *horror* of being acquainted with one of them." Neither was Laura Towne prepared to conciliate. When an affable young scion of the Rhett family made overtures to Miss Towne and said he was sorry to have been unable to call upon her, she said that that was just as well, for "our ways are not their ways, and it is troublesome to know them."[42] Most Northerners were

[40] Botume, *First Days*, pp. 230–231; Towne MS letter to her sisters, March 3, 1867.

[41] Beaufort *Republican*, February 13, 1873; the series on the history of the region was written by [Dr.] J. A. J[ohnson] and appeared from February 20, 1873, running through July 3, 1873.

[42] [?] to Emily Elliott, April 12, 1876, Elliott–Gonzales MSS; Laura Towne to "L," October 29, 1876, Towne MSS.

not responding in like manner. The death of S. C. Millett, a young carpetbagger who had steered clear of politics and advanced the commercial interests of the region by his able management of the new Port Royal railroad, was regretted by all. His eulogy in the *Port Royal Commercial* stated that under Millett's management "all" employees on the road had been "Southern boys of integrity, sobriety, honesty, and position." Millett had "spurned and despised the oppression of our poor South, as much as do the dearest of our own."[43]

The Reverend Mr. Mansfield French's son, W. M. French, had returned to Beaufort to edit the *Tribune*, and although he called himself an "independent" he followed an editorial policy that must have pleased the conservative whites as much as it displeased Laura Towne. Editor French had apparently come to some important and portentous conclusions about Southern Reconstruction. Commenting upon the hearty reception in Boston and New York of the famous rebel military unit, the Washington Light Infantry of Charleston, he saw it as a sign of a reaction:

There can be no doubt but what this reactionary feeling in favor of those who sought the dissolution of the Union, is a manifestation of the sympathy felt by the best classes at the North for a kindred people who, they are convinced, have for the last ten years been subject to state governments forced upon them of the most degraded nature.

Moral? Those same Northerners would help the return of decent government, and

. . . whatever elements obstruct the attainment of so desirable an end, whether ignorance, lust of power or greed of plunder will be thrust aside. If a suspicion gains ground that the colored vote is subversive of the best interests of an important section of the union, because controlled by bad men, the handwriting on the wall indicates that the same power that bestowed the right of suffrage will not hesi-

43 *Port Royal Commercial*, March 19, 1874.

tate to withdraw it for the benefit of the descendants of those who fought at Eutaw and Bunker Hill a century ago to found this republic.[44]

The nation was preparing to celebrate its centennial, and the spirit of peace and concord was general. On the Fourth of July Laura Towne wrote to a faithful friend in Philadelphia and tried to imagine the excitement that would mark the celebration in her native city. She did not envy her friends there, however, for sitting at her home on the islands she could enjoy the wonderful sea breeze "in utter quiet" and reflect upon "our hundred years of progress. I can imagine it all as glorious as I please." Laura Towne would not enjoy such a complacency again, for although she seemed unaware of the ominous implications of sectional reconciliation, she should have understood that the Sea Islands were a powderkeg in the summer of 1876. Her instincts had been more accurate fifteen years before, when she had enjoyed the sea breeze in Newport on a quiet Sunday afternoon, with the thunderheads of civil war looming on the horizon. Then she had sensed that the nation was "waiting for something—some great, terrible time."[45]

Two months earlier, on May 3, 1876, Editor French had informed his readers in the *Tribune* of "an event which seems almost incredible: that the Democracy of Beaufort County, so long dormant has awakened from its slumbers for a sufficient length of time to rub its sleepy eyes, get on its feet and meet in a Convention for the purpose of electing delegates" to the state party convention. French was glad to see that "some of the best citizens of the county" were taking part, welcomed the advent of the two-party system, and rejoiced "that a wealthy and intelligent class of citizens, who for years have abstained from taking part in public affairs are about to abandon their policy of inactivity and thereby add new zest to the next political campaign." Democratic clubs, he

[44] Beaufort *Tribune*, June 23, 1875.
[45] Towne to Francis Cope, July 4, 1876, and Towne MS letter to [?], May 26, 1861, Towne MSS.

observed, were being organized all over the county.[46] Editor French seemed as unaware as Laura Towne of the impending counterrevolution. The Democratic clubs were arming themselves, they were wearing red shirts, and they intended to banish the Republican party from South Carolina.

After a fall campaign notorious for the fraudulent practices and violence of both parties, the Democrats, with the cooperation of the federal government, accomplished their purpose. The attempt to remodel South Carolina along the lines of Massachusetts was officially interred. The North would not protest when their "kindred people" snatched the reins of political power from Northerners and Negroes, nor lift a hand to prevent the "redemption" of the state where Reconstruction began first and lasted longest. By 1876 even a few Negroes and carpetbaggers who had been associated with the Port Royal movement seemed ready to acquiesce to the counterrevolution. Tax Commissioner William Brisbane made a public announcement of his conversion in September before the elections: "I intend to vote for [Wade] Hampton. Why? Because I think I can strike more effectually against the combined effort to destroy the material interests of our State; and because he has promised, if he is elected, that the rights of the colored man, as defined in the thirteenth, fourteenth and Fifteenth Amendments, shall be respected. . . ." Martin R. Delany, a talented radical Negro leader who had been prominent on the islands during the war, also backed Hampton for governor. Editor French made his sympathies clear on every page of his journal, remarking with satisfaction that "many men are changing their political faith who were thought to be incorrigible."[47]

But not all evangels were "redeemed," or "reconciled" to the overthrow of their hopes. Reuben Tomlinson went North and attempted to rouse popular indignation against President Ruther-

[46] Beaufort *Tribune,* May 3, 1876.

[47] *Ibid.,* September 27, 1876; Simkins and Woody, *South Carolina During Reconstruction,* p. 511.

ford Hayes, the Republican whose elevation to office had been part and parcel of the compromise that returned South Carolina to the rule of the white native population of the state. In vain did Tomlinson suggest that under the administration of Republican Governor Daniel Chamberlain the state had already been well on the way to good government and honest reform; in vain did he point to the violence that had marked the overthrow of the Republican party. He was astonished that the North should have acquiesced to a policy "which nullified some of the most important results of the war." For Tomlinson the Southern Question was not settled. Was the Federal government not failing in its "promises to protect the millions of colored people at the South in their civil and political rights?" He pointed out that "States rights and home rule in the South mean the right of the rich and intelligent and powerful to trample under foot the poor and ignorant and weak."[48]

Protests availed little, for the nation was almost as weary of Reconstruction as were South Carolina Bourbon Redeemers. Laura Towne wrote in anger and sadness to Francis R. Cope, a faithful supporter of her school. She drew a mild reproof:

We feel very sorry that the prospect for the colored people of S. Carolina appears to you so dark. But how is it to be helped? Force may for awhile restrain the passions of men, [but] it is at least questionable whether the evil resulting does not overbalance the good. We never contemplated when we took the freed blacks under the protection of the North that the work was to be for an unlimited time. We hoped that if for a few years we lent them a helping hand, self interest, if not a sense of right, would prompt the Southern whites to do their duty by them. That in this we have been disappointed is partly their fault,

[48] Tomlinson was active in the North for several years following the campaign of 1876, attempting to draw public attention to the dangers inherent in the triumph of the Democrats in South Carolina for the Negroes. See the Boston *Advertiser*, January 28, 1878, for the speech from which the quotations are taken.

partly ours in permitting so many disreputable men to take the office of protectors and so bring discredit on the whole system.

Mr. Cope thought that "all protective systems" were "unsatisfactory" and that "no business and no individual can stand firmly till he learns to stand alone."[49] His attitude was the one most acceptable to men in the North who regarded themselves as moderate and enlightened on public issues.

Reconstruction had begun first on the Sea Islands, and it did not end there, suddenly, with the victory of Wade Hampton for the governorship in 1876. Well into the evening of the century Negroes in Beaufort County were a political force, and the two old rivals, W. J. Whipper, carpetbag Negro, and Robert Smalls, ex-slave, were regularly returned to the state legislature. Smalls was United States Congressman from 1875 to 1879 and served again to complete a vacated term in 1884. He was reelected for his last full term in 1884.[50] Near the end of the century, however, the story of Negro participation in South Carolina political life came to an end. In 1895, under the leadership of Governor Ben Tillman, a constitutional convention was held, and South Carolina effectually nullified the Fifteenth Amendment by erecting such requirements for voting that Negroes saw the futility of even trying. True to its reputation as the strongest black district, Beaufort had sent five of the six Negro representatives present at this convention, Whipper and Smalls among them. With wit and skill the two men eventually obliged the delegates to drop the cant about establishing fair practices of universal application with regard to suffrage; they pressed the issue forward until one white delegate said, in exasperation, "We don't propose to have any fair elections. We will get left every time." Robert Smalls had his chance to say the many good things that could be said for the radical constitution of 1868, which had, after all, served nearly twenty years after

[49] Francis Cope to Laura Towne, November 19, 1877, Towne MSS.
[50] George Brown Tindall, *South Carolina Negroes, 1877–1900* (Columbia, South Carolina, 1952), p. 55, and Appendix, "Negro Members of the South Carolina General Assembly after Reconstruction," pp. 309–310.

the resumption of white control. He pleaded no special defense for his race, but asked only "an equal chance in the battle of life." He was proud to be a Negro. "I stand here the equal of any man." It was brave whistling in the wind. The new constitution was adopted, and by 1903 a citizen of Beaufort reported that even though literate male Negroes in the county numbered 3,434 to 927 white voters, the "registration officials do not allow registered Negro voters to outnumber the whites."[51]

There always remained about Beaufort and the islands special reminders of their unique history during the Civil War. Among the schoolchildren there was an impressive number of Rufus Saxtons, Matilda Saxtons, and Edward Pierces. There was even a John Andrew. In the great Union cemetery in the center of the town lay the numbers of men who had died in the ineffectual but sanguinary fighting in the Department of the South. Every year at the Memorial Day celebration the remaining Northerners resident gathered to decorate the graves. H. G. Judd contributed an ode, as he had always done; and Laura Towne noted with grim pride the inscription of the monument: "Immortality to thousands of the brave defenders of our Country from the Great *Rebellion*." She admitted that it was "out of fashion now to use such plain words, but there they stand! right in the midst of the rebels, in granite." Gradually, however, time eroded some of the granite even from Laura Towne's heart, and she undertook a few social exchanges with the "native" whites, as she called them. Although she never was "redeemed," Laura Towne became a good neighbor, and her virtues were extolled by "natives" both black and white.[52]

The islanders could no longer vote, but in a signal respect they

[51] *Ibid.*, pp. 81–89, quotations, in order, from pp. 87, 86, 88.

[52] Laura Towne to her sisters, June 1, 1879, Towne MSS. Lily Ellis Fripp, to her sister-in-law, Emily Fripp, wrote of Miss Towne's neighborly acts to her in an undated letter written sometime shortly after January 18, 1883. The letter is in the Ellis Family Papers in the South Caroliniana Library, University of South Carolina. For names of schoolchildren, see *Freedmen's Record*, IV (March, 1868), 39.

were more fortunate than other Negroes of the South. They owned their own land, and upon it they could support themselves. They came in time to constitute a "black yeomanry," although they did not prosper as their best Northern and Southern white friends had hoped they might. They had been granted a chance to become free and independent in a span of years when even the most able and experienced white Sea Island planters were at a loss to meet the terrible readjustments required of them. They had had to help restore prosperity to a region that had been in an unfavorable competitive position even before the war, and to achieve this in spite of a national depression, the loss of the fine seed that had been the main element in successful long-staple cotton farming, and the capture of the long-staple cotton market by the producers in other parts of the world. Unfortunately for the freedman, these events had coincided with his entry into the political picture, and most observers, North and South, in explaining the problem, had seized the simple but inadequate excuse that the freedmen were not working. The readjustments indicated were exactly what the agricultural experts pointed out: a shift to more diversified farming; the raising of hay and truck produce; and the increasing use of commercial fertilizers. Because of lack of capital the changes were slow in coming, but they did in time take place. Although the freedmen continued to farm the long-staple crop they knew and understood, taking their chances on getting a sufficient money return to pay taxes while subsisting themselves with their corn and vegetables, the larger farmers began the shift to short-staple cotton very shortly after the war.

The Negroes of the low country were much assisted in maintaining their independent status by the opening in 1867 of phosphate mines along the rivers and estuaries. Frequently the young men went to "the rock," as they called the mines, leaving the farming of the little ten-acre plots to their wives and children. Edward Philbrick had been correct in his prediction that these tiny estates would be encumbered by excessive subdivision and lawsuits and that the acreages would diminish in size to the extent that they were no longer suitable for staple agriculture. But the remedy had appeared with the disease. Even by 1888 a Gideonite who returned to the islands for a visit reported that a New England firm regularly shipped early garden truck from the islands direct to Northern ports. After 1870 truck farming came to be a more and more important economic activity. Two great calamities eventually spurred the readjustment to its final stages; a great tidal wave in 1893, which wreaked havoc upon the central islands; and the arrival of the boll weevil in 1918. Thereafter the long-staple cotton crop disappeared, making room for new crops better suited to the new institutions of freedom and small landownership.[53]

The Sea Islanders had learned the lessons of freedom, and they became, in their own way, as self-governing as many a small New England town. The church remained for them a greater force in the conduct of men than man-made law, a law with which they would now have less and less to do. Scholars who studied the islands closely in the 1920's found that nearly all disputes were settled by committees within the churches and that among "members" the collective wisdom of the elders constituted the recognized law and reduced crime to a minimum. The Baptist church was essentially democratic; its elders were the choice of the local members, and it was the only denomination that had a considerable following on the islands. To the islanders, the secular law was the "unjust" law; the church law was the "just" law.[54]

The efforts of Gideon's Band had not gone for nothing, although Pierce's evangels might not have understood the fruit of

[53] Charles Howard Family [MS] History, pp. 108–109, 198–199, 201–202; Tindall, *South Carolina Negroes*, p. 93. The Beaufort County Census Report for 1868 (S.C. MS Census, in S.C. State Archives) lists only 220,614 acres planted in long-staple cotton, as opposed to 7,036,957 acres in short-staple. Market garden produce was valued for 1868 at above two million dollars.

[54] Johnson, *Social History*, pp. 209–210; T. J. Woofter, *Black Yeomanry* (New York, 1930), pp. 239–240.

their labor. The freedmen had become self-supporting, if not wealthy. They paid their taxes, and they took care of their local troubles with aplomb. In addition to owning their land, they enjoyed yet another advantage over many American Negroes, North or South, at the end of the century. Living almost isolated from their white neighbors on the mainland, they were spared contacts at a time when race relations in America reached their most disgraceful depths. Perhaps Suzie King Taylor, far away in Boston, experienced more painful knowledge of the frightful abuse of her people than her old neighbors on the islands ever endured. In 1902 she wrote her reminiscences of the life she had led as a little slave girl on St. Simon's Island, how she had come to Beaufort, "liberated," and had worked as a laundress and unofficial schoolteacher for the first Negro troops. She remembered that "glorious day" on the Smith plantation when the Sea Islanders had first heard the Emancipation Proclamation. At the time of writing she knew that Negroes traveling in the South always rode second-class, and that small excuse was required to set off a lynching bee. She knew that in the South the time had come again when there were few liberties of Negroes that white people were bound to respect. She could not understand. "There is no redress for us from a government which promised to respect all under its flag. It is a mystery to me."[55]

There was really no mystery. The nation had forgotten. Thomas Wentworth Higginson, who wrote the introduction to Mrs. Taylor's little book, had even in 1863 feared for the "ultimate fate" of the liberated Negroes, remembering that "revolutions may go backward."[56] The regression had simply taken longer than Higginson had imagined it might.

[55] Suzie King Taylor, *Reminiscences of My Life in Camp* (Boston, 1902), p. 61.

[56] Thomas W. Higginson, *Army Life in a Black Regiment* (Cambridge, 1900), pp. 63–64.

NOTES ON SOURCES

I. MANUSCRIPTS

THE STORY OF PORT ROYAL IS THE STORY OF ANTISLAVERY MEN and women at work to give substance to their dream of human equality. They worked in a practical situation at a particular place that was familiar to newspaper readers of a hundred years ago but has been largely lost to posterity, with the exception of specialists in Civil War and Reconstruction history. Without the availability of a large body of manuscript sources, it is doubtful if their story could be told, for many of the missionaries on the islands were too young to have had a public part in the ante-bellum abolition movement, and few became famous enough in later life to entitle them to biographies. Even for those who later achieved distinction in other fields, their unique role in the war dwindled in personal significance as the cause of Negro equality became, at the close of the century, less fashionable. Because the opportunities that opened at Port Royal resulted from the politics of war, the names of many prominent public figures are woven into the developments on the islands; but even for their biographers the great events of wartime in the nation's capital threw the part these figures played in the little world of Port Royal into the shade. As a consequence, even for the greater personalities involved in the story, the letters and diaries, published and unpublished, developed into the most fruitful sources of information.

The letters and diaries of the missionaries, however, constitute the single indispensable category of primary material. The sheer volume of these writings, covering as they do so small a geographic area, is ample testimony to the importance the evangels attached to their work. In sifting these rich sources, I soon found that there was an attractive bonus held out for careful reading. The focus of many sympathetic and perceptive eyes, over a period of several years, upon the individual Negroes who were reborn in freedom during the turmoil of war sometimes gave these usually mute participants in the struggle a real dimension of personality. In some fortunate instances I even met the same individuals in another context, as slaves particularly mentioned in the diaries and letters of the ante-bellum planters of the islands. These ante-bellum materials were of a value that transcends the number of times they have been cited, for they bared the outlines and the basic presumptions of the slave system on the islands in a manner that was essential to understanding the response of the freedmen to their new opportunities.

The manuscript collections that have been most useful in reconstructing the attitudes, motives, and accomplishments of the evangels at Port Royal are widely scattered. At Fisk University the voluminous records of the American Missionary Association are housed and are presently being catalogued. They constitute an extremely important source for understanding the evangelical missionaries. The William F. Allen manuscript diary is at the State Historical Society of Wisconsin, extant in typescript only, since the original has been lost. It dates from the fall of 1863 through 1864 and is the work of a sensitive and perceptive teacher. The William Channing Gannett Papers at the University of Rochester have proved most helpful; they include not only Gannett's own diaries but also letters from other Port Royal superintendents and teachers, lists of Gannett's pupils, and the financial statements regarding his use of the fund he set up from his profits in 1863. The correspondence of J. Milton and Esther Hawks in the Library of Congress represents the close connection between the social experiment and the first Negro regiments. Beginning as a plantation superintendent, Dr. Hawks became a surgeon in the 1st South Carolina Volunteers. His wife, also a physician, taught school and nursed wounded soldiers. The Thomas Wentworth Higginson Manuscripts in the Houghton Library at Harvard University also show these connections, for Higginson, an officer in a Negro regiment, was on friendly and sympathetic terms with numbers of the teachers and superintendents. The "Charles Howard Family Domestic History" is a privately typed, reproduced, and bound collection that includes the reminiscences of Thomas Dwight Howard, teacher on Hilton Head Island. Copies of the History may be found in The Johns Hopkins University Library and in the Southern Historical Collection at Chapel Hill.

The Arthur Sumner Papers and the Laura Towne Papers are presently located at the Penn Community Center, Frogmore, St. Helena Island, South Carolina, but will shortly form a part of the Southern Historical Collection at Chapel Hill. They reveal two entirely different personalities who shared a talent for the incisive comment. They are both in typescript copy. The Towne Papers consist of letters sent and received and a diary covering the entire war and Reconstruction periods. Arthur Sumner's correspondence covers the war period only.

The Edward Atkinson Manuscripts in the Massachusetts Historical Society and the James Miller McKim Manuscripts, which are a part of the antislavery collection at Cornell University, fill a special niche. They not only include numerous letters from teachers and superintendents but also show the organizational aspects of the missionary work. The McKim correspondence includes numerous letters from Edward Pierce, Laura Towne, and Reuben Tomlinson, as well as McKim's letterbooks as corresponding secretary for the American Freedmen's Union Commission. In no collection is the close connection between the Port Royal work and the abolition movement so clearly seen. The Atkinson Manuscripts include important letters from Edward Philbrick, as well as the records of the earliest phase of work of the Boston Educational Commission. The subsequent records of this organization and its successor, the New England Freedmen's Aid Society, are also in the Massachusetts Historical Society, as a part of the Sturgis–Hooper Papers. These materials include the minutes of the meetings of the General Committee and the Teachers' Committee, and four volumes of daily records, with abstracts of letters received and sent.

The Edward Pierce Papers at the Houghton Library constitute only two volumes and yielded only a few letters of direct bearing upon the Port Royal story. The memoirs of Joseph W. Parker, D.D., a vice-president of the New England Freedmen's Aid Society, are available in typescript upon request to Mrs. Perce Bentley, Phillipsburg, New York. One significant item came from the McKim–Maloney–Garrison Manuscripts at the New York Public Library. A single letter dated March 3, 1863, from Nathan Brown to an unknown correspondent, provided salient information on the denominational makeup of the New York contingent in Gideon's Band. It is in the South Caroliniana Library at the University of South Carolina.

Of the collections of writings of individuals who supported the Port Royal enterprise but were not themselves part of it, the papers of John Murray Forbes, in the Massachusetts Historical Society, are perhaps of most interest, affording as they do a good picture of a man who was concerned with the public aspects of the emancipation movement and who had an almost religious devotion to the principles of laissez-faire economics. The Weston Family Papers in the Boston Public Library show a consistent interest in Negro education on the part of an old abolitionist family. The Samuel Gridley Howe Manuscripts and the James Freeman Clarke Manuscripts reveal the same background and continuity of interests but have been of infrequent use in this study. The Clarke Manuscripts are in the Houghton Library, and there are Howe manuscripts both in the Houghton and in the Massachusetts Historical Society.

The manuscript collections of several public figures have been of much assistance. They are the John Albion Andrew Papers at the Massachusetts Historical Society; the Salmon P. Chase Papers at the Library of Congress; the Samuel Francis Du Pont Papers, which are in the Henry Francis du Pont Winterthur Collection, Group 9, at the Eleutherian Mills Historical Library, Greenville, Wilmington, Delaware; and the Charles Sumner Papers at the Houghton Library.

The diaries and papers of a number of Sea Island planters have proved extremely helpful in reconstructing the slave system as it operated on the islands. The Elliott–Gonzales Papers and the John Edwin Fripp manuscript diaries at Chapel Hill, North Carolina, have been especially illuminating. The first represents the collective experience of an extremely wealthy and influential family, stretching from the ante-bellum period through Reconstruction. Especially exciting are the letters to William Elliott from two slave foremen who were to all intents and purposes carrying on the farming on Elliott's estates. The Fripp diaries are rich in information on Sea-Island cotton planting and include much information on slavery. They are also the evidence of a lifetime devotion to farming. Also in the Southern Historical Collection at Chapel Hill are the diaries of David Gavin and John Berkeley Grimball, which, although they were less helpful, yielded a few items of interest on the practice of slavery in the low country.

Equal in interest to the Fripp diaries and the Elliott–Gonzales Papers is the large Thomas B. Chaplin Manuscript Diary at the South Carolina Historical Society in Charleston. Chaplin's diary covers the period between 1845 and 1860, with a long entry dated 1886 that tells the bitter story of a planter whose lands were confiscated. An introspective and unhappy man, Chaplin had the habit of re-reading his own diary from time to time, and he penciled into its margins acidulous and revealing comments upon his own former attitudes. I believe the existence of this diary has gone largely unnoticed by historians, and it is a valuable document in social history. Also in the South Carolina Historical Society are a typescript copy of the Plantation Manual of James H. Hammond and the Thomas Aston Coffin Papers. The latter do not cover the period of this study but afford a few interesting sidelights on the ante-bellum years. These Coffin papers were discovered in the attic of the Coffin Point plantation by Charles P. Ware, carried North, and eventually returned to South Carolina. At the South Caroliniana Library in Columbia are found the Ellis Family Letters and the John Jenkins Manuscripts, both offering some help in reconstructing ante-bellum life in Beaufort, as well as a few letters covering the war and Reconstruction years.

A single letter to his father from a Union soldier named Warren Bulton was also discovered at the South Caroliniana Library; it reveals the contemptuous attitude of one Union soldier toward the late slaves of the islands. The Edward Stoeber Papers, a small collection in the South Caroliniana Library, yielded a few interesting items on the land controversy, for Stoeber was an aide to Rufus Saxton and an officer in the Freedmen's Bureau. This collection includes the petition of the Edisto Island planters for the restoration of their estates. The Richard Skinner Papers consist of only a few items, but they include an interesting pair of letters on wartime life on the islands, written by a staff officer to General David Hunter. They are in the Southern Historical Collection at Chapel Hill, as are the William Harris Garland Papers. The latter have been of use to this study, though they are not at any point cited. They reveal clearly the anomalous situation of the small class of skilled white mechanics in an aristocratic milieu. The Slave Narrative Collection, in the Rare Book Room at the Library of Congress, yielded a number of items, the recollections of slaves of the islands who experienced the events recorded in these pages. Although a single picture may not outweigh a thousand words, I have found the William G. Reed Photograph Album, in the Beaufort Township Library, of inestimable help in visualizing wartime Beaufort. Reed was accommodating enough to annotate carefully his pictures of missionaries, buildings, and the peculiarities of Sea Island scenery.

The archival materials of outstanding importance are found in the Fiscal Branch of the United States Archives. The Records of the Fifth Special Agency include a volume of papers entitled the Port Royal Correspondence, and the large body of documents dealing with Restricted Commercial Intercourse. The latter include Letters Sent and Letters Received by Edward Pierce, Daybooks of Captured and Abandoned Property, and miscellaneous office papers. Equally important are the Records of the United States Direct Tax Commission for South Carolina, including the boxes of ignored pre-emption claims, records of the certificates of sales to Heads of Families and Soldiers, notebooks covering the tangled legal history of the Tax Commission, minutes of the meetings of the Commission, petitions, letterbooks, and correspondence exposing the internal clashes of the Commission. The War Records Office of the National Archives is the repository of the vast collection of the Bureau of Refugees, Freedmen, and Abandoned Lands. The Education Division was the most profitable source of information about Port Royal. The Synopses of School Reports, in two volumes, include the valuable short histories of the freedmen's aid societies. In the State Archives at Columbia, South Carolina, the Manuscript State Census Reports were found useful in determining the conditions of agriculture and landownership before and after the war. The Slavery Petitions and Correspondence for the ante-bellum period and the Education Petitions and Correspondence for the period between 1866 and 1877, in the same repository, were also quite useful.

II. DOCUMENTS

Of the published documentary sources, the voluminous *Official Records of the War of the Rebellion* constitutes the main repository of information about the Department of the South and the related work of General Saxton and the missionaries. Pre-eminent among these are the Reports of the Freedmen's Inquiry Commission, *OR*, Series 3, Vols. III and IV. Saxton's important December 30, 1864, letter to Edwin Stanton is also found in the latter volume. The same records have been consulted throughout with regard to the use of Negro troops in the Department of the South. The *Senate Executive Documents* also include much relevant material, especially the *Letter of the Secretary of the Treasury, January 25th, 1863, Transmitting the Report of A. D. Smith, Tax Commissioner*, SED, 37th Congress, 3rd session; No. 26. The *United States Statutes at Large* were consulted for the laws relating to the confiscation of Confederate property. The final settlement of the legality of the certificates of sale under the Direct Tax laws is found in U.S. Supreme Court *Reports* for the October term, 1878, *DeTreville* v. *Smalls*, 98 U.S. Lincoln's Instructions to the Direct Tax Commissioners of September 16, 1863, are in the *House Executive Documents*, 40th Congress, 2nd session; No. 146. The United States Census Reports were also consulted.

The following published reports were also of some use: the *Semi-Annual Reports of Schools for Freedmen* (Washington, 1866–1870), edited by J. W. Alvord; *Letters from the South Relating to the Condition of the Freedmen, Addressed to Major General O. O. Howard* (Washington, 1870), by J. W. Alvord; and *Report of Brevet Major General O. O. Howard to the Secretary of War, October 20, 1869* (Washington, 1869).

III. PAMPHLETS

The publications of the freedmen's aid societies constitute a valuable source, the pamphlet literature being especially significant for the earlier phases of the work because the monthly publications of these societies did not begin until 1865. The pamphlets are voluminous, and no attempt will be made to include here all the references consulted. Among the more significant publications of the Educational Commission of Boston and its successor organization, the New England Freedmen's Aid Society, are the following: *First Annual Report of the Education Commission, May, 1863* (Boston, 1863); *Second Annual Report of the New England Freedmen's Aid Society* (Boston, 1864); *Address to the Public by the Committee of Correspondence of the Educational Commission* [n.p., n.d., but probably Boston, March, 1862]; *Constitution of the Educational Commission* [n.p., n.d., but probably Boston, March, 1862]; F. J. Child, *The Port Royal Free-Black Community* [a broadside of the Boston Educational Commission, signed by Child, October 27, 1862, n.p., n.d.]. The *Extracts from Letters Received by the Educational Commission of Boston, From Teachers Employed at Port Royal and Its Vicinity* (Boston, April, 1862) was succeeded at irregular intervals by *Second Series of Extracts . . .* (Boston, June, 1862); *Third Series of Extracts* . . . (Boston, June, 1863); *Fourth Series of Extracts of Letters from Teachers and Superintendents of the New England Educational Commission* (Boston, January, 1864); and *Fifth Series of Extracts from Letters of Teachers and Superintendents of the New England Freedmen's Aid Society* (October, 1864).

A sketch of the history of the Philadelphia freedmen's organization is found in *Pennsylvania Freedmen's Relief Association* [n.p., n.d., but signed March 1, 1864]; see also *An Address Delivered by James Miller McKim at Sansom Hall, July 9, 1862* (Philadelphia, 1862), *Report of the Proceedings of a Meeting Held at Concert Hall, Philadelphia, on Tuesday Evening, November 3, 1863* (Philadelphia, 1863), and *Circular of the Port Royal Relief Committee* (March, 1862). For the New York National Freedmen's Aid Society, see the *Annual Reports*, especially *Annual Report of the New York National Freedmen's Aid Society of New York, with a Sketch of its Early History* (New York, 1866). Other small publications of the society are *Constitution of the National Freedmen's Relief Association* (New York, 1862), and *National Freedmen's Relief Association Organized in the City of New York on the 22nd of February, 1862* (New York, 1862). *A History of the American Missionary Association: Its Churches and Educational Institutions among the Freedmen, Indians and Chinese* (New York, 1874) was also found to be helpful.

Of the other numerous pamphlets that were of more than passing interest but were not publications of the aid societies, the following deserve mention: [J. K. Blackman], *The Sea Islands of South Carolina: Their Peaceful and Prosperous Condition. A Revolution in the System of Planting* (Charleston, 1880); Benjamin F. Butler, *Character and Results of the War* (Philadelphia, 1863); Ellis, Britton, & Eaton Company, *Proposition to Employ Liberated Negroes* (Springfield, Vermont, December, 1861); Emancipation League of Boston, *Facts Concerning the Freedmen, Their Capacity and Their Destiny* (Boston, 1863); *First Anniversary of the Proclamation of Freedom in South Carolina, Held at Beaufort, S.C., January 1, 1864* (Beaufort, S.C., 1864); *First Mohonk*

Conference on the Negro Question, June 4, 5, 6 (Boston, 1890); [Justus Clement French], *The Trip of the Steamer Oceanus to Fort Sumter and Charleston, S.C., Comprising the Incidents of the Excursion, the Appearance at that Time of the City, and the Entire Programme of the Exercises of Re-raising the Flag over the Ruins of Fort Sumter, April 14, 1865* (Brooklyn, 1865); Thomas P. Knox, *Startling Revelations from the Department of South Carolina, and Exposé of the So Called National Freedmen's Relief Association* (Boston, 1864); James McKaye, *The Mastership and Its Fruits* (New York, 1864); Edward L. Pierce, *The Two Systems of Government Proposed for the Rebel States, a speech of Edward L. Pierce at the Town House, Milton, October 31, 1868* (Boston, 1868); and Edward Atkinson, *Cheap Cotton by Free Labor,* (2nd edition; Boston, 1861).

IV. PERIODICALS AND NEWSPAPERS

Of primary importance in tracing the attitudes of the freedmen's aid societies were their periodical publications. The New England Freedmen's Aid Society published the *Freedmen's Record* from February, 1865, through December, 1868. The January, 1865, issue of this periodical was called the *Freedmen's Journal,* and after a single issue the title was altered. The New York National Freedmen's Relief Association published the *National Freedman* from February, 1865, through September, 1866. The Pennsylvania Freedmen's Relief Association published the *Pennsylvania Freedmen's Bulletin* from February, 1865, through February, 1868. Making citations from this periodical after the *American Freedman* began appearing is difficult, for the Pennsylvania journal appeared in the same binding with the *American Freedman* and carried the volume number of the latter, but it maintained an independent system of pagination.

The newspapers that have been examined for their entire period of publication are the Beaufort *Free South,* the Port Royal *New South,* the Beaufort *Tribune,* the Beaufort *Republican,* and its successor, the *Port Royal Commercial and Beaufort County Republican.* The *New South* and the *Free South* were wartime publications, and the other three were published on the islands during the Reconstruction period. The Boston *Commonwealth* was examined from the beginning of its publication to the end of the war. Also important to this study were the earliest issues of the New York *Nation*, which was launched at the end of the war by individuals closely connected with the freedmen's work. Other newspapers consulted for special dates, or as a check for public reaction to events at Port Royal, were the Boston *Advertiser*, the Boston *Evening Post*, the New York *Tribune*, the *New York Times*, the New York *Herald*, the *Independent*, the *Liberator*, and the Charleston *Daily Courier*.

V. THESES AND DISSERTATIONS

Several unpublished theses and dissertations have proved helpful from the standpoint of their analyses of individuals and movements, as well as in the clues they afforded as to the manuscript collections upon which they drew. Especially useful were William H. Pease's "William Channing Gannett; A Social Biography" (unpublished doctoral dissertation, University of Rochester, 1955) and Lewis Pinckney Jones's "Carolinians and Cubans: The Elliotts and Gonzales, Their Work and Their Writings," in two parts (unpublished doctoral dissertation, University of North Carolina, 1952). I also found help in Richard Bryant Drake's "The American Missionary Association and the Southern Negro, 1861–1888" (unpublished doctoral dissertation, Emory University, 1957), and Katherine Smedley's "The Northern Teacher on the South Carolina Sea Islands" (unpublished master's thesis, University of North Carolina, 1932).

VI. BOOKS AND ARTICLES ON SPECIAL SUBJECTS
A. MISSIONARY DIARIES, REPORTS, AND ACCOUNTS

Among published materials used, the most important single category includes the diaries and recollections of the missionaries who lived and taught on the islands during the Civil War and Reconstruction. Including many letters from Edward Pierce, William

Gannett, Charles and Harriet Ware, and several others, is the collection edited by Elizabeth Ware Pearson, *Letters from Port Royal* (Boston, 1906). Rupert Sargent Holland (ed.), *Letters and Diary of Laura M. Towne* (Cambridge, 1912) is useful, but the editor occasionally deleted from the originals certain of Miss Towne's more pungent phrases berating the "rebels." Also important are Mary Ames, *From a New England Woman's Diary in Dixie in 1865* (Springfield, Massachusetts, 1906); Elizabeth Hyde Botume, *First Days Amongst the Contrabands* (Boston, 1893); Ray Allen Billington (ed.), *The Journal of Charlotte L. Forten* (New York, 1953); Mrs. A[usta] M. French, *Slavery in South Carolina and the Ex-Slaves, or, the Port Royal Mission* (New York, 1862); Henrietta Stratton Jaquette (ed.), *South After Gettysburg: the Letters of Cornelia Hancock, 1863–1868* (New York, 1957); Henry Noble Sherwood (ed.), "The Journal of Miss Susan Walker, March 3rd to June 6th, 1862," in *Quarterly Publication of the Historical and Philosophical Society of Ohio*, VII (January–March, 1912), 1–48.

Direct accounts of the Port Royal experiment, made at the time by people involved or closely related to the work, are found in Charlotte Forten, "Life on the Sea Islands," *Atlantic Monthly*, XIII (May, 1864, and June, 1864), 587–596, 666–676; [William Channing Gannett, co-author with Edward Everett Hale], both "The Freedmen at Port Royal," *North American Review*, CI (July, 1865), 1–28, and "The Education of the Freedmen," *North American Review*, CI (October, 1865), 528–549. See also Charles Nordhoff, *The Freedmen at Port Royal* (New York, 1863); [Edward L. Pierce], "The Contrabands at Fortress Monroe," *Atlantic Monthly*, VIII (November, 1861), 626–640; "The Freedmen at Port Royal," *Atlantic Monthly*, XII (September, 1863), 291–315; and A. W. Stevens (ed.), *Addresses and Papers by Edward L. Pierce* (Boston, 1896).

B. ARMING THE NEGRO

The work of forming the first Negro fighting units was so interrelated with the freedmen's work at Port Royal that the letters and diaries of officers in Negro regiments are important. For published sources of this nature, see Thomas Wentworth Higginson's *Army Life in a Black Regiment* (Cambridge, 1900) and "Letters of Dr. Seth Rogers, 1862, 1863," in *Massachusetts Historical Society Proceedings*, Vol. XLII (Boston, 1910). Dr. Rogers' letters would be important if only for his incomparable vignette of Colonel James Montgomery. For the account of a liberated slave woman who worked with the black regiments as a teacher, nurse, and laundress, see Suzie King Taylor's *Reminiscences of My Life in Camp* (Boston, 1902). For two histories of the part of Negro soldiers in the Civil War, written by contemporaries who fought with them in the Department of the South, see Luis F. Emilio's *History of the Fifty Fourth Regiment of Massachusetts Volunteer Infantry* (Boston, 1891), and the more general study of George W. Williams, *A History of Negro Troops in the War of the Rebellion* (New York, 1888). The most complete modern account is Dudley Taylor Cornish's *The Sable Arm: Negro Troops in the Union Army, 1861–1865* (New York, 1956).

C. OTHER MILITARY HISTORIES AND SOLDIERS' DIARIES

Because the Department of the South was, in the first analysis, a military post and a naval station, I found the following works useful: Daniel Ammen, *The Atlantic Coast* (New York, 1898); Richard Sedgwick West, Jr., *Mr. Lincoln's Navy* (New York, 1957); Clarence Edward Macartney, *Mr. Lincoln's Admirals* (New York, 1956); and Hazard Stevens' *The Life of Isaac Ingalls Stevens*, 2 volumes (Boston, 1900). The published letters and diaries of white soldiers and officers stationed at Port Royal often provided insights as to the public estimation of the evangels, and in this respect the following were of significance: John Chipman Gray and John Codman Ropes, *War Letters 1862–1865* (Boston and New York, 1927); William Thompson Lusk, *War Letters* (New York, by the author, 1911); Oscar Osburn Winther (ed.), *With Sherman to the Sea, The Civil War Diaries and Reminiscenses of Theodore Upson* (Baton Rouge, 1943). The letters of Charles Francis Adams, Jr., written from Port Royal, are in

Worthington Chauncy Ford (ed.), *A Cycle of Adams Letters,*
1861–1865, 2 volumes (Boston, 1920).

D. WORKS ON SEA ISLAND NEGRO CULTURE AND RELIGION

The Sea Island Negroes have been of perennial interest to so-
ciologists and anthropologists; consequently, there is a large body
of literature relating to their social customs and folk literature. Of
this large body of writings I have found the following most illuminating in the course of my research: A collection of songs
made by Port Royal evangels, William F. Allen, Charles P. Ware,
and Lucy M. Garrison, *Slave Songs of the United States,* first
published in New York in 1867 and reprinted in New York in
1929; William R. Bascom, "Acculturation among the Gullah Negroes," *American Anthropologist,* XLIII (January–March, 1941),
43–50; Guion Griffis Johnson, *A Social History of the Sea Islands*
(Chapel Hill, 1930); Guy B. Johnson, *Folk Culture on St.*
Helena Island (Chapel Hill, 1930); Elsie Clews Parsons, "Folk
Lore of the Sea Islands of South Carolina," *Memoirs of the Amer-*
ican Folk-Lore Society, Vol. XVI (Cambridge, Massachusetts,
1923); Lorenzo Dow Turner, *Africanisms in the Gullah Dialect*
(Chicago, 1949); Gold Refined Wilson, "The Religion of the
American Negro Slave, His Attitude toward Life and Death,"
Journal of Negro History, VIII (January, 1923), 41–71; Thomas
J. Woofter, *Black Yeomanry* (New York, 1930). The reader of
the preceding pages will recognize that I have had a distinct preference for allowing the Sea Islanders to tell their views of life
through their songs and stories, and consequently I have made
more frequent reference to the Allen–Ware–Garrison collection
of songs and the Parsons collection of folk stories than to recent
analyses of Sea Island culture. The diaries of the missionaries
themselves have been invaluable in this respect. I have nevertheless profited from the works I mention above. Turner's book on
the Gullah dialect deserves more attention than it has received
from historians.

Melville J. Herskovits' *The Myth of the Negro Past* (New

York, 1941, and Boston, Beacon Paperback, 1958) has been a center of controversy since its first appearance. Whether one accepts the whole freight Herskovits obliges his thesis to bear on the strength of African cultural survivals, it is past caviling that there were many evidences of the African past in the remote Sea Islands a hundred years ago. Except for a few of the folk superstitions which, however interesting and exotic, were handicaps that the white masters did little to counter, the African heritage was one of strength and dignity.

E. SLAVERY

The conditions of slavery on the islands afforded in many instances a gloomy affirmation of the conclusions of Kenneth M. Stampp in his *The Peculiar Institution* (New York, 1956). In his attack on the subtler psychological effects of the institution, Stanley M. Elkins is deserving of high praise for his *Slavery, A Problem in American Institutional and Intellectual Life* (Chicago, 1959). Although my findings do not bear out all his conclusions, especially his thesis as to the fundamental alteration of personality effected in many instances by the "closed system" that American slavery indeed was, I found his book at all times stimulating and useful in that it posed fresh and profitable lines of thought. Frank Tannenbaum's *Slave and Citizens; The Negro in North America* (New York, 1947) was also the richer for having side-stepped the threadbare question of the morality of slavery. Of special use on the economic aspects of slavery and its "profitability" was Alfred H. Conrad and John R. Meyer, "The Economics of Slavery in the Ante Bellum South," *Journal of Political Economy*, LXVI (April, 1958), 95–122. Planters' diaries and records from the island region seem to confirm Conrad and Meyer's conclusions that, in spite of the special problems associated with agriculture, the income derived from the sale and transfer of slaves, by means of traders or through the more respectable channels of white family-slave emigration, was an important financial asset to the island planters. While attacking the problem of "profitability" from a more sophisticated measurement of capitalized rent, and challenging certain of Conrad and Meyer's assumptions, Yasukichi Yasuba, in "The Profitability and Viability of Plantation Slavery," *The Economic Studies Quarterly*, XII (September, 1961), 60–67, has also concluded that slavery was not, from an economic standpoint, ready for extinction in the years before the war.

Of more specific application was the old work by H. M. Henry, *The Police Control of the Slave in South Carolina* (Emory, Virginia, by the author, 1914). Three general studies of the Negro undergoing the metamorphosis to freedom, which was at once a joy and trial, were consulted from point to point. See John Hope Franklin's *From Slavery to Freedom* (New York, 1947); E. Franklin Frazier's *The Negro Family in the United States* (Chicago, 1939); Bell Irvin Wiley's *Southern Negroes, 1861–1865* (New York, 1938); and Benjamin Quarles's *The Negro in the Civil War* (Boston, 1953).

In the voluminous literature of the pro-slavery argument, two works were consulted because of the particular locale familiar to the authors. See Nehemiah Adams's *A South-Side View of Slavery; or, Three Months at the South in 1854* (Boston, 1854), and the letters of Richard Fuller in Richard Fuller and Francis Wayland, *Domestic Slavery Considered as a Scriptural Institution* (New York, 1854). Frances Anne Kemble's *Journal of a Residence on a Georgian Plantation in 1838–1839* (London, 1863), afforded much information as to the conditions of life of the Sea Island slaves and a valuable point of reference as well, for her book appeared at the height of the missionary activities on the islands, and the justice of its severe arraignment of the fugitive masters was much discussed among the evangels.

F. TRAVELERS' ACCOUNTS

In addition to the Kemble diary mentioned above, the letters, diaries, and accounts of other travelers in the Sea Island region were significant for their insight into slavery as practiced there. Especially perceptive are the accounts of Frederika Bremer, a

Scandinavian woman of remarkable intellect who spent some
time on the islands shortly before the outbreak of war. See her
Homes of the New World, 2 volumes (New York, 1854), as
well as Adolph B. Benson (ed.), *America in the Fifties; Letters
of Frederika Bremer* (New York, 1924). Sir Charles Lyell's *A
Second Visit to the United States of North America*, 2 volumes
(New York, 1849) also yielded a few anecdotes of specific Sea
Island application. William H. Russell in his famous *My Diary
North and South*, 2 volumes (London, 1863), gives a number of
distinguished pages to a Sea Island visit just at the outbreak of the
war. The travelers' accounts for the postwar period are numerous,
but those I found useful for the region under study were Sidney
Andrews, *The South Since the War, as Shown by Fourteen
Weeks of Travel and Observation in Georgia and the Carolinas*
(Boston, 1866); Sir George Campbell, *White and Black, The
Outcome of a Visit to the United States* (London, 1879); Edward
King, *The Southern States of North America* (Glasgow, 1875);
Stephen Powers, *Afoot and Alone: A Walk from Sea to Sea*
(Hartford, 1872); Whitelaw Reid, *After the War: A Southern
Tour, May 1, 1865 to May 1, 1866* (Cincinnati, 1866); John
Townsend Trowbridge, *A Picture of the Desolated States; and
the Work of Restoration, 1865–1868* (Hartford, 1868). James
Shepherd Pike's *The Prostrate State: South Carolina under Negro
Government* (New York, 1874) is of little value unless Robert
Franklin Durden's *James Shepherd Pike; Republicanism and the
American Negro, 1850–1882* (Durham, 1957) is read for an un-
derstanding of Pike's disgruntlement with the progress of radical
government.

G. AGRICULTURE

No study of any phase of ante-bellum Southern agriculture
could be complete without a consultation of Lewis Cecil Gray's
unique contribution, *The History of Agriculture in the Southern
United States to 1869*, 2 volumes (Washington, 1933). His treatment of Sea-Island cotton culture in the second volume is brief

but based upon all the relevant sources. Of special importance is
Alfred Glaze Smith, Jr.'s excellent work, *Economic Readjustment of an Old Cotton State; South Carolina, 1820–1860* (Columbia, 1958). One could wish for such an able study of several
other states. Chalmers S. Murray's *This Our Land: The Story of
the Agricultural Society of South Carolina* (Charleston, 1949)
contains picturesque detail and indicates the possibility that a study
of more use to scholars could be made from the materials available
on the subject. Frederick Law Olmsted's *A Journey in the Sea-
Board Slave States* (New York, 1856) provided valuable observations on slavery and other economic features of ante-bellum
South Carolina. Edward Atkinson's "The Reign of King Cotton,"
Atlantic Monthly, VII (April, 1961), 451–465, was representative of the attitude of economic liberals of the day. A recent work
of merit that I found useful on the economic problems of the state
before the war was Douglass C. North's *The Economic Growth
of the United States, 1790–1860* (Englewood Cliffs, New Jersey,
1961). Guion Griffis Johnson's study mentioned above, *A Social
History of the Sea Islands* (Chapel Hill, 1930), includes much
valuable material on agriculture as well as on slavery. T. J. Woofter's *Black Yeomanry* (New York, 1930) brings the agricultural
history of the Sea Islanders up to recent times.

VII. BIOGRAPHIES AND PUBLISHED DIARIES OF
PUBLIC FIGURES

Published letters, diaries, and biographies of figures great and
small have been extremely helpful in piecing out the contacts of
the many individuals who at one time or another played a significant role in the Port Royal story. I have consulted Roy P. Basler
(ed.), *The Collected Works of Abraham Lincoln*, 8 volumes and
index (New Brunswick, 1953), for special orders from the President concerning Port Royal. *The Diary of Edward Bates, 1859–
1866*, edited by Howard K. Beale, which appeared as a part of
the American Historical Association *Annual Report* for 1930,
Vol. IV (Washington, 1933), was found helpful on a few occa-

sions. The materials dealing with Chase were especially important. David Donald (ed.), *Inside Lincoln's Cabinet, The Civil War Diaries of Salmon P. Chase* (New York, 1954) was of great assistance. Of less use was the *Diary and Correspondence of Salmon P. Chase*, a part of the *Annual Report of the American Historical Association, 1902*, Vol. II. The biographical treatments of Chase were found useful in the following order: Marva Robins Belden and Thomas Graham Belden, *So Fell the Angels* (Boston, 1956); Albert Bushnell Hart, *Salmon P. Chase* (Boston, 1899); Robert Bruce Warden, *An Account of the Private Life and Public Services of Salmon Portland Chase* (Cincinnati, 1874).

Other biographies and autobiographies and collected letters and diaries used were Oliver Otis Howard's *Autobiography*, 2 volumes (New York, 1908); Sarah Forbes Hughes (ed.), *Letters and Recollections of John Murray Forbes*, 2 volumes (Boston, 1899); John Greenleaf Pearson, *The Life of John A. Andrew* (Boston, 1904); *Memoirs of William T. Sherman*, 2 volumes (New York, 1875); James Petigru Carson, *Life, Letters and Speeches of James Louis Petigru* (Washington, 1920); William J. Grayson, *James Louis Petigru* (New York, 1866); Earl Conrad, *Harriet Tubman* (Washington, 1943); Harold Francis Williamson, *Edward Atkinson, The Biography of a Liberal* (Boston, 1834); Oscar Sherwin, *Prophet of Liberty, The Life and Times of Wendell Phillips* (New York, 1958). A more recent biography of Phillips, shorter but more perceptive, is Irving H. Bartlett, *Wendell Phillips: Brahmin Radical* (Boston, 1961). Dorothy Sterling's biography, *Captain of the Planter, The Story of Robert Smalls* (New York, 1958), although written for young people, is based upon a study of the sources and was useful to me on several points in Smalls's early life.

Of less use, but important in each case for a few salient points, particularly concerning the lives of the less famous people at work at Port Royal, were the following: Benjamin F. Butler, *Autobiography and Personal Reminiscences* (Boston, 1892); James L. Bowen, *Massachusetts in the War, 1861–1865* (Springfield, Mass., 1889), which includes biographical information about Saxton; Vincent Yardley Bowditch, *Life and Correspondence of Henry Ingersoll Bowditch* (Boston, 1902); Harold Dean Cater (ed.), *Henry Adams and His Friends: A Collection of his Unpublished Letters* (Boston, 1947), containing information and a few letters from Adams' friend and brother-in-law, Edward Hooper; Ward Thoron (ed.), *The Letters of Henry Adams* (Boston, 1936), also containing prefatory material on Marian Hooper's brother, but weakened by the editor's failure to describe the special kind of service Edward Hooper was involved in during the war or even to state how important the freedmen's work was at that time to the future Mrs. Adams herself. She was a steady contributor of amounts ranging from $500 upward to the New England Freedmen's Aid Society. Ernest Samuels' *Henry Adams, The Middle Years* (Cambridge, 1958) is also of some help.

Also worthy of mention is J. H. Cuthbert's biography of a Sea Island minister and planter, *Life of Richard Fuller, D.D.* (New York, 1878). It is wholly laudatory and had to be used with discretion. See also Thomas Wentworth Higginson, *Contemporaries* (Boston, 1899); Elizabeth Merritt, *James Henry Hammond, 1807–1864* (Baltimore, 1923); Edward L. Pierce, *Memoirs and Letters of Charles Sumner*, 4 volumes (Boston, 1877–1893); Laura E. Richards, *Letters and Journals of Samuel Gridley Howe*, 2 volumes (Boston, 1906–1909); Laura A. White, *Robert Barnwell Rhett: Father of Secession* (New York, 1931); John L. Thomas, *The Liberator; William Lloyd Garrison* (Boston, 1963); Jean Halloway, *Edward Everett Hale: A Biography* (Austin, Texas, 1956); James Freeman Clarke, *Anti-Slavery Days* (New York, 1883). *The Correspondence of Thomas Carlyle and Ralph Waldo Emerson, 1834–1884* (Boston 1883–1884) yielded a few points of interest. Two diaries from the South were consulted with profit, for the impact of the invasion upon the Southerners and their reactions in the crisis. See Arney Robinson Childs (ed.), *The Private Journal of Henry William*

Ravenel, 1858–1887 (Columbia, South Carolina, 1947), and the inimitable diary of Mary Boykin Chesnut, now in two editions, each including some mutually exclusive entries. See Isabella D. Martin and Myrta Lockett Avary (eds.), *A Diary from Dixie, as Written by Mary Boykin Chesnut* (New York, 1905), and Ben Ames Williams (ed.), *A Diary from Dixie by Mary Boykin Chesnut* (Sentry [paperback] Edition; Boston, 1961).

The Massachusetts Historical Society *Proceedings* yielded biographical information concerning a number of figures important in the New England freedmen's movement. See especially, in the second series, Vol. XVIII (1903–1904), 363–364, for a memoir on the life of Edward Pierce. The American Antiquarian Society *Proceedings* [new series], XII, 197–210, also contains a memoir of Pierce. The *Dictionary of American Biography* (New York, 1928), edited by Allen Johnson and others, was helpful for data on individuals, as were the *American Annual Cyclopedia and Register of Important Events* (New York, 1861–1902), and Frank Moore (ed.), *The Rebellion Record*, 11 volumes and supplement (New York, 1861–1868). William Still's old history, *The Underground Rail Road* (Philadelphia, 1872), yielded biographical information on John Hunn and James Miller McKim.

VII. GENERAL HISTORIES AND MONOGRAPHS

Two general studies of the war written by contemporaries proved helpful on several points: Edward McPherson, *The Political History of the United States of America During the Great Rebellion* (Washington, 1865), and Horace Greeley, *The American Conflict*, 2 volumes (Hartford, 1864). More recent general works of some bearing are David Duncan Wallace, *A Short History of South Carolina* (Chapel Hill, 1951), and Allan Nevins, *War Becomes Revolution* (New York, 1960). Katherine M. Jones has compiled a collection of excerpts from primary accounts and descriptions of the Sea Island region through its entire history from the Spanish discoveries until the present time. See her *Port Royal Under Six Flags* (Indianapolis and New York, 1960).

John S. Reynolds, *Reconstruction in South Carolina, 1865–1877* (Columbia, 1905) yielded an interesting point on the career of Reuben Tomlinson.

Several books on special phases of South Carolina history were used as background studies. The most important of these were Francis Butler Simkins and Robert Hilliard Woody, *South Carolina During Reconstruction* (Chapel Hill, 1932) and George Brown Tindall, *South Carolina Negroes 1877–1900* (Columbia, South Carolina, 1952). See also Walter Allen, *Governor Chamberlain's Administration in South Carolina* (New York, 1888), and Hampton Jarrell, *Wade Hampton and the Negro* (Columbia, 1949).

Other important books dealing with the national scene during the period under consideration have been valuable for facts and insights: James G. Randall, *The Civil War and Reconstruction* (Boston, 1937), is the standard text on the whole time-span it covers, but it had become much dated until the appearance of a revised edition in 1961 by David Donald, who has rewritten large sections of the work, bringing the chapters on Reconstruction into line with more recent scholarship. See James G. Randall and David Donald, *The Civil War and Reconstruction* (2nd edition, revised; Boston, 1961). Eric L. McKitrick's *Andrew Johnson and Reconstruction* (Chicago, 1960) is an important recent work that challenges many of the old presumptions about the early period of Reconstruction. See also T. Harry Williams, *Lincoln and the Radicals* (Madison, Wisconsin, 1941), and Kenneth M. Stampp, *And the War Came* (Baton Rouge, 1950).

The Freedmen's Bureau and the related subject of the goal of landownership for the emancipated Negroes have recently received able treatments. The best work on the Bureau is George R. Bentley's *A History of the Freedmen's Bureau* (Philadelphia, 1955), largely supplanting Paul S. Peirce's older study, *The Freedmen's Bureau, A Chapter in the History of Reconstruction*, a part of the *State University of Iowa Studies in Sociology, Economics, Politics, and History*, Vol. III, No. 1 (Iowa City, 1904).

Laura J. Webster's *The Operation of the Freedmen's Bureau in South Carolina*, in the *Smith College Studies in History*, Vol. I, Nos. 1 and 2 (Northampton, 1915–1916), yielded an important clue as to the location of the manuscript records of the New England Freedmen's Aid Society. For the legislative history of the attempt to secure national planning for Negro landownership, see LaWanda Cox, "The Promise of Land for the Freedmen," in *Mississippi Valley Historical Review*, XLV (December, 1958), 413–440. Also of importance is John Cox and LaWanda Cox, "General O. O. Howard and the 'Misrepresented Bureau,' " *Journal of Southern History*, XIX (November, 1953), 427–456. The microcosm at Port Royal seems to verify in the one instance the authors' conclusion that the Bureau was not an important tool of the Congressional Radicals. Many of the evangels at Port Royal argued, indeed, that in their haste to restore order in the disturbed Sea Island region most of the Bureau officials in their locality were, after the spring of 1867, willing to sacrifice the rights and interests of the freedmen to those of the planters. Alrutheus Ambush Taylor's *The Negro in South Carolina During the Reconstruction* (Washington, 1924) was also of some use. James G. Randall's *Constitutional Problems under Lincoln* (New York, 1926) was helpful on the legal basis of confiscation.

Articles and monographs that line out the economic aspects of the questions that have been considered in the text are Stanley Coben, "Northeastern Business and Radical Reconstruction; a Reexamination," *Mississippi Valley Historical Review*, XLVI (June, 1959), 67–90, and William B. Hesseltine, "Economic Factors in the Abandonment of Reconstruction," *Mississippi Valley Historical Review*, XXII (September, 1935), 191–210. For the attitudes of Northern business interests on slavery and the coming of the war, see Philip S. Foner, *Business and Slavery* (Chapel Hill, 1941). Bernard Mandel's *Labor: Free and Slave* (New York, 1955) provided information on the attitudes of Northern laboring classes toward emancipation. Henry L. Swint's "Northern Interest in the Shoeless Southerner" in *Journal of Southern His-*

tory (November, 1950), pp. 457–471, develops the point that many Northern liberals hoped that the new labor system would provide new markets in the South for Northern manufactures.

Professor Swint brings out the same idea in his book *The Northern Teacher in the South, 1862–1870* (Nashville, Tennessee, 1941). In tracing the economic affiliations of Northern sponsors of freedmen's work, the study perhaps underemphasizes the fact that many of the same men were involved in numerous other philanthropic endeavors that would have had less direct bearing upon the development of Northern industry. I have found Charles Chester Cole's *The Social Ideas of the Northern Evangelists* (New York, 1954) quite useful in explaining the motivation and ideals of the evangelical wing of the Port Royal endeavor.

On the Freedmen's Inquiry Commission, closely related as to sponsorship with the freedmen's work at Port Royal, the best work is John G. Sproat's "Blueprint for Radical Reconstruction," *Journal of Southern History*, XXIII (February, 1957), 25–44. John Eaton's old account, *Grant, Lincoln, and the Freedmen* (New York, 1907) yielded testimonials as to the influence of the Port Royal Experiment in the subsequent arrangements for liberated slaves in other sectors of the war. On the Northern attitudes toward the development of war aims, see Edith Ellen Ware's old but still useful work, *Political Opinion in Massachusetts During the Civil War and Reconstruction* (New York, 1916), in the *Columbia University Studies in History, Economics, and Public Law*, Vol. LXXIV. Bray Hammond's "The North's Empty Purse, 1861–1862" in the *American Historical Review*, LXVII (October, 1961), 1–18, investigates the financial crisis that existed in the first year of the war. For Northern attitudes in the wake of the Kansas Wars, see C. Vann Woodward, "John Brown's Private War," in *America in Crisis*, edited by Daniel Aaron (New York, 1952). David L. Cohn's *The Life and Times of King Cotton* (New York, 1956) yielded a salient point or two on the crisis of evacuation and destruction of cotton with the Northern invasion. Wesley B. Knight's "Forty Acres and a Mule and a Speller," in *History of Education Journal,* VIII (Summer, 1957), 113–127, points out the total inadequacy of the educational efforts made by the Federal authorities but emphasizes the connection between the development of a system of public education in the South and the war-born efforts for freedmen's schools. Edwin D. Hoffman's article, "From Slavery to Self-Reliance," *Journal of Negro History,* XLI (January, 1956), 8–42, is a short account of the Port Royal story, with an emphasis upon the struggle for land. William H. Pease's "Three Years among the Freedmen: William C. Gannett and the Port Royal Experiment," *Journal of Negro History,* XLII (April, 1957), 98–117, is an expansion of a chapter in the dissertation mentioned above and a good treatment of the efforts of one evangel at Port Royal. Clyde Vernon Kiser's *Sea Island to City* (New York, 1932) tells of the migrations of St. Helena Island Negroes to Northern cities.

Although it is nowhere mentioned in the footnotes, I am indebted to C. Vann Woodward's "Equality, America's Deferred Commitment," *American Scholar* (Autumn, 1958), pp. 459–472, which first started me thinking seriously of those steps that led America to assume a moral obligation which, in the final event, the country was unwilling to discharge.

APPENDIX

It is possible to make an estimate of Philbrick's financial result, although I have not found a detailed statement. William Allen records that Philbrick states his expenses as running to $50,000, counting land, labor, cargo charges, and presumably interest to the Boston investors who had advanced money to pay teachers and labor and to purchase the plantations (Allen MS diary, November 23, 1863, p. 27, typescript). This figure is probably a generous estimate, for at 6 per cent interest on an approximate advance from the Boston Concern of $30,000 (plantation cost, $7,000; labor, $20,000; and teachers, $3,000), the interest paid was only $1,800. An interest of $1,800 plus labor cost of $20,000, plus teachers' salaries at $3,000, brings the expense of operation up to a mere $41,000, leaving what is perhaps an excessive estimate for cargo and marketing charges, $9,000. It is unlikely that there was an interest charge on the final expenses; rather, the costs were probably deducted from the marketed cotton. Even if Philbrick is allowed the $50,000 figure, however, as the cost of operation, he made an astonishing profit. He had produced 73,000 pounds of ginned Sea-Island cotton, for which he received in no case less than $1.50 per pound, and in some cases above $2.00. Edward Atkinson must have been very much pleased, as he had written Philbrick on the nineteenth of May, 1862, reminding him that in ordinary times Sea-Island cotton brought between 40 and 60 cents per pound, ginned, and that although the long-staple market had not advanced in price as rapidly under the war scarcity as the short-staple, he thought the price might reach 80 cents by the end of 1862 [Atkinson MSS]. By the end of 1863 the price had nearly doubled. Taking $1.80 as a reasonable estimate of Philbrick's market price for 73,000 pounds of cotton, and the generous estimate of $50,000 as cost, he netted $81,000 for the year's operations.

INDEX